NEW PROCLAM

NEW PROCLAMATION YEAR B, 2009

EASTER TO CHRIST THE KING

ERIK M. HEEN
HENRY G. BRINTON
KAROLINE M. LEWIS
DAVID F. WATSON

DAVID B. LOTT, EDITOR

FORTRESS PRESS
MINNEAPOLIS

NEW PROCLAMATION
Year B, 2009
Easter to Christ the King

Library of Congress Cataloging-in-Publication Data
The Library of Congress has catalogued this series as follows.
New Proclamation: Year B, 2009 Easter to Christ the King.
    p. cm.
    Includes bibliographical references.
    ISBN978-0-8006-2066-0 (alk. paper)
      1. Church year. I. Moloney, Francis J.
    BV30 .N48 2001
    2511.6‹dc21 2001023746

Manufactured in the U.S.A.
12   11   10   09   08   1   2   3   4   5   6   7   8   9   10

Contents

Preface   ix
    David B. Lott

The Season of Easter
Erik M. Heen

Introduction to the Season of Easter   1

Resurrection of the Lord / Easter Day
    April 12, 2009   5

Resurrection of the Lord / Easter Evening
    April 12, 2009   14

Second Sunday of Easter
    April 19, 2009   21

Third Sunday of Easter
    April 26, 2009   29

Fourth Sunday of Easter
    May 3, 2009   35

Fifth Sunday of Easter
    May 10, 2009   42

Sixth Sunday of Easter
    May 17, 2009   49

Ascension of the Lord
    May 21, 2009   57

Seventh Sunday of Easter
    May 24, 2009   66

Day of Pentecost
    May 31, 2009   74

The Season after Pentecost / of Ordinary Time
Henry G. Brinton

Introduction to Trinity Sunday through Proper 11   83

Holy Trinity Sunday / First Sunday after Pentecost
    June 7, 2009   85

Second Sunday after Pentecost /
Eleventh Sunday in Ordinary Time / Proper 6
    June 14, 2009   94

Third Sunday after Pentecost /
Twelfth Sunday in Ordinary Time / Proper 7
    June 21, 2009   102

Fourth Sunday after Pentecost /
Thirteenth Sunday in Ordinary Time / Proper 8
    June 28, 2009   110

Fifth Sunday after Pentecost /
Fourteenth Sunday in Ordinary Time / Proper 9
    July 5, 2009   117

Sixth Sunday after Pentecost /
Fifteenth Sunday in Ordinary Time / Proper 10
    July 12, 2009   125

Seventh Sunday after Pentecost /
Sixteenth Sunday in Ordinary Time / Proper 11
    July 19, 2009   132

The Season after Pentecost / of Ordinary Time
Karoline M. Lewis

Introduction to Proper 12 through Proper 19   139

Eighth Sunday after Pentecost /
Seventeenth Sunday in Ordinary Time / Proper 12
    July 26, 2009   142

Ninth Sunday after Pentecost /
Eighteenth Sunday in Ordinary Time / Proper 13
    August 2, 2009   152

Tenth Sunday after Pentecost /
Nineteenth Sunday in Ordinary Time / Proper 14
    August 9, 2009   160

ELEVENTH SUNDAY AFTER PENTECOST /
TWENTIETH SUNDAY IN ORDINARY TIME / PROPER 15
    AUGUST 16, 2009   167
TWELFTH SUNDAY AFTER PENTECOST /
TWENTY-FIRST SUNDAY IN ORDINARY TIME / PROPER 16
    AUGUST 23, 2009   174
THIRTEENTH SUNDAY AFTER PENTECOST /
TWENTY-SECOND SUNDAY IN ORDINARY TIME / PROPER 17
    AUGUST 30, 2009   182
FOURTEENTH SUNDAY AFTER PENTECOST /
TWENTY-THIRD SUNDAY IN ORDINARY TIME / PROPER 18
    SEPTEMBER 6, 2009   189
FIFTEENTH SUNDAY AFTER PENTECOST /
TWENTY-FOURTH SUNDAY IN ORDINARY TIME / PROPER 19
    SEPTEMBER 13, 2009   196

THE SEASON AFTER PENTECOST / OF ORDINARY TIME
DAVID F. WATSON

INTRODUCTION TO PROPER 20 THROUGH PROPER 28   205
SIXTEENTH SUNDAY AFTER PENTECOST /
TWENTY-FIFTH SUNDAY IN ORDINARY TIME / PROPER 20
    SEPTEMBER 20, 2009   207
SEVENTEENTH SUNDAY AFTER PENTECOST /
TWENTY-SIXTH SUNDAY IN ORDINARY TIME / PROPER 21
    SEPTEMBER 27, 2009   215
EIGHTEENTH SUNDAY AFTER PENTECOST /
TWENTY-SEVENTH SUNDAY IN ORDINARY TIME / PROPER 22
    OCTOBER 4, 2009   223
NINETEENTH SUNDAY AFTER PENTECOST /
TWENTY-EIGHTH SUNDAY IN ORDINARY TIME / PROPER 23
    OCTOBER 11, 2009   230
TWENTIETH SUNDAY AFTER PENTECOST /
TWENTY-NINTH SUNDAY IN ORDINARY TIME / PROPER 24
    OCTOBER 18, 2009   238
TWENTY-FIRST SUNDAY AFTER PENTECOST /
THIRTIETH SUNDAY IN ORDINARY TIME / PROPER 25
    OCTOBER 25, 2009   245

ALL SAINTS' DAY / SUNDAY
  NOVEMBER 1, 2009
    HENRY G. BRINTON   253
TWENTY-SECOND SUNDAY AFTER PENTECOST /
THIRTY-FIRST SUNDAY IN ORDINARY TIME / PROPER 26
  NOVEMBER 1, 2009   260
TWENTY-THIRD SUNDAY AFTER PENTECOST /
THIRTY-SECOND SUNDAY IN ORDINARY TIME / PROPER 27
  NOVEMBER 8, 2009   267
TWENTY-FOURTH SUNDAY AFTER PENTECOST /
THIRTY-THIRD SUNDAY IN ORDINARY TIME / PROPER 28
  NOVEMBER 15, 2009   274
CHRIST THE KING / REIGN OF CHRIST /
LAST SUNDAY IN ORDINARY TIME / PROPER 29
  NOVEMBER 22, 2009
    KAROLINE M. LEWIS   281
THANKSGIVING DAY
  NOVEMBER 26, 2009 (USA) / OCTOBER 12, 2009 (CANADA)
    HENRY G. BRINTON   290

CALENDAR

APRIL 2009   297
MAY 2009   298
JUNE 2009   299
JULY 2009   300
AUGUST 2009   301
SEPTEMBER 2009   302
OCTOBER 2009   303
NOVEMBER 2009   304

PREFACE

For over three decades Fortress Press has offered an ecumenical preaching resource built around the three-year lectionary cycle that provides first-rate biblical exegetical insights and sermon helps, a tradition that this new edition of *New Proclamation* continues. Focused on the biblical texts assigned by the three primary lectionary traditions—the Revised Common Lectionary (RCL), the lectionary from the Episcopal Book of Common Prayer (BCP), and the Roman Catholic Lectionary for the Mass (LFM)—*New Proclamation* is grounded in the belief that a deeper understanding of the biblical pericopes in both their historical and liturgical contexts is the best means to inform and inspire preachers to deliver engaging and effective sermons. For this reason, the most capable North American biblical scholars and homileticians are invited to contribute to *New Proclamation*.

New Proclamation has always distinguished itself from most other lectionary resources by offering brand-new editions each year, dated according to the church year in which they will first be used, and featuring a fresh set of authors. Yet each edition is planned as a timeless resource that preachers will want to keep on their bookshelves for future reference for years to come. Both longtime users and those new to the series will also want to visit this volume's new companion Web site, www.NewProclamation.com, which offers access not only to this book's contents, but also commentary from earlier editions, up-to-the-minute thoughts on the connection between texts and current events, user forums, and other resources to help you develop your sermons and enhance your preaching.

This present volume of *New Proclamation* covers the lections for the second half of the church year for cycle B, from Easter Sunday through Christ the King/ Reign of Christ Sunday. This volume also follows the time-honored series format, including the following elements and features:

- *New Proclamation* is published in two volumes per year, with a large, workbook-style page, a lay-flat binding, and space for making notes.

- Each writer offers an introduction to her or his commentary that provides insights into the background and spiritual significance of that season (or portion thereof), as well as ideas for planning one's preaching during that time.
- The application of biblical texts to contemporary situations is an important concern of each contributor. Exegetical work is concise, and thoughts on how the texts address today's world, congregational issues, and personal situations have a prominent role.
- Although each lectionary tradition assigns a psalm or other biblical text as a response to the first reading, rather than as a preaching text, brief comments on each responsive reading are included to help the preacher incorporate reflections on these in the sermon.
- Boxed quotations in the margins highlight themes from the text to stimulate the preaching imagination.
- A calendar at the end of the book will help preachers plan their worship and preaching schedules through the seasons of Easter and Pentecost/Ordinary Time.

As has become the custom of *New Proclamation,* the writers for this latest edition represent both a variety of Christian faith traditions and multiple academic disciplines. Erik Heen, a senior New Testament scholar who teaches at Lutheran Theological Seminary at Philadelphia, brings his keen interest in how the Bible is actually read and understood in parishes and homes to the Easter texts. Henry G. Brinton, a Presbyterian minister in Fairfax, Virginia, whose reflections on contemporary religious life have appeared in *The Washington Post* and *USA Today,* addresses the opening weeks of Ordinary Time with a particularly homiletical voice unusual for this series. Two younger New Testament professors wrap up the volume by drawing on their fresh research on the Gospels of Mark and John. Karoline Lewis, who teaches homiletics at Luther Seminary, attends especially to preaching through the Bread of Life Discourse in John 6. David Watson, a United Methodist elder who teaches at United Theological Seminary in Ohio, elicits provocative insights on the Mediterranean culture of shame and honor in his Markan commentary. We are grateful to each of these contributors for their insights and their commitment to effective Christian preaching, and are confident that you will find in this volume ideas, stimulation, and encouragement for your ministry of proclamation.

David B. Lott

THE SEASON OF EASTER

ERIK M. HEEN

In the three-year lectionary, "Year B" is the year of Mark. Yet texts from Mark have been rare in the long Lenten period leading up to Easter. They are rarer still in the season of Easter. Only the "endings" of Mark appear as alternative Gospel readings for Easter Day (Mark 16:1-8 in RCL and BCP) and the Day of Ascension (the "Longer Ending" in BCP and LFM). Rather than Mark, one gets a steady diet of the Gospel of John, as is usual in the Easter season, interspersed with readings from chapter 24 of Luke (Easter Evening, Easter 3, Ascension Day). In this round of texts, the first readings come not from the Old Testament as is the usual practice throughout the church year, but from the Acts of the Apostles, a convention that is common to all three years of the lectionary during Easter. Missing from the Easter texts, therefore, are the typological relationships between the first lesson and the Gospel text found in many Sunday readings in other seasons of the church year. Outside of the Psalms, the linkage between promise (Old Testament) and fulfillment (New Testament) is not to be found unless it is drawn in the New Testament texts themselves (Joel 2:28-32, for example, quoted in Acts 2:17-21 on the Day of Pentecost). What is perhaps most distinctive about Year B in the Easter season is that, beginning with the Third Sunday of Easter, we encounter a continuous reading of the First Letter of John.

This Eastertide, then, we are saturated with the language and imagery of the early Johannine community (John, 1 John) while simultaneously invited into Luke's portrayal of the earliest period of the church in Acts. In the first two weeks

ERIK M. HEEN

we listen to John's account of the resurrection appearances and the gift of the Spirit (20:19), texts shared with Years A and C of the lectionary. A portion of the "Good Shepherd" text (John 10:11-15) occurs on Easter 4. The Gospel readings of the next three weeks offer excerpts from Jesus' farewell discourse (John 13–17), texts that prepare us for his return to the Father (the Ascension of Our Lord).

In the Easter readings from Acts we get no further than Peter's sermon to Cornelius's household (Acts 10), which is introduced on Easter Sunday (the narrative continues on Easter 6). The readings from Acts range backwards from chapter 10, which narrates the inclusion of the Gentiles in the mission of the church epitomized by the conversion of Cornelius. After Easter Sunday we are engaged by the description of the commonality of the early church (Acts 4:32-35, Easter 2), Peter's sermon on Solomon's portico (Acts 3:12-19, Easter 3), his defense before the Jewish Council (Acts 4:5-12, Easter 4), and the wonderful story of the Ethiopian eunuch (Acts 8:26-40, Easter 5). The readings from Acts culminate in quick succession with Acts 1 on the Day of Ascension and Acts 2 on Pentecost, as is usual in all three years of the lectionary.

The readings for Easter in Year B, in weaving together texts from the Johannine school and Luke-Acts, provide the interpreter with some narrative and theological challenges. This is, in part, because the church year is patterned after the chronology of Luke-Acts. In Luke-Acts the death of Jesus is followed by the resurrection. After forty days comes the Ascension (Acts 1:3), followed ten days later by the outpouring of the Spirit on Pentecost (2:1). In the Gospel of John the clarity of this timeline is lacking. The cross, in John, is not only the instrument of Jesus' death, but also the moment of his exaltation (John 3:14); the gift of the Spirit does not occur fifty days after the resurrection (Pentecost), but on the day of the resurrection and only to the disciples (minus Thomas) gathered in the upper room (John 20:19). Because the church year's progression of festivals (Easter, Ascension, Pentecost) privileges the chronology of Luke-Acts, many churchgoers assume that Luke-Acts provides the standard against which other New Testament traditions about post-Easter events should be harmonized. When this is done, the theological insights of John with regard to Jesus' death/exaltation and resurrection/ascension can get lost, subsumed by the dominance of the Luke-Acts story line.

Although the differences in the narrative structures of the passion, death, and exaltation of Jesus among the Gospels may cause moderns some discomfort, this has not always been the case. The early church was well aware of the many differences in chronology among the four Gospels. These discrepancies were not perceived as problematic, or at least not in the same way as they would become in the post-Reformation period. That is because the ancient exegetes shared a similar education with those who wrote the Gospels. They understood that the

Gospels were rhetorical documents. Schooled in the arts of rhetoric, the early exegetes knew that in order to respond adequately to the pastoral needs of diverse communities of faith, individual Gospel narratives needed to witness to different facets of the revelation of God in Christ. Ancient biblical interpreters were quite aware that the Gospels were neither written nor were to be heard as "history" as we have come to understand the discipline in the post-Enlightenment period. Augustine, for example, simply assumed that the authors of the Gospels were given the freedom to shape the chronology of the narrative in ways that served the theological purposes of each individual Gospel.

It is quite appropriate that the church year gives prominence to the chronology of Luke-Acts. Our worship life needs its own overarching narrative structure. But this ordering of our liturgy need not come at the expense of the fourfold richness of the Gospel narratives. The ancients were better at holding these interpretive dynamics (liturgical order, biblical variety) in play than we are. One of my goals in the exegetical comments that follow is to respect the narrative integrity of John as it interfaces with Luke-Acts as well as the church year's liturgical movement from Easter to Whitsunday. The exegetical comments are written in such a way that the "horizontal" dimension of the lectionary texts is stressed more than the "vertical" dimension. Rather than focusing on the common themes that the day's appointed readings suggest, the reader is pushed to consider how these individual texts link up with the larger narratives of John or Luke-Acts (or, in the rare case, Mark).

The reader should be informed that I am interpreting these lectionary texts not only as a New Testament exegete but also as a confessing member of the church catholic. I have been formed by the Lutheran theological tradition in which the conciliar articulations of Nicea (the Trinity) and Chalcedon (the two natures of Christ) are assumed, justification by grace through faith is construed as the *scopus* (target) of Scripture, and the Word of God is known to engage one in terms of both law (judgment) and gospel (promise). What Lutherans call the "theology of the cross"—the understanding that the crucifixion of Jesus on a Roman cross reveals the unimaginable mercy of God as well as the depth of human sin—is central to my own understanding of the Christ event.[1] All these theological loci I understand as arising from Scripture itself, rather than forming some sort of interpretive grid that is imposed upon it. I am, in other words, pursuing what is increasingly called the "theological interpretation" of biblical texts.[2] Although I have been formed in a particular theological tradition, my hope is that my reading of the texts that follow is ecumenically sensitive.

In addition to these issues that shape my engagement with the lectionary texts of Year B of the Easter season, I will bring, from time to time, insights from the history of interpretation to the biblical texts under discussion. Scripture has been well served by exegetes throughout the life of the church. We are richer to the extent that we are aware of their readings that, taken together, make up what George Lindbeck some time ago called the "classical narrative reading" of the "story-shaped" church. As Lindbeck himself modeled, the recovery of the classical hermeneutics of the church in the context of postmodernity does not eliminate the need for critical reflections upon either the biblical texts or the history of their ecclesial interpretation.[3] The comments that follow seek to merge the best of both traditions, that is, the classical hermeneutic of the church and the methods of higher criticism.

Notes

1. For a succinct treatment of the *theologia crucis* see Douglas John Hall, *The Cross in Our Context: Jesus and the Suffering World* (Minneapolis: Fortress Press, 2003).

2. See Erik M. Heen, "The Theological Interpretation of the Bible," *Lutheran Quarterly* 21 (2007): 373–403.

3. See, for example George Lindbeck, "The Story-Shaped Church: Critical Exegesis and Theological Interpretation," in *The Theological Interpretation of Scripture: Classic and Contemporary Readings*, ed. Stephen E. Fowl (Cambridge: Blackwell, 1997), 39–52.

RESURRECTION OF THE LORD / EASTER DAY

APRIL 12, 2009

Revised Common (RCL)	Episcopal (BCP)	Roman Catholic (LFM)
Acts 10:34-43 or	Acts 10:34-43 or	Acts 10:34a, 37-43
Isa. 25:6-9	Isa. 25:6-9	
Ps. 118:1-2, 14-24	Ps. 118:14-29 or	Ps. 118:1-2, 16-17, 22-23
	118:14-17, 22-24	
1 Cor. 15:1-11 or	Col. 3:1-4 or	Col. 3:1-4 or
Acts 10:34-43	Acts 10:34-43	1 Cor. 5:6b-8
John 20:1-18 or	Mark 16:1-8	John 20:1-9
Mark 16:1-8		

FIRST READING
ACTS 10:34-43 (RCL, BCP)
ACTS 10:34A, 37-43 (LFM)

The first reading from Acts this Easter season consists of Peter's sermon to the household of Cornelius, a Roman army officer. It represents a section of a narrative stretching from 10:1 to 11:18 that should be read in its entirety since it relates Luke's portrayal of the "official" beginning of the church's mission to the Gentiles (see also the discussion of the Ethiopian eunuch, the first lesson of Easter 5). In Acts, this mission is based on a revelation from God to Peter (10:11-16) that Gentiles should not be forced to conform to the basic requirements of Jewish law, for instance, circumcision and dietary restrictions. Where today's lesson ends (v. 43), the text is picked up again in Easter 6 (10:44-48), in which a "second Pentecost" for the benefit of the Gentiles is related, forming a bridge between the beginning and the ending of the Easter season. Through the story of the conversion of Cornelius, Easter Sunday looks ahead to observe the fruits of the resurrection. For Luke, the most remarkable transformation affected by the proclamation of the gospel of Christ crucified and risen is the inclusion of Gentiles into the people of God (see 11:18).

In Acts, the conversion of Paul occurs in chapter 9. In chapter 10, in some tension with Paul's own account of Peter's relationship to the mission to the

Gentiles (Gal. 2:7-8), Luke has Peter taking the lead in this effort. While in Joppa, a coastal city, Peter has a vision in which he was instructed to eat animals that were categorized by Jewish law as unclean; a new commandment is given by God: "What God has made clean, you must not call profane" (Acts 10:15). Simultaneously Cornelius, a Gentile patron of the Jewish community in Caesarea (a coastal city north of Joppa and the seat of Roman power), was instructed by an angel to send for Peter. Peter responds, citing his dream and the command of God (vv. 28-29). The pattern here is reminiscent of the relationship between Jesus and the centurion of Luke 7:1-9. Both centurions are patrons of Judaism and men of some status and rank who defer to the representatives of the gospel (Jesus/Peter). Jesus' characterization of the Roman officer, a representative of an occupying power known for its brutality, is astounding: "Not even in Israel have I found such faith" (Luke 7:9). Cornelius, it seems, is cut from the same (and, one might imagine, rare) cloth—a pious Roman officer. After the meeting between Peter and Cornelius comes the text for today, a sermon preached to Cornelius and his extended household as well as others whom Cornelius had invited into his home to hear Peter (v. 24). It is Peter's last missionary speech. Paul and Barnabas are commissioned in chapter 13. It is they who carry the work among the Gentiles further. In Acts, Peter is the bridge between the mission to the Jews and the mission to the Gentiles. He has come a long way, both from his days as a fisherman in Galilee and the betrayals of Jesus that marked his discipleship during the passion of Christ.

> In Acts, Peter is the bridge between the mission to the Jews and the mission to the Gentiles.

The sermon begins with a bold statement of God's impartiality (v. 34; cf. Rom. 2:10-11); historic Israel is no longer favored in the same way as before Peter's vision. Jesus has been sent as *Lord of all* (v. 36). This proclamation of God in Christ is characterized in terms of "peace" (v. 36; cf. Luke 2:14) and begs the question of what this "peace" consists. Here it signals, in particular, that the wall that has separated Jew and Gentile has been removed; where there was enmity, precisely because of the death and the resurrection of Christ, concord and harmony is possible. For Luke, the offer of forgiveness of sins and reconciliation with God can be extended even to those who find themselves deeply embedded in the power politics of the Roman Empire, as was the centurion Cornelius. All who "fear God" and do "what is right" (v. 35) are recipients of the "grace and peace" (compare too the favorite greeting of Paul, for example, Rom. 1:7) due God's favored clients. This "peace," ironically, does not mean an absence of conflict in the lives of those who assemble around Christ. The gospel continues to resist evil and is, in turn, resisted by evil. The peace that comes from God is a gift experienced in the midst of life's painful struggle with sin and death. One cannot imagine that Cornelius had it easy as a Roman army officer *and* a disciple of Christ. It is not peace with the *world*, but peace with *God* (Col. 1:20) that is given, a gift that can lead to the reconciliation among peoples kept separate by human sinfulness. It is, as Paul says, a "peace that passes all understanding" (Phil. 4:7 RSV).

ISAIAH 25:6-9 (RCL ALT., BCP ALT.)

For discussion of this text please see the first reading (RCL) for the Resurrection of the Lord, Easter Evening, below.

RESPONSIVE READING
PSALM 118:1-2, 14-24 (RCL)
PSALM 118:14-29 OR 118:14-17, 22-24 (BCP)
PSALM 118:1-2, 16-17, 22-23 (LFM)

Psalm 118 is a hymn of thanksgiving to God who has done great things for the people of God. The early Christians read the psalm christologically as expressing a prophetic statement of Christ's Easter exaltation (for example, vv. 15-18). Many of its verses are cited or alluded to in the New Testament. Two in particular are often quoted: verse 22 ("The stone that the builders rejected has become the chief cornerstone" (see the first lesson of Easter 4), and verse 26, which is the messianic acclamation of the crowd on Palm Sunday: "Blessed is he who comes in the name of the LORD." The repeated theme of verses 15-16 (the "right hand of the LORD") symbolizes the Lord's power extended throughout the world. The theme of verses 17-18 is that the power of the Lord (made effective through Christ's resurrection from the dead) means life and not death: "I shall not die, but I shall live." This is the Easter gospel: God's promise of new life is given in Christ who, now at the right hand of God, "has become my salvation" (v. 14). For this we can join with the psalmist, who begins and ends this hymn by praising God, and say: "O give thanks to the LORD, for he is good; his steadfast love endures forever" (vv. 1, 29).

SECOND READING
1 CORINTHIANS 15:1-11 (RCL)

The second reading comes from Paul's most extended discourse on the resurrection, 1 Corinthians 15:1-58. At the end of his reflections, Paul summarizes his understanding of the resurrection by citing Isaiah 25:8 and Hosea 13:14: "'Death has been swallowed up in victory.' 'Where, O death, is your victory? Where, O death, is your sting?'" (vv. 54-55).

In the section assigned for Easter Sunday, Paul relays what many scholars believe to be one of the earliest creeds of the church (vv. 3-5; "I handed on to you as of first importance what I in turn had received"). The creed clearly expresses that Jesus died "for our sins" (v. 3; compare to Isa. 53:4-5 LXX). Though there is no "theory" of atonement expressed here, it is apparent that God received the execution of Jesus as a sacrifice for sin. That is, the creed assumes that a radical alienation exists between God and human beings because of human rebellion and sinfulness, the penalty for which is our death (see, for example, Gen. 3:3), a penalty that Christ assumes through crucifixion. As Paul says in 2 Corinthians 5:21: "For our sake he made him to be sin who knew no sin, so that in him we might become the righteousness of God." Though this understanding lies at the heart of the early Christian proclamation, it may be quite foreign to many who find themselves in church on Easter Sunday. It is a challenge of Easter preaching to celebrate the Festival of the Resurrection while being faithful to the depth of the confessional understanding of that event. Paul himself, however, may provide some suggestions for preaching Christ on Easter. In his correspondence, Paul uses a wide range of metaphors to try to articulate the effects of Jesus' death. Joseph Fitzmyer, while discussing Paul's theology in Romans, lists the following, all of which bring out different aspects of the death and resurrection of Christ: justification, salvation, reconciliation, expiation (a wiping away, rather than a "propitiation" for sins), redemption, freedom, new creation, sanctification, glorification, pardon.[1] To this we might add "exchange" as found in 2 Corinthians 5, cited above. For Paul, Jesus' death is not only a sacrifice for past sins, but is also the event that liberates one from the bondage to sin so that our lives might be lived in the freedom given in Christ. Jesus' death reveals not only our sinfulness, but also the depth of the mercy of God that, received in faith, justifies us (makes us righteous) before God. Through our baptism into Christ we are created anew, enabled to love God and serve the neighbor with joy. In short, Paul's understanding of what God has done in Christ ranges beyond that of atoning sacrifice. These other metaphors would be appropriate to explore in the context of Easter—the festival of the new life discovered in Christ.

> For Paul, Jesus' death is not only a sacrifice for past sins, but is also the event that liberates one from the bondage to sin so that our lives might be lived in the freedom given in Christ.

In 1 Corinthians 15, Paul is neither trying to "prove" the reality of resurrection nor is he arguing against those who do not "believe" in the resurrection. Rather, he cites what is the common confession of the church—"Christ died, was buried, and on the third day was raised"—in order to counter *misguided* notions about resurrection in the Corinthian community, especially the idea that one does not need to die to partake fully in the benefits of Christ's resurrection. Paul is arguing that resurrection is *from the dead*; our victory in Christ is fully experienced only upon our physical death. Here Paul is a representative of what has been called the "inaugurated eschatology" of the early church that is often expressed in the formula "already/not yet." Those who have been baptized into the death and resurrection of Christ (Rom. 6:1-14) *already* experience the kingdom of God that has been inaugurated in the ministry, death, and resurrection of Christ. Though it is indeed a real transformation from death to life, it is a process that is *not yet* completed. It awaits our death and the "coming of Christ" (v. 23), whose own resurrection is not the end of the story, but the beginning.

COLOSSIANS 3:1-4 (BCP, LFM)

The Colossians text harkens back to 2:12, "when you were buried with Christ in baptism, you were also raised with him through faith in the power of God, who raised him from the dead." Though Paul will often speak of our resurrection as largely a *future* event (for example, Rom. 6:5; see the above discussion on 1 Corinthians 15), Colossians and Ephesians (see, especially, Eph. 2:6) speak of the movement of baptism, from death to life, in terms of our *present* co-enthronement with Christ. The metaphor strives to express how it is that we participate in the new life made available to us through the resurrection of Christ. Left to ourselves, we seek the things that are below, not "above," lists of which are given in 3:5-9. Ironically, when we "seek the things that are above," we are freed to enjoy God's good earth (3:10-17). Asceticism—the notion that we can progress spiritually by means of a rejection of the world—cannot be legitimated by reference to Colossians (see 2:16, 18). Those things that are "left behind" by means of our exaltation with Christ are those things that in themselves are hostile to God, including a world-negating spirituality. So, what do people do who are now raised with Christ? Among other things, they read the Bible and sing, things done in the liturgy of the church as it assembles to praise God: "Let the word of God dwell in you richly; teach and admonish one another in all wisdom; and with gratitude in your hearts sing psalms, hymns, and spiritual songs to God" (3:16).

ACTS 10:34-43 (RCL ALT., BCP ALT.)

For discussion of this text, please see the first reading (RCL, BCP, LFM) for the Resurrection of the Lord, Easter Day, above.

1 CORINTHIANS 5:6B-8 (LFM ALT.)

For discussion of this text, please see the second reading (RCL, BCP, LFM alt.) for the Resurrection of the Lord, Easter Evening, below.

ERIK M. HEEN

THE GOSPEL
JOHN 20:1-18 (RCL)
JOHN 20:1-9 (LFM)

The twentieth chapter of John supplies both the Easter Gospel text (vv. 1-18) and that of the Second Sunday of Easter (vv. 19-31). As one approaches this chapter, the exegete must remember that the Fourth Gospel maps the events of crucifixion, resurrection, ascension, and Pentecost (the gift of the Holy Spirit) in a manner that sets it apart from the more familiar narrative progression in Luke-Acts (see the introduction, above).

Structurally, John 20:1-18 consists of the accounts of Mary Magdalene's encounter with the empty tomb (vv. 1-2) and the risen Jesus (vv. 11-18) that "bookend" the story of Peter and the Beloved Disciple's (BD) footrace to the tomb to confirm Mary's initial report (vv. 3-10). The text moves from the "dark" of 20:1 (see also 1:4-5) to the "light" of recognition (20:16).

In John, Mary is alone in her early-morning journey to the tomb that she discovers has been disturbed. She understands that Jesus' body has been removed, though she does not know how or why; perhaps by grave robbers? Mary cannot imagine at this point that "resurrection" might "explain" the empty tomb. She reports her discovery to Peter and the BD, who literally run to inspect the evidence for themselves. The BD arrives first but simply peers in. Peter impulsively, as is his nature, enters the tomb. Both disciples perceive the burial wrappings/cloth left behind (20:5-7). It is on the basis of this evidence that the BD, and apparently not yet Peter, "saw and believed" (v. 8) that Jesus had been raised from the dead. That is, the BD came to understand that Jesus' body had not been physically removed by human agency. Who would undress a dead body before transporting it? In this context the Gospel narrator goes to some length to note that the

> The disciples' prior knowledge of Scripture had not allowed them to interpret Mary's report in terms of God's resurrection of Jesus.

disciples' prior knowledge of Scripture had not allowed them to interpret Mary's report ("empty tomb!") in terms of God's resurrection of Jesus (v. 9). The Jewish canon of Scripture alone did not help the disciples make sense of the empty tomb. It is the BD's deduction from the evidence in the tomb that leads him to this belief; the experience of the crucified and risen Lord is the hermeneutical key that unlocks the deep meaning of Holy Scripture. What was true of the earliest church remains true for us. Christ, crucified and risen, remains at the center of the Old as well as the New Testament.

Mary is back at the tomb in verse 11, though we are not told how or why she returned. Weeping, she encounters two angels at either end "where the body of Jesus had been lying." Still grieving, Mary turns from the angels and encounters the resurrected Jesus, though she does not recognize him. Only when Jesus, the Good Shepherd, calls out her name does recognition occur (10:3). We can assume at this point that Mary's sorrow turns into joy (16:20). She returns to the disciples and becomes the first witness of the resurrection, recounting what Jesus had said to her.

The statement of Jesus to Mary in verse 17 ("Do not hold on to me, because I have not yet ascended to the Father") has puzzled exegetes through the centuries. This is the case because later in chapter 20 (on the following Sunday) Jesus requests that Thomas *touch* his wounds. However one resolves the tension between the two commands, it is clear that in John Jesus' mission is not complete until he returns to the Father (16:10). The counterpoint to the descent of God in the incarnation is the ascent of Jesus as the Glory of God (17:5), an ascent that is epitomized in John by means of Jesus' exaltation on the cross (3:14, 12:34). For the community to experience the fullness of new life in Christ, crucified and risen, it is necessary that Jesus return to the Father. Though it is clear that the nature of relationship between the disciples (symbolized here by Mary) and Jesus will be transformed upon Jesus' "going up" to the Father, it is also clear that this "ascent" does not mean that God has removed Jesus from the community of believers. Counterintuitively, John claims that the return to the Father ensures continual mediation of the Son of Man (1:51). After his ascent to God, Jesus can still be touched (20:27)! In some post-apostolic faith communities, an extension of Thomas's experienced "physicality" of the spiritual body of the ascended Lord is the belief that the real presence of the Word is made "visible" in eucharistic celebration (6:51). Any theological vision that perceives that the finite can contain the infinite is, of course, actually a matter of faith and not sight (20:29).

> Counterintuitively, John claims that the return to the Father ensures continual mediation of the Son of Man. After his ascent to God, Jesus can still be touched!

The stories of the encounter of Mary, Peter, and the BD with the empty tomb, and Jesus' subsequent resurrection appearance to Mary, illustrate the Gospel of John's persistent claim that normally (as in, without faith) "seeing is *not* believing." Not only the empty tomb or Scripture (20:8), but even an appearance of the resurrected Jesus can easily be misinterpreted! Belief that the Crucified One is the full revelation of God is confirmed only by means of the new life that accompanies it (20:31), a new life that contains its full measure of human sorrow as well as the joy that is experienced when the One who has defeated death calls out the names of those who grieve seemingly without hope. The word, then, *does* something; it gives life. As in the case of Lazarus, it calls us out from our tombs (11:43). The word of God, as the Protestant orthodox would say, is efficacious.

The festival of Easter celebrates Christ as the true hope given to a despairing world. The resurrection assures us that death does not have the last word. The word of God calls forth a joy that, though marked by the cross (20:16), is evidence of the gift of eternal life God has spoken into a world darkened by its own fall from grace. Easter celebrates, as John himself puts it, that "The light shines in the darkness, and the darkness has not overcome it" (1:5 RSV). Easter light, wherever and whenever it shines, breaks forth from the murky chaos of a world numbed by nonexistence. On Easter morning God yet again says, "Let there be light," and wherever this word is heard, "There is light" (Gen. 1:3).

MARK 16:1-8 (RCL ALT., BCP)

In Mark there are no "resurrection appearances" as there are in the other Gospels. There is only the empty tomb (v. 4) and the young man (compare to 14:51-52) who tells Mary Magdalene, Mary the mother of James, and Salome (see 15:40) that Jesus "has been raised," and that he is going to Galilee "just as he told you" (Mark 14:28). The women flee in fear, as had the disciples at his arrest (14:50), and say "nothing to anyone." Not a very satisfactory ending to a Gospel narrative, it would seem.

Yet the faithful reader of Mark knows that the story of Jesus' resurrection has been told in a way that upends and transforms everything. As Jesus was brought from death to life—transfigured to God's glory—through *God's* initiative (see 9:2-8), so too now is the world itself, and everything in it. In this transformation, one discovers that the cross is not only an instrument of death, but also gives hope to a deeply suffering world. It is the tree of life (Rev. 22:2). If we find ourselves responding to this "upending" word about the crucified Jesus with faith, we have received, Mark tells us, a gift beyond all measuring, one that the disciples themselves did not possess until *after* the death and resurrection of Jesus (see, for example, Mark 8:31-32).

We know from other sources that, eventually, the disciples do return to Galilee and there encounter the resurrected Lord (se, for example, Mark 14:28). The abrupt ending of Mark does not so much direct these original disciples back to *their* Galilee of the beginning of the Gospel story (1:9), but sends us to *our* Galilee. Yet note: it is no longer the same place. The everyday world we inhabit has been transformed by means of our encounter with the word about the crucified and risen Lord. We have experienced the baptism for the forgiveness of sin (1:4). We know that death and the devil has been defeated (3:27), that creation itself is undergoing renewal (note Jesus' "exorcism" of the sea in 4:39), that the eschatological banquet, presided over by the risen Lord, is ours to enjoy. . . . The Gospel of Mark testifies that Jesus, crucified and risen, has revealed to those that have eyes to see and ears to hear (4:9, 23, 8:18) that the way of the cross is also the way of life (8:34).

> The everyday world we inhabit has been transformed by means of our encounter with the word about the crucified and risen Lord.

Note

1. Joseph A. Fitzmyer, *Romans*, The Anchor Bible, vol. 33 (New York: Doubleday, 1992), 116–24.

RESURRECTION OF THE LORD / EASTER EVENING

APRIL 12, 2009

Revised Common (RCL)	Episcopal (BCP)	Roman Catholic (LFM)
Isa. 25:6-9	Acts 5:29a, 30-32 or Dan. 12:1-3	Acts 10:34a, 37-43
Psalm 114	Psalm 114 or 136 or 118:14-17, 22-24	Ps. 118:1-2, 16-17, 22-23
1 Cor. 5:6b-8	1 Cor. 5:6b-8 or Acts 5:29a, 30-32	Col. 3:1-4 or 1 Cor. 5:6b-8
Luke 24:13-49	Luke 24:13-35	Luke 24:13-35

FIRST READING

ISAIAH 25:6-9 (RCL)

As Easter follows upon the death of Jesus, so Isaiah 25 follows upon Isaiah 24. Chapter 24 describes God's wrathful judgment upon evil: "The earth is utterly broken, the earth is torn asunder" (v. 19). Chapter 25 is a hymn of praise sung to Yahweh for the salvation of the world. Life replaces death; joy replaces sorrow. At the center of this vision is the celebration of Yahweh's establishment of the kingdom of God, which involves a divine enthronement (24:23). The Gentile nations are invited to come to the great eschatological feast (25:6) that will occur on Mount Zion (in other words, Jerusalem; Isa. 24:23), at which the finest wine and food are served. The pilgrimage of Gentiles *to* Jerusalem, then, is a central motif of Isaiah's eschatological vision (for example, Isa. 56:6-8, 60:3, 66:18-23). At this feast celebrating Yahweh's victory over cosmic evil, the shroud of mourning that accompanies the human experience of mortality is destroyed (v. 7), and death is swallowed up forever (v. 8).

This text from Isaiah was read by the early Christians through the lens of their experience of the Easter exaltation of Christ that followed close upon the hard days of Jesus' arrest, trial, and crucifixion. Paul quotes Isaiah 25:7 in his great chapter on the resurrection from the dead at 1 Corinthians 15:54; John of Patmos quotes verse 8 at Revelation 17:7 and 21:4. Rather than a text describing the sovereignty of Yahweh, the early Christians perceived that Isaiah 25 spoke of the blessings that flow from the enthronement of *Jesus* to the right hand of God. First among these benefits was that death's stranglehold on humanity was broken (see, for example, Matt. 22:44; 1 Cor. 15:25-28).

The reality that Gentiles were responding in faith to the proclamation of Christ crucified and risen was a confirmation that the prophecy of Isaiah was being fulfilled through the mission of the early church (see, Matt. 2:2, 8:11). The new age had broken in; the day of the Lord was at hand. In particular, the table fellowship of the assembly—the Lord's Supper—was a realization of Isaiah's vision. Jews and Gentiles sat together at the table of the Lord. It was a fellowship that not only harkened back to the feedings and table fellowship of Jesus' historical ministry, but was also understood to be a foretaste of the great feast to come (Luke 14:15, 22:18; Rev. 19:9). It is in this meal, above all, that the Lord continues to make "*for all peoples* a feast of rich food, a feast of well-aged wines" (v. 6, italics mine). It is a feast that honors the mystery of the Paschal Lamb that has been sacrificed for us (see this evening's sec-

> The Lord's Supper is a feast that honors the mystery of the Paschal Lamb that has been sacrificed for us.

ond lesson, below). It is also a feast in which we encounter the Exalted One as we invite those whom we meet on our journey *away from* (not *to*!; see today's Gospel text) the holy mountain (Jerusalem) to dine with us as disciples of the crucified and risen Lord of all.

ACTS 5:29A, 30-32 (BCP)

This speech, given by Peter before the Sanhedrin in Jerusalem, closely resembles an earlier one (4:8-12; see the first lesson of Easter 4, below). In it Peter replies to the council's charge that the early Christians did not follow their orders to desist from teaching in the name of Jesus (vv. 27-28). But the disciples had been freed from prison by an angel who explicitly told them to proclaim again the word about Jesus in the Temple (vv. 19-20)! In response to Peter's words, the famous Pharisee Gamaliel argues for a wait-and-see policy that the Sanhedrin subsequently adopts (5:38-39). The disciples are flogged and let go (5:40).

At the heart of Peter's speech (v. 30) is a reference to Deuteronomy 21:22-23, which functioned as a "proof text" *against* the claim that Jesus was the Messiah of Israel. Deuteronomy 21:23 succinctly notes: "anyone hung on a tree is under God's curse." The question this text put to the early church was, of course, "How could the Messiah be 'under God's curse'?" The answer is given, with explicit reference to Deuteronomy 21:22-23, by Paul in Galatians 3:13: "Christ redeemed us from the curse of the law by becoming a curse for us."

ACTS 10:34A, 37-43 (LFM)

For discussion of this text, please see the first reading (RCL, BCP, LFM) for the Resurrection of the Lord, Easter Day, above.

DANIEL 12:1-3 (BCP ALT.)

The verses in this Daniel text are alluded to often in the New Testament to describe the anguish that accompanies the birth pangs of the new age (Matt. 24:21, 25:46; Mark 13:19; Rev. 7:14, 16:18). The notion of a book of life (v. 1) is developed in Revelation (see, Rev. 3:5, 13:8, 20:12), as is the apocalyptic rising of the figure of Michael (Rev. 12:7). The notion of the raising of both the unrighteous as well as the righteous at the day of the Lord winds its way back to this text as well (John 5:29; Acts 24:15). Less often noted in Daniel than such apocalyptic motifs is the clear gospel note it sounds. This text is no exception. The "great prince, the protector of your people, shall arise" and "your people shall be delivered" (v. 1). The dead shall arise (Matt. 27:52) and the righteous before God shall "shine like the stars . . . for ever and ever" (Dan. 12:3; see also Matt. 13:43; Phil. 2:15). The word of God, though it confronts and judges sin wherever it might be found, does not let death have the last say. The message of Easter is that the risen Christ is victorious over sin and death! Those who are baptized into the death and resurrection of Christ—the firstborn of the dead (Rev. 1:5)—are given the promise of new life. We live out of this hope, though we "sleep in the dust of the earth," that we too "shall awake . . . to everlasting life" (v. 2).

> The word of God, though it confronts and judges sin wherever it might be found, does not let death have the last say.

RESPONSIVE READING

PSALM 114 (RCL, BCP)

The psalm begins by reminding the people of God of their deliverance from Egypt as well as God's ongoing graceful presence among them (v. 2). The blessing of Israel through the exodus entailed the sovereign God's transformation of nature. The threatening waters of death parted; the mountains and hills responded in playful movement. Yet, in the face of a power that can bring living water from dead rock (v. 8), the hills not only skip like lambs, but the earth itself also trembles in awe (v. 7).

The early Christians recognized in this poem the figure of Christ, through whom God affected a new exodus, a liberation from the bondage of sin. In the death and resurrection of Christ, both God's sovereignty over all creation as well as God's unique presence within Israel is asserted anew through the mission of the church. In response to God's renewed sovereignty, the waters of chaos are stilled, the sea itself flees "at the presence of the LORD" (v. 5). John of Patmos saw, in the vision that is placed at the very end of the canon, that the benefits of Christ's exaltation as sovereign Lord truly are of cosmic scale: "I saw a new heaven and a new earth; for the first heaven and the first earth had passed away, *and the sea* [of chaos] *was no more*" (Rev. 21:1, italics mine).

PSALM 136 (BCP ALT.)

This psalm praises God for God's steadfast love as recounted in specific deeds—from creation, through the events of the exodus, to the settlement of Israel. From a Christian perspective, verses 23-24 give voice to the salvation effected in Christ. The refrain, "For his steadfast love endures forever," is a most appropriate response to the good news of Easter.

PSALM 118:14-17, 22-24 (BCP)
PSALM 118:1-2, 16-17, 22-23 (LFM)

For discussion of this text, please see the responsive reading (RCL, BCP, LFM) for the Resurrection of our Lord, Easter Day, above.

SECOND READING

1 CORINTHIANS 5:6B-8
(RCL, BCP, LFM ALT.)

This lesson provides us with a rich expression of Paul's understanding of the benefits of Easter in Christian community. The text is sandwiched between admonitions Paul sends to the assembly at Corinth to maintain high moral standards after he learns that a member of the church is involved in an incestuous relationship (5:1). The reference to "a little yeast leavens the whole batch" (v. 6) expresses metaphorically the danger to the entire assembly when such behavior is tolerated. Chapter 5 ends with the steely instruction, "Drive out the wicked person from among you."

Though it is important to note the deep concern that Paul has for proper social behavior among Christians, Easter Evening may not be the occasion to educate the congregation on Paul's perspective on various vices (the "malice and evil" of v. 8; see also v. 11) or the benefits of living a virtuous life (the "sincerity and truth" of v. 8). The New Testament scholar and Bishop of the Church of Sweden, Krister Stendahl, often made reference to "The Ten Commandments of Biblical Preaching." Number ten on that list is, "No moral lessons on high holy days." There are other aspects of this text that may be more appropriate to consider within the context of Easter than congregational self-discipline. Primary among them are: (*a*) the manner in which the festival of Passover informs Paul's understanding of the death of Jesus, and (*b*) the clear expression that ethical transformation in the life of the Christian is made possible *because of* the sacrifice of Christ. The theological syntax of the text is, as Rudolf Bultmann pointed out long ago, that the indicative (justification) is the foundation of the ethical imperative—"Become what you are!"[1]

Though not as explicitly as John's declaration, "Behold, the lamb of God that takes away the sin of the world" (John 1:29 RSV), Paul's pronouncement (". . . you really are unleavened. For our paschal lamb, Christ, has been sacrificed," v. 7) reflects the early Christian understanding that Jesus' death is appropriately understood in terms of the narrative and rituals of Passover (consider Paul's interpretive use of the Day of Atonement in Rom. 3:25). Passover is, of course, the great Jewish festival that celebrates the deliverance of the Israelites from Egyptian captivity. This story of Israel's liberation was understood typologically by early Christians in terms of the deliverance of humanity from the bondage of sin by means of the death and resurrection of Christ. Two details of this Old Testament narrative are taken up in today's text. The first is the Passover lamb. The blood of a lamb was used to mark the homes of the Israelites so that God would "pass over" them as destruction fell upon the Egyptians (Exod. 12:23). The second is the bread that remained unleavened because of the haste of the exodus (Exod. 12:34). In the Passover festivals that commemorated these events, a lamb was sacrificed (Exod. 12:27), and Jewish homes were cleaned of all leaven (in other words, yeasted dough; Exod. 13:3). The critical events of the Christian story, of course, took place *during* Passover, including the Last Supper and the death of Jesus. In today's text, Paul understands Jesus' death in terms of the sacrifice of the Passover lamb, an act that not only redeems humanity from the bondage of sin but also cleanses the body

> By means of Christ, "our paschal lamb," the assembly itself is graced with the holiness of a temple.

of Christ from leaven, here understood as evil. By means of this deliverance one is freed to enjoy a new life in Christ and a new kind of holiness/purity is made possible: "You really are unleavened!" (v. 7). Indeed, by means of Christ, "our paschal lamb," the assembly itself is graced with the holiness of a temple: "God's temple is holy, and you are that temple" (3:17).

In early Christianity, the celebration of the Lord's Supper could be understood as the Passover meal (Mark 14:16). The eucharist was, literally, a "festive" meal that gave thanks to God as it remembered the liberation from bondage to sin effected by the sacrifice of the Paschal Lamb, a deliverance made real by the promised presence of Christ as Lord of the supper. This Easter Evening, then, let us respond to the invitation Paul first extended to his congregation in Corinth, "Let us celebrate the festival!" (v. 8). Easter is the festival of Christ's exodus from death to life, a journey that Christ himself invites us to participate in. One of the many remarkable things about *this* exodus journey is that it has a meal at its heart, where Christ himself feeds us with unleavened bread, so that we too might "become what we are."

COLOSSIANS 3:1-4 (LFM)

For discussion of this text, please see the second reading (BCP, LFM) for the Resurrection of the Lord, Easter Day, above.

ACTS 5:29A, 30-32 (BCP ALT.)

For discussion of this text, please see the first reading (BCP) for the Resurrection of the Lord, Easter Evening, above.

THE GOSPEL
LUKE 24:13-49 (RCL)
LUKE 24:13-35 (BCP, LFM)

The Emmaus text, unique to Luke in the New Testament canon (cf. Mark 16:12-13), is a remarkable story, full of reversal and irony. Two disciples (only one of whom, Cleopas, we know by name) are walking away from Jerusalem despondent over the events that led up to and included the crucifixion of Jesus (v. 17). The reader is aware that Jesus has been raised from the dead (24:1-11), but, though the disciples themselves have this information (vv. 22-24; see also 9:22, 18:31-34), they do not believe it or, perhaps better, simply cannot "grasp what was said" (18:34), either with regard to Jesus' suffering and death or his subsequent resurrection. As the disciples are discussing the events that have Jesus at their center, he joins them on their journey. Jesus is literally in their midst, but they do not recognize him (compare to John 20:14-15, 21:4). The risen Christ, then, after admonishing them of their inability to understand the meaning of the recent events, "interpreted to them the things about himself in all the scriptures" (v. 27). At the core of the Christ-centered teaching given to these disciples "slow of heart to believe all that the prophets have declared" is the necessity of the suffering and death of the Messiah that would come before his glorification (v. 26). Even after this critical lesson in hermeneutics, the disciples still do not recognize Jesus. It is only when Jesus is at table with them and "took bread and gave thanks, broke it, and gave it to his disciples" do they perceive Jesus. For these disciples, then, the "real presence" of the resurrected Jesus is known finally in the breaking of bread. Though this is one of the dominant motifs of the narrative, the exegete should note that upon returning to Jerusalem the disciples learn that the Lord also "appeared to Simon" (v. 34; see also 1 Cor. 15:5). The risen Lord is not limited to one place, to one mode of "appearing," to one group of people.

On the day of Easter, on which the church extends its hospitality to many that normally do not assemble around the "Word, Bath, and Meal," one of the more remarkable reversals of this text should not be missed.

> Luke is instructing us that hospitality to the stranger provides an opportunity to encounter Christ. The host becomes guest and vice versa.

It is Cleopas and the other disciple's offer of hospitality, "Stay with us" (v. 29), that provides the occasion for the risen Lord to offer them, in turn, the grace of his presence as he becomes host of the meal they share together. Here Luke is instructing us that hospitality to the stranger provides an opportunity to encounter Christ (consider also Matt. 25:34-40; Heb. 13:2). The host becomes guest and vice versa.

The hospitality that allows the world to experience the grace of Christ's presence does not end in worship. Though we are there nourished by the word, we are also sent out into the world. In this Easter Evening service, the Latin of the old Roman Catholic liturgy sung at Vespers—*Mane, Nobiscum Domine* ("Stay with us, O Lord")—may sum up our longing, as well as that of the disciples on the way to Emmaus, to remain in the presence of the resurrected Jesus, and have him remain with us. Yet note, after the breaking of the bread, when "their eyes were opened, and they recognized him," Jesus vanished from their sight (v. 31). This did not distress the disciples. It energized them. The encounter with the risen Christ turned the disciples around. "At that same hour," the text says, they headed back to Jerusalem. There, as they shall soon learn, the resurrected one has rather ambitious plans for them. The task given to them is expressed in verse 47: "repentance and forgiveness of sins is to be proclaimed in his name to all nations." We, as were Cleopas and his companion, are guests of Christ's graceful presence, so that we might be strengthened in order to witness to the world, in word and deed, of God's unconditional, merciful hospitality grounded in the forgiveness of sins.

Note

1. Rudolf Bultmann, *Theology of the New Testament*, vol. 1 (New York: Scribners, 1951), 332.

SECOND SUNDAY OF EASTER

APRIL 19, 2009

Revised Common (RCL)	Episcopal (BCP)	Roman Catholic (LFM)
Acts 4:32-35	Acts 3:12a, 13-15, 17-26 or Isa. 26:2-9, 19	Acts 4:32-35
Psalm 133	Psalm 111 or 118:19-24	Ps. 118:2-4, 13-15, 22-24
1 John 1:1—2:2	1 John 5:1-6 or Acts 3:12a, 13-15, 17-26	1 John 5:1-6
John 20:19-31	John 20:19-31	John 20:19-31

FIRST READING

ACTS 4:32-35 (RCL, LFM)

The readings from Acts continue in this account of the "commonality" of the post-Pentecost church in Jerusalem. It is similar to the description that follows Luke's sketch of the first converts Peter makes, listed at three thousand, in Acts 2:42-47. Luke's purpose here is twofold. On the one hand, he wants to honor this period of the early church's commitment to the social ideals that stem from the outpouring of the Spirit (Acts 2). In doing so Luke describes how the solidarity of the first converts to the mission of the gospel is concretized in radical mutuality. The church lives out the sabbatical-year ideal described in Deuteronomy 15; those who have material wealth liquidate their assets, turning them over to the apostles so that they can be "distributed to each as any had need" (v. 35). The spirit of the risen Christ creates a new community by tearing down walls that had separated individuals in the past (for example, between wealthy dominant patrons and poor subordinate clients). The result is that "the whole group of those who believed were of one heart and soul" (v. 32). On the other hand, though Luke praises this commitment to radical commonality of the early church, he also describes how the practice could not be sustained. Following the positive example of Barnabas (vv. 36-37) comes the traumatic narrative of Ananias and Sapphira (5:1-11). They die because they deceive the apostles concerning the extent of their wealth. In chapter 6, the apostles themselves are portrayed as favoring one group

(Aramaic-speaking Jewish Christian widows) over another group (Greek-speaking Jewish Christian widows) in the daily distribution of food. Even the apostles could not maintain the "commonality" ideal.

Though Luke commends those who practice a radical divestment on account of the gospel as well as the egalitarianism that results, a much more common pattern of discipleship in Luke-Acts is reflected in Christian patrons who, while not divesting completely of their economic or social advantages, use their material resources and position within society to provide ongoing support for the mission of the church (see, for example, Luke 3:10-14, 8:1-3, 10:25-37, 14:7-14). House churches need houses to meet in! There is more than one model of discipleship in Luke-Acts. The more successful one is the one that is, on the surface, less radical. In Luke-Acts, patrons of the second model (who remain embedded in the structures of wider society) give generously *without* expecting that their contribution will buy undue influence in the affairs of the church. Such "giving" breaks completely with the normal Greco-Roman conventions of the patron/client relationship where gifts from those of means *always* came with various strings attached. Clients in antiquity simply deferred to patrons and their interests. In another context, I have called Luke's understanding of patronage, which has been transformed by the gospel of the crucified Christ, "*radical* patronage," precisely because it is so different from that which normally structured Greco-Roman society.[1] Luke's understanding of Christian patronage, in fact, "upends" the privileges of power that usually accompany patronal gifts. The Christian inversion of the normal flow of power in the patron/client relationship is, in fact, symbolized in verse 35: the patronal gifts are "laid at the apostles' feet." Luke is teaching here. The power of patrons, which in antiquity was all-reaching, *in the church* must *always* be subservient to the apostolic witness. Gifts given to the church, in other words, need to be received as true gifts (*charis*), given freely, with no strings attached. The model that structures this notion of stewardship is the "servant leadership" proclaimed by Jesus in Luke 22:24-26. Beyond this, of course, is the model of the grace given to us by God in the ministry, death, and resurrection of the Son. In this action of divestment, God acts as no normal patron would. God's power is revealed in what the world considers to be patronal weakness. As Luke rather simply puts it in 6:35 of his Gospel, God "is kind to the ungrateful and the wicked. Be merciful [then], just as your Father is merciful."

> Gifts given to the church, in other words, need to be received as true gifts (*charis*), given freely, with no strings attached.

ACTS 3:12A, 13-15, 17-26 (BCP)

For discussion of this text, please see the first reading (RCL, LFM) for the Third Sunday of Easter, below.

ISAIAH 26:2-9, 19 (BCP ALT.)

This text is a song of celebration for God's victory over God's enemies (vv. 2-6), an event that becomes the basis for trusting in the Lord (vv. 7-9). The remarkable verse 19 comes in the midst of recounting the deep distress and pain of the earth and its inhabitants. It expresses the promise that suffering and death is not the end of one's life in God. God shall resurrect the righteous to a fullness of life, in which there is no decay or death. This is a cause for celebration: "O dwellers in the dust, awake and sing for joy!" (v. 19).

Responsive Reading
PSALM 133 (RCL)

Psalm 133 is one of the "Song of Ascents" that were sung during Old Testament pilgrimages to Jerusalem to observe the annual festivals. Zion (Jerusalem; v. 3) is where the presence of God is most fully experienced as the people of God give thanks and praise for the gifts of God that bring them together. This psalm celebrates the unity that can be seen, heard, and tasted as all gather in Jerusalem as one family: "How very good and pleasant it is when kindred live together in unity!" (v. 1). In Jerusalem the people of God eat festive meals as one body. They live and worship together as one people, sharing the holiness of God—the very presence of God—that overflows like "the precious oil on the head, running down upon the beard, on the beard of Aaron, running down over the collar of his robes" (v. 2).

The image of joyful unity resonates with the mutuality of the early Christian community in Jerusalem described in today's first lesson from Acts (compare to John 17:22). In addition, the psalm gives voice to the experience of the Christian assembly as it comes together to worship God present in Word and Sacrament. As fellow disciples of Christ, brought together in the New Israel of God (Heb. 8:8), we can approach our assemblies with the confidence that there we also shall experience the grace of God, "For there the LORD ordained his blessing, life forevermore" (v. 3).

PSALM 111 (BCP)

This hymn of thanksgiving for God's "wonderful deeds" (v. 4) in delivering and sustaining the people of God states succinctly many of the attributes of God revealed in Christ, crucified and risen. God's "righteousness endures forever" (v. 3). God is "gracious and merciful" (v. 4), faithful and upright (v. 8), and has "sent redemption to his people" (v. 9). The psalm clearly suggests that "fear of the

LORD" is part of the proper relationship to God (vv. 5, 10; see alo Prov. 1:7, 9:10; Job 28:28). It is a fear that does not exclude the "delight" that comes in studying (*darash*, "seeking out") the works of the Lord (v. 2), a study that has Holy Scripture at its heart.

PSALM 118:2-4, 13-15, 22-24 (LFM)
PSALM 118:19-24 (BCP ALT.)

For discussion of this text, please see the responsive reading (RCL, BCP, LFM) for the Resurrection of the Lord, Easter Day, above.

SECOND READING
1 JOHN 1:1—2:2 (RCL)

This Sunday begins the consecutive reading of 1 John that will continue for the remainder of the Easter season. A majority of the letter is covered in these six weeks, though much is also left out (2:3-19, 3:8-15, 4:1-6, 5:7-8, 14-21), some of which includes passages that reveal the depth of conflict that had developed in the Johannine community. Probably written toward the end of the first century C.E., 1 John comes from a community that held the Gospel of John in high regard. Like that of the Gospel of John, its language, though simple, conveys deep theological insight. The saying sometimes attributed to Augustine, "the Gospel of John is deep enough for an elephant to swim in and shallow enough for a child not to drown," is an appropriate description of 1 John as well.

The community 1 John represents has experienced the trauma of division from within (2:18-19). Though it is not clear the exact nature of the dispute that led to schism, the conflict had to do with a denial, by some members of the Johannine community, of the true humanity of Jesus (4:3). Part of what 1 John does is encourage its readers to remain faithful to the gospel as it has been transmitted, from earliest time of the church, with regard to the incarnate "reality" of Jesus.

> Christ, the eternal Word of the Father, is present in the preached word that not only testifies to the Incarnate One, but also creates life anew.

Today's text resonates clearly with the language of the Gospel of John. In 1 John 1:1, "the beginning" refers not to Genesis 1 (as in John 1:1), but to Jesus' ministry. The claim is that the Johannine community's Rule of Faith stems from Christ himself, "what we have looked at and touched with our hands." Also, pointing back to John 1:1 is the claim that the Son, Jesus Christ (v. 3), is the Word (*logos*), here described both as the "eternal life that was with the Father and revealed to us" (v. 2), as well as the word that is proclaimed in the community. Christ, the eternal Word of the Father, is present in the preached word that not only *testifies* to the Incarnate One, but also *creates* life anew. It is a word that, like the word of God spoken at the beginning of all things, creates life out of nothing.

In verse 6, "light," one of the primary metaphors of the Johannine tradition, is introduced. God is described as *light* that illumines darkness (compare to John 1:4). The impetus for illumination of our condition, then, comes directly from God. This imagery (light/darkness) is combined with a reflection on sin (that which separates us from God). Sin, in the Johannine tradition, though it can refer to moral indiscretions of various kinds (for example, 1 John 1:9), is primarily understood in terms of the *response of unbelief* to the revelation of God in Christ (John 16:9). "Walking in darkness" (v. 6), though it may refer to an individual who commits "sins," more generally describes the state of not recognizing the light of God that is in Christ (John 1:5).

Response to the Word of God (Christ) involves the entire person, which includes "doing" the commands of Christ. In the Johannine tradition, such loyalty to the Word of Life is centered in Jesus' commandment to "love one another" (John 13:34, 15:12), a command that will be explicitly introduced in 1 John 3:11. "Fellowship" (1:7) is the manifestation of such love, also expressed as "walking in the light." True "knowledge" of Christ, therefore, can only be experienced within the serving fellowship of Christian community.

> Response to the Word of God (Christ) involves the entire person, which includes "doing" the commands of Christ.

The sacrificial death of Jesus, which makes such fellowship possible, is introduced in verse 7 and discussed further in 2:2. For John it is precisely the death of Jesus that does what we, left to ourselves, never can manage. It forgives our sin, reconciling us with God and with one another. The death of Jesus effects the "atonement" (or "expiation," *hilasmos*) not only for us, "but also for the sins of the whole world." The cosmic scope of the Johannine vision should not be missed.

First John 1:8-9 has been incorporated into various liturgical confessions of sin of the church catholic, and may have served such a function in the Johannine community. The formula clearly emphasizes the role of God in the process of absolution. These verses also point to one of the paradoxes of Johannine Christianity. On the one hand, there is the expectation that members of the body of Christ will inevitably sin. The need to confess that sin is, therefore, noted as well as the possibility of forgiveness for Christ's sake. On the other hand, as expressed in the second reading for next week, 1 John also claims that those who are of God will not sin (1 John 3:9). One way of thinking about this tension is to observe the different notions of "sin" noted above. The primary understanding of 1 John is that "Sin" (with a capital "S") is *unbelief*. Sin of this nature leads to death, is not compatible with life in Christian community (1 John 3:14), and may be immune to "confession" (see today's Gospel text). Such "Sin" is of a different nature than the "sins" (with a little "s," as in, indiscretions) that plague all those in Christian community. Both notions of sin reflect the brokenness of human life, but in different ways.

1 JOHN 5:1-6 (BCP, LFM)

For discussion of this text, please see the second reading (RCL) for the Sixth Sunday of Easter, below.

ACTS 3:12A, 13-15, 17-26 (BCP ALT.)

For discussion of this text, please see the first reading (RCL, LFM) for the Third Sunday of Easter, below.

THE GOSPEL
JOHN 20:19-31 (RCL, BCP, LFM)

The Gospel text for the Second Sunday of Easter (20:19-31), a continuation of the Easter text (20:1-18), contains three parts. The first episode (vv. 19-25) occurs on the evening of Easter Sunday (without Thomas) and relates the Fourth Gospel's understanding of Pentecost (the gift of the Holy Spirit). The second episode (vv. 26-29) occurs a week later and highlights Thomas's full confession of faith, "My Lord and My God." The pericope closes with a statement of the purpose of Jesus' "signs" as well as the Gospel that narrates them (vv. 30-31). The signs are written "that you may come to believe."

On Easter evening, after the events of that day as narrated by John (see the Gospel text for Easter morning, 20:1-18, above), the disciples meet behind "locked doors" for "fear of the Jews" (note: "the Jews" here stand for all who are in opposition to Christ and are not to be equated with Jewish people past or present). With remarkably concise language John relates how Jesus appeared to the disciples (v. 19a), bids them "peace" (vv. 19b, 21), shows them the marks of his death (v. 20), gives them the gift of the Holy Spirit—an event of new creation analogous to that of Genesis 2:7 (v. 22)—and commissions them as apostles (v. 21) with the particular ministry of the forgiveness (and retention) of sins (v. 23).

The ministry with which Jesus commissions the disciples (v. 21) is remarkable in that it is, in effect, a continuation of his own ministry. As Jesus was sent by the Father (3:17), so now he, too, sends the disciples; as Jesus was commissioned with the ministry of forgiveness (1:29), so now are the disciples given this task. It is the Holy Spirit that grants the church the authority, the power, and the ability to continue this ministry in the name of the Crucified One, a gift understood in John in terms of the functions of the Paraclete (14:16, 26, 15:26, 16:7). In John this gift of the Spirit is given in conjunction with the resurrection on Easter Sunday. It is a commission that belongs to the entire church, not to a select group within it. Given the prominence of the "forgiveness of sin" to this ministry, one should also note that "sin" in the Fourth Gospel functions differently than it often does in the theological vernacular in contemporary North America. Sin in John is understood not so much as our moral failure as our inability to receive the revelation of God in Christ. Sin is what makes it so difficult for us to perceive in Jesus' ministry, death, and resurrection the activity of God. If sin, then, is our blindness to God's reaching out to us in Christ, what does it mean to "forgive" or "retain" such sin? John would answer, perhaps somewhat counterintuitively, that the primary obligation of the church in this area is simply to preach the gospel. In so doing, the word, experienced as both judgment (12:48) and grace (1:14, 17), is offered to a sinful and needy world. In so proclaiming the gospel the actual ministry of Jesus is continued (15:22); judgment or forgiveness is a function of the individual responses to the gospel rightly proclaimed.

> Sin in John is understood not so much as our moral failure as our inability to receive the revelation of God in Christ.

The next episode relates Jesus' appearance to Thomas who had not been with the rest of the disciples when they experienced Jesus' presence a week earlier on Easter Sunday evening (20:24-29). In this encounter Thomas provides the ultimate confession of belief in the Gospel of John, "My Lord and my God!" (v. 28). This confession comes from one who earlier had limited insight into the identity and mission of Jesus (11:16, 14:5), a flaw also found in the other disciples. Though Thomas's response to the disciples' confession (v. 25) has earned him the nickname "Doubting Thomas," such is a misnomer. One should remember that the other disciples did not believe the testimony of Mary Magdalene either (v. 18). Their response to her report of encountering the risen Jesus was to lock themselves up "for fear of the Jews" (v. 19). The fact is, belief came to all of the disciples in the same way, on three different occasions (to Mary, to "the other disciples," to Thomas), as a result of experiencing the actual risen Christ. The Beloved Disciple is the lone possible exception here (20:8). Rather than highlighting the "doubt" of Thomas, it seems that the Fourth Gospel is narrating how remarkable is the gift of faith to those who "have not seen and yet have come to believe" (v. 29). If one experiences faith, one is in possession of a gift that is more precious than that given to those who were historically closest to Jesus.

> If one experiences faith, one is in possession of a gift that is more precious than that given to those who were historically closest to Jesus.

Exegetes have long pondered over the tension that exists between the commands given by the risen Lord to Mary ("Do not hold on to me, because I have not yet ascended to the Father," v. 17) and to Thomas ("Put your finger here and see my hands. Reach out your hand and put it in my side," v. 27). One possible resolution of this tension is to posit that when Jesus appears to Thomas, Jesus has actually returned to the Father. That is, Jesus' earthly ministry is complete. The gift of the Holy Spirit is given (v. 22); the church has been commissioned to carry on the ministry of Christ (vv. 21-23). Only after the completion of the Son's ministry by means of the descent *and* ascent of Jesus is a full confession of his person and work possible. It is such a confession that Thomas gives.

Note

1. Erik M. Heen, "Radical Patronage in Luke-Acts," *Currents in Theology and Mission* 33, no. 6 (2006): 445–58.

THIRD SUNDAY OF EASTER

Revised Common (RCL)	Episcopal (BCP)	Roman Catholic (LFM)
Acts 3:12-19	Acts 4:5-12 or Mic. 4:1-5	Acts 3:13-15, 17-19
Psalm 4	Psalm 98 or 98:1-51	Ps. 4:2, 4, 7-8, 9
1 John 3:1-7	John 1:1—2:2 or	1 John 2:1-5a
	Acts 4:5-12	
Luke 24:36b-48	Luke 24:36b-48	Luke 24:35-48

FIRST READING

ACTS 3:12-19 (RCL)
ACTS 3:13-15, 17-19 (LFM)

This reading gives us roughly the first half of Peter's third "speech" in Acts (see 1:16-22, 2:14-36, 38-39), which runs to 3:26. It is delivered in the beautiful Solomon's Portico of the Jerusalem Temple (3:2, 11), the site of Peter's first miracle in Acts (the healing of "a man lame from birth," v. 2) that immediately precedes the sermon. The miracle is reminiscent of one done by Jesus (Luke 5:17-26) and suggests that Jesus' power (Acts 2:22) has been transferred to the apostles by virtue of his ascension and the subsequent gift of the Spirit. The healing ministry of Jesus is being carried on by the church that witnesses in his name (v. 16).

The speeches of Peter in Acts, including this one, are representative of the proclamation of the early church. Because this sermon is set so early in the post-Pentecost period, it is addressed to a specifically Jewish audience and highlights the rejection of Jesus (vv. 13-15). These verses have, in combination with similar New Testament texts, legitimated Christian violence upon Jews throughout much of the church's long history. Given the specific claim in verse 15 that "you killed the Author of life," the text must be handled with great care and sensitivity.

Two mitigating factors in today's text soften the harshness of the indictment against the role of "the Jews" in the arrest and trial of Jesus (compare to Luke 23:13-24). The first is the observation that they "acted in ignorance" (v. 17) and hence the sin is pardonable (Luke 23:34; Acts 7:60, 13:27, 17:30; see also

1 Cor. 2:8). The second is the necessity of Jesus' suffering (v. 18). God (not "the Jews") is the ultimate agent behind the events of the Passion (compare to Mark 10:33; John 18:4, 19:11). The agency of God in this matter brings into focus the importance of Isaiah 53 to the early church's understanding of the Passion of Christ as the fulfillment of prophecy. The ignorance of those who were implicated directly in Jesus' death (the crowd; the rulers) is, therefore, both understandable and forgivable. The section ends with a call to repent and turn to God (v. 19).

The syntax of verse 16 is, unfortunately, not very straightforward. One can focus, however, on the phrase "faith in his name." Here "in his name" refers to the effective, empowering representation of Jesus in word and deed. "Faith," then, has a specific content ("Jesus"), given expression by the sermon ("he who was handed over, killed, raised from the dead"). Note that it is a faith that has many ties to the life of Israel. In the sermon, for example, Peter uses seven Old Testament titles to describe the significance of Jesus: "Servant" (see the last "servant song" of Isa. 52:12—53:13), "Holy One" (properly a title of God), "Upright One," "Author of Life" (in contrast to Barabbas, the murderer, v. 14), "Prophet," "Messiah," and "Offspring of Abraham" (v. 25). The power to bring those born blind to "perfect health" (v. 16) comes through the "faith" of Israel made new "in the name" of Jesus.

> The power to bring those born blind to "perfect health" comes through the "faith" of Israel made new "in the name" of Jesus.

ACTS 4:5-12 (BCP)

For discussion of this text, please see the first reading (RCL, LFM) for the Fourth Sunday of Easter, below.

MICAH 4:1-5 (BCP ALT.)

This text is typologically keyed, in various ways, to the Gospel text for today. "Peace" is a prominent theme, illustrated by the famous verse 3: "they shall beat their swords into plowshares." The instruction imparted on the mountain of the Lord (Zion/Jerusalem; v. 2) is the christological interpretation of Scripture (Luke 24:44-45). The inclusive and universal stretch of the gospel (v. 1) is proclaimed (Luke 24:47).

PSALM 4 (RCL)
PSALM 4:2, 4, 7-8, 9 (LFM)

The psalm, which has traditionally been used as a prayer before bed (consider vv. 4a, 8), is a meditation upon one wrongfully accused (v. 2). The psalm interacts thematically with the first reading, which describes the wrongful accusation of Jesus who was "handed over and rejected in the presence of Pilate" (Acts 3:13). In spite of the hardship and suffering that untruths cause, the psalm voices a strong trust in God who hears prayers that call out in midst of distress (vv. 1, 3b). Thanksgiving is expressed for the "room" God gives to those who are troubled (v. 1), and for the "gladness" (v. 7) that is found in the knowledge that one's righteousness is judged by God and not by the standards of the world. Success in the eyes of the world, in which one might enjoy honor (v. 2) and material abundance (v. 7), does not indicate one's status before God. It is only those who "put their trust in the LORD" (v. 5) that experience God's *shalom* (v. 8), the peace and well-being that comes only from God. It is a peace that invokes the response, even in troubled times, "You alone, O LORD, make me lie down in safety" (v. 8).

PSALM 98 OR 98:1-5 (BCP)

For a discussion of this text, please see the responsive reading (RCL, LFM) for the Sixth Sunday of Easter, above.

SECOND READING
1 JOHN 3:1-7 (RCL)

The second reading for this Sunday is made up of two quite different sections. Verses 1-3 extol "what the love of God has given us." Verses 4-7 speak of sin as "lawlessness" and the impossibility of one who "abides" in Jesus to sin. On the surface of it the last claim, contradicts last week's reading from 1 John, "If we say that we have not sinned, we make him a liar, and his word is not in us" (1:10). The difference between the two texts has exercised biblical scholars a great deal and will never be resolved to everyone's satisfaction. It may simply be that the term *sin* in the two texts refers to quite different things (see last week's discussion).

Today's text from 1 John resonates deeply with the theological world of the Gospel of John. The "love of God" is a unique emphasis of the Johannine tradition (John 3:16), as is the language that describes the followers of Jesus as "children of God" (John 1:12). To be born of God (John 1:13, 3:3), of course, gives the initiative of salvation to God. (It is difficult to give birth to oneself!) Given the strong language of discipleship in 1 John, it is good to remember that the creation of the family of God, with its expression of fellowship (1 John 1:3, 7) and love for one another, is ultimately God's doing. Though "already" transformed by the love of God, the community is still "not yet" perfected (v. 2). Completion of the work of God awaits the final revelation of God on the day of the Lord. Here 1 John expresses the classic eschatological position of the wider New Testament. The kingdom of God has already been inaugurated by the ministry, death, and resurrection of Christ, as well as the gift of the Spirit. The kingdom of God is, however, "not yet" fully realized in the assembly of those called out by the gospel, and shall not be until the exalted Christ is revealed (v. 2).

> The kingdom of God is "not yet" fully realized in the assembly of those called out by the gospel, and shall not be until the exalted Christ is revealed.

The meditation on sin, beginning at verse 4, continues beyond the boundaries of the lectionary pericope to the end of chapter 3. At its center is a reflection on what it means to "abide" (*menō*) in Christ, a characteristic verb of the Johannine tradition. To abide in Christ means to "dwell" or, perhaps better, "remain" in Christ. A central metaphor in the Gospel of John that illustrates this notion is the "vine": "I am the vine, you are the branches. Those who abide in me and I in them bear much fruit, because *apart from me you can do nothing*" (John 15:5; see the Gospel text for Easter 5, below). Righteousness (1 John 3:7) only comes as a fruit of abiding in Christ, a state that necessarily involves one's fellowship in Christian community. John could not conceive of a Christianity that is so individualized that membership in a specific assembly of believers is considered optional. Sin, then, is "lawlessness"—rebellion against God—that attacks the fellowship of the body of Christ through behavior that reveals "those who do not love their brothers and sisters" (3:10; see also 2:19).

> John could not conceive of a Christianity that is so individualized that membership in a specific assembly of believers is considered optional.

In many parishes, the first portion of this passage from 1 John (vv. 1-3) will be received more willingly than the second portion (vv. 4-7). The last verses of the text will strike many contemporary Christians as unnecessarily harsh. That is because it provides commentary to the insight of John 15:5, "apart from me you can do nothing" (consider Heb. 11:6), a theological perspective that goes against the grain of the North American myth of individualism where independence and autonomy are largely uncontested values. The apocalyptic tenor of these verses, which suggests the alternative to life in Christian community is not "value-neutral" but places one in opposition to Christ, will also strike many as foreign.

If taken seriously, these verses express both the high privilege (vv. 1-3) of sharing God's righteousness as well as the responsibility that comes with discipleship lived out in Christian community. The combination requires a state of vigilance with regard to our ability to betray our inclusion into the body of Christ by allowing piety to cloak our own tendency to "lawlessness," our own revolts against Christ, not only before others but even to ourselves.

1 JOHN 1:1—2:2 (BCP)
1 JOHN 2:1-5A (LFM)

For discussion of this text, please see the second reading (RCL) for the Second Sunday of Easter, above.

ACTS 4:5-12 (BCP ALT.)

For discussion of this text, please see the first reading (RCL, LFM) for the Fourth Sunday of Easter, below.

THE GOSPEL
LUKE 24:36B-48 (RCL, BCP)
LUKE 24:35-48 (LFM)

The Gospel text for today follows directly upon the story of Cleopas and his companion's encounter with the risen Christ on the way to Emmaus on Easter Sunday (24:13-35). These two join the other disciples (including the eleven apostles in Jerusalem) that evening. As those assembled piece together the various experiences of the separate groupings into a common narrative—the women's encounter with the angels at the empty tomb (24:1-10), the Emmaus experience of scriptural and sacramental revelation, and Peter's experience of the risen Christ (v. 34)—the reality of the resurrection begins to sink in. Suddenly, in the midst of this gathered community, the risen Jesus stands and grants it "Peace" (compare to John 20:19, 26). This peace was proclaimed from heaven upon the Word's incarnation (Luke 2:14), was operative in Jesus' ministry as the kingdom of God was moving forward, and was even mentioned by the crowd on Palm Sunday (19:38, 42).

The initial response of the disciples, though it moves toward "joy" (v. 41), is one of fright, confusion, and even disbelief. Even though they had been prepared for this encounter by Jesus' transfiguration into glory (9:28-32) as well as their own recounting of recent events, they still cannot fathom the experience. It is an understandable reaction. They encounter the Jesus they once knew, whom they can see and touch, with whom they can eat. Yet he is not the same. He has been transformed by suffering unto death, the marks of which his glorified body still carries (vv. 39-40; compare John 20:27). He is resurrected by God to *new* life that involves also an exaltation into glory at the right hand of God; God's own Son (1:32, 35, 3:22, 9:35) is co-enthroned with God (22:69). This crucified and risen Jesus, therefore, is also *kyrios*, Lord of heaven and earth, "and of his kingdom there will be no end" (1:33). Given all this, it is understandable that the disciples and apostles would be set back on their heels by Jesus' sudden presence in their midst. Luke's narrative reminds us that the incarnation of God, the very assumption of humanity by God for the sake of our salvation, breaks open all the religious categories we employ to try to talk about it. It is *this* Christ—fully human, fully divine—whom the church worships (24:52), that graces these disciples with his real presence. Given the nature of the encounter, it is not surprising that, as Luke puts it, "while in their joy they were disbelieving and still wondering" (v. 41).

> Luke's narrative reminds us that the incarnation of God, the very assumption of humanity by God for the sake of our salvation, breaks open all the religious categories we employ to try to talk about it.

It is important to note the teaching that Jesus does in this context. He begins, as he did with the disciples on the way to Emmaus, with the interpretation of Scripture (vv. 44-46; see alo vv. 26-27, 32). Specifically, he draws out the manner in which "everything written about me" in the Old Testament "must be fulfilled" in his ministry, death, resurrection, and ascension. He teaches the church what has been called "the christological interpretation of Scripture." Then the risen Lord adds in verse 47 what is in fact a commission to the church, the completion of which must wait upon the gift of the Spirit at Pentecost: "that repentance and forgiveness of sins is to be proclaimed in his name to all nations." This charge, with its stunning reach and universality ("to all nations"), given to this small group of Jews (the core group of which are Galileans) assembled in Jerusalem is simply astounding. Like the resurrection itself, it too broke all categories these men and women were socialized to think in, to feel with, and to act through. Clearly, the transition is being made from the time of the ministry of Jesus, directed largely to the people of Israel, to something larger, even more remarkable—the ministry and witness of the church. The new age is breaking into this world in a new way with the peace the Risen One now speaks into existence.

FOURTH SUNDAY OF EASTER

MAY 3, 2009

Revised Common (RCL)	Episcopal (BCP)	Roman Catholic (LFM)
Acts 4:5-12	Acts 4:(23-31) 32-37 or Ezek. 34:1-10	Acts 4:8-12
Psalm 23	Psalm 23 or 100	Ps. 118:1 + 8-9, 21-23, 26 + 21 + 29
1 John 3:16-24	1 John 3:1-8 or Acts 4:(23-31) 32-37	1 John 3:1-2
John 10:11-18	John 10:11-16	John 10:11-18

FIRST READING

ACTS 4:5-12 (RCL)
ACTS 4:8-12 (LFM)

These readings are a part of a text that runs from 4:1 through 4:22. Peter and John have been arrested (v. 3; see also 5:18-42; 12:3-18) because of a string of events that began with their healing of a crippled beggar in the Jerusalem Temple (3:3-10). The number of those who have responded to the word in this early period of the church after Pentecost has grown to five thousand (4:4). The rapid growth of the church is a source of worry for the Jewish leadership that has detained Peter and Paul for questioning. The specific reasons for the detention are explicitly given in verse 2: the disciples are "teaching the people and proclaiming that in Jesus there is the resurrection of the dead." The arrest comes at the instigation of the Sadducees, an aristocratic Jewish group that the New Testament associates closely with the Temple, from whom the high priest was selected. The Sadducees were also distinguished among Second Temple Jews by their denial of the resurrection (Luke 20:27; Acts 23:8). They, among all Jewish sectarians, would be most scandalized by a gospel that asserts "that in Jesus there is the resurrection of the dead."

In the trial scene that constitutes today's pericope, in addition to Peter and John, the man who has been healed is also present, apparently held as "state's evidence" (v. 9). So are a variety of Jewish leaders. Though Peter and John are ostensibly on trial, as is often the case in New Testament trial scenes, the roles of prosecution and defense are reversed by means of irony. Peter accuses the leadership of the *rejection* and crucifixion of God's *chosen one,* Jesus (vv. 10-11). The Jewish leadership is on trial for not perceiving the "resurrection power" at work in the apostolic ministry of the church. The question the leadership addresses to Peter and John is self-indicting: "By what power or by what name did you do this?" (v. 7). The leadership does not dispute the healing of the cripple; they are worried about its source. Peter's response is that the healing comes from Jesus (v. 10), echoing the claims of 3:16. The inability of the Jewish leaders to discern the activity of God "in the name of Jesus" (in other words, that which effectively represents Jesus) suggests also their inability to provide proper oversight for God's people. Luke implies that leadership has passed over to the Twelve (6:2), even though this group, symbolized by Peter and John, seems spectacularly unprepared by origin and education to lead with wisdom. It was, after all, comprised of "ordinary and uneducated men" (v. 13). Luke is making it clear that it is the Holy Spirit who calls forth individuals for leadership in the church. One's preparation for that leadership may be quite unconventional when viewed from the perspective of "the world." One mark of that leadership is the "boldness" (*parrhēsia,* v. 13; see the second lesson for Easter 5, below) exhibited by Peter, speaking the truth in the teeth of power. Christian leadership does not cringe from advocacy and witness outside the walls that provide sanctuary for the assembly.

The reversal movements of the trial scene are given voice by the citation of Psalm 118:22 at verse 11. This psalm was an important and often cited text in early Christianity. It is an "oracle of God" that speaks to: (*a*) the rejection of Jesus that, in turn, (*b*) provided the foundation for a new "building" by God, known by a variety of names (for example, the church of Christ, or the household or temple of God; see Eph. 2:19-22). Here "cornerstone" is not to be thought of in the modern sense of a stone that serves as a dedicatory placard with date and inscription, but according to its ancient meaning—a critical, load-bearing stone that was necessary for the structural integrity of the building, often placed at the junction of two walls. Remove a cornerstone and the building collapses. The rejected one is the cornerstone of God's new creation.

> Christian leadership does not cringe from advocacy and witness outside the walls that provide sanctuary for the assembly.

The last verse (v. 12) of the reading introduces "salvation" (*sōtēria*) for the first time in Acts, a favorite term of Luke's. *Sōtēria* is a cognate of the verb *sōzō* (to save/to heal), used, for example, in verse 9 to describe the healing of the cripple. To be "saved" can, in addition to "being delivered from evil," mean "to be brought to health and wholeness." In Luke's eschatological vision, such healing is possible only in the church, among those that assemble "in the name of Jesus."

This vision of deliverance/salvation is corporate, bringing together into a new wholeness both those who have been oppressed by various evil forces (human and supernatural) as well as those of power who have been transformed by the gospel (see discussion of "radical patronage" in the first reading for Easter 2, above). Such healing of patrons and clients "in the name of Jesus" began in Jesus' ministry (for example, Luke 8:1-3, 4:18-19) and continues in the proclamation and witness of the church of Christ. The disciples were heard to say, "In Jesus there is the resurrection from the dead" (4:2), a statement that deeply worried the leaders of the status quo. The rejected stone becomes the foundation of a new construction in which new life, new wholeness, new possibilities are found. The invitation to such life is still ours to give to a world in need of healing/salvation (1 Pet. 4:4-5).

ACTS 4:(23–31) 32–37 (BCP)

For discussion of this text, please see the first reading (RCL, LFM) for the Second Sunday of Easter, above.

EZEKIEL 34:1–10 (BCP ALT.)

This text describes the need for God to take on the role of shepherd (ruler, king) over Israel directly, as expressed at 34:11, "I myself will search for my sheep, and will seek them out." The designated and commissioned leadership has become corrupt (v. 3), has turned its back on the needs of the people whom it ruled with a violent hand (v. 4). The people are not assembled around the word of the Lord, nor are they nourished by it. The result is that they are scattered, exposed, without protection, vulnerable to all the forces that prey on the weak, including those who were entrusted with their care. The critique is harsh and just. Ezekiel speaks a prophetic word not only for the need of the Good Shepherd (God incarnate in Christ) to be enthroned as sovereign and compassionate King, but also to all those in authority, entrusted with the care of the vulnerable. This includes the leadership of the church, at all levels.

RESPONSIVE READING
PSALM 23 (RCL, BCP)

Though well known, this psalm's core metaphor—"shepherd"—carries the danger of being domesticated by those in modern, urban environments. In antiquity, the work was hard and dangerous, largely without honor. One was always on the move, working in the interfaces between what was known and unknown. Yet, oddly, the term in ancient Israel was used also of kings and even of God. The image was particularly associated with God's activity in bringing the people of Israel out of Egyptian captivity, into the promised land (for example, Ps. 77:20), and from Babylonian exile back to Judah (see, Isa. 40:11). The "shepherd" metaphor in ancient Israel was complex, not easily domesticated.

For Christians, Jesus is the "Good Shepherd" (see, for example, Matt. 2:6; Mark 6:34; John 10:11; Heb. 13:20; 1 Pet. 2:25). In Christ, one lacks nothing ("I shall not want"), and receives much. One gift is the remarkable confidence in the protection of Christ even though one might walk "through the valley of the shadow of death" (v. 4, KJV). Another gift is the Lord's Supper, the "table prepared" (v. 5) by the Good Shepherd himself for nourishment in the midst of a hostile world. John of Patmos, quoting verse 2, paraphrases the hymn as he speaks of Christ's role as protector and guide to those of faith (Rev. 7:16-17): "They will hunger no more, and thirst no more; the sun will not strike them, nor any scorching heat; for the Lamb at the center of the throne *will be their shepherd, and he will guide them to springs of the water of life,* and God will wipe away every tear from their eyes (italics mine)."

PSALM 100 (BCP ALT.)

This processional psalm of praise and thanksgiving (v. 4) invites the assembly into the very presence of God (v. 1). The psalm is used in worship on Good Shepherd Sunday because of verse 3b: "we are his people, and the sheep of his pasture." The hymn invites all of creation to join with the people of God in this praise of the goodness, steadfast love, and faithfulness of God.

PSALM 118:1 + 8-9, 21-23, 26 + 21 + 29 (LFM)

For discussion of this text, please see the responsive reading (RCL, BCP, LFM) for the Resurrection of the Lord, Easter Day, above.

SECOND READING
1 JOHN 3:16-24 (RCL)

The preacher should take note of two verses that lie just outside this pericope. Verse 11, "For this is the message you have heard from the beginning, that we should love one another," reveals a commandment that is central to today's text. Also, in verse 12, the murderer Cain is introduced, who presents a bold contrast to

Jesus who "laid down his life for us" (v. 16). Given the sibling conflict that has torn the Johannine church community apart (2:19), the model of Christ giving his life for others (rather than Cain's taking of a life) stands out all the more in relief (consider John 15:12-13). The threat to the Christian family is coming not so much from "without" but from "within." Hence, Johannine Christians are exhorted to "lay down our lives for one another" (v. 16). This would seem to be an impossible request. Yet one very practical example follows in verse 17 with regard to *how* one might give up one's "life" (*bios,* translated "riches" in 2:16 and "world's goods" in 3:17) for another: *by helping a brother or sister in need!* Note that the impetus for such giving comes from God. If those with material resources share with those who lack them, this grace is an expression of "God's love" experienced "in truth and action" (v. 18).

First John reveals the disconnect between those who profess love ("in word or speech," v. 18) but do not find it within themselves to live for others. This is the situation most of us find ourselves in more often than not. Thankfully, two reassurances are given to us in this text. The first is that *when* we do the right thing, the actions themselves can be of comfort to us (v. 19). The second is that when we are convicted by the guilt that comes from our inability to live out the commandment to love others, God's compassion is "greater than our hearts" (v. 20). Our sin does not have the last word with God. God continues to reach out to us even when we fail to respond properly to God's invitation. This is, by no means, "cheap grace." It is a grace that is experienced in the life of those who, as Lutherans tend to put it, are simultaneously "saint and sinner." Led by the promise of God's forgiveness, we are encouraged to confess our sins (2:8), assured that we will be nourished by the gospel, so as to continue to risk being God's agents of reconciliation in "truth and action" to a world that is not supportive of such activity. Verses 21-22 indicate that our ability to experience such "boldness" (*parrhēsia;* see the second reading for Easter 5, below) before God and neighbor is itself a gift of God's love (see 4:7-9, 17). It is a gift that enables us to respond to the enormity of the grace of God revealed in Christ through our ties with one another. It is our recognition of and trust in God's love for us that frees us to dare being of real service to our neighbor.

> Our sin does not have the last word with God. God continues to reach out to us even when we fail to respond properly to God's invitation.

The insight of verse 22, that "we receive from God whatever we ask," suggests that we should request in prayer what is "pleasing" to God. That which most pleases God is "faith" (for example, John 3:16, 6:29). A faith that is active in love not only resists the values of the world (1 John 5:4), but is victorious over them. For John such faith is possible only when one "abides" in an assembly called out of the world by God, graced by the presence of God's Spirit (4:1-7) to risk real, creative relationships.

1 JOHN 3:1-8 (BCP)
1 JOHN 3:1-2 (LFM)

For discussion of this text, please see the second reading (RCL) for the Third Sunday of Easter, above.

ACTS 4:(23-31) 32-37 (BCP ALT.)

For discussion of this text, please see the first reading (BCP) for the Fourth Sunday of Easter, above.

THE GOSPEL

JOHN 10:11-18 (RCL, LFM)
JOHN 10:11-16 (BCP)

The Gospel text is a continuation of Jesus' Shepherd Discourse, the last public teaching of Jesus in John. Next comes the Farewell Discourse spoken privately to his disciples (John 14–16). Both pericopes of the Shepherd Discourse (10:1-10, 10:11-18) are integral portions of a section of the Gospel of John that runs from 9:1 to 10:19, the heart of which is the healing miracle of the man born blind (9:1-12). It is clear that Jesus addresses this speech to the Pharisees (9:41). They are largely as antagonistic toward him (see 7:32, 48) as they are toward the blind man (9:34). The negative comparison between the "Good Shepherd" and the "hired hand" in today's text sets Jesus against those who were claiming leadership positions over the people of Israel.

Though this pericope does not cite any particular Old Testament text, it has long been recognized that the Shepherd Discourse alludes to many portions of Scripture that use pastoral imagery to describe the "shepherding" of Israel by God as well as by God's anointed representatives, both good and bad (for example, Jer. 23:1-4; Zech. 11:15-17, 13:7-9; Isa. 40:10-11). In Ezekiel 34:1-10 (see the alternative BCP first reading for today, above), one finds examples of poor shepherds who not only do not care for the sheep but exploit them, as they look out for their own interests. In the absence of good leaders, God takes over as shepherd (Ezek. 34:11-16). God, in turn, hands the leadership over to the anointed one, David (Ezek. 34:23-24). This pattern can be discerned in John 10:11-18. The characteristics of the "hired hand" echo that of the poor leadership of Ezekiel. God, having assumed direct rule of Israel, hands over its shepherding to Jesus (not David). Jesus' "goodness" is exhibited in his deep care for the flock's well-being, to the extent that he is willing to lay down his life for it (v. 15; see also Zech. 13:7-9), a clear reference to the crucifixion. In this text, then, attributes that the "pastoral" tradition of the Old Testament assigns to God describe Jesus' involvement with Israel. "I am the good shepherd" (v. 11) is, then, a claim of divine status. The fact that Jesus in this text can claim power over life and death, and even be the agent of his own resurrection (v. 18), indicates the complete union of God and the Son in the work of salvation. A bit further in chapter 10, after coming back to the shepherding imagery, Jesus simply says, "The Father and I are one" (10:30), a claim that leads to charges of blasphemy against Jesus. Today's text also states that Jesus' relationship to the church is based in this close relationship to the Father (vv. 14-15). This is spoken of in terms of "knowledge," a knowledge that is deeply relational: "I *know* my own . . . just as the Father *knows* me (italics mine)". "Knowledge" in John is not something abstract but realistic, concrete, grounded in love and mutuality. It flows from the love of God through Christ to abide in the church. Christ, who shares this mutuality *both* with God and with humanity, is the only and perfect mediator between heaven and earth (see John 1:51; Heb. 13:20). The extent of the range of the recipients of this grace should not be missed. The flock of this "good shepherd" is not only Israel, but all of humanity (v. 16; see also 3:16). The famous "there will be one flock, one shepherd" of verse 16, in other words, goes beyond modern ecumenical interests in the visible unity of the church. According to John, it expresses God's intent for all (see 12:32).

> The fact that Jesus can claim power over life and death, and even be the agent of his own resurrection, indicates the complete union of God and the Son in the work of salvation.

The Vulgate Latin of "I am the Good Shepherd" is *Ego sum pastor bonus.* As is well known, the English term *pastor* comes from the Latin for "shepherd." But note, the only "pastor" in today's gospel is Christ. It is *God's* activity through the "pastoring" of Jesus Christ that is being stressed. The self-sacrificial emptying of Christ for our salvation is not, I would suggest, being suggested as a model for congregational leadership. The warning of the text against functioning as a "hired hand" in positions of church leadership may be more appropriate advice! Still, I would argue, that rather than explicitly giving models of church leadership, the text intends to impress upon us—all of us, clergy and lay—that we are members of the same flock, attentive to the same voice that calls out to us (v. 16; 10:27-29). In this Easter season, it is good to remember that it is the risen Lord who calls to us, as Christ did to Mary Magdalene on Easter Sunday (10:16). Though Mary was alone when that word was spoken, and the parable of the lost sheep speaks of God's search for the lone stray (Luke 15:3-7; Matt. 18:12-14), today's text suggests that the risen Christ also speaks to us as a flock in a fold, assembled around Word and Sacrament. One promise of the text, seen from this perspective, is that even pastors of Christ's church might be graced by the presence of Christ in the liturgical actions of the assembled people of God through which even they are nourished and well cared for, readied to follow the *Pastor Bonus* wherever Christ might lead.

FIFTH SUNDAY OF EASTER

MAY 10, 2009

Revised Common (RCL)	Episcopal (BCP)	Roman Catholic (LFM)
Acts 8:26-40	Acts 8:26-40 or Deut. 4:32-40	Acts 9:26-31
Ps. 22:25-31	Ps. 66:1-11 or 66:1-8	Ps. 22:26-27, 28 + 30, 31-32
1 John 4:7-21	1 John 3:(14-17) 18-24 or Acts 8:26-40	1 John 3:18-24
John 15:1-8	John 14:15-21	John 15:1-8

FIRST READING
ACTS 8:26-40 (RCL, BCP)

Chapter 8 of Acts reveals—from a Jewish perspective—the reach of the gospel into untraditional areas, Samaria to the north and Gaza to the south. Surprising sorts of individuals respond—a magician (8:9-13) and an African governmental official. In the story of Philip's encounter with the Ethiopian eunuch, the progress of the gospel announced by the risen Jesus in Acts 1:8 continues. Although the Cornelius story (chapter 10) is traditionally thought to initiate the mission and conversion of Gentiles, one can make a case that this powerful, highly connected black African of ambiguous sexual identity is the first "Gentile" convert in Acts, proleptically indicating the range and inclusive reach of the gospel of Jesus Christ that stretches "to the ends of the earth" (1:8). In doing so, the great prophetic vision of Isaiah (11:11, 56:3-5) and Zephaniah (3:9-12) is realized; on the day of the Lord, God's faithfulness is publicly acknowledged by all of humanity, symbolized by "the nations'" eschatological journey to Jerusalem.

As we encounter him, the eunuch is far from home (a five-month journey), perhaps a "God-fearer"—a non-Jew attracted to the God of Israel—returning from his pilgrimage to Jerusalem. As a "eunuch" he would not have been eligible to participate fully in the temple cult (Deut. 23:1). Hence, his eschatological pilgrimage would have been, to this point, without resolution. This treasurer of the court of the Ethiopian queen is literate (highly educated) and reading Scripture.

The text is one of the Suffering Servant songs of Isaiah, critically important texts for the church, understood as prophetic articulations of the necessity of Jesus' suffering and death. These events, though central to the salvation narrative, were highly confusing to both Jew and Greek, for different reasons (1 Cor. 1:23). Philip helps the eunuch to understand the Isaiah texts by informing him that Jesus was the one who went through the unjust and humiliating suffering described (Acts 8:32-33). The outcome was not the tragedy the surface of Isaiah's text narrates, but the gift of new life (11:18), available in baptism into the death and resurrection of Christ (consider Rom. 6:1-14). In a sense, Philip does for the Ethiopian eunuch what the risen Christ did for the disciples on the road to Emmaus (Luke 24:27). Philip gives the eunuch the key to the interpretation of Scripture—Christ himself. The eunuch's response of faith to this introduction to a *christological* interpretation of Isaiah is a request for baptism. The contemporary church, as did the ancient one, needs to take the eunuch's question to heart: "How can I understand unless someone guides me?"

The story is about the Ethiopian, but it is also about Philip who comes into prominence in Acts after being introduced in chapter 6. There he is one of the seven "deacons" whom the apostles commission for a particular duty: they are to oversee the daily distribution of food, which the apostles had managed so poorly. In chapter 8, however, Philip is functioning in a much wider capacity than intended by the apostles. He is an apostolic witness to the power of the gospel in word and deed and a skillful interpreter of Scripture. Earlier in chapter 8, in Samaria, Philip preached, exorcized demons, and did miracles (8:4-13). Though the apostles

> The contemporary church, as did the ancient one, needs to take the eunuch's question to heart: "How can I understand unless someone guides me?"

had one idea of what constituted Philip's mission for which they laid hands on him (6:6)—"to wait on tables" (6:2)—the Holy Spirit had other tasks in mind. Christian ministry often jumps out of the boxes we place it in. Philip is, in fact, the quintessential missionary. He moves at a moment's notice to witness to Jesus as revealed in the word of God, working with joy across cultural lines. He is not above the undignified mad dash to a moving chariot so that the gospel might catch up to it. And the result? The end of the reading describes it well: "The eunuch went on his way rejoicing. But Philip found himself [transported some twenty miles to the north by God] at Azotus. And as he was passing through the region, he *kept preaching* [imperfect tense] the good news . . ." italics mine.

ACTS 9:26-31 (LFM)

This text follows Acts' account of the conversion of Paul (9:1-19) and his initial preaching in Damascus that got him into trouble with the authorities. The result was that Paul, rather ignobly, slipped out of town by being lowered out of the town's fortification wall in a basket (9:20-25). In Jerusalem, the followers of Jesus fear Paul because of his reputation as a violent persecutor of the church (9:21). As in Damascus, Paul preaches and "argues" (v. 29) Christ with the result that his life is again in danger.

The text goes out of its way to note that Paul proclaimed the gospel of Jesus Christ "boldly" (vv. 27, 28). That is, he does so without fear for his life, speaking the scandalous word of the cross in the teeth of power. Paul's zeal for Christ parallels his former zeal for the traditions of his ancestors (Gal. 1:13-14). Ironically, both in Damascus and in Jerusalem, his escape is effected by those whom he had formerly persecuted.

DEUTERONOMY 4:32-40 (BCP ALT.)

This passage extols the greatness of God because of the exodus (vv. 34, 37-38; see Exod. 1–15) and the revelation at Horeb (Mt. Sinai) that was mediated through fire (vv. 33, 36; see Exod. 19–24, esp. 24:17), a reminder that God is not to be represented by idols (Deut. 4:15-16). Central attributes of God are affirmed, for instance, "the LORD is God; there is no other besides him" (v. 35). The mighty acts of God that are remembered require acknowledgment in a confession of faith (v. 39). Central to the passage is an expression of one's obligation to observe *torah*, that is, the instruction or commandments of God (v. 40), which provides a link to the Gospel text (John 14:15, 21, 23).

RESPONSIVE READING
PSALM 22:25-31 (RCL)
PSALM 22:26-27, 28 + 30, 31-32 (LFM)

Psalm 22 is most often thought of in terms of the Passion; Jesus uses the words of the psalm to express his lament to God (see, for example, Mark 15:24, 29, 34). But Psalm 22 contains two sections: (*a*) a prayer for help (vv. 1-21) that is followed by (*b*) a song of praise for help given (vv. 22-31). In this psalm, Christ not only prays in his affliction, but also praises God for his deliverance. Just before today's pericope we hear Christ, in the words of the psalmist, say: "For he [God] did not despise or abhor the affliction of the afflicted; he did not hide his face from me, but heard when I cried to him" (v. 24). We recite with the resurrected Christ the song of praise in this season of the church. Easter follows Lent.

In verse 27 the reach of the gospel is prophetically revealed, "All the ends of the earth shall remember and turn to the LORD," a vision that is fulfilled in the story from today's first lesson of the Ethiopian eunuch. The gospel ranges through the entire cosmos; the good news in Christ envelops even the dead (v. 29). Still, it is as near to us as is the praise of God in the congregation (v. 25) and the meal of the Eucharist, where "the poor shall eat and be satisfied" (v. 26).

PSALM 66:1-11 OR 66:1-8 (BCP)

This is a psalm of praise that celebrates the awesome deeds of God done on behalf of God's people. The deeds are symbolized by the parting of the Red Sea (v. 6), in which the waters of chaos that threatened the people of God with death are held at bay. The suffering and trial of the people of God are noted in verses 10-12, experiences that are attended to by God through prayer (vv. 16-20).

SECOND READING

1 JOHN 4:7-21 (RCL)

This text is, in many ways, the high point of the letter, culminating in verses 9-10. Many commentators compare these verses favorably to 1 Corinthians 13, Paul's better-known poem in praise of love. In our text for today, the Nestle-Aland Greek text of verses 7-10 is offset in stanzas, indicating the editors' sense of its poetic structure. In them the heart of Johannine theology is expressed: God's reaching out in Christ to a world alienated by sin to bring it back to a life centered in God (consider John 3:16). The text clearly stresses the initiative of God in this movement (v. 10), reiterated in the succinct verse 19, "We love because he first loved us." For John the "love" that is revealed in this movement—from God to the world—is the only appropriate model for Christian love. "Love" among humans is redefined in terms of the Christ event. The text is clear that such love is not something that we bring naturally to God or to one another (v. 10). It is grounded in the death of Christ, received by God as an expiation (v. 10, *hilasmos*, a "wiping away," which the NRSV translates as "atoning sacrifice") of human sin. Love of this kind comes to us at a great cost to God. To receive it in faith necessarily transforms our own understanding of love (given to us by the wider culture), allowing us, as John puts it, to "live through" Christ (v. 9). This notion of love, grounded in the willing

> The love of which John speaks is centered in the truth (about God) and action, that is, deeds.

self-sacrifice of God in Christ, could not be more different than that "love" projected upon us by contemporary North American culture, much of which is self-centered, sought out primarily to satisfy one's own narcissistic desires and needs. Much of our culture's "love" talk centers in the interior world of self and its affects and feelings. Interestingly, there is no such "emotive" center to the love of which John speaks. It is a love that is centered in the truth (about God) and action, that is, deeds (3:18). In fact, according to John, if one is not actively engaged in loving the world and its people "through Christ," then any claim either to know or to be known by God is simply false. To love God is to discover oneself involved in God's ongoing love of the world (in general) and Christian assembly (in particular). In fact, it is *only* in the expression of such service to the world that God is known, even seen (vv. 12, 20-21). The logic of verse 20 is pretty down to earth: "for those who do not love a brother or sister whom they have seen, cannot love God whom they have not seen."

With verse 13 a shift in tense occurs, from that which speaks of God's love active in Christian community in the past, to that which occurs in the present. John, who speaks so passionately about the *practical* aspects of faith active in love, here privileges the role of one's *confession* of faith (vv. 14-15). It is clear to John that unless one witnesses correctly to the meaning of the Christ event, one cannot clearly understand one's responsibilities in the world. Our ability to love one another is dependent upon our prior understanding of how God has loved us. Here again the text challenges some of our basic assumptions about "love"—for instance, that it is primarily a thing of the "heart."

One of the remarkable gifts that come with the experience of the gospel's transforming power is the assurance—the "boldness" (*parrēsia*; cf. 2:28, 3:21; a word that we have encountered more than once in these Easter readings)—before God and the world. As John says, "perfect love casts out fear" (v. 18). To love the world is risky and difficult business, as is working for its reconciliation. This God knows well, from the inside out. A special charism, then, comes to those who witness to the power of the gospel, lived out in love.

A special charism comes to those who witness to the power of the gospel, lived out in love.

It is a boldness unknown to the world, a confidence made perfect in nonviolent, nonretaliatory weakness (2 Cor. 12:9). It is a weakness through which—precisely because it places its trust in the mercies of God—all fear of the world is cast out, and victory over the world is won.

1 JOHN 3:(14-17) 18-24 (BCP)
1 JOHN 3:18-24 (LFM)

For discussion of this text, please see the second reading (RCL) for the Fourth Sunday of Easter, above.

ACTS 8:26-40 (BCP ALT.)

For discussion of this text, please see the first reading (RCL, BCP) for the Fifth Sunday of Easter, above.

THE GOSPEL

JOHN 15:1-8 (RCL, LFM)

The Gospel text (15:1-8) is continued next Sunday (15:9-17). Both texts together constitute Jesus' use of the extended metaphor of the "vine" to describe the relationship of the Father to the Son and of both to the church. The pericope functions within Jesus' Farewell Discourse (John 14–16), in which Jesus prepares his disciples for his crucifixion and departure to the Father, an event that is imminent (17:1). The theological content of today's Gospel text also overlaps with the second reading for today from 1 John and provides, in the figure of the vine, a wonderful illustration of the homily on love in 1 John.

The figure of the vine is an allegory to which Jesus provides the interpretive code. He is the vine, the Father is the vinegrower (or "farmer," who prunes/cleans by means of the word, v. 3), and Jesus' disciples are the branches. All three are necessary for the production of fruit, which may be understood as the community's faithful response to God's word lived out through works of love. In a manner similar to that of last week's Gospel, centered on the figure of the Good Shepherd and his flock, today's Gospel uses an illustration from the everyday life of peasant agriculture that resonates deeply with the Old Testament. In the Old Testament, Israel is described in terms of vine imagery, often with devastating criticism (for example, Isa. 5:1-7; Ezek. 17:6-8, 19:10-14; Ps. 80:8-16; Jer. 2:21; Hos. 10:1). Jeremiah 2:21 is typical: "I planted you as a choice vine, from the purest stock. How then did you turn degenerate and become a wild vine?" God tends the vine with care, yet it still produces "wild grapes" (Isa. 5:4). In using this imagery, Jesus is making the claim that he represents the true Israel. God's promises are now resting on him; good fruit is to be found only on this vine. This leads to the

> Jesus makes the claim that he represents the true Israel. God's promises are now resting on him; good fruit is to be found only on this vine.

remarkable claim that "apart from me you can do nothing (v. 4)." Only by being in relationship to Jesus (v. 5) will a person produce fruit (see also Heb. 11:6). The similarly remarkable claim of verse 7 ("If you abide in me, and my words abide in you, ask for whatever you wish, and it will be done for you;" compare to v. 16) assumes the one who has responded to the word is part of a Christian community grounded in service to neighbor.

Throughout this pericope the very characteristic Johannine verb "abide" (*menō*), sometimes translated "remain" (e.g., RSV, NET), is much used. It provides the grand theme of chapter 15 of John: Jesus gives instructions of how to "remain" with him after his departure (vv. 26-27). It is the same term used to describe the Spirit's "abiding" with Jesus after his baptism (see 1:32-33) and the food that "remains" to eternal life (6:27). In the previous chapter "abide/remain" language also describes the relationship between the Father and the Son (14:10), as well as the gift of the Spirit given to the community (14:17). In our passage for today, it is clear that this "abiding" in Christ is anything but static. It is productive; it leads to works of love.

> The word of the cross "prunes" the life of discipleship in that it gives it a cruciform shape.

The "pruning/cleaning" function of the word (v. 3) is worth reflecting over. The "word" (*logos*) is, in John, a deep metaphor for the activity of God (for example, 1:1, 14). The word that is spoken by God in Christ, of course, also involves the cross (3:14-16). This word of the cross "prunes" the life of discipleship in that it gives it a cruciform shape. It eliminates certain possibilities (such as, self-aggrandizement, 5:44, 12:25, 43), while it encourages others (for example, service of the neighbor, 13:14, 34). The word that Jesus, crucified and risen, speaks to the church can be, then, heard both as: (*a*) "judgment" against the ways of the world, as well as (*b*) gospel, in that it reveals an alternative way of being, made possible through the cross, by means of cleansing baptism (1:33, 13:8) into the body of Christ (the Vine, the very temple of God, 2:21). God's word is ever efficacious. Its pruning work is never done. Yet the word is also experienced daily in the life of those who abide in the love of God as "joy" (v. 11). Ultimately, however, as Jesus reminds us, this work of the word of God is not about us, but about the "farmer." The fruits of the Vine, the good works that result from faith, are to glorify God: "My Father is glorified by this, that you bear much fruit and become my disciples" (v. 8). To abide in Christ is, then, to make the glory (*doxa*) of God visible to the world.

JOHN 14:15-21 (BCP)

This text is one of the five texts that speak of the promise of the Paraclete (also called the Advocate, the Holy Spirit of vv. 15-16) in the Gospel of John (see the commentary below on the RCL Pentecost Gospel text).

SIXTH SUNDAY OF EASTER

MAY 17, 2009

Revised Common (RCL)	Episcopal (BCP)	Roman Catholic (LFM)
Acts 10:44-48	Acts 11:19-30 or Isa. 45:11-13, 18-19	Acts 10:25-26, 34-35, 44-48
Psalm 98	Psalm 33 or 33:1-8, 18-22	Ps. 98:1, 2-3, 3-4
1 John 5:1-6	1 John 4:7-21 or Acts 11:19-30	1 John 4:7-10
John 15:9-17	John 15:9-17	John 15:9-17

FIRST READING

ACTS 10:44-48 (RCL)

This text is a continuation of the Easter Sunday reading in which we heard Peter's sermon to those gathered in the Roman centurion Cornelius's home. The sermon begins with the famous statement that "God shows no partiality" (v. 34); God extends salvation to all through Christ. Today's pericope describes "the Gentile Pentecost" that marks the opening of the mission to the Gentiles in Acts. Up to this point, with the exception of the Ethiopian eunuch (see last week), the mission of the church has been directed largely to the Jewish cultural sphere. Note also that the conversion of Cornelius follows upon that of Saul/Paul related in chapter 9 and stands in some contrast to it. Paul's initial response to the gospel, as a Jew "zealous" for the traditions of his ancestors (Gal. 2:14), was to persecute the church. His eventual conversion, based on a revelation of the risen Jesus (9:5), represents a 180-degree turnaround. The patron Cornelius, a devout Gentile friendly to the traditions and people of Israel, on the other hand, responds at once in faith to the word about Jesus. The radical inclusivity of the gospel is inscribed in these accounts of conversions of both friends (Cornelius) and enemies (Paul) of God's mission of reconciliation. As bewildering as was Paul's conversion to those whom he had persecuted (9:21), so, too, was the fact that God would pour out the Spirit on Gentiles (10:45). The Spirit of God works in stunningly unconventional ways. The bottom line for Luke in retelling these narratives is to indicate how God is

49

working variously through the Holy Spirit to establish the kingdom of God, a kingdom marked by the full inclusion of Gentiles, through faith in Jesus. Cultural boundaries are transgressed in a scandalous way; something new is created.

The text for today begins as the descent of the Holy Spirit interrupts Peter's preaching at the conclusion of his speech. The Spirit's presence, as observed by the Jewish Christians, is manifested by means of the "speaking in tongues and extolling [or praising] God" of the gathered Gentiles. These are marks of the Spirit's presence similar to those revealed in the first Pentecost (see 2:4, 11). Though the gift of speaking in tongues is usually associated with the outpouring of the Spirit, the second gift should not be ignored—that of the *praise* of what God has done in Jesus. Indeed, one might claim that the true *worship of God* is the reason *why* the gift of the Holy Spirit is given to the church; the gift of tongues—however it might be understood—is also to serve this end (see 2:11; 1 Cor. 14:26-28).

Peter responds to the gift of the Spirit to the Gentiles assembled in Cornelius's house by requesting that they be baptized (11:17). The sheer gratuity of this benefaction that comes directly from God to the Gentiles should not be missed. Its meaning is clear. The outpouring of the Spirit of God "on all flesh" (2:17-21) as free gift by means of the word about Jesus is *the* sign of the in-breaking of the new age into the world.

> The outpouring of the Spirit of God "on all flesh" as free gift by means of the word about Jesus is *the* sign of the in-breaking of the new age into the world.

The multiculturalism of the church signals that God's reconciliation project of the last days (2:17) has begun in earnest. It is the shared experience of the Spirit that binds this very diverse community of Jews ("from every nation," 2:9-11) and Gentiles together, symbolized by their baptisms into the same name, that of "Jesus."

Connections are made in the text between the proclamation of the word (which actually forms Christian assembly), the centrality of baptism (which gives the church its fundamental identity in Christ), and the unity of the body of Christ (which is found in the abiding presence of God's Spirit). Interestingly, the gift of the Spirit actually interrupts Peter's proclamation about Jesus (v. 44), transforming Peter's words into the efficacious word that *does* something—it creates a new people of God. The experience of this gift of the word leads to the spontaneous praise of God. That Peter remained in this new Christian community for several days after his experience of the "Gentile Pentecost" indicates that there is no longer any thing that prohibits the full communion (shared common life) of Jew and Greek (or even a Roman soldier) in the body of Christ (see Gal. 3:26-28; Eph. 2:11-22).

For discussion of verses 44-48, see above. For discussion of verses 34-35, please see the first reading (RCL, BCP, LFM), for the Resurrection of the Lord, Easter Day, above.

ACTS 11:19-30 (BCP)

The persecution in Jerusalem that follows the stoning of Stephen (8:1) has scattered the church, driving the early followers out of the historic land of Israel into the Greco-Roman cultural sphere, thus providing an opportunity for wider evangelism. Among the cities they find refuge in is Antioch, one of the great urban centers of the East. There the mission to the Greeks, for the first time, begins in earnest (v. 20). When the remnant of the church in Jerusalem hears of this success, they send the talented Barnabas, who retrieves Saul (Paul) from Tarsus, his hometown, where Saul had been brought for his safety (9:30). The text indicates the remarkable success of the mission to the Gentiles based in Antioch by reporting that it was there that the movement ("the Way"; 9:2) received, for the first time, a Greek name—"Christian" (*christianos*).

In verses 27-30, a famine that occurred during the time of Claudius, emperor of Rome (41–44 C.E.), provided the opportunity for the solidarity of the Greek-speaking and Aramaic-speaking missions of the church to take concrete form. A collection was taken up for those in distress in Judea, delivered from Antioch by Barnabas and Saul. The commonality of the early church in Jerusalem (2:44) moves to a higher, international level. The newly made members of the body of Christ roll up their sleeves to help a church in need. Though the word of God came to the Hellenists by means of the "established" church in Jerusalem, it was the "other"—the "Greek"—that provided hospitality and needed care to the "elders" (v. 30).

ISAIAH 45:11-13, 18-19 (BCP ALT.)

The text describes the unusual and unexpected ways that God works for the salvation of the world, including the use of the Persian king Cyrus to effect the return of the people of God from exile (v. 13).

RESPONSIVE READING

PSALM 98 (RCL)
PSALM 98:1, 2-3, 3-4 (LFM)

This is a hymn of praise because "[the LORD] has done marvelous things" (v. 1) and because God's continuing judgment is just (v. 9b). In particular it celebrates the *victory* of "the right hand of God" (v. 1), which has "revealed his *vindication* in the sight of all nations" (v. 2). The Greek LXX translates the "victory" of the NRSV as *sōtēria* ("salvation"). Similarly, behind "vindication" lies *dikaiosynē* ("righteousness"). So the New American Standard Bible can translate verse 2 as, "The LORD has made known His *salvation*; He has revealed His *righteousness* in the sight of the nations." It is through such LXX terms that Paul understands the verse christologically while incorporating it into his statement of the theme of Romans at 1:16-17, as does Luke in his citation in the *Nunc dimittis* (Luke 2:30-31). From the New Testament perspective the hymn celebrates *Christ* as the revelation of God's faithfulness and saving righteousness, not only to Israel (v. 3), but to all of creation (vv. 4, 7-9). In particular, the fact that God's righteousness is revealed to the "nations" (v. 2) is understood by New Testament theologians to refer to God's outreach to the Gentiles effected through the death and resurrection of Jesus. The psalm is well matched with today's first reading, which relates the "Gentile Pentecost" of Acts 10. The "new song" (v. 1) that the church sings is a hymn to God in thanksgiving for Christ, the Savior, the very Righteousness of God (see Rev. 5:9-14, 14:3).

PSALM 33 OR 33:1-8, 18-22 (BCP)

This psalm is a hymn of praise because God is trustworthy (vv. 4, 21). God's promises are the only source of all hope (vv. 18, 22) and gladness (v. 21). God is just, faithful, and upright. God will, because of God's "steadfast love" (vv. 5, 18), deliver one from death (v. 19). Though God looks with special favor on "the people whom he has chosen" (v. 12), God is sovereign Lord of all peoples and "fashions the hearts of them all" (v. 15). The universal reach of God's love of all that is created is worthy of exuberant praise. This psalm is a possible lection for the day of Pentecost, which links the gift of God's renewal of the "hearts of all" (v. 15) with the outpouring of God's Holy Spirit upon "all flesh" (Acts 2:17; Joel 2:28-32 LXX; see also Jer. 31:33-34; Heb. 8:8-13; Rom. 2:15; John 6:45).

1 JOHN 5:1-6 (RCL)

The "family" or "kinship" language that has been much in evidence in 1 John continues in today's reading. The text begins (v. 1) with the characteristic Johannine claim that those who have been given the gift of belief in Jesus as the incarnate Christ ("come in the flesh," 4:2) have been born anew by God (John 1:12-13, 3:3; 1 John 2:29, 3:9, 4:7). The initiative here lies with God. The response of belief originates in the extraordinary act of God in Christ through which we become God's adopted children (compare Rom. 8:15-16; Eph. 1:5). In what follows, John's "familial logic" is displayed. John makes the claim that those who love the parent (*gennēsanta*), love the children (*gegennēmenon*). This is the obverse of the claim in 4:20, that those who do not love their brothers and sisters cannot assume to love God. "Love" here is understood in terms of one's relational obligations in Christian community, "For the love of God is this, that we obey his commandments" (v. 3; see also Mark 12:30-31; Rom. 13:9; Gal. 5:14; James 2:8). Then comes the remarkable expression of verse 3b, "And his commandments are not burdensome." This is similar to the Matthean claim, "For my yoke is easy, and my burden is light" (Matt. 11:30). The power of the gospel is discovered, in part, by being so transformed that the tough, relational work of living in community is not experienced as a burdensome duty, but as a gift of God. Here as elsewhere, much of what the gospel of Christ crucified offers us is counterintuitive; it goes against our instincts. So too is the claim that the reconciling work of Christ carried out in church assemblies, which also bear the wounds of the world's conflicts, represents, as John says, a "victory that conquers the world." It is precisely "faith" (v. 4) that makes this possible. The one who "believes that Jesus is the Son of God" (v. 5) has conquered the world, in that through belief we are liberated from the hold the world has on us, especially as it defines our obligations to our neighbor. This suggests that the radical individualism of the present-day North American context, which understands any demand our neighbor's life places upon us as a restriction of our own freedom, is not inevitable. One thinks here of Luther's understanding of how the gospel frees us to be of service to our neighbor within and without the body of Christ. It is God's grace that allows us to experience this service, not as a painful duty, but as an expression of our "calling" by God.

New language is introduced in verse 6 ("water, blood, testimony"). Exegetes are divided about the meaning of the terms "water and blood" in reference to Christ. Options include: (*a*) Jesus' own baptism/death, (*b*) the sacraments of the people of God (baptism/eucharist), and (*c*) the death of Jesus (John 19:34). Given

The power of the gospel is discovered by being so transformed that the tough, relational work of living in community is not experienced as a burdensome duty, but as a gift of God.

that the efficacy of the sacraments of the church are founded in the atoning death of Jesus (1:7, 2:2), perhaps one need not make a choice among these possibilities. If the "Spirit is the one that testifies" (v. 6), and the Spirit can be thought of in terms of the Paraclete (John 14:16, 26, 15:26; see also 1 John 2:1), then what is in view here is the "real presence" of Christ that "abides" in the church. The sacraments of the body of Christ (water and blood), in other words, "testify to" as well as mediate the gift of eternal life given in Christ (v. 11). They are the word made visible, made "testimony" of what God has done and continues to do in Christ.

1 JOHN 4:7-21 (BCP)
1 JOHN 4:7-10 (LFM)

For discussion of this text, please see the second reading (RCL) for the Fifth Sunday of Easter, above.

ACTS 11:19-30 (BCP ALT.)

For discussion of this text, please see the first reading (BCP) for the Sixth Sunday of Easter, above.

THE GOSPEL
JOHN 15:9-17 (RCL, BCP, LFM)

Last week's Gospel text (John 15:1-8) began with Jesus' declaration that "I am the true vine." Today's Gospel picks up where last week's text ended. Verse 11 provides a point of transition between the two pericopes and, in doing so, introduces the notion of "joy" (*chara*). The Johannine love commandment, which we have encountered before in this Easter season, is stated anew in verse 12 (compare to 13:34; 1 John 2:7-11, 3:11, 23; 2 John 5) and is repeated at the end of the pericope for emphasis (v. 17). The content of such love is illustrated strikingly by Jesus' own death (v. 13; cf. 10:15). A remarkable revelation comes in verse 14 when Jesus says that he considers his disciples "friends" (*philos*), not "servants" or "slaves" (*doulos*). This is followed in rapid fashion with the reminder of God's election of the church, and God's promise to be faithful to the requests of the elect, which is a restatement of a promise encountered in last week's text (15:7) that surfaces elsewhere in the Johannine literature (see 14:14, 16:23; 1 John 3:22, 5:14-15). A few words about each of these subjects are in order.

The purpose of the fruit (v. 16) borne out of the love of the community for one another is the glorification of God (v. 8). One should remember that this "love" (*agape*) of which the Gospel and letters of John speak is not based in emotion, but rather in the often difficult deeds of service extended to the neighbor, the world, and God. Even though "love" may not be an emotion for John, the gift discovered in the active witness of the assembly to the love of God is. Through the esteeming of others (love) one discovers "joy"—the experience of gladness. Such joy is a Johannine theme (3:29, 16:20ff., 17:13; 1 John 1:4). In John "joy" is well aware of its opposite (sorrow, pain; 16:20), for it is the joy of the Crucified One who has won the victory over sorrow and death by passing through both. The joy that is in the community of which John speaks is the joy of Christ—("I have said these things so that *my* joy may be in *you*," v. 11). Such a joy, made possible by the resurrection of Christ, can withstand the hatred of the world, experienced as persecution on account of the gospel (15:18-25).

> In John "joy" is well aware of its opposite, for it is the joy of the Crucified One who has won the victory over sorrow and death by passing through both.

The Greek word for "friend" is *philos* (v. 13), the cognate of the verb *phileō*, often translated in English as "to love." In Greek, then, the "love" language continues throughout today's Gospel text on "friendship." It is important to note how radical is the shift from *doulos* (slave, servant) to *philos* (friend) that Jesus explicitly models. Most relationships in antiquity reflected the dynamics of what social-scientific criticism of the New Testament calls "patrons" and "clients." In this relational pattern, the patron was clearly dominant, the client was subordinate. The archetypal form of such relationships was that between a master and a slave, though it also patterned most interactions between free citizens. Ancient society was hierarchical; one carefully related to those above and below in the social pecking order. "Friendship" between equals was a rare thing, simply because equality was mostly absent in the social relations of antiquity. The values of this patronage system are severely criticized in the New Testament. It is, for example, precisely this patron/client dynamic that Jesus upends in the foot-washing ritual (John 13), where the greater (Jesus) serves the lesser (the disciples). This leveling of the social order effected in the ministry of Jesus continues in today's text. The disciples become true friends of Jesus because Jesus has shared all things with them, including his intimate knowledge of God, something a patron would never do with a client (v. 15). Knowledge, after all, is power. The bramble of a grape "vine" is the perfect illustration of such radical mutuality: "I am the vine, you are the branches" (15:5). Lest the image of the intertwined branches and vine somehow erase the distinction between Christ and his friends, we are reminded in verse 16, "You did not choose me but I chose you."

"The Father will give you whatever you ask him in my name" (v. 16). This verse, taken out of the context of Jesus' discourse on the true vine and understood solely in terms of God rewarding a disciplined prayer life by fulfilling specific requests, has wreaked all sorts of spiritual havoc through the centuries. It is important to note that today's Gospel is followed by a discussion of the world's hatred of the church. That which God promises to give, in response to prayer "in the name" of the Crucified One, is precisely the power to love the world even though the world responds to that love with hatred (15:25). Through its proclamation of the gospel in word and deed, the church continues to witness to the power of the Word and its salvific purpose: "For God so loved the world. . . . God did not send the Son into the world to condemn the world, but in order that the world might be saved through him" (3:16-17).

The work of this love, joyfully active in word and deed, has passed from vine to branches—empowered by the promises of God, pruned by the cross of Christ—in order that the vine might continue to be fruitful in God's work of salvation.

> The disciples become true friends of Jesus because Jesus has shared all things with them, including his intimate knowledge of God, something a patron would never do with a client.

Though scholars are of different minds about the presence of sacramental imagery in the Gospel of John, one may perceive resonances with baptism and the Eucharist in the vine discourse. Inclusion into this vine (the body of Christ) comes by baptism ("you have already been cleansed by the word that I have spoken to you" (v. 3). At the heart of the Lord's Supper (through not explicitly present in John) is the remembrance of the sacrifice of the body and blood of Jesus. So also, the Vine himself reminds us that "no one has greater love than this, to lay down one's life for one's friends" (v. 13). We abide in the vine that is Jesus, in part, by means of our participation in his sacramental body and blood (John 6:56).

ASCENSION OF THE LORD

Revised Common (RCL)	Episcopal (BCP)	Roman Catholic (LFM)
Acts 1:1-11	Acts 1:1-11 or Ezek. 1:3-5a, 15-22, 26-28	Acts 1:1-11
Psalm 47 or Psalm 93	Psalm 47 or 110:1-5	Ps. 47:2-3, 6-7, 8-9
Eph. 1:15-23	Eph. 1:15-23 or Acts 1:1-11	Eph. 4:1-13 or 4:1-7, 11-13
Luke 24:44-53	Luke 24:49-53 or Mark 16:9-15, 19-20	Mark 16:15-20

FIRST READING

ACTS 1:1-11 (RCL, BCP, LFM)

Given the significant overlap between the last chapter of the Gospel of Luke and the first chapter of Acts (for example, the two accounts of Jesus' ascension in Luke 24:50-53 and Acts 1:9-11), the first reading and the Gospel text for today can be thought of as one extended pericope. Actually, some details of the texts would be better understood if the sequence of the readings were reversed. For instance, the unspecified promise of Luke 24:49 is given concrete expression in Acts 1:4-5—the baptism by means of the Holy Spirit that occurs on the day of Pentecost.

The beginning of the Acts pericope (1:1-5) includes a concise review of Luke's first volume. It also lays out the chronology of death, resurrection, and ascension that is particular to the Lukan narrative. The risen Jesus was with the disciples for forty days before ascending to the Father (v. 3); the outpouring of the Spirit occurs ten days later (on Pentecost, in other words, fifty days after Passover). It is this Lukan chronology that patterns the liturgical church year. The early church, however, had a variety of ways of thinking about the exaltation of Jesus, an occurrence that is, ultimately, a mystery. No one description of it suffices. In some of the liturgical fragments of the early church preserved in the New Testament (for example, Phil. 2:5-11; also Eph. 1:20-23, the second reading for today) the lines between resurrection and exaltation are not as clear as they are in Luke's narrative. That is because the early church also understood that the *resurrection* (not only the "ascension") represented the entering of Christ into the glory of God. Here Psalm 110:1, the most often-cited text of the Old Testament in the New, in one movement articulates the exaltation of Jesus from death to co-enthronement with God in heaven (see also Luke 20:42, 22:69, 24:26; Acts 2:32-35). The resurrection appearances of Jesus, even in Luke, can be understood, therefore, as the revelation of the risen Jesus from his glorified state with the Father, somewhat in line with John's thinking on the matter (see my comments on John 20 on Easter Sunday and Easter 2, above).

One detail of today's first reading much discussed by exegetes is the question the apostles ask Jesus in verse 6: "Is this the time when you will restore the kingdom to Israel?" A common apocalyptic expectation of the period was that a restoration of Israel to its former political glory would occur in the end times (see Luke 24:21). The resurrection of Jesus was a confirmation that the end times were upon Israel, yet the expected restoration had not begun. This puzzles the apostles.

Jesus teaches that *God's* eschatology is different from our apocalyptic projections, however biblically based they may be.

In answering the disciples' question, Jesus shifts the focus from political expectations to the coming mission of the church; the apostles (and through them, the church) has critically important work to do. The extent is described in verse 8: "to the ends of the earth." Once again Jesus teaches that *God's* eschatology is different from our apocalyptic projections, however biblically based (as were those of the apostles) they may be. Indeed, Jesus' understanding of the future pushes us back into an engagement with the world in ways we might not appreciate, in order to carry out the hard tasks of God's ongoing reconciliation of the world through the witness and work of the gospel.

The imagery used in Luke-Acts to describe the ascension of Jesus is based on Daniel's vision of the Son of Man (Dan. 7:13-14). Part of what Luke is saying by this use of Daniel is that the exaltation of Jesus occurs "according to the Scriptures." Scripture, understood as the word of God, is the living voice of God that appropriately interprets the Christ event.

Though the vision of the ascension, couched in Daniel's apocalyptic imagery, seems to imply the removal of Jesus from earth, this is clearly not Luke's intent. Jesus is continually present in the remainder of Acts—represented by his "name"—in the proclamation of the gospel, as well as in the sacraments of baptism and the Eucharist. Even after the ascension, Jesus is "seen" by Stephen (Acts 7:55-56) and Paul (9:1-9). Rather than removing Jesus, the ascension actually makes possible the gift of the Spirit on Pentecost (2:33). Somewhat counter to our everyday notions of common sense, Luke understands that the exaltation of Jesus makes Christ more fully present, by means of the Spirit active through the ministry of the church, to more individuals than Jesus' historical ministry allowed. Luke well understood that the primary gift of the Spirit—the forgiveness of sins—is dependent upon the atoning death of the Incarnate One and his exaltation to God's presence (see Luke 24:46-47; Acts 5:31, 20:28; John 16:7-11).

The point of the ascension is not that our focus should be upon Jesus in "heaven," but that our energies are directed, with the help of the Holy Spirit, to the mission and witness of the church here on earth. The question of the "two men in white robes" put to the disciples is intended to be heard by us as well: "Why do you stand looking up toward heaven?" (v. 11). By this question the two angels are simply repeating what Jesus earlier told his apostles. The work of the church is to be done upon the earth until that time when Jesus "will come again in glory to judge the living and the dead."

EZEKIEL 1:3-5a, 15-22, 26-28 (BCP alt.)

Ezekiel's vision of the glory of God is anything but straightforward. It has exercised the imaginations of exegetes (for instance, Rev. 4:2-6) and mystics (such as, the Jewish Merkavah tradition) throughout the ages. It is variously referred to as the "chariot vision" or the "throne vision" because of references to (a) something like a divine chariot pulled by "four living creatures" (vv. 15–22) and (b) the divine throne of verse 26 (see also Rev. 5:6-8, 6:1, 6, 7:1, 11, 14:3, 15:7, 19:4). The text suggests that the movement of the chariot was from earth to heaven (vv. 19, 21) and hence became an image of the ascension of Jesus. The "human form" enthroned (v. 26) has been read, in conjunction with such texts as Psalm 110:1, as that of Christ. Though the vision of the glory of the exalted Lord itself may be confusing, it resolves, in an act of remarkable divine accommodation to human limitations, into "the voice of someone speaking" (v. 28). The unutterable, incomprehensible glory of God is a word that can be heard and believed. This is the mystery of the incarnation that ironically "transcends" even the ascension of Jesus—the exalted Christ is present among us in Word and Sacrament.

RESPONSIVE READING
PSALM 47 (RCL, BCP)
PSALM 47:2-3, 6-7, 8-9 (LFM)

Psalm 47 is read in all three years of the lectionary on the Day of Ascension. It is one of the "enthronement psalms" of ancient Israel that were used on festive occasions to celebrate the declaration of God as "King." As an ancient Near Eastern king was enthroned at the beginning of a new year (announced by the trumpet blast of v. 5) with the acclamation of the nation, so God's rule over earth (vv. 2b, 7a) is lifted up in liturgical celebration. The enthroned earthly king, then, is a figure of the divine Lord, who sits above *all* principalities and powers "on his holy throne" (vv. 8-9; compare 1 Pet. 3:22).

In the church, this psalm is read in terms of the exaltation/ascension of Christ. Christ has "gone up" (v. 5)—an image of enthronement in the psalm (v. 8)—to become "king of all the earth." The "christological hymns" of the New Testament (such as, Phil. 2:6-11; Col. 1:15-20; Eph. 2:14-16), which speak of the enthronement of Christ in heaven "at the right hand of God" (see also Ps. 110:1), are fulfillments of the psalmist's invitation to the church to "Sing praises to God, sing praises; sing praises to our King" (v. 6), as is the subsequent hymnody of the church.

PSALM 93 (RCL ALT.)

Another of the "enthronement psalms" (see Psalm 47 above), this hymn praises the establishment of God's rule. God is "robed" with majesty and strength (v. 1); God is enthroned "on high" (v. 4). The poem suggests that it is the creation of the world that provides the foundation of God's eternal rule; God continues to govern the earth with kingly majesty and fairness: "your decrees are very sure" (v. 5). Creation and God's reign (that is, the kingdom of God) are therefore inextricably connected; the trustworthiness of God underlies both. As the medieval Aristotelians would say, God is the efficient *and* instrumental cause of all creation as well as the *re*-creation that is effective through Christ. The exalted, ascended Lord, present in the church, is the same Word through whom all things were created (John 1:4). The liturgical fragment of the early church we have preserved in Ephesians 1:20-23 of today's second reading is a restatement of the enthronement psalms, as is the great hymn of Colossians 1:15-20 (compare to Rev. 19:6), which confesses: "[Christ] is the image of the invisible God, the firstborn of all creation; for in him all things in heaven and on earth were created, things visible and invisible, whether thrones or dominions or rulers or powers—all things have been created *through* him and *for* him."

> The exalted, ascended Lord, present in the church, is the same Word through whom all things were created.

PSALM 110:1-5 (BCP ALT.)

Psalm 110:1 is the most often-cited Old Testament verse in the New Testament. It lies at the very earliest level of tradition of early Christianity's response to the death and subsequent exaltation of Jesus: "The LORD [*kyrios*, that is, God] says to my lord [*kyrios*, that is, Christ], 'Sit at my right hand until I make your enemies your footstool.'" It is the origin of the creedal statement, "He ascended into heaven and is *seated at the right hand* of the Father," that articulates Christ's co-enthronement with God and installation into the divine office of sovereign Lord of all. Similarly, Psalm 110:4 is the origin of Hebrews' typological understanding of the exalted Christ as the high priest who makes continual intercession for us before God: "You are a priest forever according to the order of Melchizedek" (Heb. 6:20, 7:17). Both verses, in their New Testament usages, assume the atoning significance of the death of Jesus (for example, Heb. 10:12).

SECOND READING

EPHESIANS 1:15-23 (RCL, BCP)

Ephesians 1:15-23 is one *long* sentence in Greek. Formally it represents a prayer of thanksgiving (vv. 15-16) that moves into a prayer of intercession for the community (vv. 17-18). The passage ends with an expression of the high Christology and ecclesiology of Ephesians that many believe reflects early liturgical and creedal formulations of the church (vv. 20-23). On this day that the church celebrates the ascension of Christ, the last two verses are particularly important to consider: "And [God] has put all things under [Christ's] feet and has made him the head over all things for the church, which is his body, the fullness of him who fills all in all."

The revelation that the church universal is the body of the ascended Christ who "fills all in all" challenges simplistic understandings of the exaltation of Christ that reduce the ascension to a physical, bodily removal of Jesus to heaven. One way of paraphrasing Ephesians' hymnic material might be by means of Luther's understanding of the "ubiquity" of the glorified Christ. Luther held that Christ in his glorified state, though everywhere, is not everywhere to be found. One is assured, however, that Christ can be found where "the gospel is purely preached and the holy sacraments are administered according to the gospel."[1] Specifically, Luther understood the expression "the right hand of God" to indicate God's omnipresence. The exalted Christ shares this metaphysic with God the Father. Luther sees this attribute revealed in New Testament texts:

> When St. Stephen saw Jesus (Acts 7:55), he did not say that he came down from heaven, but he saw him standing at the right hand of God. When Paul, in Acts 9:4, heard him speak, Christ did not come down from heaven. In short, the mad spirit thinks in childish terms, as if Christ went up and down. He does not understand the realm of Christ

which is in every place, and as Paul says, fills all in all (Eph. 1:23). We are not bidden to search out how it can be that our bread becomes and is the body of Christ. It is the Word of God that says so. We hold to that and believe it.[2]

However one's theological tradition may parse the details of the ascended Christ's presence in the church, the mystery of the ascension is that, through the exaltation of Christ to the right hand of God "in the heavenly places" (v. 20), God has empowered Christ to be more fully and more powerfully (v. 21) present to the world through the mission of the church than he was during Jesus' historical ministry.

There is much that could be said about the thanksgiving and prayer that introduces the creedal affirmation of Christ's exaltation of verses 20-23. Two observations will suffice. The first is that the gifts of God have *already* been given in Christ, to be received in faith. That is, the initiative for salvation is clearly God's (see Eph. 2:8). The prayer is that by means of the Holy Spirit ("a spirit of wisdom and revelation," v. 17), those who have been enlightened through baptism might come to recognize the "hope to which God has called you" (v. 18), that is, one might experience the grace of faith in the promises of God—"the riches of God's glorious inheritance among the saints." Second, the gospel is a great "power for us who believe" (v. 19; see also Rom. 1:16-17). It is the word of life, which defeats death and the devil. As Ephesians goes on to say: "But God, who is rich in mercy, out of the great love with which he loved us even when we were dead through our trespasses, made us alive together with Christ—by grace you have been saved—and raised us up with him and seated us with him in the heavenly places in Christ Jesus." (2:4-6). On the festival of the Ascension of the Lord, we celebrate these remarkable benefits won by Christ and, by the grace of God, given to the body of Christ. Through Christ's ascension the church is taken up into the economy of salvation of the triune God.

> Through Christ's ascension the church is taken up into the economy of salvation of the triune God.

EPHESIANS 4:1-13 OR 4:1-7, 11-13 (LFM)

This text from Ephesians, by means of a creative interpretation of Psalm 68:18, links the ascension of Christ with gifts given to the people of God (v. 8b). Of primary importance is the gift of unity (vv. 3, 13). The church should reflect the unity that exists within the Trinity—one God, Father (v. 6), Son (v. 5), and Spirit (v. 4). Other gifts are listed (v. 11; compare to 1 Cor. 12:4-11); all serve the purpose of "building up the body of Christ" (v. 12).

For discussion of this text, please see the first reading (RCL, BCP, LFM) for the Ascension of the Lord, above.

THE GOSPEL
LUKE 24:44-53 (RCL)
LUKE 24:49-53 (BCP)

If one compares Luke's account of the ascension in Acts 1 with that of Luke 24, some rather startling differences emerge. In Luke 24 it seems as though the ascension occurs on the *evening* of Easter day and at *Bethany* (v. 50). In Acts we find the traditional chronology of forty days between Easter and the day of ascension (Acts 1:3). In Acts, the place is given as the Mount of Olives (1:12). Since Luke 19:29 indicates that Bethany and the Mount of Olives are held together in the mind of Luke, the exact location of the ascension is not really an issue. Yet the exegetical tradition remains stymied as to the significant difference between the two texts with regard to the time at which the ascension occurred. In this regard, one should note that Luke is not writing "history" as we would understand it. The ascension of Jesus provides the natural *end* of the story of Jesus (volume one in Luke's two-volume narrative) and the natural *beginning* of the story of the church in the Acts of the Apostles (volume two). Though there is substantial overlap between Luke 24 and Acts 1, the ascension serves different narrative roles in each book. Also, though Luke provides the church year with a theological narrative that clearly separates the resurrection from the ascension, Luke will blur the lines between resurrection/exaltation/ascension in various ways. The difference in the timing of the ascension in Luke and in Acts, in other words, might be quite intentional. The reader is left to puzzle why this might be. Perhaps it is Luke's subtle way of letting us know that he is quite aware that the resurrection of Jesus from the dead and his exaltation to the very presence of God consists of one grand movement of reversal that defies any narrative retelling that is too cavalier about the dimensions of either time or space in which this defeat of sin and death and subsequent enthronement in power occurs. At the very least, because the discrepancy did not bother Luke, it should not bother us. Rather, it might well serve to deepen our appreciation of the Day of Ascension as a great festival of the church, one that celebrates Christ's victory over death, his return to his preexistent glory, and his naming as *kyrios* (Acts 1:21; see also Phil. 2:9), that is, one who is worthy of our worship. In today's text, having received the resurrected Christ's blessing (v. 51), the disciples do exactly that. They worship (*proskyneō,* v. 52) Jesus for the first time in the Gospel of Luke. That these Jews worship Jesus witnesses to the power of the resurrection to break open even the most sacred and protected theological tenet of Judaism, that *nothing* is coequal with God.

Before Jesus is lifted up beyond the sight line of those gathered, he continued to teach them. The teaching is based in a study of Scripture that sees Christ—the suffering Messiah of Israel (v. 46)—at its very heart. Jesus himself is *the* center of Scripture (or its *scopus*, as the Protestant Reformers would say). Then comes the shocking commission to preach "repentance and forgiveness of sins . . . in his name" to the entire world (v. 47). Out of his newly exalted status, Christ is empowered by God to send "what my Father promised" (v. 49), which in turn empowers his disciples for the tasks of taking the gospel forward into the world. In the first lesson for today we learned that the promise of the Father is the gift of the Holy Spirit. Note carefully: this promise of God turns out not to be what was expected by many to occur in the last days—the immediate restoration of Israel or the creation of a new heaven and a new earth. Rather, the promise is something that will be realized in a more hidden manner, something actually received in faith. It is the promise of the Holy Spirit through which God will establish a new covenant (Jer. 31:31-34; see also Luke 22:20) with *all* of humanity, based in the forgiveness of sin. That we, as well as the first disciples, are witnesses (v. 48) both *of* and *for* this promise of God, made real by faith, is why we have been "clothed with power from on high" (v. 49).

> That these Jews worship Jesus witnesses to the power of the resurrection to break open even the most sacred and protected theological tenet of Judaism, that *nothing* is coequal with God.

MARK 16:9-15, 19-20 (BCP ALT.)
MARK 16:15-20 (LFM)

The "longer ending" of Mark amends the Gospel by means of motifs drawn from other Gospel traditions, including resurrection appearances of Jesus to Mary Magdalene (vv. 9-11; compare to Matt. 28:9-10; John 20:11-18), two unnamed disciples (vv. 12-13; compare to Luke 24:9-11), and the gathered "eleven" disciples (Luke 24:36-43). The ascension of Jesus is reported in verses 19-20 (compare to Acts 1:11), an ascension that did not prohibit Christ from assisting the work of church in proclaiming "the message" (v. 20). In a unique tradition, among the signs that are said to accompany the progress of the gospel are "snake handling" (see also Luke 10:19) and the "drinking of poison," gifts that are still acknowledged among some contemporary Pentecostal groups.

The longer ending, echoing the Great Commission of Matthew (Matt. 28:19), portrays the universal reach of the gospel, as well as the role of baptism among the people of God (v. 16). It also emphasizes the appropriate response to the experience of Christ crucified and risen: "they went out and proclaimed the good news everywhere" (v. 20).

Notes

1. See Article 7 of the Augsburg Confession, in *The Book of Concord: The Confessions of the Evangelical Lutheran Church*, ed. Robert Kolb and Timothy J. Wengert (Minneapolis: Fortress Press, 2000), 42.

2. Martin Luther, "Against the Heavenly Prophets in the Matter of Images and Sacrament," in *Luther's Works*, ed. Helmut T. Lehmann, vol. 40 (Philadelphia: Fortress Press, 1958), 216.

SEVENTH SUNDAY OF EASTER

MAY 24, 2009

Revised Common (RCL)	Episcopal (BCP)	Roman Catholic (LFM)
Acts 1:15-17, 21-26	Acts 1:15-26 or Exod. 28:1-4, 9-10, 29-30	Acts 1:15-17, 20a, 20c-26
Psalm 1	Ps. 68:1-20 or 47	Ps. 103:1-2, 11-12, 19-20
1 John 5:9-13	1 John 5:9-15 or Acts 1:15-26	1 John 4:11-16
John 17:6-19	John 17:11b-19	John 17:11b-19

FIRST READING

ACTS 1:15-17, 21-26 (RCL)
ACTS 1:15-26 (BCP)
ACTS 1:15-17, 20A, 20C-26 (LFM)

This lesson consists of a portion of Peter's first of many speeches in Acts as well as a description of the process by which the early church replaced Judas with Matthias so that the full number of the Twelve might be regained. The interesting question is, of course, why this replacement was necessary. When other members of the Twelve die (such as James the Zebedee in Acts 12:2), they are not replaced. Similarly, the office of "apostle" is not carried on in the church beyond the first generation of leadership. In fact, in Acts, the Twelve are not mentioned after 6:2 and the title *apostle* is not used again after 16:4. After this point in the narrative, the term *elder* (*presbyteros*) is often used when speaking of Christian leadership. Why, then, is it necessary to replace Judas at this point in the narrative?

The answer lies in the symbolic significance of the number twelve. For Luke, the Twelve is a special group chosen from a wider circle of disciples (Luke 6:13). In the context of the Last Supper, Jesus, while conferring on them "a kingdom," explicitly connects the Twelve to the twelve tribes of Israel (Luke 22:28-30). This special group of disciples are new leaders—*authorized by Jesus*—of a reconstituted Israel who will also function as its judges (as will happen at Pentecost). Given the eschatological roles of the Twelve in the restoration of all things put into motion

by God through the ministry, death, and resurrection of Jesus, its integrity is a
matter of critical importance, as is evident in Luke's care in relating Matthias's
selection. It is the restoration of the Twelve that is important, rather than the
particular individual who replaces Judas. From this point on, one hears nothing
more about Matthias in Acts, nor elsewhere in the New Testament.

When Luke introduces the notion of the Twelve sitting "on thrones judging the twelve tribes of Israel" in his Gospel (Luke 22:30), the next pericope
prophesies Satan's work in Judas ("Satan has demanded to sift all of you like
wheat") as well as Peter's threefold denial (Luke 22:34). At the heart of this special group, then, are two high-profile betrayers of Jesus, Peter and Judas. By Acts
1, Peter has both been forgiven and assumed leadership of the assembly, actions
stemming from God, perhaps mediated through Jesus' resurrection appearance to
Peter (Luke 24:34). When Jesus foretells Peter's betrayal in the Gospel of Luke,
he also notes that Peter, when he has "turned back," will "strengthen his brothers
and sisters" (22:32). It is in this new role that we encounter Peter in today's text.
He has learned much from the resurrected Jesus (Acts 1:2-3). Peter even turns
to Scripture as Jesus often did, here in order to think through reasons for Judas's
defection and to move forward from it. The "why" of Judas' betrayal is revealed
in verse 16—because Scripture needed to be fulfilled (in other words, God's
providence lay behind Judas's actions). More specifically, two texts (Pss. 69:25
and 109:8) are given (in the section cut out from today's pericope) to describe the
judgment on Judas's actions as well as the need for someone to take his place. The
requirements for a true replacement are given in verses 21-22, that the person has
been with the others since the beginning (the ministry of John the Baptist) to the
end (an eyewitness to the resurrection). Lots were cast so that the decision was
taken out of human hands and given over to God (v. 24), for which there is Old
Testament precedent (see, for example, Prov. 16:33).

Once the circle of the Twelve has been restored, the pouring out of the Spirit
can occur (2:1-13), which is fittingly described in the next set of readings on the
Day of Pentecost. After Pentecost, though individual
leaders, especially Peter, take prominent positions in
the church, "the Twelve" as an entity does not. It is
mentioned once at 6:2, then there is silence (although
the "twelve tribes" are made mention of in 26:7).
One might again ask the question, Why? Once (*a*)
the Twelve are reconstituted (a symbol of the new Israel created by Jesus), and (*b*)
the gift of the Holy Spirit is given to the church (and the Twelve testify to Israel
on Pentecost), the promise of Jesus' historical ministry, which was focused largely
on Israel, is fulfilled. When the mission to the Gentiles is initiated and the transition from Peter to Paul and Barnabas occurs (chapters 9–11), a new configuration

The Twelve, even though their existence is a sign of the in-breaking kingdom of God and the new era initialed by Jesus' own ministry, represent transitional leadership.

of leadership in the church is needed. Paul, of course, was not a member of the Twelve. He never knew Jesus. In Acts 1, we are still in the hinge section between the time of Jesus and that of the evolving church. The Spirit, though active (v. 16), has not yet been poured out "on all flesh" (2:17), and hence the church has not yet begun its mission "to the ends of the earth" (1:8). The Twelve, even though their existence is a sign of the in-breaking kingdom of God and the new era initialed by Jesus' own ministry, represent transitional leadership. Once the promised gift of the Spirit (1:8) is given, God will use it to raise up new leaders, in new configurations, with new skills, for the church's mission as it moves into ever new areas. God still does.

EXODUS 28:1-4, 9-10, 29-30 (BCP ALT.)

The Gospel text for today is a portion of Jesus' "high priestly prayer." This lesson from Exodus describes the vestments that the high priest (Aaron) wears as he serves in the Temple. Aaron, as high priest, was understood by the early church to be a type of Christ. Christ bears the sins of all as he goes into his holy of holies to offer sacrifice on behalf of all humanity (see, for example, Heb. 2:17, 4:14-15, 5:4-5, 13:11-12). Christ, our high priest, the text tells us, "shall bear this judgment . . . on his heart before the LORD continually" (v. 30).

RESPONSIVE READING
PSALM 1 (RCL)

This psalm expresses the antinomy that exists between "two ways"—the way of the righteous and that of the wicked. The contrast between these ways is illustrated in today's other lectionary readings. "The LORD watches over the way of the righteous" (v. 6) resonates with Jesus' reminding the Father in John 17:12 that "I protected them in your name that you have given me." The psalm's concluding line, "the way of the wicked will perish" is illustrated by the death of Judas (Acts 1:18-20, 25; John 17:12). Note that there are no mediating shades of gray between the two groups. They are set off against each other as opposites, laying the foundation for the strong apocalyptic dualism of Jewish, and later Christian, theology.

It is important to note what sets the two groups apart. It not a particular set of behaviors judged in strictly moral terms. Rather, it is a particular orientation to the "law of the LORD." The psalm begins with a beatitude: "Blessed is . . ." (RSV). Blessed is the one whose "*delight* is in the law of the LORD" (italics mine; compare to Luke 6:20-26). Here "law" (*torah*) is best glossed as "instruction" rather than "command." The psalmist is referring to the word of God given as revelation to guide and instruct the people of God. This word includes, of course, the written Torah, the Holy Scriptures. In the context of the church, this word includes the New as well as the Old Testament. Through Scripture—a primary means of grace—God continues to engage us. The "way of righteousness" is discovered by those who respond in faith.

PSALM 68:1-20 (BCP)

The core metaphor of this psalm is of a warrior (vv. 1, 11-14, 17) whose victory assures a salvation that includes "escape from death" (vv. 19-20) and whose enthronement (v. 18) ensures a just and compassionate rule (vv. 5-6). The hymn chronicles the guidance of the people of God, from Sinai (v. 8) to Jerusalem (v. 16). The early Christians read this poem from Israel's early history in terms of the cosmic battle against evil fought by God in Christ. Although the Son is the almighty and powerful *Christus victor*, he is also Jesus, "the father of orphans and protector of widows" (v. 5), who "gives the desolate a home to live in" (v. 6). In singing this psalm, one prays that the church of the exalted and victorious Christ be empowered to continue this work in the name of Jesus (v. 4).

PSALM 47 (BCP ALT.)

For discussion of this text, please see the responsive reading (RCL, BCP, LFM) for the Ascension of the Lord, above.

PSALM 103:1-2, 11-12, 19-20 (LFM)

This psalm is a hymn of praise offered to God whose primary "benefit" is forgiveness (vv. 3, 11), epitomized in the wonderful verse 8: "The LORD is merciful and gracious, slow to anger and abounding in steadfast love." In response to the sovereign grace of God, experienced in the forgiveness of sin, one blesses (gives thanks and praise for) the gift through service to God and neighbor: "Bless the LORD, O you his angels, you mighty ones who do his bidding, obedient to his spoken word" (v. 20).

SECOND READING

1 JOHN 5:9-13 (RCL)
1 JOHN 5:9-15 (BCP)

ERIK M. HEEN

The "testimony" language we encounter in this reading is introduced in verse 6. The preacher should back up at least that far to get a sense of the larger context. It would also be good to be aware of the ongoing conversation of the Gospel of John regarding "testimony" (see, for example, John 1:7, 19, 3:11, 31-33, 4:39, 5:31-36, 8:13-17, 19:35, 21:24). Also, today's lectionary text ends at verse 13, which actually *begins* the conclusion of the letter. The boundaries of the pericope, in other words, work against rather than facilitate its interpretation. By bridging over into the conclusion of the letter, the reading does, however, end with John's testimony as to the purpose of the epistle: "I write these things . . . so that you might know that you have eternal life" (compare to John 20:31).

Important as our "testimony" (*martyria*) might be with regard to our faith, it is clear that here the initiative—again—comes from God (John 5:31-36). Our witnessing is in response to "the testimony of God that he has testified to his Son" (v. 9). According to John, God's testimony/witness to us in the life, death, and resurrection of the Son is the basis not only of our response, but of the gift received through it—eternal life (v. 11). The gift of eternal life is another way of speaking about being "born of God" (5:4). In this Easter season, one should not miss the fact that John's understanding of the testimony that Jesus gives about the Father *assumes* the resurrection, which itself is *the* witness *of God* to the possibility of life that transcends the constraints of death: "I am the resurrection and the life. Those who believe in me, even though they die, will live" (John 11:25). Given this understanding of the resurrection of Jesus as itself a central witness to the eternal life made possible in Christ, one can intuit why some formerly of the Johannine community downplayed the full *humanity* of Jesus, including his death (1 John 4:2-3; see also John 3:6). But the three witnesses to the life made possible in Christ noted in 5:8 include not only water and Spirit (in other words, new birth that comes with baptism; see also John 3:5, 4:14), but also blood (in other words, the death of the human Jesus, see also John 19:34). The Johannine writings in the New Testament are a witness to the church's confession that the incarnate Christ was truly human, who "for our sake was crucified," as the Nicene Creed puts it. According to 1 John, our testimony to God involves christological content (4:2) as well as a commitment to the Father's commands engaged through service to one's brothers and sisters in Christ.

> The testimony language of 1 John refers not only to the historical incarnation of Christ in Jesus, but also the ongoing presence of Christ in the sacraments of the church.

The sacramental life of the church, in which the everyday realities of our world (water, bread, wine) mediate to us the eternal life that has its origin in God, is "incarnational" in the same way as was the man Jesus. In my theological tradition (Lutheran), there is a very real sense that such "finite" entities (water, bread, wine) are capable of carrying the "infinite" (*finitum capax infiniti*). This being the case, even one's "spirituality"—one's experience of God—is grounded in the everyday world in which we live. Our love of God cannot be isolated from our service to other human beings and that of creation.

The testimony language of 1 John refers, then, not only to the historical incarnation of Christ in Jesus, but also to the ongoing presence of Christ in the sacraments of the church ("There are three that testify: the Spirit and the water and the blood, and these three agree," 5:8). The testimony that believers have "in their hearts" (v. 10) assumes a worshiping community that assembles not only to hear the word, but quite literally to be immersed in it in baptism, as well as fed by it in Holy Communion. "This life" that "is in his Son" (v. 11) cannot be separated out from the worshiping assembly any more than can the love of God from one's relationships within the family of God (4:21, 5:2). With such deeply incarnational and sacramental thoughts we are brought back to where we began six weeks ago in our first reading of 1 John: "We declare to you what was from the beginning, what we have *heard*, what he have *seen* with our eyes, what we have looked at and *touched* with our hands, concerning the word of life" (1:1; italics mine).

1 JOHN 4:11-16 (LFM)

For discussion of this text, please see the second reading (RCL) for the Fifth Sunday of Easter, above.

ACTS 1:15-26 (BCP ALT.)

For discussion of this text, please see the first reading (RCL, BCP, LFM) for the Seventh Sunday of Easter, above.

THE GOSPEL
JOHN 17:6-19 (RCL)
JOHN 17:11B-19 (BCP, LFM)

Today's Gospel text is the middle portion of Jesus' "high priestly prayer" that concludes the farewell discourse (chapters 14–17) set within Jesus' last meal with his disciples. One should read all of chapter 17, at least, in order to situate

ERIK M. HEEN

today's verses in the flow of this section. It is critical, for instance, to note that Jesus begins the prayer to God by acknowledging that "the hour has come" (17:1; see also 13:1); the betrayal, arrest, and crucifixion follow quickly in subsequent chapters. With his departure imminent, Jesus entrusts the future of his disciples directly to God. On the simplest narrative level this text describes Jesus sitting at table with his disciples at the end of his ministry. He turns to the Father in prayer and asks that God protect (vv. 11–15) and sanctify (vv. 17–19) his followers. Yet, as is typical for John (for example, 2:22, 4:23, 5:25, 16:32), the text also reveals not only the Last Supper of the historical Jesus, but also the eschatological perspective of the church of the glorified Christ. Jesus is "the resurrection and the life" (11:25) before his death!

The sense of time in this text is elastic, incorporating past, present, and future. Jesus' prayer is offered not only for his original disciples, but also for the church of every subsequent time.

In today's text Jesus, while clearly present with those who accompanied him in his historical ministry, is also in the process of going to the Father (v. 11b; italics mine). Even more remarkably, he is "no longer in the world" (v. 11). The sense of time in this text is elastic, incorporating past, present, and future. Jesus' prayer is offered not only for his original disciples, but also for the church of every subsequent time.

The intercessory petitions offered up to God on behalf of the church (vv. 11–19) are introduced by a summary of Jesus' ministry: "I made your *name* known" (v. 6), that is, Jesus has revealed the character and identity of God. Here, too, John's sense of time extends beyond the narrative's present. It is not only in Jesus' ministry that God's "name" is revealed, but most particularly in Jesus' death and resurrection. The "oneness" of the Father and the Son in these events is also underlined in our text, a unity that Jesus prays will extend to the community itself (v. 11; see also vv. 21–23). That is, the love *of God* for the world is most poignantly revealed in the death *of Jesus* (15:13, 3:16), a love that the *church* is commissioned to proclaim in word and deed to the world (v. 18).

If the elasticity of time in these verses is somewhat challenging to the interpreter, so, too, is that of place. In particular, the term *world* (*kosmos*) seems unstable. That is because it is being used to refer to different realities. On the one hand, "the world" simply refers to the place where humans live (see v. 11). On the other hand, the term symbolizes that which is set in opposition to God (see v. 14). In verses 14–15, for example, you have the two uses piling up on each other. The three uses of the term *world* in verse 14 (the disciples do not "belong to the *world*") refer to that which is hostile to God. "World" in verse 15, however, simply refers to the physical world—"I am not asking you to take them out of the *world*." One way to paraphrase what is intended by this fluid use of "world" is to say that the disciples are "in" the world (place), but not "of" the world (in other words, not rebelling against God by rejecting Jesus).

The first petition of Jesus' farewell prayer is for the *protection* of the church. It is not a ministry of suffering to death that Jesus wishes upon his followers, but a "joy" (*chara,* v. 13, 16:22) grounded in the gifts that flow from the resurrection *from* the dead. From a historical perspective, it is remarkable that none of Jesus' early disciples lost their lives on account of their association with Jesus either during his ministry or in the days immediately following Jesus' execution at the hands of the Romans, with the exception of Judas (v. 12). Though it is clear that difficult times lay in store for some of his followers in the years ahead (see, for example, 16:2, 21:19), not all discipleship would lead to martyrdom (21:22). In the context of Jesus' farewell prayer that speaks of his death in terms of his *glorification* (17:1), it is good to remember that the first of Jesus' signs through which he revealed his *glory* (2:11) occurred during a wedding feast in Cana, where an entire community was transformed by the presence of one who turned ordinary water into the wine of the eschatological feast. The everyday "world" is transformed by the presence of the Lord (*doxa*) from a sphere of obligation and duty into a joyful celebration.

> The everyday "world" is transformed by the presence of the Lord from a sphere of obligation and duty into a joyful celebration.

DAY OF PENTECOST

May 31, 2009

Revised Common (RCL)	Episcopal (BCP)	Roman Catholic (LFM)
Acts 2:1-21 or Ezek. 37:1-14	Acts 2:1-11 or Isa. 44:1-8	Acts 2:1-11
Ps. 104:24-34, 35b	Ps. 104:25-37 or 104:25-32 or 33:12-15, 18-22	Ps. 104:1 + 24, 29-30, 31 + 34
Rom. 8:22-27 or Acts 2:1-21	1 Cor. 12:4-13 or Acts 2:1-11	1 Cor. 12:3b-7, 12-13 or Gal. 5:16-25
John 15:26-27; 16:4b-15	John 20:19-23 or John 14:8-17	John 20:19-23 or John 15:26-27; 16:12-15

First Reading

ACTS 2:1-21 (RCL)
ACTS 2:1-11 (BCP, LFM)

Luke's Pentecost narrative covers the entirety of Acts 2. Verses 1-4 describe the actual event; verses 5-12 give the response of those who observed the descent of the Holy Spirit; verses 14-36 hold Peter's explanation to the question posed at verse 12, "What does this mean?"; and verses 37-47 describe the conversion and baptism of three thousand who favorably responded to the first Christian "sermon" preached by Peter. Though today's lectionary text stops at either verse 21 (RCL) or verse 11 (BCP, LFM), Peter's sermon drives forward to the summary statement of 2:36: "Therefore, let the entire house of Israel know with certainty that God has made him both Lord and Messiah, this Jesus whom you crucified." In this speech, Peter is fulfilling Jesus' promises, not the least of which is that the Twelve will judge the twelve tribes of Israel (Luke 22:28-30; see also Acts 26:7) and that the Spirit will provide a witness to Jesus in Jerusalem (1:8).

Pentecost is one of the three great pilgrimage festivals of Second Temple Judaism (Passover, Pentecost, Feast of Booths), occurring fifty days after Passover. Today's text makes it clear that Jerusalem is full of those who have come from all over the world. Following immediately after the restoration of the Twelve (Acts 1:21-26; see Easter 7, above), the early church (presumably the 120 mentioned at 1:15) gathers in a house in Jerusalem. There, what had been foretold by John the Baptist (Luke 3:16) and promised by the resurrected Jesus (Luke 24:47; Acts 1:8) is fulfilled. The church experiences a baptism, as John had said, "with the Holy Spirit and fire." In the presence of Jews assembled from all over the world, it is revealed that God's promises can be believed; the death of Jesus and his subsequent exaltation has made the gift of the Spirit possible. Guided by the Holy Spirit, the church will be able to carry out the mission assigned to it—to proclaim the forgiveness of sins in the name of Jesus to the ends of the earth (Luke 24:47; Acts 1:8).

> Guided by the Holy Spirit, the church will be able to carry out the mission assigned to it–to proclaim the forgiveness of sins in the name of Jesus to the ends of the earth.

The manifestation of the gift of the Spirit in verse 4 is described as "speaking in other languages." This is often, in church tradition, harmonized with "speaking in tongues," that is, glossolalia (see 1 Cor. 14:6-33), in which ecstatic utterances need interpretation in order to be understood. Here, however, the inspired speech is immediately understood by those assembled in their native languages (v. 11), a sign of the universality that will characterize the mission of the early church. Still, even though the *words* were understood, their meaning (as well as that of the charismatic display) was not. Peter's sermon (2:14-36), which incorporates many Old Testament texts important to the early church's understanding of the Christ event (such as Joel 2:28-32 LXX and Pss. 16:8-11, 110:1), interprets the events for those outside the faith.

Having received the gift of the Spirit on Pentecost, whatever the apostles do in Acts from this point forward will occur under its guidance. As the message about the "Lord and Messiah" moves forward by means of the church's witness, though it remains the same, its audience becomes radically different. The guidance of the Spirit is necessary to provide both: (*a*) continuity with the ministry of Jesus and (*b*) the creativity necessary as the church struggles to adapt to the evolving mission field, one that will soon include not only the diversity of Diaspora Judaism but also Gentiles. Though the narrative of Acts begins in Jerusalem, it ends in Rome!

EZEKIEL 37:1-14 (RCL ALT.)

In this vision of the valley of dry bones come to life, the "spirit of the LORD" functions as a refrain (vv. 1, 5, 6, 8, 9, 10, 14). It is precisely God's spirit, breathed upon a dead people, that gives them new life (see also Ezek. 36:26-28). The vision becomes reality on the day of Pentecost.

ISAIAH 44:1-8 (BCP alt.)

The spirit of God poured out upon the people of God nourishes them like water "upon the thirsty land" (v. 3), bringing forth luxurious growth like "willows by flowing streams" (v. 4). Such was the experience of the New Testament church of the gifts that flowed from Pentecost. It is the promise of God that the presence of the Spirit of God will cause the contemporary church to flourish as well.

Responsive Reading
PSALM 104:24-34, 35b (RCL)
PSALM 104:25-37 or 104:25-32 (BCP)
PSALM 104:1 + 24, 29-30, 31 + 34 (LFM)

In language that is reminiscent of Genesis 1, Psalm 104 praises God the creator of the earth and provider of all that is in it. The section that begins today's reading marvels at the diversity and depth of God's good creation. It moves on to describe creation's total dependence on God for sustenance (vv. 27-28) and the giving of God's spirit, which from the time of the ancient church has been associated with Pentecost: "When you send forth your spirit, they are created; and you renew the face of the ground" (v. 30). The psalm ends expressing the desire that the continued singing of praise to (and "meditation" on) the Lord be received as pleasing (v. 34).

The psalm expresses the deep and varied ways in which God is present to a creation that is utterly dependent upon God for all things. The "spirit" (*ruah/ pneuma*) of God given in baptism does not pull us away from our grounding in God's good creation. Indeed, it empowers us to be of service to that creation, discovered in revitalized relationships with "nature" as well as our neighbors. Through the Spirit that is poured out on the church on Pentecost, God is calling not only humanity, but all creation, back to God's intent for it, until "the earth is satisfied with the fruit of [God's] work" (Ps. 104:13).

PSALM 33:12-15, 18-22 (BCP alt.)

For discussion of this text, please see the responsive reading (BCP) for the Sixth Sunday of Easter, above.

ROMANS 8:22-27 (RCL)

Romans 8:18-21 provides an important introduction to today's text. These verses acknowledge the repercussions within creation that originated from humanity's fall from grace, described succinctly in God's address to Adam in Genesis 3:17: "cursed is the ground because of you." As a consequence of Adam's disobedience, not only did sin and death enter into the relationship between human beings and God, but creation itself was "subjected to futility," experiencing a "bondage to decay" (Rom. 8:20-21). The futures of humanity and creation are inextricably bound up together. Since the fall, all of nature longs for a restoration to that which God intended in the act of creation, that is, a freedom experienced in: (a) a restored (nonexploitative) relationship with human beings, and (b) the banishment of corruption and decay (v. 21). As those in the church look forward to the resurrection of the body and a final victory over death (1 Cor. 15:54), so, too, creation yearns for a restoration to a paradise lost long ago. One of the gifts of the Spirit given to Christian community, then, is the awareness of the pain and suffering that has come upon creation as a consequence of human sin. One's "sanctification," in the time before the end, entails new relationships not only with God and fellow human creatures, but also with creation itself. What God has begun in the death and resurrection of Christ and the outpouring of the Spirit, is nothing less than the creation of a "new heaven and a earth" (Rev. 21:1; 2 Pet. 3:13; see also Isa. 11:6-9; Gal. 6:15; 2 Cor. 5:17; Rev. 22:1-5). The cosmic scope as well as the "ecological" dimensions of the restoration that God is effecting through the eschatological outpouring of the Spirit should not be missed.

> One of the gifts of the Spirit given to Christian community is the awareness of the pain and suffering that has come upon creation as a consequence of human sin.

The gift of the Spirit and its many benefits (see, for example, 1 Corinthians 12–14; Gal. 5:22) was experienced by the early Christians as confirmation that the new age—the kingdom of God—had broken into this world through the ministry, death, and resurrection of Jesus. Equally amazing as the cosmic dimensions of the transformation underway and the actual diversity of gifts showered upon the church was the fact that the Spirit was experienced not in terms of "power" (in other words, of our spiritual perfection), but in "weakness" (v. 26; see also 1 Cor. 1:25; 2 Cor. 12:9). The use of the "childbirth" metaphor to describe the present state of the church as well as creation (vv. 22-23; see also John 16:20-22; Mark 13:8; 1 Thess. 5:3; Rev. 12:1-6) suggests that the outpouring of God's creative Spirit inevitably draws the ire of powers that remain hostile to God. The church of the new age will suffer on account of the gospel. But the church also, in its vulnerability and perceived weakness, where suffering and pain makes the redemption in Christ anything but evident (v. 24), will be sustained by the Spirit of God in different ways. Christian "hope" (vv. 24-25) is, in fact, a gift of the Spirit of God. Such hope is something distinct from what the word often expresses in North American popular culture, where it means "wishful thinking"—for instance, in the statement "I hope it doesn't rain tomorrow." Christian hope is based in the promises of God that are sustained in the body of Christ by

> Christian hope is based in the promises of God that are sustained in the body of Christ by means of the Holy Spirit.

means of the Holy Spirit. In addition to a hope that sustains in difficult times, a second gift of the Holy Spirit that comes to us in our weakness is the help that comes to us in prayer (vv. 26-27). The invocation "Abba! Father" (v. 15) is such a gift. In our status as adopted children of God we are included in the body of Christ and can pray in the Spirit of the Son, "Father," and know that we are heard, "because the Spirit intercedes for the saints according to the will of God" (v. 27; see also 1 John 2:1; Heb. 7:25).

The range and diversity of the gifts of the Spirit of God are remarkable. Those expressed in today's text represent just the tip of the iceberg. They stretch from our awareness of the pain of creation, to our adoption as children of God (through baptism) who are taught to pray by the very wisdom of God. All this wonderful diversity, however, has a center. The Spirit of God, Paul reminds us, is the same Spirit of Christ (v. 9; Rom. 1:4; Phil. 1:19). The gifts of the Spirit are the same gifts made real to us in Jesus, crucified and risen, through whom God is revealed and we are made new. In this movement of the Spirit of God toward us, we are brought back into proper relationship with God and our fellow human beings. We are also reminded of our responsibility to exercise just stewardship over God's good creation (Gen. 1:26-31). That we are able to so as we wait patiently, in hope, for "what we do not see" (v. 25), is also a gift of God's own Spirit.

1 CORINTHIANS 12:4-13 (BCP)
1 CORINTHIANS 12:3B-7, 12-13 (LFM)

The close relationship between Ascension and the Day of Pentecost may be seen in the second readings chosen by the LFM for these festival days: Ephesians 4 (Ascension) and 1 Corinthians 12 (Pentecost). Both texts move from a statement of the unity of the Trinity (Eph. 4:4-6; 1 Cor. 12:4-6) to the spiritual gifts given to the church for "the common good" (for example, 1 Cor. 12:7). In today's text the "body" is the primary metaphor of the unity the gifts are to serve that, though it is made up of many parts, is "one" (v. 12). The expression of this unity is the confession of the church, which 1 Corinthians 12 gives in perhaps its earliest and simplest form: *kyrios Iēsous*, "Jesus is Lord" (v. 3b). The gifts of the Spirit, active in the body of Christ, can be nothing else than the Spirit of Christ (see Rom. 8:9).

ACTS 2:1-21 (RCL ALT.)
ACTS 2:1-11 (BCP ALT.)

For a discussion of this text, please see the first reading (RCL, BCP, LFM) for the Day of Pentecost, above.

GALATIANS 5:16-25 (LFM ALT.)

In these verses, Paul expresses his understanding of the strong antimony between the "flesh" (*sarxs*) and the "spirit" (*pneuma*). Paul understood the goodness of creation and God's intent that we be fully embodied creatures. The "body" (*sōma*) is, therefore, highly valued by Paul. "Flesh" in Paul's thought is something different. It belongs to the old Adam; it constitutes desires that lead us to rebel against God (see Rom. 5:19), to do violence to our neighbor, and to tear apart fragile communities (vv. 19-21, 26). The "fruits of the spirit" (vv. 22-23) lead us back to God's intent for embodied and relational human life. Elsewhere Paul notes, "the law of the Spirit of life in Christ Jesus has set you free from the law of sin and of death" (Rom. 8:2). The Spirit has set us free *from ourselves* (in other words, the desires of our "flesh"), precisely to serve the neighbor in his or her need. Such work is the "fruit of the Spirit" poured out on Pentecost and made real in our baptisms, "so we too might walk in newness of life" (Rom. 6:4).

THE GOSPEL
JOHN 15:26-27; 16:4B-15 (RCL)
JOHN 15:26-27; 16:12-15 (LFM ALT.)

John often refers to the third person of the Trinity as the Paraclete (*paraklētos*, translated as "Advocate" in the NRSV and in other versions as "Comforter," "Helper," or "Counselor"). Today's Gospel text is found midway in Jesus' Farewell Discourse (John 14-17), when Jesus is with his disciples at their last supper together. It presents three of the five texts in which Jesus speaks of the promised Paraclete (14:16-17, 14:26, 15:26, 16:7-11, 16:12-15). In our text, Jesus describes how the Paraclete, "who proceeds from the Father and the Son," as the Nicene Creed paraphrases John 15:26, will extend knowledge of the benefits of God's work that his death and ascension completes (see also 4:34, 5:36, 17:4). It is Jesus' promise that though "his hour has come to depart . . . to the Father" (13:1), by means of the gift of the Holy Spirit, he shall always be present to the church as its guide and teacher (16:13). Jesus also promises that the Paraclete will continue Jesus' role as revealer of that which is opposed to God (16:8-11). Thus, the Holy Spirit makes the incarnate Word of God efficacious in the world by means of what the Lutheran theological tradition terms law (the revelation of human sin) and gospel (belief in the promises of God). In this portion of the Farewell Discourse Jesus instructs his disciples that what may look like the end of the incarnation (his death) provides the opportunity for God not only to extend—in a way that transcends any spatial or temporal limits—the good news of Jesus Christ to a world ignorant in its unbelief, but also to ensure Christ's continuing presence among those who believe that in the Christ event the love of God for the world is revealed. It is the realization of these promises that we celebrate on Pentecost Sunday.

In 16:7, Jesus instructs the disciples that the gift of the Spirit is dependent upon his death (see also 7:39). What is exceptional about Jesus' statement is not the revelation of his imminent departure, but the claim that "it is to your advantage that I go away." The "advantage" is realized in multiple ways. In the first place, it is only through the death and ascension of Jesus that the work of God in Christ is completed. John speaks of these events as Jesus' "glorification" that "glorifies" God (17:1). Here "to glorify" means to make visible the presence of God, as did the *kavod/doxa* in the Old Testament (Exod. 33:18—34:8; see also John 1:14). It is specifically in Jesus' death and exaltation that God's love for—as well as God's judgment of—the world (16:8-11) is made most fully visible. Second, Jesus' departure is advantageous because only after Jesus' return to the Father will the gifts that come with the Holy Spirit be given to the church. These gifts are centered in the experience of the real presence of Christ—crucified and risen—in the ministries of Word and Sacrament. In addition, Jesus promises that the Paraclete will "teach you everything, *and remind you of all I have said to you*" (14:26, italics mine). One of the tasks of the Spirit in the church, then, is to make the church mindful of the word of God. In John's understanding, this incorporates not only the words of the historical Jesus (2:22), but also Scripture itself (12:16). Yet the Paraclete not only *reminds* the church of what Paul called the "oracles of God" (Rom. 3:2), but also *guides* it in the proper interpretation of them (16:12-13). Here it is important to note that the gift of the Paraclete is given to the church as community, not to individuals. The often hard and contentious work of scriptural interpretation in the church is, Jesus promises, guided by the Holy Spirit.

> It is specifically in Jesus' death and exaltation that God's love for—as well as God's judgment of—the world is made most fully visible.

In the Lutheran tradition, as noted above, the word of God is understood as encountering the world in terms of both law and gospel. The manner in which today's text speaks of how the Paraclete "prove[s] the world wrong about sin and righteousness and judgment" (16:9) is similar to the word's ongoing function as "law," which exposes human sin, unrighteousness, and the tendency of humans to usurp *God's* perogative of judgment. Here, in John, "sin" is understood not in moral terms, but in the inability to believe that Christ crucified and risen reveals the innermost heart of God (16:9). The exaltation of Jesus to the right hand of God also proves the world wrong about "righteousness" in that it reverses the world's understanding of what righteousness before God might look like (death on a cross). The Paraclete reveals the world's misguided "judgment" about both sin and righteousness in that it leads not to life as God intended but, ironically, to blindness as to the purposes of God (9:40) and even violence against them (see 10:33). The Spirit of God, in other words, by means of the word of the cross, judges the world's instincts about sin, righteousness, and judgment and exposes them as "wrong."

> In John, "sin" is understood not in moral terms, but in the inability to believe that Christ crucified and risen reveals the innermost heart of God.

In 14:16 and 14:26, Jesus promises that *God* will send the Paraclete. In 16:7, *Jesus* promises that he himself will send the Holy Spirit. Exegetes have long seen in these texts the mystery of the Holy Trinity at work: Father, Son, and Holy Spirit are united in the economy of salvation. The Day of Pentecost is the festival that celebrates the triune God's great gift of the second (14:16) Advocate to be with us forever: the Holy Spirit. This grace of God empowers the church to testify publicly on behalf of Jesus (15:26) in a world that remains hostile to this good news. It exposes the sin and unrighteousness of the world while it guides the church in "all the truth" (16:13) centered in the Word of God, crucified and risen. In doing so, it ensures the continuing presence of Jesus, in word and deed, among the people of God and, through its witness, to the world.

JOHN 20:19-23 (BCP, LFM)

For discussion of this text, please see the Gospel (RCL, BCP, LFM) for the Second Sunday of Easter, above.

JOHN 14:8-17 (BCP ALT.)

For discussion of this text, please see the Gospel (BCP) for the Fifth Sunday of Easter, above.

THE SEASON
AFTER PENTECOST /
OF ORDINARY TIME

TRINITY SUNDAY THROUGH PROPER 11
HENRY G. BRINTON

Halford Luccock was a respected professor of preaching at Yale Divinity School. One day in class a student preached a long, seemingly endless sermon. When he finally sat down, Luccock's first observation was not about the sermon, but was about a small bandage affixed to the student's chin. "How did you cut your chin?" he asked. The student replied, "When I shaved this morning I was thinking so hard about my sermon that I cut my chin." Luccock then advised, "Next time think about your chin and cut your sermon!"

Luccock was probably a great fan of the Gospel of Mark. It's short, clear, and to the point. The lessons from Mark that begin on Proper 6, immediately after the celebration of Holy Trinity Sunday, offer the preacher a marvelous opportunity to preach a sermon series that moves in quick succession from *parable* to *storm stilling* to *healing* to *rejection* to *discipleship* to *the death of John the Baptist* to *compassion for a crowd*. Over the course of six Sundays, in a season uninterrupted by religious holidays, the congregation can explore the Galilean ministry of Jesus with a focus that is difficult to maintain during other periods of the year. The Gospel passages for this season also give the preacher a clear and compelling theme to develop, during a time in which summer Sundays can feel disjointed and disconnected, without a unifying purpose.

So what insights into the public ministry of Jesus are offered by Mark from Proper 6 to Proper 11? On the first Sunday, Jesus tells two stories about growth—the parables of the growing seed and the mustard seed—and in both cases he gives

God the credit for the development of the seeds into fully grown plants. This insight runs counter to our American work ethic and challenges us to focus less on human striving, and more on faith and vision. One week later, Mark directs our attention to the stilling of the storm and assures us that Jesus can calm our troubled spirits and give us power over our problems so that we will not panic or lose hope when chaos is raging in or around us. On the third Sunday in this series, Jesus heals a woman and saves a child, revealing that he has been put here for a purpose—to save us from iniquity and illness, sin and death. Like a divine superhero, he carries the power of God into the very middle of human life, and we are invited to respond by putting our faith in him.

On Proper 9, Jesus is rejected by the people of Nazareth, and the disciples discover that they are facing a very rocky road. In similar fashion, followers of Christ today have to anticipate resistance and be prepared to overcome obstacles as they stand up for what they believe in and do the Lord's work in some hard-to-reach places. The question for the day is "What Would Jesus Drive?" The next Sunday, the Gospel lessons diverge, with the BCP and LFM focusing on the mission of the Twelve, and the RCL dealing with the death of John the Baptist. John becomes the first to lose his life for the Lord, setting an example for disciples who live by the standards of the kingdom and show willingness to lose their life for Christ's sake and for the sake of the gospel. On the final day of this six-week series, Proper 11, Jesus shows compassion for a crowd of needy people and responds to their condition by teaching and healing them. We are invited to do what we can to support international Christian mission efforts that are focused on preventing the "diseases of poverty"—tuberculosis, malaria, and AIDS. It is important to have compassion for others, because Jesus has compassion for us.

The Gospel of Mark is clear and concise, giving us a highly concentrated dose of the saving work of Jesus and his disciples. The six weeks following Holy Trinity Sunday provide us with an opportunity to witness the awesome and unlimited power of God in Jesus, and invite us to trust that Christ is at work today to overcome any of the forces of chaos threatening to hurt us in body, mind, or spirit. These passages are good spiritual medicine for congregations in need of healing and hope.

HOLY TRINITY SUNDAY / FIRST SUNDAY AFTER PENTECOST

JUNE 7, 2009

Revised Common (RCL)	Episcopal (BCP)	Roman Catholic (LFM)
Isa. 6:1-8	Exod. 3:1-6	Deut. 4:32-34, 39-40
Psalm 29	Psalm 93 or	Ps. 33:4-5, 6 + 9,
	Canticle 2 *or* 13	18-19, 20 + 22
Rom. 8:12-17	Rom. 8:12-17	Rom. 8:14-17
John 3:1-17	John 3:1-16	Matt. 28:16-20

FIRST READING

ISAIAH 6:1-8 (RCL)
EXODUS 3:1-6 (BCP)
DEUTERONOMY 4:32-34, 39-40 (LFM)

Synesthesia Spirituality

Synesthesia is a neurologically based phenomenon involving an expansion of everyday sensory perceptions. It's an experience in which one type of stimulation creates the sensation of another, such as when the hearing of a sound results in the seeing of a color. When a woman with synesthesia hears a truck backing up, making a "beep-beep-beep" sound, she sees the beeps as a series of red dots. When a man with synesthesia looks at a string of numerals, he experiences the fives as being a different *color* than the twos. Although this blending of different senses is unusual, it is not a disorder, and the majority of people with synesthesia are glad to have the ability. It can sharply improve their memory, and it may even enhance their creativity. Synesthesia is seven times more common among artists, novelists, and poets, and it helps their creative work.[1]

Now it is hardly a news flash to say that people experience life in different ways. We all know that young people have different perceptions than older people, and women see many things differently than men. But the challenge for us, whether we are young or old, male or female, is to expand our perception of who God is and what God wants us to do. We can do this through synesthesia spirituality—spirituality that goes beyond our normal expectations.

85

The prophet Isaiah may have experienced synesthesia when he entered the Temple in Jerusalem (RCL). He walked into his place of worship and encountered the awesome reality of the Lord in sight, sound, smell, touch, and taste. He *saw* the Lord "sitting on a throne" (Isa. 6:1). He *heard* one seraph call to another, "Holy, holy, holy is the LORD of hosts" (v. 3). He *smelled* the smoke that filled the house of the Lord and *felt* the pivots on the thresholds shake (v. 4). He even *tasted* the live coal that the seraph put on his mouth to blot out his sin (vv. 6-7). This is a much more sensational encounter with God than most of us experience on a given Sunday in church. Our perceptions of the Lord are usually on the level of quiet stirrings, not thundering spectacles. And yet, we cannot dismiss the experience of the prophet Isaiah, a man who grasped the truth of God's power and purity and grace and love through his expanded sensory perceptions. Nor can we ignore the significance of Moses at the burning bush, where "the angel of the LORD appeared to him in a flame of fire out of a bush" and "God called to him out of the bush, 'Moses, Moses!'" (Exod. 3:2, 4, BCP).

> Our perceptions of the Lord are usually on the level of quiet stirrings, not thundering spectacles.

If truth be told, we all *hunger* for this kind of experience. We would love for God to crack open our normal worship and let us see, hear, feel, and taste God's glory! We would be thrilled to hear the Lord speak to us out of a burning bush and discover that the place we are standing "is holy ground" (Exod. 3:5). Our problem today is not that we grasp too much of God, but that we experience too *little* of God. But if we expand our hearts and minds so that we can encounter God in fresh ways, then we discover a Lord who is extraordinary, not ordinary. God is holy, high, and lofty—on a throne, lifted up. The Lord is speaking out of a burning bush, revealing the divine self to be the God who was, and is, and is to come—"the God of Abraham, the God of Isaac, and the God of Jacob" (Exod. 3:6).

Synesthesia spirituality begins with confession. When we enter God's presence, we sense that we are unworthy to stand before the Lord and we discover what Isaiah was going through when he said, "Woe is me! I am lost, for I am a man of unclean lips, and I live among a people of unclean lips" (Isa. 6:5). We know why Moses had to remove his dirty sandals in the vicinity of the burning bush (Exod. 3:5). And we begin to understand why it makes sense to get ourselves in line with the agenda of this awesome and almighty God, doing our best to "keep his statutes and his commandments," for our own well-being and for that of our descendants after us (Deut. 4:40, LFM).

All three of these lessons from Isaiah, Exodus, and Deuteronomy call us into a fresh encounter with an extraordinary Lord. They give us an experience of synesthesia spirituality by expanding our perceptions of who God is, and what

God is calling us to do. This Lord of power and purity is also a God of grace and love, seen when Isaiah is given a taste of a burning coal in the Temple—this experience removes his guilt and blots out his sin (Isa. 6:6-7). The Almighty is a God who forgives us so that we can perform a mission in the world, as Isaiah and Moses did—one that is in line with God's healing and liberating work. Isaiah sees a vision of God in the Temple and responds by saying, "Here am I; send me!" (Isa. 6:8). Moses encounters God in a burning bush (Exod. 3:1-6), and goes on to call his people to a new way of life (Deut. 4:39-40).

These lessons for Trinity Sunday remind us that there are no limits to how we can experience God and no limits to what these encounters will inspire us to do in lives of mission and service.

These lessons remind us that there are no limits to how we can experience God and no limits to what these encounters will inspire us to do in lives of mission and service.

RESPONSIVE READING

PSALM 29 (RCL)
PSALM 93 (BCP)
PSALM 33:4-5, 6 + 9, 18-19, 20 + 22 (LFM)

Naming the Unnameable God

Today's psalms focus on God as Creator, the one who makes heaven and earth and all that is, seen and unseen, including each one of us. "The voice of the LORD is over the waters," says Psalm 29:3 (RCL), "the God of glory thunders, the LORD, over mighty waters." The word of God is powerful and creative, and it was the voice of God over the waters of chaos that brought the universe into being. As Genesis tells us, God said, "Let there be light"—and there was light (1:3). "By the word of the LORD the heavens were made," says Psalm 33:6 (LFM), "and all their host by the breath of his mouth." The LORD "has established the world; it shall never be moved" (Ps. 93:1, BCP). To focus on God as Creator is appropriate for Trinity Sunday, where the names Creator, Redeemer, and Sustainer can be used to describe the functions of the Triune God.

But naming the unnameable is the perennial challenge of this day in the church year. The story is told of St. Augustine walking along a Mediterranean beach, contemplating the Trinity. He saw a young child running back and forth with a bucket, moving between the sea and a hole she had dug. He stopped and asked the child what she was doing. "I'm putting the giant sea into my little hole," she exclaimed. Then it dawned on Augustine that he was trying to do the same: to put the great identity of God into his little, human brain.

SECOND READING

ROMANS 8:12-17 (RCL, BCP)
ROMANS 8:14-17 (LFM)

The God Who Dances

In just a few short verses in Romans 8, Paul mentions all three persons of the Trinity: "the Spirit of God" (v. 14), "Abba! Father" (v. 15), and Jesus Christ (v. 17). The relationship between these three forms the foundation of our relationship with God, and it is clear that Paul wants all who are led by the Spirit of God to understand that they are children of God. He writes to the Christians in Rome, "you have received a spirit of adoption," and makes the case that "When we cry, 'Abba! Father!' it is that very Spirit bearing witness with our spirit that we are children of God, and if children then heirs, heirs of God and joint heirs with Christ" (vv. 15-17). It is through adoption, made possible by the power of God the Holy Spirit, that we become part of God's family—special, precious, chosen children whom the Lord has given new life. We are not servants, nor are we hired hands—we are now children of a holy, loving, saving God.

But why do you suppose that the Lord wants to adopt us? It would seem to make sense to keep imperfect people like ourselves at somewhat of a distance. My hunch is that God desires these relationships because relationship is at the heart of the Trinity: God is a Father, Son, and Holy Spirit, three persons in an eternal, loving relationship with one another. John of Damascus, a Greek theologian of the seventh century, came up with an understanding of the Trinity based on *perichoresis*, a Greek word meaning "dancing around," as in the choreography of a ballet.[2] Father, Son, and Holy Spirit are not like three sovereigns on three thrones, but instead are like three dancers holding hands, dancing together in perfect love, freedom, and harmony. They are deeply one, but at the same time they are three. They are what they are in relation to each other—in a shared purpose, and in a mutual love, for all eternity. For God, ultimate reality is found in relationship. It's all in the family.

> Father, Son, and Holy Spirit are like three dancers holding hands, dancing together in perfect love, freedom, and harmony.

That's the key to our relationship to the Trinity. Our Lord invites us to enter into relationship with the Trinity, to join the Lord's never-ending dance, and to become part of God's family. We are not asked to understand the triune God on Trinity Sunday, but instead to join the Father, Son, and Holy Spirit in their *perichoresis*. The challenge for us in twenty-first-century America is to turn off the computer or television, and find joy in people—instead of in technology. Growth will come as we commit ourselves to doing the hard work of reconciliation, instead of giving up on others and trusting only in ourselves. Closeness to God will be experienced as we accept the invitation to join the dance of Father, Son, and Holy Spirit with childlike joy.

THE GOSPEL
JOHN 3:1–17 (RCL)
JOHN 3:1–16 (BCP)
MATTHEW 28:16–20 (LFM)

Living on Trinity Drive

In the town of Bowie, Maryland, the Jewish synagogue had a very unfortunate address. Instead of being located on Maple Lane or First Street or some other road with a meaningless name, the synagogue was placed on Trinity Drive. *Trinity Drive*: A street that makes you think of God as Father, Son, and Holy Spirit. The same awkwardness would be created by the placement of a Roman Catholic Church on "John Calvin Avenue," or a Presbyterian Church on "Mohammed Lane." While these names are important to particular faith communities, they are not equally revered by all. Muslims are particularly devoted to Mohammed, Presbyterians are indebted to Calvin, and it is Christians—rather than Jews—who see God as a Trinity. In Bowie, the name problem was eventually solved by a change of address. The synagogue is still located on Trinity Drive, but the mailing address is now listed as "Torah Lane."

On Trinity Sunday, we are challenged to reflect on our uniquely Christian understanding of God. We sing about it in the hymn "Holy, holy, holy, Lord God Almighty . . . God in three persons, Blessed Trinity." We affirm it in the Apostles' Creed: "I believe in God, the Father almighty, creator of heaven and earth. I belive in Jesus Christ, God's only Son, our Lord, who was conceived by the Holy Spirit." We confess it every time we baptize a person in the name of the Father, and of the Son, and of the Holy Spirit, as the LFM Gospel reading instructs us to do (Matt. 28:19). The Trinity is central to our understanding of who God is, and even very young Christians know who the three persons of the Trinity are. When my daughter was six years old, I came across her pretending to baptize her dolls in the name of the Father, Son, and Holy Spirit.

Since we know who our God in three persons *is*, it is important on Trinity Sunday to take a look at what this God in three persons *does*. Just as God exists as Father, Son, and Spirit, God *acts* as Creator, Redeemer, and Sustainer. God is experienced by us as the Lord who creates us and gives us life, redeems us from captivity to sin, and sustains us through the many challenges of life. This view of God does not replace our understanding of God as Father, Son, and Holy Spirit; instead, it is a functional view of God that can deepen our devotion to the Trinity.

Kenneth E. Bailey, an author and lecturer in New Testament Studies, makes a strong connection between the Trinity and the visit of the Jewish leader Nicodemus to Jesus in John 3, the RCL and BCP Gospel readings. Bailey points out that Nicodemus makes three speeches to which Jesus gives three replies. In addition, Jesus introduces each reply with the phrase "Amen, amen, I say to you" (NAB; the NRSV states, "Very truly, I tell you". Whenever this phrase appears, something of supreme importance is being said. The first amen statement provides critical information about God, the second tells of the Spirit, and the third illuminates the person of Jesus.[3]

After Nicodemus approaches Jesus with the respectful greeting, "Rabbi, we know that you are a teacher who has come from God" (John 3:2), Jesus replies with the words, "Very truly, I tell you, no one can see the kingdom of God without being born from above" (v. 3). What Jesus actually says is "you must be born *ánōthen*"—a Greek word with a dual meaning, translated either "from above" or "anew." To be born *ánōthen* speaks of both a time of birth ("anew") and the place from which the new birth is generated ("from above"). So what Jesus is saying is that we must accept a radical new birth that is generated by God—a birth that is both new and from above.

> Jesus is saying that we must accept a radical new birth that is generated by God—a birth that is both new and from above.

Jesus is affirming that God is the Creator, the deity who gives us birth. According to Bailey this bold and striking phrase is "a clear New Testament example of female imagery used to describe God who is Spirit and thereby neither male nor female. If we are 'born of God' then God in some sense gives birth like a woman."[4] Bailey notes that the Canaanites had male and female deities, but Israel did not. Instead, the prophets used both male and female imagery to enrich their understanding of God, as did the authors of the New Testament. Scripture calls God *Father*, defining the term in Hosea 11:1 ("When Israel was a child, I loved him") and Luke 15:23-24 ("Let us eat and celebrate; for this son of mine was dead and is alive again"). But the Bible also says that God will "cry out like a woman in labor" (Isa. 42:14), and the psalmist states that he is comforted "like a weaned child with its mother" (Ps. 131:2). So God is neither male nor female, but instead a Creator God who gives birth to children in a way that is both "anew" and "from above."

Unfortunately, Nicodemus doesn't comprehend what Jesus is saying. "Can one enter a second time into the mother's womb and be born?" he stammers in confusion, getting the picture of being born "anew" but missing the whole meaning of being born "from above." Sometimes when we speak of being "born again" we make the same mistake: We understand Jesus' words on only one level. We focus on being "born again" to the exclusion of being "born from above"; we simplify the expression down to only one meaning, and link it to an individual's private moment of conversion. But there is a divine depth and mystery and power in what Jesus says that can never be captured in one definition—these words envision what biblical scholar Gail O'Day calls a "new mode of life for which there are no precedents, life born of water *and* the Spirit, life regenerated through the cross of Jesus."[5]

Jesus tries to expand his visitor's vision by saying, "Very truly, I tell you, no one can enter the kingdom of God without being born of water and Spirit" (John 3:4-5). With these words, Jesus' focus shifts from God the Creator to God the Sustainer. Suddenly, a second person of the Trinity is on center stage, and Jesus says to Nicodemus, "Do not be astonished that I said to you, 'You must be born from above.' The wind blows where it chooses, and you hear the sound of it, but you do not know where it comes from or where it goes. So it is with everyone who is born of the Spirit" (John 3:7-8). In Greek, the word *pneúma* is used for both "wind" and "spirit," so when Jesus says, "The wind blows where it chooses," he is also saying, "The Spirit blows where it chooses." His point is that the Spirit is a new wind that is blowing powerfully through the land, beyond the control of Nicodemus and the Pharisees and any other human group.

The Spirit of God continues to blow where it chooses today. It sustains faithful people and gives life to the church, sometimes in the face of incredible hardship. Bailey points to the Mekane Yesus Church of Central Ethiopia, which in his lifetime has grown from fifty thousand to four million members. He notes that the South Sudan has suffered and endured more than forty years of war with more than three million people dead. "Yet, over that same period the Church has grown beyond anyone's fondest hopes. Entire tribes are now Christian and African villages once Muslim are finding answers to life's deepest questions through faith in Jesus."[6] The sustaining power of the Spirit can be felt by us as well, if we open ourselves to its power in our times of need.

> The Spirit of God continues to blow where it chooses today. It sustains faithful people and gives life to the church, sometimes in the face of incredible hardship.

In the third of his "amen" statements, Jesus says, "Very truly, I tell you, we speak of what we know and testify to what we have seen; yet you do not receive our testimony" (v. 11). In this section, he is focusing on himself, a third person of the Trinity—God the Redeemer. He speaks of how he descended from heaven and will soon be lifted up, and concludes with the words, "For God so loved the world that he gave his only Son, so that everyone who believes in him may not perish but may have eternal life (v. 16). God the Redeemer, seen in Jesus Christ, is the one who buys us back from slavery to sin, much as in ancient times a redeemer was designated to travel to a foreign country and buy his people out of slavery. We today are not in bondage to some foreign power—rather, we are enslaved to sin, and we need our God to bring us back to himself.

"It is important to note," writes Brian Abel Ragen, an English professor in Illinois, "that the idea of a redeemer, a savior, is impossible without the idea of a fallen humanity. You cannot be saved if you are not lost. You cannot be redeemed if you are not in hock. You cannot be freed if you are not enslaved. American culture, even in its churches, avoids the idea of real sinfulness." He goes on to say that "We believe not in sin and forgiveness but in illness and recovery. It is the endless message of our culture that everyone is basically good and that most of our problems will be solved when we realize this—in other words, when we build up our self-esteem."[7]

Ragen points out that in many hymnals, the lyrics of hymns are changed to reflect this shift. In some versions of "Amazing Grace," for example, the words "That saved a wretch like me" have been changed to "That saved and strengthened me." Christians should be appalled, argues Ragen, "to see their own hymns weakening the one Christian doctrine that can be verified from the television news . . . human depravity." We are sinful people, and we see this in the news, in our colleagues, in our families, and in ourselves. We are desperately in need of a redeemer. Fortunately, God did not send the Son into the world to condemn the world, but to be the Redeemer, "in order that the world might be saved through him" (v. 17). When we find ourselves lost in selfishness and captive to sin, we have a way back—through faith in the Redeemer.

"Every religious system has some form of Incarnation," writes Bailey. "For Judaism, God came down, entered a burning bush and spoke to Moses [see the BCP first reading, Exod. 3:1-6, above]. For Islam, God gave one section after another of the Quran to the angel Gabriel and sent him to recite those uncreated chapters in Arabic to the person of Muhammad." Bailey makes the case that the person of Jesus is to Christians what the Qur'an is to Muslims—both contain the very speech of God. God came to us in Jesus the Redeemer and revealed "not merely the words of God, but the life and love of God."[8]

In John 3, we are told of a Father who gives birth, a Spirit that blows freely, and a Son who rescues us from captivity to sin and death. As Christians, we should think of our address as Trinity Drive, a place where God is always at work as Creator, Sustainer, and Redeemer. Just as on the night that Nicodemus visited Jesus, our Lord is creating new life, sustaining us in times of challenge, and redeeming us from bondage to the powers that threaten to destroy us.

Notes

1. Shankar Vedantam, "When Sound is Red: Making Sense of Mixed Sensations," *The Washington Post*, October 14, 2002, A12.

2. Shirley C. Guthrie, *Christian Doctrine* (Louisville: Westminster John Knox, 1994), 91.

3. Kenneth E. Bailey, "John 3:1-15: Jesus and Nicodemus," *The Presbyterian Outlook*, February 11, 2008, http://www.pres-outlook.com/reports-a-resources/42-lenten-resources/6870.html, accessed July 18, 2008.

4. Ibid.

5. Gail O'Day, "The Gospel of John," in *The New Interpreter's Bible, Vol. 9: Luke–John* (Nashville: Abingdon, 1995), 548–55.

6. Bailey, "John 3:1-15."

7. Brian Abel Ragen, "A Wretch Like Who?" *America*, January 29, 1994.

8. Bailey, "John 3:1-15."

SECOND SUNDAY AFTER PENTECOST

ELEVENTH SUNDAY IN ORDINARY TIME / PROPER 6
JUNE 14, 2009

Revised Common (RCL)	Episcopal (BCP)	Roman Catholic (LFM)★
Ezek. 17:22-24 or 1 Sam. 15:34—16:13	Ezek. 31:1-6, 10-14	Ezek. 17:22-24
Ps. 92:1-4, 12-15 or Psalm 20	Psalm 92 or 92:1-4, 11-14	Ps. 92:2-3, 13-14, 15-16
2 Cor. 5:6-10, (11-13), 14-17	2 Cor. 5:1-10	2 Cor. 5:6-10
Mark 4:26-34	Mark 4:26-34	Mark 4:26-34

FIRST READING

EZEKIEL 17:22-24 (RCL, LFM)
EZEKIEL 31:1-6, 10-14 (BCP)
1 SAMUEL 15:34—16:13 (RCL)

A Tale of Two Trees

In both Ezekiel 17 and 31, the prophet uses the image of a cedar to illustrate the fate of a nation. In chapter 31 (BCP) the word of the Lord comes to Ezekiel and instructs him to say to Pharaoh, the king of Egypt, "Consider Assyria, a cedar of Lebanon, with fair branches and forest shade, and of great height, its top among the clouds" (v. 3). This tree gave shade to all the great nations of the world, but because "its heart was proud of its height" (v. 10), God cast it out and allowed it to be destroyed. By contrast, in Ezekiel 17 (RCL, LFM), God takes "a sprig from the lofty top of a cedar" and plants it on a high and lofty mountain—Mount Zion (v. 22). This sprig is the people of Israel, restored to their homeland after a period of exile in Babylon, and God's promise is that they will grow strong and bear fruit in their time of restoration.

★In Roman Catholic tradition, the Second Sunday after Pentecost is the Solemnity of Corpus Christi (Body and Blood of Christ). The texts for that day may be found in *New Proclamation Commentary on Feasts, Holy Days, and Other Celebrations,* ed. David B. Lott (Minneapolis: Fortress Press, 2007).

The image of a tree experiencing growth and fruitfulness is inspiring, especially to people living in a harsh and arid environment. But Ezekiel is careful to give God the credit for this vitality, not the people of Israel themselves. "All the trees of the field shall know that I am the LORD," says God through the prophet. "I bring low the high tree, I make high the low tree; I dry up the green tree and make the dry tree flourish. I the LORD have spoken; I will accomplish it" (17:24). It is God who determines the future of nations, whether a high tree (Assyria) is brought low, or a low tree (Israel) is made high. In the alternate RCL lesson, God chooses a sapling named David to be king over Israel, telling Samuel not to look on "the height of his stature" (1 Sam. 16:7). All through Ezekiel, God passes judgment on Israel and

> It is God who determines the future of nations, whether a high tree (Assyria) is brought low, or a low tree (Israel) is made high.

the other nations of the world for a variety of idolatries and hostilities, but at the end of the book there is a beautiful vision of restoration for the people of Israel and the Temple, one that is made possible by an outpouring of God's spirit (see the vision of the valley of dry bones in Ezekiel 37).

When the people return home, they will "become a noble cedar," predicts the prophet. Under the strength and serenity of this tree "every kind of bird will live; in the shade of its branches will nest winged creatures of every kind" (17:23), in a kind of peaceable kingdom. God expects the people of Israel to "put away violence and oppression, and do what is just and right," including the use of honest balances and measures in commerce (Ezek. 45:9-12). "God promises peacemaking," says biblical scholar Walter Brueggemann. "That peacemaking by God only happens, however, when there is truth-telling—costly, urgent and subversive. That is the work of the church. The issue, since Ezekiel, is clear: When we lie, we die. When we speak truthfully about human reality, God sends us peace."[1]

RESPONSIVE READING

PSALM 92:1-4, 12-15 (RCL)
PSALM 92 OR 92:1-4, 11-14 (BCP)
PSALM 92:2-3, 13-14, 15-16 (LFM)
PSALM 20 (RCL ALT.)

A Tree Grows in Jerusalem

This song for the Sabbath day is the only psalm assigned to a particular day of the week, and it begins by lifting up some of the distinctive activities of this day: giving thanks to the Lord, singing praises to the Most High's name, declaring God's steadfast love in the morning and God's faithfulness by night (Ps. 92:1-2).

In verses 12-15, the psalmist turns to a description of those who are in right relationship with God, using the image of stately trees to illustrate their uprightness. "The righteous flourish like the palm tree, and grow like a cedar in Lebanon," writes the psalmist (v. 12), suggesting that they are rooted in the worship life of the Temple by describing them as "planted in the house of the LORD" (v. 13). Their vigor and vitality is captured in the verse, "In old age they still produce fruit; they are always green and full of sap" (v. 14)—an image that should bring a smile to the face of any faithful senior citizen! But these lines ultimately bring glory to God, not to the Lord's righteous followers. Like Psalm 20 (the RCL alternative), Psalm 92 focuses on God's sovereignty, and because of this the strength and height of these trees is testimony that "the LORD is upright; he is my rock, and there is no unrighteousness in him" (v. 15). The psalm evokes the first lines of the Westminster Shorter Catechism: "Q. What is the chief end of man? A. Man's chief end is to glorify God and to enjoy him for ever."

SECOND READING

2 CORINTHIANS 5:6-10, (11-13), 14-17 (RCL)
2 CORINTHIANS 5:1-10 (BCP)
2 CORINTHIANS 5:6-10 (LFM)

Reconciliation at the Rugby Game

Paul begins the fifth chapter of his Second Letter to the Corinthians with a description of what it means to live by faith (vv. 1-10), and then he shifts gears and focuses on the ministry of reconciliation (vv. 11-21). While the BCP and LFM passages fall within the first section, the RCL lection bridges the two and includes several critical insights into the nature of Christian life: "we walk by faith, not by sight" (v. 7), and "if anyone is in Christ, there is a new creation: everything old has passed away; see, everything has become new!" (v. 17).

So, what does it mean to walk by faith and be part of Christ's new creation? For Paul, this resurrection-powered life includes making a constant effort to please God (v. 9), and regarding no one "from a human point of view" (in Greek, regarding no one "according to the flesh [*sarx*]" (v. 16). Those who are in Christ, and part of his new creation, are no longer trapped in an earthly existence, but have been freed by the resurrection to see neighbors in a new light and participate in Christ's ministry of reconciliation. They walk by faith instead of sight, and as they walk this way they can see a whole new world.

For Paul, this resurrection-powered life includes making a constant effort to please God, and regarding no one "from a human point of view."

A glimpse of this new creation was seen in South Africa in the mid-1990s.
Nelson Mandela had been elected the country's first black president in 1994, after
spending decades as a leading opponent of apartheid, the country's official policy
of racial segregation. In 1964, the white government had locked him up for life,
but in 1990 he was released—and then elected president. In 1995, South Africa
hosted the Rugby World Cup Tournament. Now rugby was a white man's game,
and the South African team was entirely white—a white team, representing a
country that was 80 percent black. It also had a team symbol—a leaping gazelle
called a "springbok"—that reminded most black South Africans of the country's
racist history.

What did Nelson Mandela do? He showed up at a press conference wearing a
rugby jersey and cap with a springbok on it. He said, "These are our boys now.
They may all be white, but they're our boys, and we must get behind them and
support them in this tournament." The next day, the Springbok coach took his
team to the prison where Nelson Mandela had spent nearly three decades of his
life behind bars. The coach said, "This is the cell where Nelson Mandela was
imprisoned. He was kept here for twenty-seven years by the racist policies of our
government. We tolerated his imprisonment for all those years, and yet he has
backed us publicly. We can't let him down."

The tournament opened, and the Springboks played beyond everyone's expectations. In fact, they made it into the final game. President Mandela was in the
stands, wearing a Springbok jersey. During time-out, he brought a South African
children's choir out of the stands, and they led sixty-five thousand people in the
singing of a black African miners' song. When the Springboks took the field, they
were unstoppable, and they won the World Championship. And for the next
twenty-four hours, whites danced with blacks in the streets of South Africa—for
the first time, they saw each other as fellow countrymen, brothers and sisters in
Christ.[2] That's walking by faith instead of sight—and entering a "new creation"
(v. 17).

THE GOSPEL
MARK 4:26-34 (RCL, BCP, LFM)

Automatic Growth

The novelist Reynolds Price has said that next to food and drink, our
most basic human need is story. Jesus knew this, and used parables throughout
his ministry to satisfy the spiritual hunger of the people who crowded around
him, aching for insight and inspiration. The director of the Center for Creative

Leadership in Greensboro, North Carolina, has told evangelist Leighton Ford that corporate values are most effectively taught not through slogans or policies put on a wall but through what he calls "value parables"—stories of people in the company whose principled actions make a difference.[3] The "value parables" of Jesus focus not on noteworthy business practices, of course, but on the coming of the kingdom of God.

In Mark 4:26-34, Jesus tells two stories about growth—the parable of the growing seed and the parable of the mustard seed—and in both cases he gives God the credit for the development of the seeds into fully grown plants. This insight runs counter to our American work ethic, which tends to link growth to hard work and adherence to the "value parables" of corporate life. In today's economy, we fear job loss through downsizing, mergers, or competition, so our natural inclination is to put in longer hours and more intense effort. In the parable of the growing seed, however (a story unique to the Gospel of Mark), "the kingdom of God is as if someone would scatter seed on the ground, and would sleep and rise night and day, and the seed would sprout and grow, he does not know how" (Mark 4:26-27). With a sense of humor, "Jesus reminds the disciples that the One waiting to grow what they sow is so capable that all they need to do after they throw the gospel on the ground is to go to bed!" writes pastor and medical doctor Richard Deibert. "Stop calculating, stop worrying about design and strategy, stop trying to crunch results. Scatter what you have and hit the sack."[4]

Clearly, human effort is not the key to the successful growth of the kingdom of God. But humans do have a role to play, by acting in faith and holding on to a vision of what God is doing in the world. In the parable of the growing seed, it is significant that the farmer gets out of bed and puts effort into scattering seed on the ground—he has faith that good seeds in good soil will bear fruit, and he embraces a vision of what the field will look like once it is full of stalks, with "the full grain in the head" (v. 28). The farmer trusts that God will give the growth, until the time for the harvest comes. In much the same way, the mustard seed in the second parable is able to grow into the largest of all shrubs not because of human effort, but because that is God's intention for mustard seeds. The human role in this process is simply sowing the seeds upon the ground (v. 31), a process that is defined in the parable of the sower as sowing "the word" (v. 14). "Taken together, the parables teach that it is not the work of the disciples to create the kingdom," writes American Baptist minister and communications professor Robert Stephen Reid; "theirs is only to act on what they have been told to do. It is the work of the 'Word' to effect the kingdom."[5]

These parables illustrate the growth of the kingdom of God, but they illuminate important aspects of our spiritual growth as well. For us to develop a fully formed Christian faith, it is critically important for us to focus less on human striving, and more on faith and vision. To drive this point home, Jesus emphasizes the autonomy of the growing process—Deibert points out that in verse 28, Jesus describes the process as effortless, "the earth produces of itself [*automatos*]," actually using the word from which we get our English word *automatic*. In striking contrast to our American work ethic, Jesus makes the point that it is while we sleep—absolutely independent of us—that the seed of God's kingdom germinates and grows to maturity.[6] This automatic growth leaves us with the challenge of developing our faith and our vision—in particular the visualization of good growth and good harvests. "If you visualize the wrong thing," warns leadership expert Stephen Covey, "you'll produce the wrong thing."[7] Covey tells the story of Charles Garfield, a psychologist who has done extensive research on peak performers in the worlds of athletics and business. He has also studied peak performance in the NASA program, watching the astronauts rehearse everything on earth, over and over again in a simulated environment, before they blast off and go into space. His research reveals that almost all of the world-class peak performers are visualizers—"they see it; they feel it; they experience it before they actually do it," writes Covey. "They begin with the end in mind."[8]

For us to develop a fully formed Christian faith, it is critically important for us to focus less on human striving, and more on faith and vision.

We, too, are challenged to begin with the end in mind—to have faith in the growth of the kingdom of God, and to visualize good fruit and abundant harvests. Although our human efforts to sow the seed of God's word may seem insignificant at first, the promise of the parable of the mustard seed is that "the smallest of all the seeds on earth" will grow into "the greatest of all shrubs" (vv. 31-32). Notice that the seed grows into a great shrub, not a great tree—even fully grown, the plant is small by earthly standards. In his book *Making the Small Church Effective*, Carl Dudley celebrates the value of "mustard seed" congregations: "In a big world, the small church has remained intimate. In a fast world, the small church has been steady. In an expensive world, the small church has remained plain. In a complex world, the small church has remained simple. In a rational world, the small church has kept feelings. In a mobile world, the small church has been an anchor. In an anonymous world, the small church calls us by name—by nickname!"[9] It is clear that even small churches produce abundant quantities of good fruit.

More significantly for the world around us, this mustard shrub "puts forth large branches, so that the birds of the air can make nests in its shade" (v. 32)—this is a vision of God's kingdom as a place of hospitality and harmony, protection and peace. "The 'way of the sower' will subsequently be revealed as the way of nonviolence," writes activist and theologian Ched Myers: "servanthood become leadership, suffering become triumph, death become life."[10] Such a surprising

100

THE SEASON
AFTER PENTECOST
───────
HENRY G.
BRINTON

outcome reminds us that the kingdom of God is not within our control—it will grow, automatically, in line with God's intentions. Our challenge is to sow the seeds of God's word, have faith that the growth of the kingdom will occur, and do our best to visualize the new creation that is breaking into human life.

Mark concludes this section by saying, "With many such parables he spoke the word to them, as they were able to hear it; he did not speak to them except in parables, but he explained everything in private to his disciples" (vv. 33-34).

> Our challenge is to sow the seeds of God's word, have faith that the growth of the kingdom will occur, and do our best to visualize the new creation that is breaking into human life.

Knowing that the people of Galilee were hungry for stories, Jesus used parables to illustrate the kingdom of God, but he also "explained everything in private to his disciples." This reminds us that an important part of our vision of the kingdom comes from listening carefully to the explanations and instructions of Jesus.

"Right hearing is attentive, committed, determined, obedient hearing which bears fruit," notes New Testament scholar John Painter. "To such hearing the mystery of the kingdom of God is given."[11] So it is not enough to ponder the "value parables" of growing seeds—we also need to pay attention to the full range of Jesus' teachings, and find evidence of the automatic growth of the kingdom in all of his words. As Jesus promises at the end of his explanation of the parable of the sower, those who "hear the word and accept it" will bear much fruit, "thirty and sixty and a hundredfold" (v. 20).

Notes

1. Walter Brueggemann, "Truth-telling and Peacemaking: A Reflection on Ezekiel," *The Christian Century* (November 30, 1998), 1098.

2. Ralph Ahlberg, "The Dark Pieces and the Blessing of Communion," November 7, 2004, a sermon he preached at the First Congregational Church of Greenwich, Conn., available at http://www.fccog.org/2004sermons/sermon041107.htm, accessed July 9, 2008. See also John Carlin's book *Playing the Enemy: Nelson Mandela and the Game that Made a Nation*, and the movie adaptation, directed by Clint Eastwood scheduled, to be released in 2009, starring Morgan Freeman and Matt Damon.

3. Leighton Ford, "The Evangelist as Storyteller," *Journal for Preachers* 29 (2006): 28–29.

4. Richard L. Deibert, *Mark* (Louisville: Geneva, 1999), 41.

5. Robert Stephen Reid, *Preaching Mark* (St. Louis: Chalice, 1999), 54.

6. Deibert, *Mark*, 41–42.

7. Stephen R. Covey, *The 7 Habits of Highly Effective People* (New York: Simon and Schuster, 1989), 134.

8. Ibid.

9. Carl Dudley, *Making the Small Church Effective* (Nashville: Abingdon, 1978), 176.

10. Ched Myers, *Binding the Strong Man: A Political Reading of Mark's Story of Jesus* (Maryknoll, N.Y.: Orbis, 1988), 181.

11. John Painter, *Mark's Gospel: Worlds in Conflict* (New York: Routledge, 1997), 85.

THIRD SUNDAY AFTER PENTECOST

TWELFTH SUNDAY IN ORDINARY TIME / PROPER 7

JUNE 21, 2009

Revised Common (RCL)	Episcopal (BCP)	Roman Catholic (LFM)
Job 38:1-11 or 1 Sam. 17:(1a, 4-11, 19-32) 32-49 or 17:57—18:5, 10-16	Job 38:1-11, 16-18	Job 38:1, 8-11
Ps. 107:1-3, 23-32 or 9:9-20 or Psalm 133	Ps. 107:1-32 or 107:1-3, 23-32	Ps. 107:23-24, 25-26, 28-29, 30-31
2 Cor. 6:1-13	2 Cor. 5:14-21	2 Cor. 5:14-17
Mark 4:35-41	Mark 4:35-41; (5:1-20)	Mark 4:35-41

FIRST READING

JOB 38:1-11 (RCL)
JOB 38:1-11, 16-18 (BCP)
JOB 38:1, 8-11 (LFM)
1 SAMUEL 17:(1A, 4-11, 19-32) 32-49 OR
7:57—18:5, 10-16 (RCL ALT.)

Out of the Whirlwind

God speaks to long-suffering Job out of a whirlwind in chapter 38, offering a set of challenging questions that engage Job in a theological dialogue: "Where were you when I laid the foundation of the earth? . . . Or who shut in the sea with doors when it burst out from the womb? . . . Have you entered into the springs of the sea, or walked in the recesses of the deep?" (38:4, 8, 16). Observes Old Testament professor Norman Habel, "The starting point of theology is a vast array of questions posed by God about the cosmos and God's role in that cosmos." This section of Job reveals that God "has subdued and organized chaos to enable the existence of the living world without threat of extinction."[1] The Lord's control over creation is seen in an earth with foundation and measurements (vv. 4-5), a sea with "bars and doors" (v. 10), and a set of gates for death and deep darkness (v. 17). In the vast ecology of creation, there is nothing beyond the control of Almighty

God—not even the threatening, chaotic power of the wind and the waves. Divine power is seen to be equally effective in the alternate RCL reading, in which David overcomes Goliath by affirming that "the battle is the Lord's" (1 Sam. 17:47).

RESPONSIVE READING

PSALM 107:1-3, 23-32 (RCL)
PSALM 107:1-32 or 107:1-3, 23-32 (BCP)
PSALM 107:23-24, 25-26, 28-29, 30-31 (LFM)
PSALM 9:9-20 or PSALM 133 (RCL alt.)

Deliverance from Peril on the Sea

Psalm 107 is a communal psalm of thanksgiving to God, one in which "those he redeemed from trouble" (v. 2) give thanks for the Lord's deliverance. Verses 23 through 32 contain one of four experiences of distress described in the psalm—in this case, we learn that "Some went down to the sea in ships, doing business on the mighty waters," and ran into a stormy wind (vv. 23-27). "Then they cried to the Lord in their trouble, and he brought them out from their distress; he made the storm be still, and the waves of the sea were hushed" (vv. 28-29)—a line echoed in the Navy Hymn, "O hear us when we cry to thee, for those in peril on the sea." As is typical in thanksgiving psalms, a "picture is drawn of the past distress and the psalmist's cry for help," writes Old Testament professor Denise Dombkowski Hopkins; the description of this "pit experience helps to underscore the deliverance that God has brought about"[2] (compare Ps. 9:13-14, RCL). At the end of the section, the psalmist returns to the introductory theme of praise and thanksgiving, encouraging God's people to "thank the Lord for his steadfast love, for his wonderful works to humankind" (v. 31). God ordains this blessing, says Psalm 133:3 (RCL), "life forevermore."

SECOND READING

2 CORINTHIANS 6:1-13 (RCL)
2 CORINTHIANS 5:14-21 (BCP)
2 CORINTHIANS 5:14-17 (LFM)

Rebreathing Lessons

Rebreathers are high-tech devices used by divers to allow them to stay underwater for extended periods of time. They recycle exhaled air, scrubbing it of poisonous carbon dioxide and squeezing out every last molecule of oxygen in the tanks. With rebreathers, divers can linger for half a day without thinking about their air supply, taking the time they need to survey shipwrecks, frolic with fish, or explore undersea caves that were previously off-limits. A rebreathing apparatus is like a set of gills, permitting divers to live as though they really belonged in the water all along. It enables people to breathe like fish, turning them into a kind of a new creation—a new creation that feels equally at home on the land or in the sea.[3]

There is a rebreathing lesson in 2 Corinthians. The apostle Paul admits that he "once knew Christ from a human point of view" (5:16, BCP, LFM)—seeing him as a land-dwelling, air-breathing rabble-rouser who was rightly put to death on the cross. But now he takes a very different view. Paul has come to claim the crucified Christ as his risen Lord, and to see him as the heaven-dwelling, Spirit-breathing righteous reconciler of God and all humankind. What's more, the apostle claims that Christ is the head of a brand new creation—one in which "everything old has passed away" and "everything has become new!" (v. 17)—a creation that all Christian believers can now call home.

Talk about radical rebreathing! Jesus Christ turns us from land dwellers to heaven dwellers, and from air breathers to Spirit breathers. "So if anyone is in Christ," proclaims Paul, "there is a new creation" (v. 17). When we believe in the Lord Jesus, we enter a whole new world, a world in which love replaces hatred, acceptance replaces rejection, and cooperation replaces competition. In this new world, we Spirit-breathing believers are challenged to do the work of reconciliation—the restoration of friendship between feuding parties.

> In this new world, we Spirit-breathing believers are challenged to do the work of reconciliation–the restoration of friendship between feuding parties.

Although heaven is now our official home address, we still have work to do in this sin-sick and struggling society. Christ asks us to be Spirit breathers in an air-breathing world, using our rebreathing abilities to strive for peace in situations of conflict, and to seek to repair all sorts of strained and shattered relationships. "All this is from God," says Paul, "who reconciled us to himself through Christ, and has given us the ministry of reconciliation" (v. 18). Reconciliation is the key to life in this brand-new creation—it's the work that God began through Christ, and that we are challenged to continue. We are to do this work in our homes, our schools, our workplaces, and in our communities of faith. So our rebreathing lessons have two parts: one, be reconciled to God (v. 20); and two, perform the ministry of reconciliation (v. 18). We are to find peace with God through his Son Jesus Christ, and then go out into the world to repair broken relationships, both person to person and person to God. "Now is the acceptable time" to do this Spirit-breathing work; "now is the day of salvation!" (6:2, RCL).

Another dimension of radical rebreathing is illustrated by the RCL passage: learning to live with oxymorons, contradictions in terms. Open up any newspaper, and you'll see grocery store advertisements for "jumbo shrimp"—a classic oxymoron. Open up 2 Corinthians 6:1-13, and you'll see statements that seem like contradictions in terms as well: We are treated "as poor, yet making many rich; as having nothing, and yet possessing everything" (6:10). How are we to understand and live with these oxymorons? The secret is to realize that Paul and his fellow Christians are rich in something besides money—they may be poor in dollars and possessions, but they are rich in gifts from God: purity, knowledge, patience, kindness, holiness of spirit, genuine love, truthful speech, and the power of God (vv. 6-7). These gifts enable us to feel peaceful and grounded, even when life is full of injustice and uncertainty. Having accepted the "grace of God" (v. 1), we can understand and live with the oxymorons so well known to Paul: treated as dying, and yet alive, "as punished, and yet not killed, as sorrowful, yet always rejoicing" (vv. 9-10).

THE GOSPEL
MARK 4:35-41 (RCL, LFM)
MARK 4:35-41; (5:1-20) (BCP)

The Stilling of the Storms

Jesus is teaching at the edge of the Sea of Galilee, and when evening comes he says to his disciples, "Let us go across to the other side" (Mark 4:35). As they are making their way across the water, a great windstorm arises, causing waves to crash into the boat and swamp it. Jesus is sleeping soundly at the back of the boat, but the disciples panic and wake him, saying, "Teacher, do you not care that we are perishing?" (vv. 36-38). As early as the first century, this dramatic story became a symbol for the Christian church: a ship with a cross for a mast, sailing through the storm of life. Presbyterian pastor and medical doctor Richard Deibert writes that "Mark paints this scene, captured so powerfully by Rembrandt van Rijn in his painting *The Storm on the Sea of Galilee*, to typify the mighty challenges confronting Christian community throughout the centuries. So far in Mark's narrative, the disciples have heard their calling. Now they must know the gates of hell cannot prevail against them."[4]

But this story is more than a symbol of the church—it is also a statement about the identity of Jesus. Mark tells us that Jesus gets up from his nap in the stern, probably feeling a little cranky, rebukes the wind, and says to the sea, "Peace! Be still!" (v. 39). He rebukes the wind in the same way that he rebuked an unclean spirit in a man earlier in the Gospel of Mark (1:25). Jesus has power over the wild, dark, chaotic side of life, both in the hearts of human beings and out in the natural world. In this case, his words cause the wind to cease and the water to fall into a dead calm. Then Jesus turns to his disciples and says, "Why are you afraid? Have you still no faith?" He does not fault them for fearing the storm, writes Presbyterian pastor Gary Charles, but "for thinking the demonic forces of the sea were more powerful than he."[5] The disciples are filled with great awe and say to one another, "Who then is this, that even the wind and the sea obey him?" (vv. 40-41). The story reveals that Jesus is one who has within himself the awesome and unlimited power of Almighty God.

Eddie Rickenbacker, the American aviator, was in a plane during the Second World War that accidentally went off course, ran out of fuel, and crashed into the Pacific. He and six other men floated in a raft for twenty-four days, and how they survived is recorded in his book *Seven Came Through*. Food was gone after three days—although at one point a seagull landed on Rickenbacker's head. Eddie slowly reached up and

> Jesus has power over the wild, dark, chaotic side of life, both in the hearts of human beings and out in the natural world.

caught it, and the bird became both dinner and fishing bait. It seemed as if the men were facing certain death, but their faith in God grew—in the midst of a storm, in the darkness of night, in a time of hunger and thirst. Soon after their rescue, Rickenbacker visited some airmen in a military hospital. They had just been sent back from the front, and many of them thought they could not go on. Some had arms or legs missing, and most were broken in spirit as well as in body. Rickenbacker spoke to these airmen and told them that they must not give in to depression and defeat. Having experienced the power and goodness of God personally, he said, "If you haven't had an experience of God in your life, you get yourself one mighty quick, because with that you will have power over all your problems."[6]

The disciples are given "an experience of God" when Jesus stills the storm. They discover that even the wind and the sea obey this one who has within himself the power of Almighty God. With a word he can drive out a demon, calm a sea, or strengthen the faith of airmen floating without food in the Pacific. But this is only the first of four "storms" that Jesus confronts in chapters 4 and 5 of Mark—he goes on to show us his power over chaos in three additional dramas. First, we "sail into Jesus' person on the Sea of Galilee as the powers of the abyss pour over the gunwale of our boat," notes Deibert. Then, we "make it to the eastern shore, to the eerie country of the Gerasenes, where a soul fouled by evil lunges at our faith. We are forced back to the western shore, where a street woman stalks us. Finally, the death of a twelve-year-old child threatens to steal the last breath of our discipleship. Miraculously, we survive. And Jesus is made known to us as Lord over chaos, the living embodiment of the Sabbath calm."[7]

In all of these stories—including that of the Gerasene demoniac included in the BCP reading for today—Jesus teaches us to trust his power over all that can hurt or destroy us. The "experience of God" we have with Jesus can give us the strength we need to face and overcome our problems. As we cross the Sea of Galilee with the disciples, we do not need to fear the water that was a cringe-inducing symbol of chaos, death, and disorder to the ancient Israelites. We can trust that the Lord will answer when we cry out, "Save me, O God, for the waters have come up to my neck. . . . With your faithful help rescue me from sinking in the mire; let me be delivered from my enemies and from the deep waters" (Ps. 69:1, 13-14). As we encounter the Gerasene demoniac (5:1-20), we can trust Jesus to calm the chaos of the past; as we encounter chronic illness in the untouchable woman (5:25-34), we can trust Jesus to calm the chaos of the present; as we encounter death in Jairus's daughter (5:21-24, 35-43), we can trust Jesus to calm the chaos of the future. "In every sphere of human existence, Jesus reigns over disorder."[8]

> As we cross the Sea of Galilee with the disciples, we do not need to fear the water that was a cringe-inducing symbol of chaos, death, and disorder to the ancient Israelites.

But these victories don't come easily—we would be wrong to overlook the intensity of the struggle in the stilling of these storms. In reflecting on the story of the Gerasene demoniac, activist and theologian Ched Myers observes that the name of the powerful demonic horde, "Legion," had only one meaning in Mark's social world: a division of Roman soldiers. He notices that the rest of the story is filled with military images as well, including the use of the term *agele* for "herd" in 5:11—this term is inappropriate for pigs, who do not travel in herds, but it is often used to refer to a band of military recruits. So Jesus is not simply driving out demons here—he is doing battle. And when the demons enter the swine and are drowned in the sea, it is hard not to think of enemy soldiers being swallowed by hostile waters. As Moses sings after the Egyptian army is swallowed by the Red Sea, "The LORD is a warrior; the LORD is his name. Pharaoh's chariots and his army he cast into the sea; his picked officers were sunk in the Red Sea" (Exod. 15:3-4).[9] In all of these stories, Jesus is not simply showing power over the forces of chaos and disorder—he is doing fierce battle with them, and he is winning.

We can be thankful that Jesus stilled a variety of storms over the course of his ministry, saving people from death, illness, and demonic possession. But what kind of victory can we expect today, when Jesus is not physically by our side—in the stern of a boat, or next to the bed of a dying child? Not all of the storms we encounter in our lives will be miraculously calmed, nor will all the diseases we face be instantly cured. And so we need to answer for ourselves the questions that Jesus asks the disciples—"Why are you afraid? Have you still no faith?" (4:40)—and we have to answer these questions in a way that focuses on faith, instead of on miracles. The challenge is to have faith that Jesus loves us and is working for an ultimate good, even when waves beat around us and our boat is being swamped.

To have faith that God has created the world and is in control of it, even when chaos seems to reign and evil seems to triumph. To have faith that the Holy Spirit is giving us strength and inner peace, even when we're feeling stressed and exhausted and at the end of our ropes. Faith is what keeps us going in spite of the depressing, disappointing, and demoralizing circumstances around us, and it enables us to face an uncertain future without fear. "If it does get stormy, we can cry out for help in confidence. Jesus sleeps no more," writes James McGinnis, the founder of the Institute for Peace and Justice in St. Louis. "He can calm our frightened, turbulent spirits so we can ride out the storm together."[10]

To have faith today is to trust that Jesus will give us an "experience of God" —even though it may not involve a rescue at sea or a miraculous cure. Instead, Jesus can calm our troubled spirits and give us power over our problems, so that we do not panic or lose hope when a storm is raging in us or around us. As much as we might like Jesus to be sitting right beside us, the Gospel of Mark indicates that such physical proximity is not necessarily part of the divine plan.

> As much as we might like Jesus to be sitting right beside us, the Gospel of Mark indicates that such physical proximity is not necessarily part of the divine plan.

In fact, when the Gerasene demoniac is healed, he begs to stay with Jesus and be as close to him as the disciples. But Jesus refuses, and says to him, "Go home to your friends, and tell them how much the Lord has done for you, and what mercy he has shown you" (5:19). Jesus does not permit the physical closeness that the man desires, but sends him back to his own house to report what the Lord has done for him.[11] This is our challenge as well: to go and tell others what Jesus has done for us, instead of clinging selfishly to him.

Our assignment is to tell stories that communicate an "experience of God" in human life—stories that come from personal experience, and from the experiences of others as well. Effective preaching will always include stories of the ways that Jesus is stilling storms in human life and giving people power over their problems. So draw deeply on your own experiences, as well as the reflections of others—evangelist Leighton Ford writes that "people will remember the stories I tell long after they have forgotten the statistics I quote." This is true whether you are preaching on the stilling of the storm, or any of the other dramatic narratives in which Jesus overcomes the powers of chaos and brings peace to God's people. "I am advocating that we see the gospel as story," says Ford, "and that we understand evangelism as living and telling the Story of the One who has entered and changed our story and will do so with theirs who also encounter his story."[12] When connections are made between divine and human stories, the power of Jesus is experienced in a life-changing way.

Notes

1. Norman C. Habel, "In Defense of God the Sage," *The Voice from the Whirlwind: Interpreting the Book of Job* (Nashville: Abingdon, 1992), 33–37.

2. Denise Dombkowski Hopkins, *Journey through the Psalms* (St. Louis: Chalice, 2002), 136.

3. Kathy A. Svitil, "To Breathe Like a Fish," *Discover* (July 2000), 42ff.

4. Richard I. Deibert, *Mark* (Louisville: Geneva, 1999), 44.

5. Brian K. Blount and Gary W. Charles, *Preaching Mark in Two Voices* (Louisville: Westminster John Knox, 2002), 66.

6. Edward V. Rickenbacker, *Seven Came Through* (New York: Doubleday, 2000).

7. Deibert, 44–45.

8. Ibid., 49.

9. Ched Myers, *Binding the Strong Man: A Political Reading of Mark's Story of Jesus* (Maryknoll, N.Y.: Orbis, 1988), 191.

10. James McGinnis, "Go Out into the Deep," *Weavings* (March-April 1996), 46.

11. John Painter, *Mark's Gospel: Worlds in Conflict* (New York: Routledge, 1997), 92.

12. Leighton Ford, "The Evangelist as Storyteller," *Journal for Preachers* 29 (2006): 27.

FOURTH SUNDAY AFTER PENTECOST

THIRTEENTH SUNDAY IN ORDINARY TIME / PROPER 8

JUNE 28, 2009

Revised Common (RCL)	Episcopal (BCP)	Roman Catholic (LFM)
Wisd. of Sol. 1:13–15; 2:23–24 or Lam. 3:23–33 or 2 Sam. 1:1, 17–27	Deut. 15:7–11	Wisd. of Sol. 1:13–15; 2:23–24
Psalm 30 or 130	Psalm 112	Psalm 30:2 + 4, 5-6, 11–12a + 13b
2 Cor. 8:7–15	2 Cor. 8:1–9, 13–15	2 Cor. 8:7, 9, 13–15
Mark 5:21–43	Mark 5:22–24, 35b–43	Mark 5:21–43 or 5:21–24, 35–43

FIRST READING

WISDOM OF SOLOMON 1:13-15; 2:23-24 (RCL, LFM)
DEUTERONOMY 15:7-11 (BCP)
LAMENTATIONS 3:23-33 OR
2 SAMUEL 1:1, 17-27 (RCL ALT.)

Death Is Never God's Desire

Although traditionally attributed to King Solomon, the Wisdom of Solomon never mentions the king by name, and was probably written by a Jewish scholar close to the time of Christ, with the goal of making other Jews proud of their faith. The book begins with the assertion that people who are truly righteous never die, because after their earthly death they continue to live with God.[1] The author states that God "does not delight in the death of the living" (1:13, RCL, LFM), but instead sees the goodness of all that God has made, describing God's creatures as wholesome, with "no destructive poison in them" (v. 14). Death is not God's desire for us, but instead "God created us for incorruption, and made us in the image of his own eternity, but through the devil's envy death entered the world, and those who belong to his company experience it" (2:23-24). There is clearly a cosmic struggle going on between the life-promoting power of God and the death-dealing power of the devil, but the good news for us is that God's "righteousness is immortal" (v. 15), completely immune to the power of death. Righteousness is illustrated by the command in Deuteronomy 15 to give with generosity (BCP)—"Open your hand to the poor and needy neighbor in your land" (v. 11)—and by David's lamentation over Saul and Jonathan (2 Sam. 1:17-27, RCL). Clearly, it is not God's desire to "willingly afflict or grieve anyone" (Lam. 3:33, RCL).

Responsive Reading
Psalm 30 (RCL)
Psalm 30:2 + 4, 5-6, 11-12a + 13b (LFM)
Psalm 112 (BCP)
Psalm 130 (RCL alt.)

From Individual Deliverance to Communal Celebration

Psalm 30 (RCL, LFM) is a classic thanksgiving psalm, one that praises God for recovery from a grave illness. It recounts the story of the psalmist's distress and God's deliverance: "O LORD my God, I cried to you for help, and you have healed me" (v. 2). God brought the psalmist up from the Pit, from the land of the dead, and because of this the writer calls on others to "Sing praises to the LORD, O you his faithful ones, and give thanks to his holy name" (v. 4). Old Testament scholar Denise Dombkowski Hopkins notes that the English translation "faithful ones" comes from the Hebrew *hasidim*, which is related to the word *hesed*—used often in the psalms for God's covenant loyalty. "The *Hasidim* are those within the community of faith who keep covenant, who follow in the paths God has set out for them," she notes. "These are the ones who would understand and value the marvelous transformation in the life of the psalmist that has just occurred."[2] In psalms of thanksgiving, personal deliverance does not remain an individual experience, but quickly becomes part of the celebrations of the wider community of faith. The BCP's Psalm 112 captures the joy of this community of covenant-keepers in its opening verse, "Praise the LORD! Happy are those who fear the LORD, who greatly delight in his commandments" (v. 1); and the RCL's alternate Psalm 130 calls to the entire nation, "O Israel, hope in the LORD!" (v. 7).

> In psalms of thanksgiving, personal deliverance does not remain an individual experience, but quickly becomes part of the celebrations of the wider community of faith.

SECOND READING
2 CORINTHIANS 8:7-15 (RCL)
2 CORINTHIANS 8:1-9, 13-15 (BCP)
2 CORINTHIANS 8:7, 9, 13-15 (LFM)

FlexChurch

There's a new kind of transportation available in many cities for those who occasionally need to drive but don't want to own an automobile: It's called Flexcar. These vehicles are shared by a couple of dozen people for a $25 lifetime fee plus a monthly charge, such as five hours of driving for $35. For many people today, the sharing of an automobile is a perfect way to keep their resources and their needs in balance.[3] This is an equilibrium that we need to establish in the life of the church as well.

In 2 Corinthians, the apostle Paul challenges the church in Corinth to "excel in everything"—in faith, in speech, in knowledge, and in utmost eagerness (8:7). But in particular, he wants them to excel in what he describes as a "generous undertaking": a collection for the Christians of Jerusalem. The city of Corinth at this time is a booming economic center, prosperous and highly competitive, and the Christian church contains a cross-section of the city's economy, with laborers and slaves sitting side by side with people of leisure, wealth, and social influence. Paul makes an appeal to this community, asking them to contribute to a collection for "the poor among the saints at Jerusalem" (Rom. 15:26). He believes that need and abundance should always be kept in equilibrium within the larger Christian community, and that those who have wealth are obligated to assist those who are in need.

This is not about welfare policy, however—it's about balance. Paul takes a surprising and unexpected stand when he suggests that the rich Corinthian Christians are indebted to the poor Jerusalem Christians—yes, that's right, the *rich* are indebted to the *poor*—since the Jerusalem believers preceded the Corinthians in the faith (Rom. 15:27). Because the Jerusalem crowd has sent spiritual wealth to the Corinthians, Paul believes that it's only fair for the Corinthians to respond with a

> Paul takes a surprising and unexpected stand when he suggests that the rich Corinthian Christians are indebted to the poor Jerusalem Christians.

gift of material wealth. He wants them be a FlexChurch, one marked by the free and flexible sharing of spiritual and material resources. This is the perfect way to keep a community's abundance and its needs in balance. Paul wants the church to be as fair and free and flexible as a Flexcar program, making sure that there are always resources and support available for members of the Christian community. It is a question of "a fair balance," says Paul, "a fair balance between your present abundance and their need, so that their abundance may be for your need, in order that there may be a fair balance" (vv. 13-14).

Fair balance is the engine that drives a FlexChurch. In day-to-day life, this means simply sharing what you have. "For example, you have five apples, so you give away three," suggests Victoria Sirota, vicar of the Church of the Holy Nativity in Baltimore. And why not? "They were going to go bad before you ate them anyway." Once you begin to behave in this way, you discover that the first step in ministry is simply sharing what you have in abundance. It may be apples or computers (or even Apple computers!). It may be carpentry skills or child-care abilities or an interest in teaching English as a second language. This kind of work turns into ministry when you begin to see that it is a way of achieving balance—balance between your own personal abundance and the world's pressing needs. In time, predicts Sirota, you may start to care about other people above yourself. "In this case, you find yourself buying five apples [and then] giving them away because you know that there is a family in need and they really need fresh fruit." Your focus shifts from acquiring apples for yourself to sharing apples with others, so that both you and the people around you gain all the nourishment that is needed for a healthy life.[4] "For you know the generous act of our Lord Jesus Christ," says Paul, "that though he was rich, yet for your sakes he became poor, so that by his poverty you might become rich" (v. 9). Keeping all these things in a fair and free and flexible balance is what defines a faithful FlexChurch, and it's what gives each one of us a life worth living.

THE GOSPEL
MARK 5:21-43 (RCL, LFM)
MARK 5:22-24, 35b-43 (BCP)
MARK 5:21-24, 35-43 (LFM alt.)

Saved by a Superman

An almighty father sends his son to Earth. He puts him here for a purpose. "They can be a great people," says the father. "They only lack the light to show them the way. For this reason, above all—their capacity for good—I have sent them you, my only son." On Earth, the son fights hard for truth and justice. He displays amazing abilities and incredible insights, but sometimes he feels that his power is being drained out of him. After a dramatic battle with the forces of evil, he is killed. But then he is resurrected and ascends into heaven. He returns in a second coming. This is the story of Jesus, right? Well, yes, it is. But it is also the story of Superman. Watch the movie *Superman Returns*, and you'll see Superman's arms outstretched, as though he is being crucified, and you'll watch as he receives a wound in the side—like the spear stabbing endured by Jesus.

So maybe Jesus and Superman have quite a bit in common. Not in their costumes, but in their power to save. Jesus comes on the scene in the Gospel of Mark as a man of action: curing the sick, casting out demons, cleansing a leper, and healing a paralytic—all before he finishes calling his twelve disciples (2:13-19). Then he stills a great windstorm on the water and heals a demoniac, sending the man's numerous unclean spirits into a herd of two thousand swine (4:35—5:13). This superhero Jesus is all about saving people from illness, evil, destruction, and death—in fact, the Greek word for "save" (*sozo*) pops up again and again in this Gospel, although it is usually reduced to bland English words such as "heal" or "get well."

> The power of Jesus attracts the attention of people who are looking to be rescued by nothing less than a Superman.

The power of Jesus attracts the attention of people who are looking to be rescued by nothing less than a Superman.

First comes Jairus, a leader of the synagogue. He falls at Jesus' feet and begs him repeatedly, "My little daughter is at the point of death. Come and lay your hands on her, so that she may be made well (5:21-23)." What he really says is, "Come . . . so that she may be *saved*". Being an authentic superhero, Jesus goes with him. Then a woman, who has been suffering from terrible bleeding for twelve years, joins the crowd that is following Jesus. She and the others press in on him like a mob of adoring fans, and the woman says to herself, "If I but touch his clothes, I will be made well." (vv. 24-28) Again, what she really says is, "If I touch . . . I will be *saved*". She's like a fan of the Man of Steel, dreaming of putting a single finger on the folds of his crimson cape.

There's no doubt that this woman really needs a superhero—she is ritually unclean and financially destitute. "As a result of her physical condition of unarrestable hemorrhaging, she should—according to the levitical purity code—be perpetually segregated," notes activist and theologian Ched Myers. And she was a victim of exploitation by quack doctors as well, a perennial problem for the poor in antiquity—Mark tells us she "had spent all that she had; and she was no better, but rather grew worse" (v. 26).[5] So she reaches out, touches Jesus, and immediately her bleeding stops—she feels in her body that she has been healed of her disease. The pain, suffering, social isolation, and ritual impurity that she has endured for twelve long years is suddenly over. She has been saved!

Then the plot thickens. Like Superman in the vicinity of a piece of Kryptonite, Jesus suddenly begins to feel that his power has left him. "Who touched my clothes?" he shouts to the mob pressed in around him. Nobody answers. "Who touched my clothes?" Jesus needs to know. "Uh . . . like, *everybody*," say the disciples to themselves, wondering if their master has lost his marbles. But Jesus is looking for a particular person, an utterly unique individual who has come for one reason—to be saved by a Superman. A few more moments pass. Then the woman steps forward. Full of fear and trembling, she tells her superhero the whole truth. But instead of punishing her for his momentary power-loss, he commends her by saying, "Daughter, your faith has made you well." (Literally, your faith has *saved* you.) "Go in peace, and be healed of your disease" (vv. 29-34). Jesus stuns the woman, and all those around her, by stating that her faith has saved her. Not his clothes. Not her touch. Not anything in or on his body at all. Instead, Jesus says that her faith is the source of her healing—she is saved by her willingness to believe that Jesus is a channel of the power and the presence of God. This woman now embodies "the calm of an existence whose chaos has been ruled by the creative power of God," writes pastor and medical doctor Richard Deibert. "There at Jesus' feet, before the hushed disciples, she worships in the fullness of truth. Using three different descriptors for her grace-filled reality, Jesus emphasizes a completely new creation: *saved, peaceful,* and *whole.*"[6]

> Jesus says that her faith is the source of her healing—she is saved by her willingness to believe that Jesus is a channel of the power and the presence of God.

Then the scene shifts, in a dramatic turn so common in summer blockbusters. While Jesus is still speaking, some people come to Jairus with the news that his daughter is dead. But Jesus overhears this message and says to Jairus, "Do not fear, only believe" (vv. 35-36)—an equally valid translation would be, "Do not fear; only trust," or "Do not fear, only have faith" (v. 36). This echoes what Jesus previously said to the storm-tossed disciples, "You are still not trusting" (4:40). And to the bleeding woman, "Your trusting has saved you" (5:34). And now to Jairus, stunned by the death of his daughter, Jesus says, "Only trust" (v. 36). Asserts Delbert, "For Mark, trust is the opposite—and antidote—to fear."[7] They proceed to Jairus's house, where there is a commotion being caused by people weeping and wailing. Jesus cuts through the chaos, throws the mourners out, and enters the house with only the father, the mother, and three of his disciples. Without lengthy prayers or dramatic gestures, Jesus reaches out to the child and says, "Little girl, get up!" And immediately the girl gets up and begins to walk about (vv. 37-42). Mark tells us that the witnesses are "overcome with amazement" (v. 42), using a term for astonishment (*ekstasis*) that appears again only once in Mark—when the women are told that Jesus, too, has risen from the dead (16:8).[8]

The girl is saved by a superhero. Saved not by Superman, but by the Son of Man. Saved by the one who carries the power and presence of God into the very middle of human life. Saved by Jesus, the Christ, the Savior. Clearly, Jesus has been put here for a purpose—to save us from iniquity and illness, sin and death. He comes to us because God so loved the world that God sent the only Son, so that everyone who believes in him may not perish, but may have eternal life (John 3:16). The key is to believe in him. To rely on him. To put our faith in him. To

trust him to be our Savior. We do this when we give 10 percentage of our earnings to God's work, trusting that our needs will be met if we are faithful in our
commitments. We do this when we suffer a job loss or personal failure, but then
find a way to face an uncertain future with confidence, believing that our Lord
is always working for good in our lives. We do this when we make an effort to
be loving and forgiving . . . not because such actions are easy or gratifying, but
because Christ has always been loving and forgiving toward us. We are able to
love others because Jesus loves us.

All of these actions are based on faith, not on miracles. They are grounded in
our belief that Jesus saves us from a life of emptiness and despair when he gives us
the ability to be generous, confident, loving, and forgiving. It remains true that
we will still struggle with illness, and each of our earthly lives will end in death.
"Miracles are *not* the resource to ride out the storms of life," notes American Baptist minister and communications professor Robert Stephen Reid. "Faith is the
resource. Faith can move us to moments when we see what God can do in our
lives or maybe even see what God has been doing all along. And in that moment,
when we recognize God at work, in whatever way God works in our lives, just
maybe like Jesus' disciples, like the possessed man, like the ailing woman, like the
man with everything at stake, we too will pause, dumbfounded, to ask, 'Who
is this man?' It takes faith to ask that question. It takes faith to answer it."[9] And
when we answer, perhaps we will discover that a Savior is really far better than
a Superman.

Notes

1. Roger A. Bullard and Howard A. Hatton, *A Handbook on The Wisdom of
Solomon* (New York: United Bible Societies, 2004), 1–6.

2. Denise Dombkowski Hopkins, *Journey through the Psalms* (St. Louis: Chalice,
2002), 138.

3. Carolyn Kleiner, "Go Cars," *The Washington Post Magazine*, September 15,
2002, 7.

4. Kevin Axe, "Finding a ministry that's right for you," *Faithlinks*, February 4,
2002, http://www.livingchurch.org/news/faithlinks/2002/2/4/finding-a-minis-
try-that-8217s-right-for-you, accessed August 1, 2008 (registration required).

5. Ched Myers, *Binding the Strong Man: A Political Reading of Mark's Story of Jesus*
(Maryknoll, N.Y.: Orbis, 1988), 201.

6. Richard I. Deibert, *Mark* (Louisville: Geneva, 1999), 54.

7. Ibid., 54.

8. Myers, *Binding the Strong Man,* 203.

9. Robert Stephen Reid, *Preaching Mark* (St. Louis: Chalice, 1999), 66.

FIFTH SUNDAY AFTER PENTECOST

FOURTEENTH SUNDAY IN ORDINARY TIME / PROPER 9
JULY 5, 2009

Revised Common (RCL)	Episcopal (BCP)	Roman Catholic (LFM)
Ezek. 2:1-5 or 2 Sam. 5:1-5, 9-10	Ezek. 2:1-7	Ezek. 2:2-5
Psalm 123 or 48	Psalm 123	Ps. 123:1-2a, 2bc, 3-4
2 Cor. 12:2-10	2 Cor. 12:2-10	2 Cor. 12:7-10
Mark 6:1-13	Mark 6:1-6	Mark 6:1-6

FIRST READING

EZEKIEL 2:1-5 (RCL)
EZEKIEL 2:1-7 (BCP)
EZEKIEL 2:2-5 (LFM)
2 SAMUEL 5:1-5, 9-10 (RCL ALT.)

Speaking to Scorpions

In the thirtieth year of exile in Babylon, the book of the prophet Ezekiel begins with a vision of a chariot, culminating in the appearance of the likeness of the glory of the Lord. When Ezekiel sees this, he falls on this face and hears "the voice of someone speaking" (1:28b)—this begins the call and commissioning of the prophet, which runs from 1:28b through 3:15. The voice of God speaks to Ezekiel, and a spirit enters into him and sets him on his feet (2:2)—the same spirit that will bring life to the dry bones in Ezekiel 37. God says to him, "Mortal, I am sending you to the people of Israel, to a nation of rebels who have rebelled against me" (v. 3). Ezekiel is being sent as a messenger to the people, a job defined by the words God uses to commission him, "you shall say to them, 'Thus says the Lord GOD'" (v. 4). There are actually three parts to this commissioning: "I am sending you" (vv. 3, 4), "you shall say" (v. 4), and "they shall know that there has been a prophet among them" (v. 5). And it will be the use of the formulaic phrase, "Thus says the Lord GOD," that will signal to the people that Ezekiel is a prophet.

Australian scholar Charles Biggs stresses that this recognition "did not guarantee the people of Israel would accept what the prophet had to say (v. 7). It was more likely they would resist and reject the prophet and his words."[1] God encourages Ezekiel with the words, "do not be afraid of them . . . though briers and thorns surround you and you live among scorpions; do not be afraid of their words, and do not be dismayed at their looks, for they are a rebellious house" (v. 6). The task of a messenger is to speak God's word to the people, whether they listen or not—even when they attack like stinging scorpions. A similar mission is given to Jeremiah (1:7-8), to Isaiah (6:9-10), to the disciples of Jesus (Mark 6:7-13), and, in a sense, to David. Although a king instead of a prophet, any success that David had with the people of Israel was due to the fact that "the LORD, the God of hosts, was with him" (2 Sam. 5:10, RCL).

RESPONSIVE READING

PSALM 123 (RCL, BCP)
PSALM 123:1-2A, 2BC, 3-4 (LFM)
PSALM 48 (RCL ALT.)

Looking to God for Help

This request for mercy is grounded in the image of a servant looking to a master for help, in a relationship of complete dependency. "As the eyes of servants look to the hand of their master, as the eyes of a maid to the hand of her mistress, so our eyes look to the LORD our God, until he has mercy upon us" (Ps. 123:2). The use of both "servants" and "maid" conveys a sense of inclusiveness, writes professor of Hebrew Robert Alter, stressing that *everyone* in this community, "man and woman, looks urgently to God for a sign of grace."[2] God's gracious mercy is needed because "we have had more than enough of contempt" (v. 3)—pain has been caused by "the scorn of those who are at ease; of the contempt of the proud" (v. 4). Although we are left to wonder about the specific offenses of "the proud," the Jewish Publication Society's translation suggests that contempt has been shown by "proud oppressors." The end of this song sets the stage for Psalm 124 and its expression of thanksgiving for Israel's deliverance. As the RCL's alternate Psalm 48 makes clear, God's "right hand is filled with victory" (v. 10), and the city of God is established forever (v. 8).

2 CORINTHIANS 12:2-10 (RCL, BCP)
2 CORINTHIANS 12:7-10 (LFM)

Posttraumatic Growth

When the bomb went off on a road near Baghdad, Hilbert Caesar thought his life was over. An Army staff sergeant, Caesar was in charge of a long-range howitzer—a self-propelled gun that resembles a tank. He was out on patrol in Iraq when a roadside bomb exploded. When the smoke cleared, Caesar looked down and saw that his right leg was severed in three places, just dangling by the skin. He thought to himself, "Oh man. This is it. My life is over." But he didn't die. The insurgents responsible for the attack disappeared, and Caesar was transported to safety. At Walter Reed Hospital, his missing limb was replaced with an artificial leg of plastic and steel.

Still, he felt despair about his future. He was in pain, and was worried that he'd never be able to run again, or be attractive to women. He received word that eight men from his platoon had been killed by a car bomb in Baghdad, including one of his role models. The news was devastating. But little by little he began to shift focus. Caesar met other injured soldiers and heard them talk about their recoveries. He began to look for the best, and realized that he was fortunate to make it back from battle with just one missing limb. Caesar now completes marathons in racing wheelchairs and has found a job with the U.S. Department of Veterans Affairs. He feels that his life is just beginning, and believes that he has come out of the war with more wisdom, compassion, and appreciation for life. He is one of a number of soldiers who are returning from war feeling enhanced, instead of suffering from shattered spirits. Now this is not to say that war is desirable or healthy or good—but it can lead to personal growth. Call it "posttraumatic growth."[3]

The same thing happened to the apostle Paul after he was stabbed with a thorn in the flesh (2 Cor. 12:7). We don't know exactly what this thorn was, although scholars have suggested that it could have been anything from epilepsy to stuttering, depression to eye problems. What's important is that Paul considered this affliction to be a painful trap or torture designed to take him out of the spiritual battle plan. Back in the first century, sharpened wooden stakes were often placed in pits, with the hope that enemy soldiers would fall on them and be impaled. They were also used as a method of torture. Sharpened stakes were the roadside bombs of the ancient world, and they were described in Greek by the word *skolops*—the exact same word that Paul uses for his thorn in the flesh. So Paul was stabbed—by a messenger of Satan, he says—"to torment me, to keep me from being too elated" (v. 7). He could have given up, assuming that his life as an apostle was over. But instead, he discovered that it was just beginning. Three times he pleaded with the Lord to remove the *skolops*, but God said to him, "My grace is sufficient for you, for power is made perfect in weakness" (v. 9).[4]

Power is made perfect in weakness. As amputee Hilbert Caesar says, "It makes me appreciate life a whole lot more." In the church, it is trauma that moves us from isolation to community; we are bound together as members of the body of Christ by such trauma as illness, grief, struggle, adversity, confusion, and crisis. Trauma also shifts us from self-reliance to God-reliance. It is when we accept our weakness that the power of Christ is best able to dwell in us. "Whenever I am weak," concludes Paul, "then I am strong" (v. 10). Reliance on God moves us from weakness to strength, from agony to ecstasy, from cross to resurrection. It's a perfect power, one that is found on the other side of pain, in an experience of posttraumatic growth.

> Paul could have given up, assuming that his life as an apostle was over. But instead, he discovered that it was just beginning.

THE GOSPEL
MARK 6:1-13 (RCL)
MARK 6:1-6 (BCP, LFM)

WWJD: What Would Jesus Drive?

A group called the Evangelical Environmental Network has run ads asking the question, "What Would Jesus Drive?" It's a clever question, one that tries to get Christians to think about the morality of driving gas-guzzling sport-utility vehicles (SUVs). Members of this network believe that Jesus would never drive an SUV, because car pollution causes illness and death, and it has a particularly devastating effect on the elderly, the poor, the sick, and the young. Gas guzzlers also contribute to global warming, which can cause drought, flood, hunger, and homelessness. Yet, if you were to preach a sermon insisting that Jesus would drive a hybrid, you can easily imagine the response. Nothing inspires feedback like a strong stand in the pulpit—"That was way too political," you would hear at the church door, or "I am free to drive whatever I want!" More polite critics might say something like, "Each sermon you preach is better than the next" (sounds like a compliment . . . but think about it).

Jesus gets a similar response when he begins to teach in the synagogue in his hometown of Nazareth. Mark tells us that many who hear him take offense at him, resenting him for upsetting the status quo and trying to elevate himself—

after all, he is an ordinary carpenter (*tekton*), from a nontraditional family (he is described as "the son of Mary" rather than "Bar-Joseph," in Mark 6:3). New Testament scholar John Painter notes that the original Greek says they are "scandalized" by him (v. 3)—it seems that because he is a local boy, the people of his hometown take offense and stumble at the authority implied by his teaching and miracles.[5] They allow their preconceptions and opinions of him to get in the way of seeing who he truly is.

In a sense, Jesus sees this coming, knowing full well that prophets have no honor in their own hometowns (v. 4). But at the same time, he feels hurt by this rejection, and Mark tells us that he is "amazed at their unbelief" (v. 6). "Here, Jesus is amazed by their non-faith (*apistian*)," writes professor of religion Sharyn Dowd. "This is a development beyond the concept of faith assumed by the miracle stories just narrated. Merely recognizing that Jesus has power is not faith. Faith is confidence in the saving power of *God* as manifested in the ministry of Jesus."[6] Although the people of Nazareth recognize that Jesus is doing miraculous things with extraordinary wisdom (v. 2), they do not recognize God as the source of Jesus' power and wisdom, nor do they recognize the coming of the kingdom of God in what he is doing and saying. Activist Ched Myers observes, "Without their cooperative faith (6:6)—that is to say, their openness to a new order—Jesus can accomplish none of the 'mighty works' (6:5, *oudemian dunamin*) that have aroused the hometown crowd's suspicion."[7] Dowd compares the people of Nazareth to the seed that fell beside the path—they never take root. "Jesus' combination of human ordinariness and divine power makes no sense to them. In 8:33 Jesus will call this kind of posture 'human thinking' by contrast with 'God's thinking.'"[8]

> The people of Nazareth do not recognize God as the source of Jesus' power and wisdom, nor do they recognize the coming of the kingdom of God in what he is doing and saying.

Christians are going to face resistance when they stand up for what they believe in, sometimes from the family members and friends closest to them. Being a disciple of Christ does not always lead to love and admiration—it can sometimes result in rejection. So how can disciples prepare themselves for the rocky road that lies ahead? In light of the rejection of Jesus at Nazareth and the mission of the Twelve that follows, a surprising answer emerges from the question, "What Would Jesus Drive?" Maybe the best vehicle for him would be an SUV. Yes, a sport-utility vehicle. Not because Jesus doesn't care about the environment, but because he and his disciples are facing a very rocky road.

When the going gets tough, you need a tough vehicle—such as the Hummer H2 SUV. This smaller, commercial version of the military humvee is built for high-mobility, off-road use, enabling its occupants to go just about anywhere, including over rocks and fallen logs, and straight through streams and creeks.

Think of the rough road faced by Jesus and his disciples. When he teaches in Nazareth, Jesus is rudely rejected, but he does not let this response deter him from his mission. He immediately hits the gas and goes out among the villages, and continues his teaching. A Hummer might have helped him, because evangelism is not a coward's game. "You've got to keep going when the going gets tough," writes Warren Brown in an automotive review. "The H2 is plenty tough."[9] So that's the first answer to the question, "What Would Jesus Drive?" Something tough.

Jesus then calls the twelve disciples and sends them out two by two, with authority over the unclean spirits (v. 7)—he empowers them and sends them out to continue the activities that marked his ministry. He orders them to take nothing for their journey except a staff (v. 8)—like the wandering Israelites who live on daily manna, they are completely dependent on God's care.[10] This is a frightening mission, because the disciples know that they'll be crossing tough spiritual terrain and encountering fierce resistance. But they bravely accept the assignment, and go out into the world proclaiming that all should repent. "They are to call humanity to a reversal of thinking and action (*metanoia*)," notes Dowd, "and they are to bring God's power to bear on the demons and diseases that prevent human wholeness and oppose God's reign. They do not do this alone, but with others."[11]

> This is a frightening mission, because the disciples know that they'll be crossing tough spiritual terrain and encountering fierce resistance.

They succeed in casting out many demons, reports Mark, and in curing many who are sick (vv. 7-13), and as this work takes them over rocks and logs, streams and creeks, they might appreciate the Hummer's gargantuan 6-liter V-8 engine, with the kind of power you need to haul a trailer . . . or, says car critic Brown, "if you are a missionary like some of my friends, to bring loads of food and medical supplies to people in poor countries."[12] So that's the second answer to the question of what Jesus would drive: a vehicle that can help people to do God's work in the most remote corners of the world. Of course, for most Americans today, SUVs are used mainly to drive to the grocery store and back—they aren't taken anywhere near the places they are *meant* to go, and aren't used to haul building supplies or food or water or medicine to people in urgent need. That's a sin.

The same sort of distortion goes on in our practice of the Christian faith every day, whether we own an SUV or not. We possess wide-ranging skills and knowledge, but we use them more to help ourselves than to assist people around us. We own beautiful homes, but we concentrate more on our personal comfort than on the practice of hospitality. We are given free time in the evening and on weekends, but we focus more on shopping and on self-improvement than on performing acts of service. We have enormous wealth and material resources—more than any other nation on earth—but we feel greater passion about stocking up on things for ourselves than about sharing our abundance with others. This is not to say that any of these things are bad, just as a sport-utility vehicle is not inherently evil. The problem is that we so often *distort* what we've been given, and we put our gifts to improper use. A Hummer H2 can certainly be holy . . . but not while it is idling in the parking lot of the local convenience store.

The challenge is to practice some true "SUV spirituality": to serve Jesus by doing something tough, and by performing the Lord's work in some hard-to-reach regions. This might mean counseling homeless men and women in a local shelter, teaching English as a second language to a class of recent immigrants, giving a week of vacation to chaperone a youth summer mission trip, or acting as a foster parent to a troubled child from the community. SUV spirituality also means standing up for what you believe in as a disciple of Jesus Christ. It has never been easy to leave the comfortable road of conventional wisdom and to face the rocks and logs and other barriers that society throws in our way. Jesus offended his neighbors when he spoke with wisdom and performed deeds of power, and the first disciples had to be prepared to be rejected by the people they visited (vv. 3, 11)—they shook the dust from their feet in a gesture that might have reflected the practice of a Jew returning to Israel, shaking the dust of Gentile lands from his feet.[13] Through it all, they were SUV tough, and they stuck to their mission of spreading the gospel through word and deed.

> It has never been easy to leave the comfortable road of conventional wisdom and to face the rocks and logs and other barriers that society throws in our way.

Once again, the example of the Hummer H2 is instructive. "It seems to me," says Brown, "that Jesus was all about peace, love and forgiveness, about 'beating swords into plowshares.'" He suspects that Jesus would be thrilled by the idea of turning a military humvee into a Hummer H2—a vehicle that could be used to bring food and medicine to the poor, "instead of making nasty ol' war."[14] You can be SUV tough and carry a message of new life instead of death.

So, What Would Jesus Drive? Maybe an H2—or, better yet, a more eco-friendly Chevy Tahoe Hybrid—if he or his disciples needed to go off-road to spread the gospel, cast out demons, and heal the sick. It's important to use the proper tools for the proper work, so that we can complete the mission we have been given by Jesus Christ.

Notes

1. Charles R. Biggs, *The Book of Ezekiel* (London: Epworth, 1996), 7.

2. Robert Alter, *The Book of Psalms* (New York: Norton, 2007), 441.

3. Michael Ruane, "From Wounds, Inner Strength," *The Washington Post,* November 26, 2005, A1.

4. J. Paul Sampley, "Second Letter to the Corinthians," in *The New Interpreter's Bible, Vol. 11: Second Corinthians–Philemon* (Nashville: Abingdon, 2000), 161–68.

5. John Painter, *Mark's Gospel: Worlds in Conflict* (New York: Routledge, 1997, 96.

6. Sharyn Dowd, *Reading Mark: A Literary and Theological Commentary on the Second Gospel* (Macon, Ga.: Smith & Helwys, 2000), 60.

7. Ched Myers, *Binding the Strong Man: A Political Reading of Mark's Story of Jesus* (Maryknoll, N.Y.: Orbis, 1988), 212.

8. Dowd, *Reading Mark,* 60.

9. Warren Brown, "It's Rugged, and They're Cross," *The Washington Post*, December 8, 2002, N1.

10. Dowd, *Reading Mark,* 64.

11. Ibid., 63.

12. Brown, "It's Rugged," N1.

13. Painter, *Mark's Gospel,* 99.

14. Brown, "It's Rugged," N1.

SIXTH SUNDAY AFTER PENTECOST

FIFTEENTH SUNDAY IN ORDINARY TIME / PROPER 10

JULY 12, 2009

Revised Common (RCL)	Episcopal (BCP)	Roman Catholic (LFM)
Amos 7:7-15 or	Amos 7:7-15	Amos 7:12-15
2 Sam. 6:1-5, 12b-19		
Ps. 85:8-13 or Psalm 24	Psalm 85 or 85:7-13	Ps. 85:9-10, 11-12, 13-14
Eph. 1:3-14	Eph. 1:1-14	Eph. 1:3-14 or 1:3-10
Mark 6:14-29	Mark 6:7-13	Mark 6:7-13

FIRST READING
AMOS 7:7-15 (RCL, BCP)
AMOS 7:12-15 (LFM)
2 SAMUEL 6:1-5, 12B-19 (RCL ALT.)

An Upsetting Prophetic Word

Speaking to the Northern Kingdom of Israel, the prophet Amos delivers a powerful message of social justice, criticizing the wealthy for oppressing the poor and for failing to "let justice roll down like waters, and righteousness like an ever-flowing stream" (5:24). Unfortunately, many Christians misunderstand biblical prophecy—they think of it as fortune telling, when in fact it is truth telling. "Prophecy is not the result of seeing into the future," writes Bob Hulteen in *Sojourners* magazine. "Instead, prophecy is the faithful declaration of the implications of current actions on the future, with the hope of having an impact on both. For instance, one need not be a rocket scientist to figure out that increasing economic inequities lead to social dissolution and fragmentation. So someone with the courage to say that wealth accumulation leads to the destruction of community, and that the result will be a future awash in violence, isn't looking into a crystal ball. They're simply sensitive to inevitabilities."[1]

In Amos 7, Amos sees a vision of the Lord "standing beside a wall built with a plumb line, with a plumb line in his hand" (v. 7). God asks what Amos is seeing, and when the prophet answers "A plumb line," the Lord vows to set a plumb line in the midst of God's people Israel, to see if they are strong and straight and true. Because they have failed God's assessment, they must be torn down like a leaning wall—"the high places of Isaac shall be made desolate, and the sanctuaries of Israel shall be laid waste." God concludes by promising to rise against the house of King Jeroboam with the sword (vv. 8-10).

This prophecy upsets Amaziah, the priest of Bethel, so he complains to King Jeroboam of Israel, saying, "Amos has conspired against you in the very center of the house of Israel; the land is not able to bear all his words" (v. 10). Like messengers of God in every time and place—including John the Baptist and Martin Luther King Jr.—Amos upsets the established powers with his prophetic words. Amaziah tries to silence the prophet by sending him away to the land of Judah:

> Like messengers of God in every time and place—including John the Baptist and Martin Luther King Jr.—Amos upsets the established powers with his prophetic words.

"earn your bread there, and prophesy there; but never again prophesy at Bethel, for it is the king's sanctuary, and it is a temple of the kingdom" (vv. 12-13). But Amos responds by stating that he has been given a special commission from God, "Go, prophesy to my people *Israel*" (v. 15). He cannot prophesy to anyone but the people of Israel if he is going to remain true to God's call, and besides, he is not a career prophet. "I am no prophet, nor a prophet's son," Amos explains; "but I am a herdsman, and a dresser of sycamore trees" (v. 14). The Lord took him from following the flock to take a particular message to Israel, and he must continue on this course until his mission is complete—as a truth teller, not a fortune-teller. (For treatment of the alternate RCL text, see the commentary on the Gospel lesson.)

RESPONSIVE READING

PSALM 85:8-13 (RCL)
PSALM 85 OR 85:7-13 (BCP)
PSALM 85:9-10, 11-12, 13-14 (LFM)
PSALM 24 (RCL ALT.)

A Prayer for Restoration

The psalmist's opening statement that God "restored the fortunes of Jacob" (v. 1) suggests that Psalm 85 may have been written after the Babylonian exile, although the exile itself is never mentioned. Restoration is a key theme in the psalm, being sounded in verses that speak of forgiveness (v. 2), withdrawal of anger (vv. 3, 4), revival (v. 6), steadfast love (v. 7), peace (v. 8), and salvation (v. 9). Verse 10 contains an "allegory of the ideal moment when God's favor is restored to the land," writes professor of Hebrew Robert Alter, a bold metaphor for an era of perfect loving harmony: "Steadfast love and faithfulness will meet; righteousness and peace will kiss each other."[2] In this restored land, faithfulness and righteousness will be seen everywhere, from earth to sky, and the Lord will give good gifts as the land becomes fruitful again (v. 12). In an unusual closing image, righteousness will actually move ahead of God and "make a path for his steps" (v. 13), carving out a route for the Lord to follow as God returns to the land. (See All Saints' Day, below, for a treatment of the alternate RCL Psalm 24).

SECOND READING

EPHESIANS 1:3-14 (RCL, LFM)
EPHESIANS 1:1-14 (BCP)
EPHESIANS 1:3-10 (LFM ALT.)

Spiritual Blessings from Heavenly Places

The letter to the Ephesians opens with a long outpouring of thanksgiving—one which is, in the original Greek, a single continuous sentence from verses 3 through 14. Along with 2 Corinthians and 1 Peter, Ephesians begins with a benediction that blesses "the God and Father of our Lord Jesus Christ," and then goes on to praise God for blessing us "in Christ with every spiritual blessing in the heavenly places" (1:3). The expression "in the heavenly places" is found only in Ephesians, and it refers to the unseen spiritual world—that world that exists behind and above the material world. The heavenly places are where God has chosen us in Christ before the foundation of the world to be holy and blameless before God in love (v. 4), destined us for adoption as God's children through Jesus Christ (v. 5), offered us forgiveness of our trespasses according to the richness of divine grace (v. 7), made known to us the mystery of the divine will (v. 9), and finally marked us with the seal of the promised Holy Spirit (v. 13). New Testament professor Nils Dahl points out that the text is a unified whole: "God is the acting subject, Christ the mediator of God's action and of the benefits Christians have received and possess in Christ."[3]

> It is not hard to imagine this passage being used in the worship of the early church as a joyful doxology of the divine plan of salvation.

The sovereignty of God infuses every verse of this passage, with emphasis placed on God's choice, will, grace, wisdom, insight, good pleasure, and "pledge of our inheritance toward redemption as God's own people, to the praise of his glory" (v. 14). The focus is on God's actions "in the heavenly places" (v. 3), with mention of God's "plan for the fullness of time, to gather up all things in [Christ], things in heaven and things on earth" (v. 10). This plan includes the unification of Gentiles and Jewish Christians in the church (2:14), and will eventually involve bringing the entire history of the universe to completion in Christ. God's love for each of us is made abundantly clear by this declaration of thanksgiving, as is God's desire that we all be reconciled to God and to one another through Jesus Christ. It is not hard to imagine this passage being used in the worship of the early church as a joyful doxology of the divine plan of salvation.

THE GOSPEL

MARK 6:14-29 (RCL)
MARK 6:7-13 (BCP, LFM)

Losing It

The Gospel lessons diverge on Proper 10, with the BCP and LFM focusing on the mission of the twelve disciples (Mark 6:7-13), and the RCL dealing with the death of John the Baptist (6:14-29). Since the commentary for Proper 9 addresses the mission of the twelve disciples, this section will focus on the death of John the Baptist, while making a connection to the alternate RCL first reading, 2 Samuel 6:1-5, 12b-19 (King David dancing before the ark of God). Those who follow the BCP and LFM are encouraged to turn to Proper 9 for material on their Gospel text, while users of the RCL are invited to take a fresh look at their 2 Samuel and Mark texts through the lens of an action common to both: a dance.

Paul Taylor, the innovative American dancer and choreographer, once contributed a modern dance solo in which he simply stood motionless on stage for four minutes. He just stood still, not moving a muscle. Now it's hard to know what to say about such a dance, but one reviewer for a dance magazine responded in an appropriate way: his review consisted of just four inches of white space. He wrote nothing about nothing. The dancing we do in church tends to be quite similar to Paul Taylor's solo. What we do is nothing—we just stand still, hardly moving a muscle. Our worship of God involves our minds, our hearts, and our tongues, but rarely our whole bodies. In American churches, dancing is a rare and controversial thing. In some congregations, it is absolutely forbidden.

Our reluctance to dance in worship stands in sharp contrast to the passionate physical movements we encounter in Scripture. In 2 Samuel 6, King David and his people brought the ark of God to Jerusalem, and as they made their way to the city, "David and all the house of Israel were dancing before the LORD with all their might, with songs and lyres and harps and tambourines and castanets and

> Our worship of God involves our minds, our hearts, and our tongues, but rarely our whole bodies.

cymbals" (v. 5). It is an incredibly joyful worship experience, full of music and shouting and enthusiastic movement—you might say that David "loses it" in his energetic leaping and dancing. "How they cut loose together," writes Presbyterian author Frederick Buechner: David and God, "whirling around before the ark in such a passion that they caught fire from each other and blazed up in a single flame" of magnificence. Not even the scolding that David got from his wife Michal afterwards could dim the glory of it.[4]

David does quite a dance before the ark. It is nothing if not enthusiastic, a word that originally meant "in God" (*en theos*). It is like the dancing that Ghanaian Christians do when they bring their offerings forward, a dance of celebration and liberation and joy in the Lord. But these dances can be controversial. When an American church member witnessed a Ghanaian offering one Sunday, she said, "If they want to worship that way, fine with me. But don't bring it into my sanctuary. They were running up and down the aisle, hollering, 'I'm happy, I'm happy' . . . . Well, as I say, if they want to do that, that's their business. But why do I have to sit and listen to it?"[5] And 2 Samuel reports that David's wife Michal saw her husband dancing, and she "despised him in her heart" (v. 16). Michal was not an evil woman, she just did not understand or approve of David's enthusiasm—she did not think that "losing it" in passionate movement was an appropriate way to worship God. She would have much preferred Paul Taylor's dance solo.

So, shall we dance? It's a tough question. Mark 6 tells the story of how a certain dance was used not to praise God, but to put John the Baptist to death. King Herod is throwing himself a birthday party, and present are his courtiers and officers and the leaders of Galilee (v. 21). One of the pieces of entertainment is a dance by his daughter, and this dance so pleases Herod and the guests that he says to the girl, "Ask me for whatever you wish, and I will give it. . . . Whatever you ask me, I will give you, even half my kingdom" (vv. 22-23). So the girl goes out and asks her mother, Herodias, who has a grudge against John, "What should I ask for?" Her mother replies, "The head of John the baptizer" (v. 24). And so the little girl rushes back to King Herod and requests, "I want you to give me at once the head of John the Baptist on a platter" (v. 25). "The involvement of the young daughter is a particularly chilling detail," notes religion professor Sharyn Dowd; "it is plain that she is put by the Gospel writer into the same age group as Jairus' twelve-year-old daughter. The same word (*korasion*) is used for both. One little daughter is restored to life; one participates in a grisly murder. It is the child who adds the detail of the platter. John's head is the final course in this macabre banquet."[6]

> Michal did not understand or approve of David's enthusiasm—she did not think that "losing it" in passionate movement was an appropriate way to worship God.

King Herod is deeply grieved by this request—Mark has told us earlier that "Herod feared John, knowing that he was a righteous and holy man, and he protected him" (v. 20). Yet out of regard for his oaths and for the guests, he does not want to refuse the girl. Herod loses his head while watching the beautiful dance, and now—to keep a promise—John the Baptist is going to have to lose his. So Herod sends a soldier of the guard with orders to bring John's head, and in short order John is killed and his head is placed on a platter for the girl and her mother (vv. 26-28). Mark seems to have sympathy for Herod in this passage, telling us that the king was perplexed by John, "and yet he liked to listen to him" (v. 20). But in the end, Herod is revealed to be a weak man, one who allowed himself to be manipulated by Herodias and his daughter—a girl who is, at the least, a very willing accomplice.[7]

So the question, "Shall we dance?" cannot be answered with an easy yes or no. Dance is good if it is truly enthusiastic, truly "in God." It can even be an appropriate part of worship if it enables us to put more of our God-given bodies into our celebrations of God's goodness—if it helps us to love the Lord not only with our mind, but with all our heart, soul, mind, and strength (Mark 12:30). Our Lord wants us to feel passion, as David did, and to be willing to "lose it" in joyful praise and thanksgiving. But watch out: dance can be dangerous if it becomes a human-centered form of entertainment, cut off from God—an artistic expression that causes us to "lose our heads" and act in ways that shatter the peace, unity, and purity of the church. Herod was so captivated by the beauty and passion of his daughter's dance that he lost his connection to God, and he ended up participating in the killing of a man that he knew to be righteous and holy—one that he had even made efforts to protect.

In the end, the dance we are all challenged to join is one in which we "lose it" for Jesus and the kingdom of God. In Mark, there are two ways of life laid out for followers of Christ: The first involves "saving one's life out of fear," and the second is grounded in "losing one's life for others out of faith." New Testament professor David Rhoads stresses that Mark's narrative consistently condemns the first and promotes the second. Throughout Mark, the quest to maintain power and status is motivated by fear (see, for example, 11:18). We see that (1) the Jewish and Gentile authorities are afraid, that (2) Herod fears John the Baptist (6:20), that (3) Pilate defers to the crowd (15:15), and that (4) the Jewish authorities fear Jesus' popularity (15:10). "To protect their power and status, the authorities destroy others," says Rhoads. "Although Herod considers John the Baptist to be a righteous man, he nevertheless executes John because he does not want to break his oath to Herodias's daughter for fear of losing face before 'the most important' and 'the greatest'

> In the end, the dance we are all challenged to join is one in which we "lose it" for Jesus and the kingdom of God.

people of Galilee (6:26)."[8] Herod does not want to lose face, and so he saves his honor by making a destructive choice.

In contrast, followers of Christ are called to lose their life for others. Disciples who live by the standards of the kingdom of God are willing to lose their life for Christ's sake and for the sake of the gospel (8:35), be last of all and servant of all (9:35), and be "slave of all" (10:44). John the Baptist is the first to lose his life for the Lord he had baptized in the Jordan, and through his death he becomes a model for those who come after him—his beheading follows on the heels of a remarkably successful mission trip, notes Presbyterian pastor Gary Charles, and alerts us to the potential cost of discipleship.[9] "Truly I tell you," says Jesus in the Gospel of Matthew, "among those born of women no one has arisen greater than John the Baptist; yet the least in the kingdom of heaven is greater than he" (11:11). The challenge for us is to be willing to "lose it" in service to Christ and the kingdom: lose our inhibitions in enthusiastic praise of God, lose our selfish interests in acts of service, and lose our very lives for the sake of Christ and the gospel. Like disciples who have gone before, we will find that the words of Jesus are true: "those who want to save their life will lose it, and those who lose their life for my sake, and for the sake of the gospel, will save it" (Mark 8:35).

Notes

1. Bob Hulteen, "Once in a Millennium," *Sojourners* (July-August 1998), 65.

2. Robert Alter, *The Book of Psalms* (New York: Norton, 2007), 310.

3. Nils Alstrup Dahl, "Ephesians," in *Harper's Bible Commentary* (New York: HarperCollins, 1988), 1213.

4. Frederick Buechner, *Peculiar Treasures: A Biblical Who's Who* (New York: HarperCollins, 1979), 26–27.

5. Henry G. Brinton, *Balancing Acts: Obligation, Liberation, and Contemporary Christian Conflicts* (Lima, Ohio: CSS, 2006), 63.

6. Sharyn Dowd, *Reading Mark: A Literary and Theological Commentary on the Second Gospel* (Macon, Ga.: Smith & Helwys, 2000), 67.

7. John Painter, *Mark's Gospel: Worlds in Conflict* (New York: Routledge, 1997), 103.

8. David Rhoads, "Losing Life for Others In the Face of Death," *Interpretation* (October 1993), 360–61.

9. Brian K. Blount and Gary W. Charles, *Preaching Mark in Two Voices* (Louisville: Westminster John Knox, 2002), 100.

SEVENTH SUNDAY AFTER PENTECOST

SIXTEENTH SUNDAY IN ORDINARY TIME / PROPER 11

JULY 19, 2009

Revised Common (RCL)	Episcopal (BCP)	Roman Catholic (LFM)
Jer. 23:1-6 or	Isa. 57:14b-21	Jer. 23:1-6
2 Sam. 7:1-14a		
Psalm 23 or Ps. 89:20-37	Ps. 22:22-30	Ps. 23:1-3a, 3b-4, 5, 6
Eph. 2:11-22	Eph. 2:11-22	Eph. 2:13-18
Mark 6:30-34, 53-56	Mark 6:30-44	Mark 6:30-34

FIRST READING

JEREMIAH 23:1-6 (RCL, LFM)
ISAIAH 57:14B-21 (BCP)
2 SAMUEL 7:1-14A (RCL ALT.)

Woe to Bad Shepherds

In Jeremiah, God laments the loss of good shepherds to watch over Israel. God is especially disappointed in King Jehoiakim, who lived six hundred years before Christ. Jehoiakim abused his people through misrule, unrighteousness, injustice, and economic oppression. When the powerful pharaoh of Egypt demanded that his nation pay a hundred talents of silver and one talent of gold, Jehoiakim raised this money by levying a tax on the whole land (2 Kgs. 23:35). "It is you who have scattered my flock," charges the Lord, through Jeremiah "and have driven them away, and you have not attended to them. So I will attend to you for your evil doings, says the LORD" (Jer. 23:2, RCL, LFM). God promises to gather the remnant of the flock and to put God's people under the care of a new generation of kings—kings who will be good shepherds and will watch over their people, protect them, and keep them from getting lost (note that God takes the shepherd-king David "from following the sheep to be prince over my people Israel" in the RCL alternative reading 2 Samuel 7:8). Best of all, God will "raise up for David a righteous Branch, and he shall reign as king and deal wisely, and shall execute justice and righteousness in the land" (v. 5). And this is the name by which he will be called, says Jeremiah, "The LORD is our righteousness" (v. 6).

Christians know this Righteous Branch to be Jesus, the one who came to earth to make a connection between people and God and to help people see that their righteousness comes from God. This Lord-righteousness is the exact opposite of the self-righteousness that so dominates our society today—it is so different from the self-centered smugness that leads us to believe that we somehow deserve our good fortune. Many of us make the assumption that doing good is synonymous with doing well—we are born on third base, and we go through life believing we have hit a triple. In the face of this self-delusion, Jesus reminds us that our righteousness comes from God alone. It is God who makes us righteous—who does this through the life, death, and resurrection of our good shepherd Jesus Christ. God dwells "in the high and holy place," according to Isaiah 57:15 (BCP), "and also with those who are contrite and humble in spirit."

RESPONSIVE READING

PSALM 23 (RCL) OR 23:1-3A, 3B-4, 5, 6 (LFM)
PSALM 22:22-30 (BCP)
PSALM 89:20-37 (RCL ALT.)

Everything We Need

Most of us have little contact with sheep or shepherds, but in spite of this distance we feel a deep bond with Psalm 23 (RCL, LFM), especially the first line, "The LORD is my shepherd, I shall not want" (v. 1). The promise of this psalm is that God gives us everything we need—food, drink, shelter, protection—and it challenges us to trust God to provide for us. "For the psalmist, God is the only necessity of life, because God provides the other necessities," writes professor of biblical interpretation J. Clinton McCann Jr. The first three verses speak of the food, drink, and protection that the Lord provides, making it clear that "God keeps the psalmist alive."[1] Verse 4 affirms that God is present with protection and comfort even though the psalmist walks through "the darkest valley." Then, at the end of the psalm, the scene shifts and God the gracious host provides for the guest in the same way that the shepherd took care of the sheep, offering food, drink, shelter, and protection: "You prepare a table ... my cup overflows .... I shall dwell in the house of the LORD my whole life long" (vv. 5, 6). Since it is within God's nature to provide for God's people, offering us everything we need, "the proper response to the good news of Psalm 23 and the good news of Jesus Christ is trust," writes McCann. "Life is not a reward to be earned; it is a gift to be accepted."[2] The alternate RCL reading, Psalm 89, describes God's covenant with the shepherd-king David, while Psalm 22:22-30 (BCP) praises the Lord who provides for God's people.

SECOND READING

EPHESIANS 2:11-22 (RCL, BCP)
EPHESIANS 2:13-18 (LFM)

Breaking Down the Barriers

"For two years, I shared my home with more than 30 children, four freedom fighters, a government bureaucrat, a wife-beater, a Red Cross worker with a taste for liquor, a number of prostitutes, a madman, and all the customers of the tea shop next door." This is the story of Maria Said, a newspaper reporter who spent time doing international development in the African desert. Writing in the Christian magazine *Re:generation Quarterly*, she admits that sharing her home with such a complex crowd was not her original intention, "but rather the unexpected circumstance of living in a room with only half-walls."[3]

Can you imagine living in such a house, separated from your neighbors by nothing but half-walls? There would be physical difficulties but also spiritual benefits, because such a situation reminds us that God sent Jesus Christ to break down "the dividing wall, that is, the hostility between us" (Eph. 2:14). Jesus came to lower the barrier that had existed between Gentiles and Jews, and to "reconcile both groups to God in one body through the cross, thus putting to death that hostility through it" (v. 16). In so doing, Jesus introduced not only a new relationship between God and people, but between human beings, one to another.

Maria Said reports that in her half-wall world, one of the women who lived next door became her best friend. When the dust storms came and the lights blew out, the woman would place her candles on top of the wall so that the two of them could share the light. On nights when she worked late, Maria passed bowls of American-style food over the wall and listened as the woman and the tea shop customers tried to identify and swallow the strange meals. Each night, after they dragged their rope beds out of the hot rooms into the small courtyards, they would whisper over the wall and wish blessings for the next day. The woman called Maria "sister" and made her a part of her family. The very same thing happens to those who become brothers and sisters in Christ: "you are no longer strangers and aliens," writes Paul, "but you are citizens with the saints and also members of the household of God" (v. 19).

> Jesus came to lower the barrier that had existed between Gentiles and Jews, and to "reconcile both groups to God in one body through the cross, thus putting to death that hostility through it."

THE GOSPEL

135

SEVENTH
SUNDAY AFTER
PENTECOST

JULY 19

MARK 6:30-34, 53-56 (RCL)
MARK 6:30-44 (BCP)
MARK 6:30-34 (LFM)

Every Fifteen Seconds

A wildfire is raging. And it's wiping people out. All across Africa, an out-of-control inferno is consuming people at the rate of 5,500 per day. The death and destruction is horrifying—with men, women, and children being killed around the clock. 5,500 people every day. One person every fifteen seconds. That's why the rock star Bono, lead singer of the group U2, started jumping up and yelling "Fire!" back in 2002. He felt he needed to shout because few other people were raising the alarm. "It's not a cause," he said, "it's an emergency." The wildfire he was yelling about was not a real fire, racing across the landscape—it was AIDS (Acquired Immunodeficiency Syndrome). AIDS is the reason that an entire continent is going up in smoke.[4] Although much progress has been made since 2002, the need is still enormous. Two million Africans died of AIDS in 2006, and the number of new cases—especially among women—continues to grow, and is outpacing the introduction of treatment services.[5]

Jesus and his disciples certainly knew what it felt like to face intense and seemingly intractable human need. In Mark 6, they are traveling the countryside, casting out demons and curing the sick, and are working so hard that they are not finding time to grab a bite to eat. So Jesus calls the apostles to hop into a boat with him and go away to a deserted place, to enjoy some rest and relaxation. But the desperately needy people of the region see where Jesus is headed and hurry on ahead of him, so that when his boat hits ground there is a huge crowd waiting for him. Although he is weary, Jesus isn't annoyed that his much-deserved day off has been interrupted, he isn't irritated that these people are unable to help themselves, he isn't even frustrated that the need all around him is so enormous.

The desperately needy people of the region see where Jesus is headed and hurry on ahead of him, so that when his boat hits ground there is a huge crowd waiting for him.

No, Jesus has compassion for them (v. 34)—which means, literally, that he "suffers with" them. The Greek word for compassion, *splagchnizomai*, means to be moved with pity from the depths of one's heart. Jesus has a sympathetic awareness of their distress, combined with a strong desire to alleviate it. Mark tells us that Jesus has compassion because they are "like sheep without a shepherd; and he began to teach them many things" (v. 34). Jesus becomes their Good Shepherd, one who invites the people "to sit down in groups on the green grass" (v. 39), just like the Lord of Psalm 23 makes his sheep "lie down in green pastures"

(v. 2). Religion professor Sharyn Dowd notes that in this, the first of the two feeding miracles in the Gospel of Mark, Jesus is pictured as the faithful shepherd promised to Israel in the prophetic literature of Ezekiel 34:23 and Jeremiah 23:4. Since both Moses and David had been shepherds, the shepherd had become a metaphor for the religious and political leaders of Israel. In the covenant with David, for example, God speaks of the tribal leaders of Israel "whom I commanded to shepherd my people Israel" (2 Sam. 7:7). But the supremely faithful shepherd of Israel remained the Lord, "who stood in judgment on all human leaders."[6] It is no accident that Jesus, the Son of God, is portrayed as a compassionate and faithful shepherd.

The question for us is this: Do we feel this same sense of compassion when we hear about the devastation of AIDS in Africa? Do we "suffer with" the men, women, and children who are infected with HIV, the AIDS virus, but are unable to afford the medication that will keep them alive? Are we moved with pity from the depths of our hearts . . . or are we merely annoyed, irritated, and frustrated? In 2002, Bono toured the American Midwest with a quiet African woman named Agnes. "I am from Uganda," she told a crowd of Christians in Louisville. "I once had 10 children . . . and we were very happy." Then her husband, a migrant worker, tested HIV-positive, and Agnes couldn't afford the medication necessary to keep him alive. "We bought it until we couldn't buy it any more," she explained, "and then we watched him die, without treatment." She learned that she too was infected, but she gained access to the anti-retroviral medicines that can keep AIDS in check. But then she found out that her youngest child was suffering from AIDS, which pained her deeply. "He's innocent," she said, "and he got the HIV from me. It was very difficult to me, but I tried to gain courage, and I prayed my Lord."[7]

> It is no accident that Jesus, the Son of God, is portrayed as a compassionate and faithful shepherd.

Jesus has compassion for Agnes, and for all of his people—young and old, male and female, black and white, moral and immoral. He senses that they are sheep without a shepherd, so he teaches them and helps them and heals them (vv. 34, 53-56). According to Mark, the eschatological shepherd has arrived—Jesus is the good shepherd promised by Ezekiel, Jeremiah, and Isaiah, the one who teaches his people (v. 34b), provides them with food (v. 42), and heals their sick and injured (vv. 53-56). "He will feed his flock like a shepherd," promises Isaiah; "he will gather the lambs in his arms, and carry them in his bosom, and gently lead the mother sheep" (40:11). "I will set up over them one shepherd, my servant David," says Ezekiel, "and he shall feed them" (34:23). The feeding of the five thousand, included in the BCP lesson, reflects God's gift of manna during the exodus, and it foreshadows the Last Supper, especially in Jesus' blessing and breaking the loaves and giving them to the disciples (v. 41). This passage also contains an implicit criticism of the religious leaders who oppose Jesus, notes Dowd: "they are the irresponsible shepherds condemned by the prophets."[8] The opponents of Jesus are the shepherds criticized by Ezekiel for feeding themselves instead of the sheep, and for failing to heal the sick or bind up the injured (34:2-4).

Jesus heals everyone, without discrimination and without asking how they managed to get sick in the first place (vv. 53-56). This last point is important, because there are some people today who are quick to pass judgment on Agnes, or on her husband, for becoming infected with the HIV virus in the first place. Now it is certainly true that God will judge Agnes and her husband, as God will judge each and

> Jesus heals everyone, without discrimination, and without asking how they managed to get sick in the first place.

every human being on earth. But God will also judge us, as individuals and as a community, on how we responded—or failed to respond—to the AIDS crisis. God will ask us how we let an entire continent burst into flames, and let 5,500 of our brothers and sisters die every day. One every fifteen seconds. Men, women, and innocent children.

There is much we can do to help douse the flames that are eating up the people of Africa. We can start by supporting international Christian mission efforts that are focused on preventing the "diseases of poverty"—tuberculosis, malaria, and AIDS. Good efforts are underway to prevent these diseases and treat their victims, and Christian hospitals continue to be the source of much of the available health care in areas of maximum poverty. These institutions need our prayers and our financial support. Tragically, our Western world tends to think in terms of winners and losers, and it looks down on the poor, who can pay little for services such as health care. Those who cannot pay anything do not count at all, and are seen as losers. But for Christians, writes a member of the Christian Medical Fellowship, "any man, woman or child who is a loser is of strategic importance because Jesus came to seek and to save the lost."[9] That's an unexpected emphasis, isn't it? For Christians, losers are more important than winners, because Jesus came specifically to seek and to save the lost. Are we following in his footsteps?

It is so important to have compassion for others, because Jesus has compassion for us. Every one of us, at some time or another, has been lost, and Jesus has found us. Every one of us, in one situation or other, has been a loser, and Jesus has reached out to us and embraced us. Every one of us, over the course of our lives, has made a number of poor decisions, maybe even as life-threatening as the decisions made by Agnes and her husband in Uganda. In such situations, we cannot save ourselves, we cannot pull ourselves up by our bootstraps. Instead, we need help . . . we need mercy . . . we need compassion. "Forgive, and you will be forgiven," says Jesus in the Gospel of Luke, "give, and it will be given you" (6:37-38). If we show compassion, we will receive compassion, "for the measure you give," says Jesus, "will be the measure you get back." The giving and receiving of compassion are central elements of the Christian life, and they should never be downplayed or ignored.

Now it's true that saving 5,500 people a day is an enormous challenge—one of the biggest that the world has ever faced. But it's something that can be done, sometimes through the administration of a simple shot, one person at a time. We can support this work in the name of the One who loved, touched, and healed the suffering people of his day, and saved them from destruction. We can do it with the help of the One who assisted everyone, without discrimination, and without passing judgment on their illnesses or economic conditions. Wherever Jesus went, says Mark, "they laid the sick in the marketplaces, and begged him that they might touch even the fringe of his cloak; and all who touched it were healed" (v. 56). The time has come to put some water on the fire called AIDS. As followers of Jesus Christ, people who have received his compassion ourselves, we can do no less.

> The giving and receiving of compassion are central elements of the Christian life, and they should never be downplayed or ignored.

Notes

1. J. Clinton McCann Jr., *A Theological Introduction to the Book of Psalms: The Psalms as Torah* (Nashville: Abingdon, 1993), 128.

2. Ibid., 129–31.

3. Maria Said, "Half-Walls Between Us," *Re:generation Quarterly* (Spring 1999).

4. John Filiatreau, "Rock star in the pulpit," *The News of the Presbyterian Church (USA),* December 20, 2002, 14–17.

5. "UN Millennium Development Goals 2007 Report," DATA (debt AIDS trade Africa) Website, July 3, 2007, http://www.data.org/issues/UN_Millennium_Dev_Goals_20070703.html, accessed July 10, 2008.

6. Sharyn Dowd, *Reading Mark: A Literary and Theological Commentary on the Second Gospel* (Macon, Ga.: Smith & Helwys, 2000), 68.

7. Filiatreau, "Rock star in the pulpit," 14–17.

8. Dowd, *Reading Mark,* 68.

9. David Clegg, "Is medical mission still relevant?" *Global Connections* newsletter, June 2001.

THE SEASON
AFTER PENTECOST /
OF ORDINARY TIME

PROPER 12 THROUGH PROPER 19
KAROLINE M. LEWIS

The middle section of Ordinary Time, beginning with the Eighth Sunday after Pentecost, affords the preacher with several creative trajectories for preaching during this, the lengthiest season of the church year. While the continuous Old Testament readings provide some obvious opportunities for sermon series, another option would be to continue working through Ephesians, which was introduced on Proper 10 (Sixth Sunday after Pentecost). The second lesson for seven consecutive Sundays during the season of Pentecost is devoted to this letter, which offers a number of powerful images and metaphors for living a life in Christ. While the assigned readings for the Revised Common Lectionary leave out the challenging image of the Christian household (5:21-32), a sustained reflection on this sometimes controversial correspondence would enable renewed consideration of the letter's contribution to the Christian witness.

A second direction would be to focus on the letter of James, which occupies five Sundays in the second lesson slot beginning with Proper 18 (Fourteenth Sunday after Pentecost). It is not often that preachers, either in the pulpit or in Bible study, devote time to the "later writings" of the New Testament, those smaller books lodged between Paul and Revelation. In addition to a host of important themes concerning the relationship between faith and life, such as the nature of trials and temptations (1:2-27), love and concern for the poor (2:1-13, 4:1—5:6), and controlling the tongue (3:1-12), the letter of James presents a vital corrective to possible misreadings of Paul that suggest the apostle ever assumed faith could be separated from acts of faithfulness.

140

THE SEASON
AFTER PENTECOST
─────────
KAROLINE M.
LEWIS

Focusing on James would elevate not only the importance of understanding how Christian faith results in ethical behavior but also to what extent preachers consider what it means to preach Christian ethics or to embody ethical preaching. Preaching James offers witness to the breadth and depth of the concept of faith and its inherent collaborative character. When Paul and James are put into conversation with each other, this deepens our understanding of both and suggests the importance of the process of checks and balances, both in the writings we call Scripture and in our interpretation of them. James asks us to reflect on the significance of the life of Jesus, and particularly his teachings concerning the marginalized, as also having salvific meaning. At the same time, Paul reminds us that a community that locates faith and salvation utterly in ethical teachings and actions of Jesus' ministry denies the absolute necessity for the undeserved grace of God. The pull, both in faith and in interpreting the Bible, is frequently toward reconciling the tensions and ironing out the wrinkles. When we look for opportunities to lift up the diversity of expressions of the New Testament writers, we call attention to the intricate, diverse, and dynamic texture of Scripture. We are able to hold up the Bible, not as final answer, but as open-ended conversations into which all are invited to join. We are able to see, the biblical writers ways of thinking, and ways of doing theology, ways of addressing the complications of believing in Christ that arose from real living communities of faith that offer contemporary congregations models of theological reflection.

One final trajectory for preaching during Pentecost 2 would be to preach John 6. Propers 12 through 16 give continuous readings through this chapter in the Fourth Gospel. While a familiar response to this lectionary option is typically how one might generate five sermons on what appears to be Jesus' repetitive words, this is a remarkable opportunity to "abide" in the Gospel that is not afforded its own lectionary year. John 6 represents a typical structural pattern for John's Gospel. Jesus performs a sign (not a *miracle*, as in the Synoptic Gospels), which is followed by a dialogue between Jesus and the observers, and then a discourse from Jesus that interprets the sign. The dialogue between Jesus and the crowds, the Jews, and the disciples, and Jesus' discourse after his feeding of the five thousand and his walking on the water, are critical to proper interpretation of Jesus' actions. It is not the sign itself that is either demonstrative of Jesus' power or that which must be believed, but it is what Jesus says about it that is the revelatory moment for this Gospel. Jesus as the Word made flesh is the one who provides the words for understanding the works he does. Again, dwelling on this significant structural pattern is critical for the interpretation of John that the lectionary rarely offers. For example, this is not the case in the lectionary for the sign/dialogue/discourse in John 9–10. While John 9, where Jesus heals a man blind from birth, is read in its entirety in Year A during Lent, the discourse in John 10, where Jesus interprets this healing, is dislodged from the sign itself (John 10:1-10 is read on Easter 4 in Year A, and John 10:11-18 is read on Easter 4, Year B), when 9:1—10:21 is all one unit. In this case, the liturgical and lectional decisions have outweighed the narrative thrust of the Fourth Gospel.

The challenge, of course, is to recognize the significance of the entirety of the discourse when it appears that Jesus is simply repeating the "same old, same old." While a number of these important transitions will be noted in the commentary that follows, it is helpful to note at this point several key themes through which to read this chapter in the Gospel of John. First, preaching on these texts from John 6 could focus on the connections between this section of John and the narrative of the Israelites in the wilderness in Exodus. The preacher could focus on the theme of God's provision, the Fourth Evangelist's reinterpretation of God's relationship with God's people as expressed in the cosmic vision of this narrative vision, and the way in which New Testament writers understood God's activity in Christ as the ongoing love of God for the world (John 3:16).

A second important theme would be to explore the absence, theology, and praxis of the Lord's Supper as reinterpreted, reengaged, and reimagined by the Fourth Evangelist. While the debate over the presence, or lack thereof, of the Eucharist in the Fourth Gospel continues among Johannine scholars, the narrative reality is such that in this story of Jesus' ministry, there is a Last Supper, but no Lord's Supper. What difference does it make that what might be understood as the Lord's Supper is *here*, in chapter 6, with crowds and the Jewish leaders, and not with the disciples alone the night before his death? What difference does it make that Jesus says, "I am the bread of life," and not, "This is my body, given for you"? What difference does *this* Jesus have, this Jesus who says, "Those that eat my flesh and drink my blood abide in me, and I in them," for our understanding of the interpretation, meaning, and practice of Holy Communion? Preaching during this period in Year B offers this oftentimes-perceived stagnant season several rich prospects for bringing to light Pentecost's celebration of new life, growth, and the reality of God's ongoing presence, comfort, and help in the gift of the Holy Spirit.

EIGHTH SUNDAY AFTER PENTECOST

SEVENTEENTH SUNDAY IN ORDINARY TIME / PROPER 12
JULY 26, 2009

Revised Common (RCL)	Episcopal (BCP)	Roman Catholic (LFM)
2 Kgs. 4:42-44 or 2 Sam. 11:1-15	2 Kgs. 2:1-15	2 Kgs. 4:42-44
Ps. 145:10-18 or Psalm 14	Psalm 114	Ps. 145:10-11, 15-16, 17-18
Eph. 3:14-21	Eph. 4:1-7, 11-16	Eph. 4:1-6
John 6:1-21	Mark 6:45-52	John 6:1-15

FIRST READING
2 KINGS 4:42-44 (RCL, LFM)

It is not hard to recognize the reason for the choice of today's text from 2 Kings in light of the Gospel reading from John. The Old Testament lesson narrates Elisha's miraculous feeding of one hundred men. The first part of today's Gospel is John's version of Jesus feeding the five thousand. Given this obvious connection between the texts, it may seem strange to focus only on Elisha, yet this prophet of the Lord is a compelling witness to the presence and power of God. The feeding of the one hundred men is early on in Elisha's ministry. After Elijah is carried up into heaven (2 Kgs. 2:9-12), Elisha becomes his successor, immediately picking up the mantle of his master (2:13) and parting the waters of the Jordan. This act makes clear to the company of prophets who witness the event that Elisha is indeed the heir to Elijah's spirit and work. The parting of the Jordan is but only the first of many miracles that Elisha performs that are narrated in 2 Kings 2:1—13:25.

Repeatedly, Elisha is described as "man of God" and his works leave no doubt of this portrayal. Already in chapter 4, Elisha has provided the widow of one of the prophets with enough oil to pay off her debts (4:1-7), raised the Shunammite's woman's son (4:8-37), and purified the contaminated pot of stew so that all might eat (4:38-41). After the feeding of the hundred, his miraculous acts continue with the healing of Naaman (5:1-19a). Even after Elisha's death, he will bring back to life a dead man who only touched his bones (13:20-21).

Preaching on Elisha's miraculous feeding makes a number of important claims about God and God's work without having to eschew Elisha in favor of Jesus. The story might be situated in Elisha's overall prophetic ministry as an opportunity to consider the role of the prophets in the lives of the people of God, and especially the particularities and details that surround this prophet. In addition, Elisha's feeding of the one hundred men is yet another example of God's provision and abundance. The servant's question in 4:43 is frequently our own in response to God's promises. The servant essentially asks, "How can this be?" All-too-familiar words in the face of what we think is not possible for God, especially when we equate God's blessings with our own worth or favor. "How can this be?" is a question about God but also about ourselves. It is also important to note that the servant's words are specifically, "How can *I*?" Indeed, how can *I*? And that is exactly the point, for thus says the Lord, "They shall eat and have some left." It is not us *alone*, but God's presence and power that enable works and acts for the sake of the other beyond our imagination.

> It is not us *alone*, but God's presence and power that enable works and acts for the sake of the other beyond our imagination.

2 KINGS 2:1-15 (BCP)

Second Kings 2 launches a large section of text (2:1—13:25) typically referred to as the Elisha cycle, to whom we were introduced as the disciple of Elijah in 1 Kings 19:19-21. Second Kings is the continuation of the historical narrative of 1 Kings, and at the start, Elijah is taken up into heaven, leaving Elisha as his successor. The prophetic succession begins with Elijah and Elisha on a journey from Gilgal to Bethel, then to Jericho, and finally to the Jordan River. Second Kings 2:1 implies that this will not be an ordinary outing for master and student. Instead, we are told that the Lord is about to take Elijah to heaven. While Elisha is not aware of what is to come, his devotion to Elijah intimates that he knows that something is different. Each time they arrive at their new destination, Elijah tells Elisha, "Stay here; for the LORD has sent me . . . ," and each time Elisha's response is the same, "As the LORD lives, and as you yourself live, I will not leave you." Like Ruth's commitment to Naomi her mother-in-law (Ruth 1:16-17), Elisha will not abandon his "father" (2 Kings 2:12).

When they arrive at the banks of the Jordan River, Elijah is able to part the waters with his mantle, signaling that his prophetic role has rivaled that of Moses who was able to part the Red Sea, and marking the significance of the role that Elisha will be taking over. When they are on the other side, Elijah grants Elisha one last wish of sorts before his departure, to which Elisha responds with the request similar to that of the firstborn son's inheritance. Yet, what Elisha will inherit is not connected with land or property or wealth, but with power. As they are walking, a whirlwind bringing fire, chariots, and horses takes Elijah from Elisha. Elisha's mourning (2:12) is quickly replaced by the symbolic act of his picking up Elijah's mantle (2:13), striking the water, the water parting, and crossing the river. The transfer of power is complete.

As this first reading is paired with Mark 6:45-52 (BCP), one avenue for preaching is to explore the meaning of a theophany—the presence of God—and what this story communicates about God's presence in our lives. God retrieves Elijah in the midst of a whirlwind, or storm, which is frequently associated with the presence of God. Jesus' words to the disciples in the midst of the storm on the sea, "Do not be afraid," are also typical of a theophany. Along with fire and chariots and horses, how do we imagine God's presence? What do these images communicate about the presence and power of God? While there are no words from the Lord in this section of text, the Lord is very much present, from the very first verse to the mantle that symbolizes the power of God's chosen ones. Elisha follows in the footsteps of those who have gone before him—Moses out of Egypt by crossing the Red Sea, Joshua and the Israelites into Canaan by crossing the Jordan, and Elijah. Now Elisha, himself, in the presence of God, *becomes* the presence of God, a prophetic voice to God's people.

> What Elisha will inherit is not connected with land or property or wealth, but with power.

2 SAMUEL 11:1-15 (RCL alt.)

The RCL alternate reading is the eighth Sunday of a twelve-week series dedicated to the character of David (Propers 5–16). On either side of this week's focus on the story of David and Bathsheba are lectionary readings that present the prophet Nathan, who calls attention to the troubles and triumphs that are to come for David. Proper 11 features an oracle to David (2 Sam. 7:1-14a), and Proper 13, a parable (2 Sam. 11:26—12:13a). Nathan is first introduced in 7:2 and in addition to the significant role he plays in the aftermath of David and Bathsheba, he will play a part in the story of Solomon's succession to the throne (1 Kings 1). The selected texts in the series that follow the story of David's adultery with Bathsheba include the death of Absalom (2 Sam. 18:5-33), the death of David and Solomon's taking over of the throne (1 Kgs. 2:10-12, 3:3-14), and Solomon's dedication of the Temple (1 Kgs. 8:1-43).

The preacher who has already decided to focus on this series of texts for this summer has made her choice, but preaching on this text even without having devoted the previous weeks to the David cycle would be a worthwhile digression on its own. Admittedly, however, the story of David and Bathsheba is not without a tangible peril in the view of the preacher. This is perhaps one of the best-known yet feared events in the life of David—feared because of how frighteningly accurate it is about the faults, follies, and failures of being human. Indeed, "Comfortable congregations prefer to hear tame sermons about mustard seeds and lilies of the valleys rather than be disturbed by the genuinely human behavior of David and his court."[1]

Although the lectionary ends the pericope at verse 15, the preacher should consider reading until the end of the chapter, to include the actual death of Uriah that David orders in verse 15. The child that David and Bathsheba conceived—which David tries to cover up, first by trickery and then by Uriah's death—will also die at the hand of the Lord. Preaching on the story of David and Bathsheba will necessitate situating the event within the larger narrative of the David cycle. And it will demand careful and honest work with the text that does not try to save either David or God.

> Preaching on the story of David and Bathsheba will necessitate situating the event within the larger narrative of the David cycle.

Another important reason to preach on this text is to focus on the character of Bathsheba. How often do we get to preach Bathsheba, the object of David's desire, the advocate for David's son? While David has a number of wives, it will be Bathsheba to whom the king will go for counsel about his successor (1 Kings 1–2). It will be the son of Bathsheba, Solomon, who will become king. Yet, the preacher cannot ignore the passive portrait of her character presented in the text for this Sunday. For all intents and purposes, she is objectified, taken, and later her grief over the death of her son curtailed in favor of David's consolation (2 Sam. 12:24).[2] What does this say about David? Who is Bathsheba? What does this communicate about God? While clearly the lectionary series is devoted to the figure of David, a sermon on this text would allow Bathsheba to speak.

RESPONSIVE READING

PSALM 145:10-18 (RCL)
PSALM 145:10-11, 15-16, 17-18 (LFM)

The designated psalm for the responsive reading is the second section of this praise psalm celebrating God's goodness and provision. The likely connection to the Gospel reading for the day is verse 15, "The eyes of all look to you, and you give them their food in due season." Yet, in the very next verse, the psalmist affirms God's ability to satisfy "the desire of every living thing." In John 6:12, the people who are fed by Jesus are also described as being "satisfied." In both the Greek New Testament and the Septuagint (the Greek translation of the Old Testament), the word for "satisfy" is the same. God is the one who is able satisfy the needs and desires of God's people. What does it mean to be satisfied in our day and age? What might that look like? And why is it put forward as something that God is able to do? What does it communicate about God and God's answer to the human condition?

PSALM 14 (RCL ALT.)

Psalm 14 as a prophetic psalm is offered as the pairing with the alternate first reading, the story of David and Bathsheba. Read in this liturgical context, the psalm is an indictment against David for his immoral behavior. Psalm 14 is a worthwhile conversation partner with the first reading, for it offers several points of interest by which to enter into the dynamics of David's behavior. Yet, verses 1–3 claim the sinfulness of all of humanity because we do not seek after God and have gone astray. In what sense are we the fools who claim, by our words and deeds, that there is no God?

PSALM 114 (BCP)

God's deliverance of Israel from Egypt and provision during the exodus is celebrated by the psalmist in this brief but impressive testament to the power and presence of the Lord. The psalm affirms the Lord's dominion over everything, over the whole of the earth, so that all of creation responds. Hymnic in quality and because of the subject matter, this psalm was typically read on the last day of Passover. Psalm 114 is a marvelous example of the power of allusion in Hebrew poetry. The events to which it refers are not directly stated but are rather reimagined, renamed, reinterpreted in figurative language. This is not unlike the Fourth Evangelist's reimagination of the same events through the incarnated presence of God in Jesus.

SECOND READING
EPHESIANS 3:14-21 (RCL)
EPHESIANS 4:1-7, 11-16 (BCP)
EPHESIANS 4:1-6 (LFM)

The choice of readings from Ephesians for this Sunday is the third lection in a seven-week series of readings from this letter. If preaching on Ephesians this week, it would be important to refer to the commentary for the previous two Sundays to have a sense of the argument up to this point in the letter. 3:14–21 functions as a bridge section for the letter. The apostle returns to themes previously discussed in his correspondence, but in looking ahead to the final portion of the letter, the prayer for the recipients reintroduces and reshapes previous themes as strategies for hearing the exhortations that follow. Ephesians 4:1 signals a move in the letter from theological claim to moral commitment. These ethical and practical reflections dominate the rest of the letter and are grounded in the certain affirmation of God's activity in and through Jesus Christ. It is significant that this section follows the prayer and doxology for the readers. With these observations in mind, this section of commentary will address all three of the lectionary pericopes offered for this Sunday, in recognition of the function of 3:14-21 and the inter-relatedness of this lection with 4:1-16.

The lectionary does not include the first part of chapter 3, which offers the source for the opening phrase in 3:14, "For this reason." It would be important to incorporate verses 1-13 into discussion of and preaching on verses 14-21, to set the context for the author's prayer for the addressees. The extent of God's love evident in Christ to which the author refers in verses 3:18-19 is made visible in God's inclusion of the Gentiles into God's promises (3:1-6).

As a bridge between the first part of the letter and what follows, 3:14-15 recasts the discussion of unity (2:11-22) as grounded in the Father, which is restated in 4:4-6. The unity that Christians share is a oneness that is realized in Christ, in the Spirit, but also because all are able to call upon the Father. This oneness has a direct impact on Christian behavior as promoting the growth of the community "in building itself up in love" (4:16). The prayer also revisits the concept of love (3:17) lifted up earlier in the letter (1:15, 2:4) by describing it as the rootedness and groundedness toward strength and power in the Spirit (3:17). This becomes the mainstay of how Christians are to live, especially with one another (4:2, 16).

> The unity that Christians share is a oneness that is realized in Christ, in the Spirit, but also because all are able to call upon the Father.

3:18-19 draws on 2:1-10 and the "immeasurable riches of his grace" (2:7), which is given to all and which saves all, and looks forward to the discussion in 4:7-16 on the gifts given to each individual for the sake of the whole. The gifts that are given, whatever they are, represent in tangible and visible ways the breadth, length, height, and depth that is the fullness of God. 3:18-19 also revisits 3:1-13 and foreshadows 4:13 with the idea that the knowledge of God's actions (3:2-6), the wisdom of God (3:10), and the knowledge of the Son of God (4:13) lead to full maturity of faith that works itself out in living one's life.

THE GOSPEL

JOHN 6:1-21 (RCL)
JOHN 6:1-15 (LFM)

The introduction above called attention to Proper 12 as the beginning of a five-week continuous reading through chapter 6 of John's Gospel. It is worth noting again that this series of readings presents a unique occasion to enter into the world of the Fourth Gospel when the primary role assigned to John in the three-year lectionary is as supplement or filler to the Synoptic accounts of Jesus. Preaching continuously from John over a five-week period not only creates an opportunity for significant engagement with the themes, theology, and witness of the Fourth Evangelist's account of Jesus' life and ministry, but also makes possible that which this narrative asks of its readers—to abide in the word. The theological claim of this Gospel is that anyone who reads this Gospel and abides in its words as the Word made flesh receives the same promises that Jesus made to his first disciples, "If you continue in my word, . . . you will know the truth and the truth will make you free" (8:31-32). The better translation for "continue" is "remain" or "abide." Enabling our congregations to experience Jesus' words from the perspective of this theological commitment offers a different sense of what the Gospel lesson on Sunday morning is and means.

One way that preachers might create this experience of abiding in the word is to model in preaching on these texts from John how the Gospel itself enacts this abiding. A significant strategy for creating this experience is how the Evangelist structures the text so that *rereading* is essential.[3] That is, there are certain literary techniques at play that ask the reader to go back and reread what has come before. As a result, the reader "remains" in the text, so that the content or material being expressed is reinforced by the form that the text has taken on. When the preacher and hearer understand this dynamic at work, a number of textual relationships occur. The connections between passages in the Gospel set up mutual opportunities for interpretation that do not occur when one is bent on a linear reading so as to get to the end, as if getting to the end will provide the answer. The commentary on John 6 that follows on ensuing Sundays will regularly point out these opportunities for rereading as a way toward new imaginations and possibilities for preaching.

> The connections between passages in John's Gospel set up mutual opportunities for interpretation that do not occur when one is bent on a linear reading so as to get to the end, as if that will provide the answer.

Today's reading pairs two significant events in Jesus' ministry, both of which are recounted in all four canonical Gospels. While this attests to the probable importance of these "miracles" in the memory of the early believers, another crucial aspect of being able to read about these events in each of the four Gospels is to note where and how, and then, of course, why, each of the four writers interprets these stories for their own situation. Paying attention to redactional activity between the Synoptics is always a useful exercise, but regardless of one's conclusions concerning John's knowledge or use of the Synoptics, it is also fruitful to consider in what ways and for what reasons the Fourth Evangelist interprets these oral traditions and how the stories function in the overall narrative.

The story of the feeding of the five thousand in the Gospel of John has a number of significant details unique to this Gospel. First is the setting for the miraculous feeding. 6:4 notes that the Passover was near. John purposefully situates the feeding within the context of the Passover festival. It is important to note that in the Gospel of John there are three references to Passover being near (2:23, 6:4, 11:55), a pilgrimage festival that would be expected of any Jewish male. As a result, it is from the Fourth Gospel that we have in mind a three-year ministry for Jesus. According to the Synoptic Gospels, Jesus' ministry is one year because he goes to Jerusalem only once, at the triumphal entry, after which occurs the Temple incident. Of course, the Temple cleansing is moved forward in John's Gospel (2:13-22), to immediately following the wedding at Cana.

The next difference between John and the Synoptics is found in 6:11. Jesus himself distributes the bread and fish to the crowds, whereas in Matthew, Mark, and Luke it is the disciples who do so. This is a critical detail for Jesus' claims in the discourse. It is his very self that is the bread of life. Moreover, that which Jesus does in the feeding miracle becomes that which Jesus says in the discourse and vice versa. There is really no separating Jesus' words from Jesus' actions, which is a main claim of this Gospel. Jesus is the Word. In 6:14 the crowds claim Jesus as a prophet. This is, of course, not the true identity of Jesus but it is a significant advancement toward recognizing Jesus' identity (compare to 4:19, 9:17). Jesus walking on the water follows immediately after this sign. For John, there is no Peter, no storm stilling. Rather, this is most certainly a theophany, a revelation of God. While "I am" is also in Mark, it does not have the same force as in the story in John, where all of the absolute "I am" statements ("I am" without a predicate nominative, such as "bread of life") stand behind Jesus' revelation to the disciples in the boat (compare to 4:26, 8:24, 28, 58, 13:19, 18:5, 8). Holding these two stories together creates worthwhile directions for preaching. It is interesting to note that Jesus' "revelation" to the crowds is what he can provide to the disciples, it is who he is. In our understanding of the meaning of Jesus, both need to be held together. In a very real sense, it will be one of the disciples who will make this connection. "My Lord and my God," says Thomas (20:28). Indeed, in Jesus is everything that the Lord gives and everything that God is.

> There is really no separating Jesus' words from Jesus' actions, which is a main claim of this Gospel. Jesus is the Word.

THE SEASON
AFTER PENTECOST
————————
KAROLINE M.
LEWIS

Today's reading from the Gospel of John pairs Jesus' feeding of the five thousand and his walk across the water. The BCP alternative is to focus on just the latter according to the Gospel of Mark, even though Jesus' walking on the water follows his feeding of the five thousand in Mark and in Matthew (14:13-33), but not in Luke (9:10-17). If preaching on this text from Mark and then returning to the lectionary text from John for next week, the preacher may want to consider including Mark 6:30-44, especially in light of Mark 6:52, which references the feeding story. It is also imperative to note that Jesus' discourse in the Fourth Gospel (John 6:24-71) is best understood in the context of John's version of the feeding of the five thousand.

Given the parameters of the lection from Mark, it is helpful to compare the stories in both Mark and Matthew. Matthew's typical redaction of Mark expands Mark's version to include the interaction with Jesus and Peter. Peter's actions as the representative disciple become the central focus of the story to lift up the theme of faith. The response of the other disciples in the boat, having witnessed this event, calls attention to the concern for faith: "Truly you are the Son of God" (Matt. 14:33). Their reaction foreshadows the confession that Peter will have to make for himself at Caesarea Philippi (Matt. 16:16).

In typical Markan fashion, the story in Mark is streamlined to narrate the basic elements. Yet, preaching on this text will need to take into account the unique features of Mark's interpretation of this event in the life of Jesus' ministry. First, Mark says that Jesus came to the disciples, walking on the sea, and "meant to pass by them." Matthew omits this verse entirely, probably equally puzzled by the phrase as most contemporary commentators. What does this detail add to the story? Why would Jesus want (the verb is *thelō*, to wish or want) to go beside them (*parerchomai*)? Of course, also problematic for Matthew is the disciples' response in Mark. When Jesus gets into the boat, the wind ceased. Yet, "They were utterly astounded, for they did not understand about the loaves, but their hearts were hardened" (6:51b-52). This is not the hoped-for response, especially when the disciples have just seen Jesus feed five thousand people, walk on water, and calm the sea. The disciples not only do not understand Jesus, a characteristic of the disciples most present in Mark (8:17, 10:5), but their reaction is also equated with that of the Pharisees who stand in opposition to Jesus (3:5-6, 8:17, 10:5).

> The disciples not only do not understand Jesus, but their reaction is also equated with that of the Pharisees who stand in opposition to Jesus.

In Matthew's account, Jesus and Peter get into the boat, the wind stops, and the disciples worship him and say, "Truly you are the Son of God" (14:33). The story in Mark ends much like the Gospel itself: "They said nothing to anyone, for they were afraid" (16:8). The disciples are afraid (6:50), do not understand, and their hearts are hardened (6:52). Even when Jesus is in the boat with them, "the disciples are 'far' from Jesus in more ways than one."[4] Preaching on Mark's version of Jesus walking on the water may very well mean an exploration into paradox. As Frank Kermode writes, "Mystery and stupidity make an important conjunction or opposition; but it must be seen with all the others, denial and recognition, silence and proclamation, clean and unclean, indoors and out, lake and mountain, one side and the other side."[5] Perhaps this story is illustrative of faith's capacity to elicit both poles in the response of the believer. The question is, then, whether or not you are on land or sea, and why.

Notes

1. Rolf Jacobson, "Preaching the David Story," *Word & World* 23, no. 4 (2003): 430–38.

2. See Jo Ann Hackett, "1 and 2 Samuel," in *The Women's Bible Commentary*, ed. Carol A. Newsom and Sharon H. Ringe (Louisville: Westminster John Knox, 1998), 98.

3. For further discussion of the concept of rereading and the Fourth Gospel, see Karoline M. Lewis, *Rereading the "Shepherd Discourse": Restoring the Integrity of John 9:39—10:21* (New York: Peter Lang, 2008).

4. Robert M. Fowler, *Let the Reader Understand: Reader-Response Criticism and the Gospel of Mark* (Harrisburg: Trinity, 1996), 217.

5. Frank Kermode, *The Genesis of Secrecy: On the Interpretation of Narrative* (Cambridge: Harvard University Press, 1979), 143.

NINTH SUNDAY AFTER PENTECOST

EIGHTEENTH SUNDAY IN ORDINARY TIME / PROPER 13

AUGUST 2, 2009

Revised Common (RCL)	Episcopal (BCP)	Roman Catholic (LFM)
Exod. 16:2-4, 9-15 or 2 Sam. 11:26—12:13a	Exod. 16:2-4, 9-15	Exod. 16:2-4, 12-15
Ps. 78:23-29 or 51:1-12	Ps. 78:1-25 or 78:14-20, 23-25	Ps. 78:3-4, 23-24, 25 + 54
Eph. 4:1-16	Eph. 4:17-25	Eph. 4:17, 20-24
John 6:24-35	John 6:24-35	John 6:24-35

FIRST READING

EXODUS 16:2-4, 9-15 (RCL, BCP)
EXODUS 16:2-4, 12-15 (LFM)

The first reading finds the Israelites now in the wilderness after being set free from Egypt, after having crossed the Red Sea in escape from Pharaoh and his army. 16:1 provides the chronological setting for their arrival in the wilderness, "on the fifteenth day of the second month after they had departed from the land of Egypt." In some respects, their complaints that follow are reasonable given the circumstances. They are hungry, they are in unknown territory, and they are still in the process of getting to know God.

This is not the first time the Israelites have complained since leaving Egypt. In 14:10ff, and following, they see the Egyptians hot on their trail and they are frightened for their fate. Indeed, what will become of them if the Egyptians catch up and overtake them? They are justifiably afraid for their safety and call on Moses, "What have you done to us?" (14:11). They would rather be back in Egypt, serving the Pharaoh, than face the possibility of death by Pharaoh and the Egyptians. And this is the case for their situation now in the wilderness. They would rather be in Egypt where they had food, as much as they wanted, than to be in the wilderness and face death by hunger. In both circumstances the Lord responds: by parting the Red Sea and by providing bread from heaven, "as much as each of them needed" (16:18).

The choice of this Old Testament lesson comes by its pairing with the beginning of the Bread of Life Discourse in the Gospel text from John. Yet, on its own, this story that recounts a critical juncture in the relationship between God and God's people suggests a number of directions for preaching. While it is likely that the Fourth Evangelist had this story in mind in the reinterpretation of Jesus' feeding of the five thousand and the discourse that follows (see the discussion on the Gospel reading, below), the claims about the provision of God are equally powerful without necessary recourse to Jesus' unambiguous statement, "I am the bread of life" (6:35).

The details of the narrative are striking and each on their own evokes theological claims worth exploring in a sermon. 16:9-11 repeats the fact that the Lord has heard the complaining of the people. This is further emphasized if we include verses 7-8, where the refrain, "the LORD has heard the complaining," is repeated twice. We are meant to hear this for ourselves, in the numerous repetitions, that the Lord does indeed hear our complaints. This can be worked out in two ways. One, the recognition

> We are meant to hear for ourselves, in the numerous repetitions, that the Lord does indeed hear our complaints.

of the obvious fact that the Lord does hear us when we complain—but also that we need to complain! It is as if complaining or grumbling is expected in this relationship. This is sometimes a difficult concept to acknowledge or comprehend, both liturgically and culturally. Liturgically, in the Lutheran church (ELCA) for example, all of the lament psalms were excluded from the *Lutheran Book of Worship*. This has meant almost thirty years of the ecclesial suppression in worship life of a common and sometimes necessary response to the human condition and perceived absence of God. Culturally, we tend to look with disdain on complainers, grumblers, and whiners—and why? Surely, there must be some other way that they might communicate their dislike, discomfort, or disease than this annoying form of expression. There are certain perceptions that go along with complaining—that such people are ungrateful, pessimistic, or unhappy. The expectation is that if such people could simply stop complaining, then they would be heard. A good example of this is having small children, to whom you might frequently say, "Stop whining, stop complaining," when in reality—or at least, in their own eyes—their needs might indeed be legitimate. It is a way of being heard.

In a related way, the repetition of the statement, "The LORD has heard your complaining," may also be likened to having small children, who continue in their grumbling state, forcing the parent to say over and over again, "I heard you the first time! I heard you already! I hear you!" One cannot help but wonder if this is the same dynamic that is going on in the text from Exodus. While later in the book of Numbers God's response will not be as positive, is this not certainly true of the relationship between parent and child? It may be easy to cast blame on the Israelites for their ungrateful response, yet how many times have we said something like the following to our own children, "Do you realize how much I have already done for you?"

Whether it be reasonable or not, part of being human is to complain, to grumble, and it is up to God to determine whether or not it is justified. And it is in God's answer that we learn something about God and something about ourselves. In the process of complaining and in hearing God's response, we learn more about how to determine needs from wants, plenty from greed, sufficiency from inadequacy—a lesson that cuts across numerous levels of our lives and of which we need reminding over and over again. And in the process of complaining, we learn that when it comes to *how* God will answer and *what* God might provide, we may have absolutely no idea what that may be. When the Israelites first see the manna on the ground, they ask Moses, "What is it?" They have no clue. And while Moses' response names it according to their need, "It is the bread that the LORD has given you to eat," Israel names it *manna* (16:31), for out of what is not expected, what is not known, what is not asked of God, comes something new.

> In the process of complaining, we learn that when it comes to *how* God will answer and *what* God might provide, we may have absolutely no idea what that may be.

2 SAMUEL 11:26—12:13A (RCL ALT.)

The commentary on last week's alternative first lesson noted that these texts are part of a semi-continuous reading through the David cycle. This week's text is the Lord's response to David through the prophet Nathan following the death of Uriah. The story picks up with Bathsheba's expressed grief over the death of Uriah (11:26), yet after the appropriate length of mourning, David sends for her, marries her, and Bathsheba has a son. The fate of the firstborn son of David and Bathsheba is interrupted, or delayed, by Nathan's words, but then prophesied by Nathan, "the child that is born to you shall die" (12:14). While the lectionary ends with David's acknowledgment of his actions, "I have sinned against the LORD" (12:13a), preaching on this text should include the reality of the repercussions he suffers. His repentance will not remove his comeuppance. David will not die, but for ordering the death of Uriah, David and Bathsheba's child will die, on the seventh day of his life, before he is circumcised, before he is named. While David's life is spared, his son's is not. We are left to wonder how the chosen punishment is really any better than the alternative.

Nathan's words to David begin with a parable. David is able to see the injustice that is the point of the parable and in doing so, names his own sinfulness and the suitable penalty for his actions. While David acknowledges that the rightful sentence for the rich man's behavior toward the poor man should be death, David himself will not receive that sentence. Instead, trouble will come from within his own house (12:11), foreshadowing the rebellion of Absalom. Indeed, what follows for David's life will be a series of sad events within his own household: the rape of Tamar, the death of Amnon, the revolt of Absalom, and the death of Absalom. Through David's eyes we see how easy it is to objectify and distance our own behavior until it is brought before us in full light, until someone must say to us, until God must say to us, "You are the one."

Responsive Reading
PSALM 78:23-29 (RCL)
PSALM 78:1-25 or 78:14-20, 23-25 (BCP)
PSALM 78:3-4, 23-24, 25 + 54 (LFM)

The chosen psalm for this Sunday resonates with the first reading for the day. As a historical psalm, the psalm recounts God's gracious acts toward the Israelites in a sweepingly detailed narrative. The selectivity with which each of the lectionary traditions works intimates the aspect of the psalm each wishes to emphasize. As a result, the verses selected for the RCL reading, for example, omit any reference to the sinfulness of God's people and focus primarily on God's provision. In preaching on this psalm, it is helpful to remember the function of this particular genre of psalm. Yet, historical psalms are not "just about dry facts, old events, or a past that is just an archive. The historical psalms aren't really about history, they are about God. They teach us that our story is part of God's story."[1]

PSALM 51:1-12 (RCL alt.)

Psalm 51 is classified as an individual lament or a prayer for help, and early Christian tradition considered it one of the seven penitential psalms (Psalms 6, 32, 38, 102, 130, 143). Early editors of the psalter accredit the psalm to David, and in particular, connect it to the story of David and Bathsheba. While it is a personal acknowledgment of sin, it is also a cry for God's cleansing and pardon, for God's mercy and forgiveness. As confident as the psalmist is about the severe state of the transgressions committed, there is equal if not greater confidence in the vast breadth and depth of God's grace. In Martin Luther's commentary on Psalm 51, he writes, "It is the teaching of this passage that conscious sinners . . . should have courage, and that God the Righteous and man the sinner should be reconciled, so that in our sins we are not afraid of God but sing with David, 'Have mercy.'"[2]

SECOND READING
EPHESIANS 4:1–16 (RCL)

For commentary on this text, see the second reading for the Eighth Sunday after Pentecost, above.

EPHESIANS 4:17–25 (BCP)
EPHESIANS 4:17, 20–24 (LFM)

These verses from the letter to the Ephesians are included in the lectionaries for the BCP and LFM but not for the RCL. Instead, next week will put all three in sync again as the lections pick up at 4:25. Here, verses 17–25 focus on the new life in Christ, which is really the theme for the rest of the letter. The previous life as a Gentile is contrasted with a radically new existence and way of life in Christ. These verses and what follows in the letter recall the opening greeting, "to the saints in Ephesus." This new life because of faith in Jesus Christ demands holiness (4:24) and conduct that makes evident having heard the gospel (1:13) and being marked by the seal of the Spirit (1:13).

One striking theme in this small portion of text stands out for preaching. First, the author assumes that there is a strong correlation between what has been learned and behavior that follows. The repetition of terms having to do with knowledge call attention to the claim that what the Ephesians have learned about God through Christ makes a difference for their lives. This is made evident in the first verse of the pericope, as the Gentiles are accused of living in the futility of their minds. The word for "futility" can also be translated as "emptiness." While they obviously are in possession of minds, nothing fills them, or at least, what is there is transitory, ineffective, and pointless. There is a certain truth to this in the life of faith that is sometimes overlooked. That is, faith and even living out the Christian life are typically viewed as matters of the "spiritual" and not the "intellectual." Or, that faith does not have to do with any kind of scholarly or academic pursuits but is merely an assent to that which cannot be understood. Certainly, by its very definition faith is a suspension of logic or rational thought on many levels. Yet, this does not mean that having faith asks us to stop questioning, wondering, pursuing, and in the case of the Ephesians, drawing on what we *know* to have an impact on our lives. Faith and intellect are not mutually exclusive. As much as God asks for our heart and soul in believing, God asks for our minds as the full expression of how deeply and completely our faith is a part of us, or even wholly us.

> As much as God asks for our heart and soul in believing, God asks for our minds as the full expression of how deeply and completely our faith is a part of us, or even wholly us.

The Gospel

157

Ninth
Sunday after
Pentecost

August 2

JOHN 6:24-35 (RCL, BCP, LFM)

This section begins Jesus' discourse that interprets the signs in 6:1-21. As noted in the introduction above, this outline of sign/dialogue/discourse is important to understanding the Fourth Gospel, not simply at a literary, structural, or narrative level, but at the level of understanding the theological claims of John's narrative. The sign itself is really not the major point. Rather, because they are "signs" and not "miracles," they point *to* something and that something has to do with the revelation of God in Jesus. The portion of text for Sunday determined by the lectionary narrates the first major section of dialogue, here between Jesus and the crowd. Jesus' response to the statements and questions from the crowd represents a typical pattern in this Gospel, whereby Jesus' words are not only misunderstood by his conversation partners, but call attention to the two different levels of meaning in which Jesus and his dialoguers operate. Previously in the Gospel, Nicodemus questions Jesus' claim of needing to be born again/anew/from above by stating, "How can anyone be born after having grown old? Can one enter a second time into the mother's womb and be born?" (3:4). At the end of the conversation, Nicodemus will not be able to move to the plain of understanding where Jesus is trying to move him. After nine verses, Nicodemus's final response is, "How can these things be?" (3:9), and his status as a believer is very much questionable, even after his advocacy for Jesus (7:50-52) or his unexpected appearance to assist in the burial of Jesus (19:38-42). In John 4, the Samaritan woman who meets Jesus at the well fares much better than her male counterpart. As with Nicodemus, her first response misunderstands the level to which Jesus wants her to go: "Sir, give me this water, so that I may never be thirsty or have to keep coming here to draw water" (4:15). Yet, by the end of the conversation she has left her water jar behind, goes back to her town, and announces, "Come and see a man who told me everything I have ever done! He cannot be the Messiah, can he?" (4:29).

The same dynamic is at play between Jesus and the crowds in their dialogue about the meaning of the sign they have just witnessed, the feeding of the five thousand. As with Nicodemus and the Samaritan woman, Jesus' response to the crowds is an attempt to move them from seeing the sign to a greater understanding of who he is. At the same time, however, being able to progress to a new level in recognizing who Jesus is and where Jesus comes from is not simply a matter of intellectual pursuit. Jesus' discourses in the Gospel of John are indeed interpretations of the signs he has just performed. Yet, Jesus as the Word made flesh means that his

> Jesus as the Word made flesh means that his words are also the incarnation of God's love for the world.

words are also the incarnation of God's love for the world. The discourses are also in themselves new moments of incarnation and revelation—that is, Jesus' words are the incarnated presence of Jesus as much as he is incarnated in the flesh. The crowds, in Jesus' words and person, are experiencing the revelation of God as much as they did, and even more so, in the sign they saw.

As the first section of the discourse, this passage sets up some of the main themes that are worked out in the verses that follow. One of the most important themes of the discourse is how the Fourth Evangelist reinterprets God's gift of manna to the Israelites in the wilderness through the incarnation of Jesus. As manna was a sign of God's presence in the wilderness, Jesus is the sign of God's presence now.

> One of the most important themes of the discourse is how the Fourth Evangelist reinterprets God's gift of manna to the Israelites in the wilderness through the incarnation of Jesus.

Yet, it is this understanding—that Jesus is the sign itself—that is misunderstood. The crowd finds Jesus on the other side of the sea and Jesus is direct about why they have sought him—because they "ate their fill." The crowd is not able to see that in the sign, Jesus reveals who he is, not just what he can do. In a very real sense, this is the meaning of the manna: that in the gift of manna from heaven, God revealed not only what God can do, but also who God is. The God of the Israelites has great power and can perform mighty acts. But more importantly, the God of the Israelites loves them, desires relationship with them, and wants to dwell with them, who chooses now through the Word made flesh to live in (John 1:14) and love the world (John 3:16).

The crowd is correct in seeking Jesus. "What are you looking for [seeking]?" are Jesus' first words to his disciples (1:38), and then "Who are you looking for/ whom are you seeking?" are Jesus' first words to the mob that comes to arrest him (18:4). is a main concern for John's Gospel. Just as the Gospel itself begins with Jesus' "seeking" question "What" and ends with "Who," Jesus must reveal to the crowd that the "what" (signs) is really a "who"—Jesus himself. The crowd makes the connection between Jesus' provision in the feeding miracle and God's provision in the wilderness, but by verse 34, and the end of the pericope for today, this is all they can see: "Sir, give us this bread always." The rest of the discourse will be about Jesus' continuing revelation and whether or not the crowd (and the disciples) will be able to recognize that Jesus himself is the "what" (bread) but also that Jesus is from the Father, from heaven. Believing that Jesus is sent from God is the reason for another important theme in this section of the discourse, the meaning of the term *work*. While the crowd asks Jesus what "works" (plural) of God they should do, the only work (singular) is to believe in Jesus who was sent by God. Indeed, by the end of the discourse, even some of his disciples will not believe that in Jesus is God's presence (6:66). Yet it is this work alone that enables the greater works that are to come (see also 5:20, 14:12).

In seeking Jesus, what are we looking for? For signs, for miracles, for something that we can see, touch, taste, smell, or hear? And for whom are we looking? It is essential to note that the words of Jesus do not override the importance of the sign. Both are evidently needed and we would benefit from asking why. In many respects, the sign embodies the discourse, or we might say, it is Jesus' words made flesh. The sign, retrospect, or in rereading after the discourse, is an acting-out ahead of time of the discourse that follows. For the Bread of Life Discourse, this means that when Jesus himself feeds the crowd he is truly the bread of life. This same pattern will happen again in John 9 and 10. Jesus and the blind man become the "figure of speech" (10:6), the shepherd and the sheep, that Jesus uses to interpret the sign. We might ask, therefore, what this means for a life of faith. That is, in what ways is God acting out in our lives the words God speaks to us? In what sense do we hold on to a sign that God provides without God's words that make sense of it? Or, when do hear God's Word, speak the Word of God, place all emphasis on God's Word, yet do not recognize or live out the Word as sign? Do we limit our abiding in the Word and not realize the mutuality, intimacy, and relationship between work and Word?

Notes

1. Rolf Jacobson, "Preaching the Psalms, Part 3—Preaching the Genres," http://www.workingpreacher.org/texts.aspx?article_id=83, posted May 10, 2008, accessed July 24, 2008.

2. Martin Luther, *Luther's Works,* vol. 12, ed. and trans. Jaroslav Pelikan (St. Louis: Concordia, 1955), 319.

TENTH SUNDAY AFTER PENTECOST

NINETEENTH SUNDAY IN ORDINARY TIME / PROPER 14
AUGUST 9, 2009

Revised Common (RCL)	Episcopal (BCP)*	Roman Catholic (LFM)*
1 Kgs. 19:4-8 or 2 Sam. 18:5-9, 15, 31-33	Deut. 8:1-10	1 Kgs. 19:4-8
Ps. 34:1-8 or Psalm 130	Psalm 34 or 34:1-8	Ps. 34:2-3, 4-5, 6-7, 8-9
Eph. 4:25—5:2	Eph. 4:(25-29) 30—5:2	Eph. 4:30—5:2
John 6:35, 41-51	John 6:37-51	John 6:41-51

FIRST READING
1 KINGS 19:4-8 (RCL, LFM)

In the first reading for this Sunday we find Elijah fleeing for his life from Jezebel. If this text is chosen for preaching, it would make sense to extend the reading to include verses 1-3 in order to set up the reason for Elijah's location in the wilderness. Once again, we witness God's provision, in this case toward the prophet Elijah. The number of connections between Elijah's experience in the wilderness and the Israelites in the same predicament explains its pairing with the continued reading through the Bread of Life Discourse in John. First, Elijah finds himself in the wilderness and, like the Israelites, voices his despair over his situation. The whole congregation of the Israelites complained to Moses and Aaron, "If only we had died by the hand of the LORD in the land of Egypt, when we sat by the fleshpots and ate our fill of bread; for you have brought us out into this wilderness to kill this whole assembly with hunger" (Exod. 16:3). Elijah has similar words for God. Wishing for his own death, he says to the Lord, "It is enough; now, O LORD, take away my life, for I am no better than my ancestors." The crowd will grumble over Jesus' words in John (6:41, 43).

*In the Episcopal and Roman Catholic traditions, churches may celebrate August 9 as the Feast of the Transfiguration (transferred from August 6). For commentary on the Transfiguration texts, see the *New Proclamation Commentary on Feasts, Holy Days, and Other Celebrations,* ed. David B. Lott (Minneapolis: Fortress Press, 2007).

Second, as for the Israelites, God supplies Elijah with the sustenance necessary for his journey ahead. Elijah eats and drinks, not once but twice in response to the angel's command to "Get up and eat." And the cakes and water made available by the Lord give him enough strength to survive forty days and forty nights. In John 6:35, Jesus will state specifically that he is the bread who has come down from heaven, and whoever comes to Jesus will never be hungry or thirsty. Third, Elijah's journey through the wilderness takes him to Mount Horeb (Sinai), where the law was given to Moses and the Israelites. Jesus' ministry is described as doing the will of God (6:38; see also 4:34, 5:30, 12:27).

2 SAMUEL 18:5-9, 15, 31-33 (RCL ALT.)

The alternative first lesson, which has been a semi-continuous reading through the David cycle, brings us to the death of Absalom. To do justice to the story in preaching would include reading the entirety of chapter 18. The narrative details of the events leading up to and following Absalom's death contribute significantly to the mood and suspense of the drama. While 18:5 provides David's direct command to spare Absalom in battle, verses 1-4 emphasize further David's absence in the whole affair. David wants to go with his army to quell Absalom's rebellion; however, his men dissuade David from marching with them by reminding David that he is king, after all, and should stay behind. Verse 4 stands out, "The king said to them, 'Whatever seems best to you I will do.' So the king stood at the side of the gate, while all the army marched out by hundreds and by thousands." *All* the army marched out, leaving the *king*, not David, at the gate of the city. David then gives the order not to harm Absalom to Joab, Abishai, and Ittai, each of whom is the commander of one of the three groups into which David had divided the army (18:2). This leaves no uncertainty that the entire army should know the plan.

The lectionary suggests reading verses 5-9 to provide the setting for Absalom's death in verse 15, but the narrative leading up to the actual killing of Absalom calls attention to the deliberateness and determination that surround the event. Riding on a mule through the forest, Absalom gets stuck in an oak, "and he was left hanging between heaven and earth" (18:9). This is more than a literal description of Absalom's predicament. Suspended between heaven and earth is the state of his life. A man finds Absalom, reports it to Joab, who wonders why Absalom was not struck down then and there. Joab is not interested in weighing the consequences for the man if he had indeed killed Absalom. Wasting no more time, as if saying, "Oh for heaven's sake, I'll do it myself," the narrative comes to a screeching halt as Joab's

> Absalom's death is not in the collision and chaos of a battlefield but by the murdering hand of one.

each step unfolds. Only after Joab stabs Absalom *first* do any of Joab's men join in the attack (v. 15). Absalom's death is not in the collision and chaos of a battlefield but by the murdering hand of one.

The lectionary pericope then skips to David's reaction to his son's death (vv. 31-33), but between the sounding of the trumpet (v. 16) and the final announcement to the king about his son's death the tension builds and the reader is put in the same place of waiting as David. Joab sends an outsider to give David the news and we are brought painstakingly slowly to David's response. The first word of 18:33 in Hebrew is the verb "deeply moved," which has a sense of "quake, shake, tremble." David's grief is visible as well as audible, as he cries out for Absalom three times and as "my son" no less than five times in verse 33. David the king, from the beginning of the chapter, is now—as no other time before—David the father.

DEUTERONOMY 8:1-10 (BCP)

This passage from Deuteronomy follows the reiteration of God's law in the Ten Commandments (5:1-21), the *Shema*, "Hear, O Israel" (6:4-9), and the reciting of God's acts of deliverance in the exodus (7:17-26). The section of text from chapter 8 specifically recalls the wilderness wanderings and the gift of manna, which explains its connection to the Gospel lesson for this Sunday.

On its own, however, it is a striking witness to the relationship between God and God's people thus far. On the brink of entering into the promised land, the Israelites are reminded of all of the goodness of God. The pericope might best be extended to end with verse 11, "Take care that you do not forget the LORD your God, by failing to keep his commandments, his ordinances, and his statutes, which I am commanding you today." "Do not forget" bookends the call to "remember" (8:2). How easy it is to forget what God has done, which the Israelites are called to remember, but it is important to note that "don't forget" also follows what God *will* do. The Lord is bringing them "into a good land, a land with flowing streams, with springs and underground waters welling up in valleys and hills, a land of wheat and barley, of vines and fig trees and pomegranates, a land of olive trees and honey, a land where you may eat bread without scarcity, where you will lack nothing, a land whose stones are iron and from whose hills you may mine copper" (8:7-9). The details of the land that God has promised emphasize narratively how easy it will be for the Israelites to get caught up in the goodness, able to eat their fill, with the difficulties far behind them. And so, it is as if God says to God's people: Will you

> The details of the land that God has promised emphasize narratively how easy it will be for the Israelites to get caught up in the goodness, able to eat their fill, with the difficulties far behind them.

remember me, or will you forget? Will you forget what I have done for you? And will you forget when you leave the "great and terrible wilderness" (8:15) behind, when you cross the Jordan into the land that I promised your ancestors? O my people, will you forget *me*?

RESPONSIVE READING

PSALM 34:1-8 (RCL, BCP)
PSALM 34:2-3, 4-5, 6-7, 8-9 (LFM)

This week begins three consecutive weeks of responsive readings that move through the entirety of Psalm 34 (1-8, 9-14, 15-22). Psalm 34 offers praise and thanksgiving for God's goodness. With this theme of the goodness of God, "those who seek the LORD lack no good thing" (34:10), this psalm illuminates the other readings for the day. Putting this psalm together with the first reading and the Gospel creates a reverberation of this claim about God, and if read responsively, allows the congregation to enter into the praise and thanksgiving of the Israelites long ago. This act of praise—of sharing the words of God's people—not only unites generation to generation, but also in giving voice to the goodness of God, it affords greater meaning to what "having no want" (34:9) can look like. Psalm 34 is also an invitation: "taste and see." This invitation links us to God's people, for we, too, are invited to experience God's goodness, to discover what it means to lack no good thing.

Eugene Peterson's version of the Bible, *The Message*, offers the following reading for verse 8, "Open your mouth and taste, open your eyes and see how good God is."[1] There is a certain wisdom in this interpretation. Recognizing God's goodness means that we must look to God (v. 5). To what extent is experiencing the goodness of God possible when we do not first turn to God, fear the Lord, and cry for help (v. 17)?

PSALM 130 (RCL ALT.)

Psalms 120–134 in the psalter have the same superscription, "A Song of Ascents," which commentators link to the three pilgrimage festivals (Passover, Weeks, Booths) as being used by pilgrims either on their way to Jerusalem or during the feast itself. The RCL alternative responsive reading is Psalm 130, which is meant to follow in both form and function the death of Absalom, for the psalm echoes David's cry from the depths of his despair and his own offenses. As early hymns in the church were considered sermons on particular texts, Martin Luther's hymn on Psalm 130 is one example of the interpretation of this psalm into the

164

THE SEASON
AFTER PENTECOST
───────
KAROLINE M.
LEWIS

lives of God's people. Luther's interpretation of the first two verses of the psalm capture the twofold dynamic at work between our own sinfulness (depths) and God's mercy: "Out of the depths I cry to you; O Lord God, hear me calling. Incline your ear to my distress in spite of my rebelling."[2]

SECOND READING
EPHESIANS 4:25—5:2 (RCL)
EPHESIANS 4:(25-29) 30—5:2 (BCP)
EPHESIANS 4:30—5:2 (LFM)

In our reading through Ephesians during Pentecost, this section of the letter continues the focus on what life in Christ should look like. The BCP and LFM lectionary readings from Ephesians encompass some or all of the section prior to the set pericope for this Sunday (BCP 4:17-25; LFM 4:17, 20-24), but the RCL skips these verses entirely. Preaching through the RCL readings on Ephesians would suggest either including the omitted verses or incorporating them (see the second reading for the Ninth Sunday after Pentecost, above) into the logic of 4:25—5:2.

The most extraordinary claim in this section of the letter comes at the end of the pericope: "be imitators of God" (5:1). This imperative enacts the rereading of what has come before through the lens of a completely different perspective. At stake for a new life in Christ is the striking claim that we are called to be imitators of God. It is one thing to consider such niceties as speaking the truth (4:25), putting away anger and bitterness (4:31), being kind, tenderhearted, and forgiving (4:32). It is quite another thing to consider these characteristics as those of God. In fact, being called to imitate God appears nowhere else in the New Testament and a sermon that explored the meaning, function, and possibilities of this charge alone would be well worth the effort for both preacher and congregation.

> At stake for a new life in Christ is the striking claim that we are called to be imitators of God.

THE GOSPEL
JOHN 6:35, 41-51 (RCL)
JOHN 6:37-51 (BCP)
JOHN 6:41-51 (LFM)

John 6:35 (RCL) functions as a bridge verse between the portion of the Bread of Life Discourse from last week (6:24-35) to this week's segment. Verse 35 introduces for the first time Jesus' claim, "I am the bread of life." It is worthwhile to set the parameters of the pericope as verses 35–51. Jesus' claim in verse 38 is central to this discourse and to the Gospel as a whole, "For I have come down from heaven, not to do my will, but the will of him who sent me." Recognizing from where Jesus came and who sent him is essential for understanding the ministry and meaning of Jesus. Moreover, verse 38 makes explicit what was implicit in verse 33, "For the bread of God is that which comes down from heaven and gives life to the world."

On one level, this verse is a crucial juncture in the discourse from the perspective of the connections the Fourth Evangelist is making between Jesus and God's provision for the Israelites through Moses, sent by God. It reveals something about God, that God is continually looking for ways to sustain God's people, to nourish the relationship between them, to feed them not only with bread, but also with knowledge of God's love. In Jesus as God, "bread of life" is even more than we thought it to be. It is God's constant desire to give life in any way possible. As a result, there is new understanding of Jesus' words, "I will raise that person up on the last day"

> In Jesus as God, "bread of life" is even more than we thought it to be. It is God's constant desire to give life in any way possible.

(6:44) and "Whoever believes in me has eternal life" (6:47). While it is certainly true that Jesus' *resurrection* is implied in these verses, they also contain meaning of Jesus' *ascension* for the life of the believer. Jesus came down from heaven and will return to the Father at the ascension and this is the same promise that is given to believers. Jesus' return to the Father means that the believer will abide in this intimacy between father and son (14:2-3, 23). This is a central claim of this Gospel and what is revealed in particular in verses 41–51. It is this very claim of Jesus, "I am the bread that came down from heaven," to which the crowd takes issue (6:41), not that Jesus said, "I am the bread of life." By putting these two things together, *the bread* and *coming from heaven*, Jesus is revealing not only what he *does* (provide life), but who he *is* (from God). "I came down from heaven" must be heard in light of verse 40 and 44, "I will raise them up." Recognizing Jesus' origins, from where he comes and to where he must return, means the same for those who believe in him.

Another crucial aspect in the interpretation of this part of the discourse is to read verses 47 and 48 together because the one offers a corrective of a misinterpretation of the other. While we might think that Jesus' claims of life are limited to future life with Jesus and God, on the last day, at the resurrection/ascension, verse 48 comes in to correct this. That is, Jesus is the bread of life, not in the future, but here and now. The Word becoming flesh brings into the present the promises of the future. In this realized eschatology, the abundance of life with God is possible now, this God who chose to make God's home with us, who chose to "tabernacle" with us (1:14). This is the radical claim of the incarnation. God's commitment to the "everydayness" of human existence signifies that *now* means something.

A final entry into this text might take a cue from the psalm. The invitation to "taste and see" is exactly Jesus' invitation in this discourse. Indeed, it is this invitation that Jesus extended to the first disciples, "Come and see" (1:39). The Samaritan woman at the well returns to her town and invites them to "come and see" (4:29). "Taste and see" is fully realized in 6:51, which is the first time the term *flesh* is used in the discourse. In a sense, this is strikingly fitting for this Gospel, whose most sweeping claim is the incarnation. The senses of incarnated life come to full expression in this narrative of Jesus. Here, and more graphically later, in the discourse, we are invited to taste. In John 9:1—10:21, the healing of the man blind from birth, the emphasis is on sight and hearing (9:7, 27, 10:3-5), and indeed, Lazarus will come out of the tomb (11:43-44) and Mary will recognize Jesus (20:16) when they hear their names called by Jesus. The story of Lazarus also calls attention to smell (11:39) and the story of Thomas emphasizes the importance of touch (20:24-29). Believing in Jesus is a full sensory experience, a fully incarnated, fully embodied faith that is not about assent to doctrine, for faith in this Gospel is never a noun but always a verb: to believe, active, living, doing, and being, just as God became in Jesus.

> This is the radical claim of the incarnation. God's commitment to the "everydayness" of human existence signifies that *now* means something.

Notes

1. Eugene Peterson, *The Message* (Colorado Springs: NavPress, 2005).

2. Martin Luther, "Out of the Depths I Cry to You," *Evangelical Lutheran Worship* (Minneapolis: Augsburg Fortress, 2006), #600.

ELEVENTH SUNDAY AFTER PENTECOST

TWENTIETH SUNDAY IN ORDINARY TIME /
PROPER 15
AUGUST 16, 2009

Revised Common (RCL)	Episcopal (BCP)	Roman Catholic (LFM)
Prov. 9:1-6 or	Prov. 9:1-6	Prov. 9:1-6
1 Kgs. 2:10-12; 3:3-14		
Ps. 34:9-14 or Psalm 111	Psalm 147 or 34:9-14	Ps. 34:2-3, 4-5, 6-7
Eph. 5:15-20	Eph. 5:15-20	Eph. 5:15-20
John 6:51-58	John 6:53-59	John 6:51-58

FIRST READING

PROVERBS 9:1-6 (RCL, BCP, LFM)

Personified wisdom invites her disciples to her house, where the table is set and the feast is ready. The personification of wisdom as a woman is one of the unique features of the book of Proverbs and dominates the first nine chapters. Two speeches come from Woman Wisdom, 1:20-33 and 8:1-36 (see the first reading for the Fifteenth Sunday after Pentecost, below). The instructions and sayings of Woman Wisdom are contrasted with the "loose woman" and the "foolish woman" who offer what seems to be wise advice, but is deadly in the end. Within the context of the first section of Proverbs, the reading for this Sunday sets before us the choice between wisdom and foolishness. Preaching on this text could draw on the previous chapters in the book of Proverbs to flesh out what wisdom "looks like" and why it was and is an important concept for a life of faith. What difference does it make for living before God?

> The invitation of Woman Wisdom to her banquet is an invitation to insight for the sake of a different life.

The choice of this text to be paired with the Gospel reading makes sense on two levels. First, Wisdom provides: "Come, eat of my bread and drink of the wine I have mixed" (9:5). She prepares a banquet, as God provides, and as Jesus provides. As Wisdom before him, Jesus as the bread of life reveals his ability to offer that which lays claim on the way of life here and now. The invitation of Woman Wisdom to her banquet is an invitation to insight for the sake of a different life, "Lay aside immaturity, and live, and walk in the way of insight" (v. 6). Jesus' invitation means the same, that partaking in the feast that is his very flesh and blood gives life in him now and the opportunity to abide in him and he in us.

A second reason for the reading of this text from Proverbs in conjunction with the Gospel reading from John is the possible inference on the part of the Fourth Evangelist to communicate Jesus as *logos*, wisdom, who was in the beginning with God (John 1:1; Prov. 8:22-31). Whether or not and to what extent this explanation of the thought world of the Fourth Gospel holds sway is much debated in Johannine scholarship. At the very least, however, we are meant to see Jesus as representative of God, who invites all to a choice of life. Just as Wisdom says "come," so does Jesus, "Whoever comes to me." Coming to Jesus is connected with believing in Jesus (6:35, 37), being taught by God, and learning from the Father (6:45). At the end of the Gospel, Jesus will invite his disciples to another meal, to breakfast, where Jesus gives them bread and fish. Having gone the whole night without catching anything, Jesus has them cast their nets again and they are not able to haul the net, for their catch yields 153 fish. Sitting around a charcoal fire, Jesus says to his disciples, "Come and have breakfast" (John 21:12). And they eat of the bounty that Jesus has provided, once again. In Wisdom, in Jesus, is God's bountiful blessings for God's people. It is God saying, "I am—for you."[1]

1 KINGS 2:10-12; 3:3-14 (RCL ALT.)

This selection of texts from 1 Kings narrates David's death and introduces David's son Solomon as his successor to the throne. Even if the preacher has chosen to work through the David cycle offered in Pentecost 2, preaching on this episode would require some back story to set up the transference in power. First Kings begins with King David as "old and advanced in years" (1:1) and the need for an heir to the kingship is at stake. Adonijah, David's oldest son, comes forward and claims the throne, his very right. Moreover, he is a very handsome man (1:6)! He throws a party for himself, but not every follower of David is supportive of Adonijah, including Nathan, the prophet. Nathan sends Bathsheba to visit David, who reminds him of a fictional promise to make Solomon king. Nathan comes and concurs with Bathsheba, and at once David makes Solomon king. After a brief farewell speech to his son, the new king, we come to the first section of text for this Sunday: the death of David (2:10-12). The lection fast-forwards through Solomon's elimination of threats to the throne, including Adonijah and Joab, to the Lord's visit to Solomon in a dream at Gibeon. In the dream, God says to Solomon, "Ask what I should give you" (3:5). Solomon's response to the Lord is to ask for what would make him a good king. Indeed, this is Solomon's prayer for wisdom, the benefits of which will be demonstrated in the very next story (3:16-28). The request for wisdom also establishes a connection with the other readings for the day.

If the preacher has considered preaching through these alternate readings and has spent some time on the character of Bathsheba, this reading from 1 Kings can be another opportunity to highlight the queen and even the much less known Abishag. What is her role in this story? How are the two women, Bathsheba and Abishag, functioning in this story that seems quite overpowered by men? Where and how is their power in the midst of men who are jockeying for power? When one considers the result, that Solomon does indeed take over as king, these women play an integral role in the affairs. It is worthwhile to consider in what ways God is seen at work in the unexpected, and perhaps unaccepted, dimensions of human relationships.

> It is worthwhile to consider in what ways God is seen at work in the unexpected, and perhaps unaccepted, dimensions of human relationships.

RESPONSIVE READING

PSALM 34:9-14 (RCL, BCP ALT.)
PSALM 34:2-3, 4-5, 6-7 (LFM)

For commentary on this text, see the responsive reading for the Tenth Sunday after Pentecost, above.

PSALM 111 (RCL ALT.)

This praise psalm is general enough to fit with all of the designated readings for the day. It is typically paired with Psalm 112, which picks up where Psalm 111 left off (111:10) by extolling the blessings of those who fear the Lord. The dominant theme is the thanksgiving for the wonderful works of God. One of the interesting aspects of this psalm is its acrostic structure. Acrostics in Hebrew poetry are poems in which each half phrase begins with the following letter in the Hebrew alphabet. The creative preacher who chooses to preach on this psalm may consider organizing the sermon around the structure of the psalm, with each poetic line making the sermonic move and exploring the theological claims of the psalm.

PSALM 147 (BCP)

The last five psalms in the psalter are praise psalms, each beginning and ending with "Praise the LORD!" Walter Brueggemann notes that this psalm is one of several in the psalter that move toward a more general summation of God's profound goodness rather than thanksgiving for particular acts in Israel's history. Even the reference to the "outcasts of Israel" in verse 2 (note that the JPS translation is "exiles") does not necessarily refer to specific moments of exile, but rather "understands exile-ending as Yahweh's characteristic action."[1]

SECOND READING

EPHESIANS 5:15-20 (RCL, BCP, LFM)

In this semi-continuous reading through Ephesians in Pentecost, all three lectionaries skip over 5:3-14 to the concluding cautions found in the selected text for this Sunday. The opening verse, "Be careful then how you live, not as unwise people but as wise," connects this section of the letter to the first reading. While 5:15-20 does suggest a final unit of thought, much of the argument presented in these five verses is based on 5:3-14. The concluding verse (v. 20) alludes to 5:3-4, "Let there be thanksgiving." The thanksgiving "to God the Father at all times and for everything" works itself out not simply in formal moments of praise (v. 19) but in all that we say and do. Our thanksgiving is demonstrative of walking in the light (v. 8), for it is the visible, discernible response to all that God has done for the saints (1:1, 5:3). There is a mutuality here, between light and living, in which the light exposes how one's life is lived, but also how the way one lives is observable because of the light (v. 13). The singing and making melody to the Lord *in your hearts* (v. 19) also points to this reciprocity, for the letter has already stated that the heart is the dwelling place of Christ (3:17). Hardness of heart causes one to "become darkened" (perfect passive participle) in one's understanding, estranged from the life of God (4:18), and producing unfruitful works (5:11). Living as wise people (v. 15) means living toward what is good and right and true, which is indeed the "fruit of the light" (v. 9). Living as wise people also means being able to understand the will of

> God has desires for us, that Christ will shine on us and reveal our obedience, our wisdom, and our thanksgiving.

the Lord. The word *will* can also be translated "desire," which suggests an interesting play on the preceding lists of perceived desires of those who do not inherit the kingdom of Christ (1:4, 5, 5:5). God has desires for us, that Christ will shine on us (5:14) and reveal our obedience, our wisdom, and our thanksgiving.

JOHN 6:51-58 (RCL, LFM)
JOHN 6:53-59 (BCP)

This fourth reading from John 6 begins at verse 51, which was the final verse for last week's pericope, thus providing a bridge between last Sunday's section of text and the verses set for this Sunday's Gospel reading. The overlap of verses, while providing a necessary connection between last week and this week, indicates how difficult it is to break up Jesus' discourses into succinct and self-contained units of text. Verse 51 is a necessary lead-in to the question of the Jewish leaders in verse 52. In verse 51, Jesus uses the term *flesh* for the first time in the discourse. Not surprisingly, the Jews respond in disbelief, for what Jesus is saying does not make sense and is shocking. Yet, instead of explaining his controversial claim, Jesus ups the ante even more in verse 53, "Very truly, I tell you, unless you eat the flesh of the Son of Man and drink his blood, you have no life in you."

In fact, each verse in this section of the discourse increases the contentiousness of Jesus' claims, so much so that his disciples respond, "This teaching is difficult. Who can accept it?" (v. 60). Who indeed? In verse 54 Jesus directly states, "Those who eat *my* flesh and drink *my* blood," shifting his words from the more distant third person, "flesh of the Son of Man; drink his blood," to the explicit first-person claim, "my flesh" and "my blood." Moreover, there is a verb change in verse 54. While up until this point in the discourse, Jesus has used the verb *esthiō* for "to eat," he now uses *trōgō*, which can also be translated as "to eat" but has a much more graphic sense, having to do with the eating that animals do. The word can be translated as "gnaw" or "chew." In verse 55 Jesus states that his flesh and blood are *true* flesh and *true* blood.

Verse 56 is perhaps the central claim of this discourse. What Jesus offers in this act of eating his flesh and drinking his blood is to abide in him and "I in them." The concept of abiding or remaining in Jesus is pivotal for this Gospel as a way of expressing the intimate relationship that Jesus has with those who believe in him. Jesus' first words in the calling of the disciples are, "What are you looking for?" Their response, "Where are you staying?" makes no sense, unless this theme of abiding is realized (1:38). We might translate the question of the disciples, "Where are you abiding?" and Jesus responds, "Come and see." They came and saw where he was *abiding* and they *abided* with him that day. When the Samaritan woman at the well offers her townspeople the same invitation as Jesus to the disciples, "Come and see a man who knows all about me" (4:29), the Samaritans ask Jesus to abide with them and Jesus abides with them two days (4:40). Of course,

> The concept of abiding or remaining in Jesus is pivotal for this Gospel as a way of expressing the intimate relationship that Jesus has with those who believe in him.

the image of abiding in Jesus and the intimate relationship with Jesus and the Father that it represents receives its fullest expression in John 15 in the figure of the vine and the branches.

Jesus' statement in verse 57 is the boldest yet, for he eliminates altogether the mediums of flesh and blood: "Whoever eats *me*." Verse 58 recalls again the provision of God in the wilderness, the giving of the bread for the daily needs of the Israelites. In addition to this provision of subsistence, Jesus sets himself as the provision of abundance (10:10). This is one more example of the grace upon grace (1:16) that believers receive because of Jesus making God known (1:18). It is important to remember that the term *grace* is never used again in the Gospel outside of the Prologue (1:1-18). The rest of the Gospel shows what an abundance of grace looks like in Jesus—changing water into wine (2:1-11), the source of living water that gushes up to eternal life (4:10, 14, 7:37-39), pasture that provides life abundantly (10:9-10), the raising of Lazarus, resurrection *and* life (11:25), and the abundant catch of fish (21:11). This last abundant provision, the catch of fish, is particularly important for it comes at the very end of the Gospel, when the disciples have returned to their "day job," fishing. In this moment, Jesus reveals to his disciples that the abundance that he provides is not limited to his life, nor is it limited to their life together. The disciples will experience the abundance of Jesus even after he returns to the Father, and they will participate in the providing of this abundance as the following dialogue between Jesus and Peter will reveal (21:15-19).[3]

While the set pericope for this Sunday ends at 6:58, 6:59 is an important reminder of where this is all taking place—in the synagogue at Capernaum. It is no wonder that in 7:1 Jesus must go to Galilee and not remain in Judea, "because the Jews were looking for an opportunity to kill him." Indeed, chapters 7–8 will include some of the most disturbing and polemical confrontations between Jesus and the Jewish leaders. The setting of this discourse, within the synagogue, foregrounds the conflict between Jesus and his followers and their Jewish community. We are reminded again—as we were in the Temple incident in chapter 2 (which occurs immediately after Jesus' first sign, the wedding at Cana, and not after Jesus' entry into Jerusalem as in the Synoptic Gospels), as we were in Jesus' interaction with the Pharisee Nicodemus, as we will be when the man born blind is cast out of the synagogue (*aposynagogos*)—of the difficult realities for the Jesus movement within first-century Judaism and Roman-occupied Palestine. It is worth considering not only the emotional, political, religious, and social ramifications of following Jesus, but also that subversion has its due consequences.[4] Moreover, that Jerusalem is not postponed until the last week of Jesus' life, but is rather at the beginning, in the middle, and at the end, and that the setting for this discourse is in the synagogue, makes a particular theological claim. Jesus as the incarnate

Word of God is *where* God is supposed to be (temple, synagogue) but not *how* God is expected to be. The revelation of God in Jesus is met, and will continue to be met, with disbelief, resistance, and yes, even hatred (17:14).

One of the important aspects of this text is how to negotiate its particularities of interpretation surrounding the tradition of the institution of the Lord's Supper. While the presence, or lack thereof, of the Lord's Supper in the Gospel of John continues to be debated in scholarship, there is no doubt that what the church has come to adopt as its understanding of the meaning and theology of Holy Communion is different than what we are given in John. In John's Gospel, there is a last meal with the disciples, but the central act there is the foot washing and Jesus' farewell words to his disciples (chapters 13–16). Jesus' familiar words, "This is my body, given for you. Do this in remembrance of me," are absent. Instead, Jesus offers these words: "Eat my flesh and drink my blood." It is worthwhile to wonder how our institutions, traditions, and rituals surrounding the Lord's Supper might be influenced by Jesus' claims in this discourse. It is also important to consider that if this is the Fourth Evangelist's interpretation of this event, it is not at the end of Jesus' life, but in the middle of his public ministry. We are reminded that he himself passed out the bread and the fish to the five thousand. The gift of Jesus' flesh and blood is not associated with his death, but connected to his life. It is not a theology of remembering, but of abiding.

> Jesus as the incarnate Word of God is *where* God is supposed to be (Temple, synagogue) but not *how* God is expected to be.

Notes

1. Sharon H. Ringe, *Wisdom's Friends: Community and Christology in the Fourth Gospel* (Louisville: Westminster John Knox, 1999), 2, 60.

2. Walter Brueggemann, *The Message of the Psalms* (Minneapolis: Augsburg, 1984), 164.

3. For further discussion of the conversation between Peter and Jesus and its function in the Gospel as a whole, see Karoline M. Lewis, "'Shepherd My Sheep': Preaching for the Sake of Greater Works Than These," *Word and World* 28, no. 3 (2008): 318–24.

4. For an interesting discussion of Jesus as subversive, see George S. Johnson, "Was Jesus Subversive? Considering the 'other' reason Jesus died on the cross," *The Lutheran* (March 2008), 28–29.

TWELFTH SUNDAY AFTER PENTECOST

Twenty-First Sunday in Ordinary Time / Proper 16

August 23, 2009

Revised Common (RCL)	Episcopal (BCP)	Roman Catholic (LFM)
Josh. 24:1-2a, 14-18 or 1 Kgs. 8:(1, 6, 10-11) 22-30, 41-43	Josh. 24:1-2a, 14-25	Josh. 24:1-2a, 15-17, 18b
Ps. 34:15-22 or Psalm 84	Psalm 16 or 34:15-22	Ps. 34:2-3, 16-17, 18-19, 20-21
Eph. 6:10-20	Eph. 5:21-33	Eph. 5:21-32 or 5:2a, 25-32
John 6:56-69	John 6:60-69	John 6:60-69

FIRST READING

JOSHUA 24:1-2A, 14-18 (RCL)
JOSHUA 24:1-2A, 14-25 (BCP)
JOSHUA 24:1-2A, 15-17, 18B (LFM)

The reading from the book of Joshua comes from the last chapter of the book and calls for a renewal of the covenant with the Lord. Verses 3-13 are removed from the pericope, yet they remind the Israelites once again of the reason for the rejuvenation of their obedience to God. The review of history takes the story of God and God's people back to the covenant with Abraham and includes the newest chapter of God's deliverance in Joshua's conquest of the promised land. Verses 3-13 also focus on the Lord's presence and deliverance in the midst of the battles for Canaan. This is an essential thing to remember, for what follows in Judges is continued warfare over the land.

This passage from Joshua contains two well-known Bible verses, ones that typically find themselves on various plaques and wall hangings in our homes: "Choose this day whom you will serve," and "As for me and my household, we will serve the LORD" (24:15). Rather than being treated as pithy sayings or platitudes, these maxims might gain more meaning if resituated in their narrative context. While at this juncture the Israelites now enjoy possession of the land promised to Abraham and they promise to serve the Lord, the story will continue beyond verses of Joshua, to narrate the continued threat of enemies against the Israelites and of Israel's disobedience. Perhaps it is this very sense that is imbued in the popularity of the above principles for life. Somehow, we recognize that by placing them in our homes, we need to be reminded to serve the Lord—and the Lord only—on a daily basis. The review of God's oversight of the conquest of Canaan and the sober reality of what lies ahead is occasion for us to consider in what circumstances and for what reasons we choose to serve our God.

1 KINGS 8:(1, 6, 10-11) 22-30, 41-43 (RCL ALT.)

The RCL alternative first reading concludes the focus on David and David's kingdom with this prayer of Solomon to the Lord. The context of the prayer is the completion of the Temple. The optional verses cited for the lectionary text are selected verses from the first part of the chapter, which narrate the carrying of the ark into the Temple (8:1) and its placement in the "most holy place" of the Temple (8:6). Verses 12-21, omitted from the lection, contain Solomon's address to the people in which he affirms the promises of the Lord to David, and therefore, to the people Israel. The primary text chosen for this week is a portion of Solomon's prayer of dedication at the altar of the Lord, which continues through 8:53.

Solomon's prayer is simultaneously petition and praise to the Lord—especially poignant in the context of Solomon's greatest achievement, the construction of the Temple. It is an appropriate end to the eleven-week focus on David and his dynasty. Solomon will soon lose favor with the Lord (11:9-13) and the family reign will come to an end with the death of Solomon (11:43) and the division of the kingdom into two. Yet, at this point there is cause for celebration. In the portion of text for this Sunday, Solomon first praises God for the covenant made at Sinai and the Davidic covenant, holding these two symbols of the relationship between the Israelites and the Lord together (8:22-26). Solomon then asks God to hear the prayers of the people in and toward the house of the Lord. In 8:41-43, Solomon extends this request, that the Lord hear even the prayers of non-Israelites, "for they shall hear of your great name, your mighty hand, and your outstretched arm." The result of granting such a request is that "all the people of the earth may know your name." Truly, then, the Temple will be a house of prayer for all peoples.

> Solomon's prayer is simultaneously petition and praise to the Lord—especially poignant in the context of Solomon's greatest achievement, the construction of the Temple.

176

THE SEASON
AFTER PENTECOST
───────────
KAROLINE M.
LEWIS

One of the most striking claims in Solomon's prayer is verse 27, "But will God indeed dwell on the earth? Even heaven and the highest heaven cannot contain you, much less this house that I have built!" The Hebrew verb that the NRSV translates as "dwell" is the same verb used in 8:13, "I have built you an exalted house, a place for you to dwell forever." It can also be translated "sit" and has the sense of being enthroned. These words are a remarkable testimony to the promises of God to God's people then and now. How is Solomon's question our question? How will God dwell on earth? How will God be enthroned?

> The presence of the ark in the Temple testifies to the dwelling of God with Moses, not only here, in this holy place, but forever.

How will God make God's home among us? For the Israelites, the Temple is no less than the very dwelling of God, the very presence of God, yet Solomon's humble statement of the reality of God's magnitude reminds the Israelites and us that where God promises to be, God will be, but God will also be where God needs to be to carry out, to live out, God's incredible love for God's people. The presence of the ark in the Temple testifies to the dwelling of God with Moses, not only here, in this holy place, but forever.

Without recourse to the very same claim that we make about Jesus, that God then chose to dwell among us as a human being, the first reading can most certainly stand on its own as the basis for a sermon that explores some of the issues and questions discussed above. That being said, that this text could be read on this last Sunday with readings from John 6 imbues both texts with an extraordinary sense of the meaning of God's presence in the history of God's relationship with God's people. John 6 holds this history behind it and at the same time is the fulfillment of Solomon's witness. God's transcendent presence cannot be limited and even Jesus, the incarnated God, will die. The incarnation will come to an end. But it is John who reminds us that those who abide in the word, abide in Jesus—and know that Jesus' words to his disciples are words to us, "I am in my Father, and you in me, and I in you" (John 14:20).

RESPONSIVE READING

PSALM 34:15-22 (RCL, BCP ALT.)
PSALM 34:2-3, 16-17, 18-19, 20-21 (LFM)

For commentary on this text, see the responsive reading for the Tenth Sunday after Pentecost, above.

PSALM 84 (RCL ALT.)

177

TWELFTH
SUNDAY AFTER
PENTECOST

AUGUST 23

As a Song of Zion (see also Psalms 46, 48, 76, 87, and 122), Psalm 84 is a natural fit to follow the RCL alternative reading of Solomon's rededication of the Temple. The psalm exudes the joy that comes from worshiping in the Temple of the Lord but has as its focus the happiness that comes from dwelling with God or being in the presence of God. This psalm is traditionally thought to have been recited by pilgrims on their way to Jerusalem. Living in the house of the Lord provides security. The image of the sparrow finding a home in God's house—that even the swallow can find "a nest for herself, where she may lay her young" (v. 3)—reveals the breadth and depth of God's ability to offer shelter and refuge and lays particular claim on what God's house means.

PSALM 16 (BCP)

As a psalm of trust, the words of Psalm 16 seem to echo Joshua's call to the Israelites to maintain their loyalty to God in the face of certain obstacles. The psalmist expresses faith in the many ways the Lord provides all things good for the sake of the "path of life." At the same time, there is a palpable sense that the choice of this path needs to be front and center in life in order to be able to enjoy the refuge of God.

SECOND READING
EPHESIANS 6:10-20 (RCL)
EPHESIANS 5:21-33 (BCP)
EPHESIANS 5:21-32 OR 5:2A, 25-32 (LFM)

The sections of text for the second reading from Ephesians follow immediately on last week's pericope in the BCP and LFM. The RCL skips over this controversial section of the letter in favor of a portion of text from the last chapter of the correspondence. 5:21-33 presents the Christian household, in particular the marital relationship, on the basis of Greco-Roman household codes, an understanding of the household as a "microcosm" of the larger cultural society with roots in Greco-Roman philosophers such as Aristotle.[1] The difficulty of this presentation arises not only from the words themselves, but also in how they have been interpreted and then used as evidence for perceived God-demanded structures for human relationships. The preacher needs to give serious consideration

> The preacher needs to give serious consideration as to whether or not this passage should be read in the assembly if it will not be preached in the pulpit.

as to whether or not this passage should be read in the assembly if it will not be preached in the pulpit. For some, these words have little difference from other passages that refer to the place and role of women (see, for example 1 Cor. 11:2-16; Col. 3:18—4:1; 1 Pet. 2:13—3:7; 1 Tim. 2:8—3:13; Titus 2:1-10) and even the polemic against the Jews in John 7–8.

Several issues need to be considered if preaching on this passage from Ephesians. At the outset, the author of Ephesians first uses the term *household* in 2:19 to argue that the members of the community are members of the household of God. The metaphor is developed further, "built upon the foundation of the apostles and prophets, with Christ Jesus himself as the cornerstone. In him the whole structure is joined together and grows into a holy temple in the Lord; in whom you also are built together spiritually into a dwelling place for God." To what extent does this working out of the metaphor inform interpretation of 5:22-30? What seems to be at stake for the author in drawing upon this image again?

Second, if preaching on this passage it is essential to lengthen the pericope beyond the said versification. The use of the metaphor begins with the relationship between wives and husbands, but then extends to children and parents, slaves and masters, each of which should be equally problematic. While we hope that readers of this portion of text from Ephesians would recognize that slavery was an acceptable social norm in the ancient world, it is certainly not now. Yet, this same recognition does not always transfer to views concerning marriage. It seems quite agreeable for some interpreters to insist on the rules of submission seemingly outlined here, yet would grant the injunctions about slavery only four verses later as not applicable now. It is critical to hold the whole of this passage together for responsible interpretation of a part.

Third, the preacher at some point will need to come to a resolution about the issue of Pauline authorship for Ephesians. As one of the disputed letters, there are arguments to be made either way. The seriousness of the question of authorship has to do with the authority of the words being heard. If the author is Paul, which most congregants assume, how will the preacher be heard if part of the discussion in the sermon questions Paul's authorship?

Finally, preaching on this passage from Ephesians will necessitate a clear and thoughtful focus for the sermon and one that does not eschew the rest of the value of the letter. What is the purpose of preaching on this passage, or texts such as this? What will be the hoped for outcome, function, or import that the preacher intends to achieve? If these questions are answered on the front end, perhaps 5:21 will be able to be heard for its illustration of mutual, reciprocal, shared expression of relationship.

6:10-20 is representative of the cosmic scope of this letter (see also 1:3, 10, 20-23, 2:2, 6, 3:10) that the forces of evil and the enemies that surround the people of God necessitate full-on confrontation. This language can be representative of either the institutional realities of the latter writings of the New Testament—where heresy is more prominent, the outlook more cosmic, and the "church" more stabilized, ordered, institutionalized—or an apocalyptic viewpoint. But the language might also be the viewpoint of the Old Testament, writings from the Dead Sea Scrolls, and Greco-Roman philosophy, especially Roman battle. The imagery is thoroughly battle driven: "the armor of God" (vv. 11, 13), "belt of truth and breastplate of righteousness" (v. 14), "shield of faith" (v. 16), "helmet of salvation" and "sword of the Spirit" (v. 17). There is no mistaking the meaning of the metaphor here as the elements of war are piled up on top of one another. In our times, however, this image of combat and crusade, even for the sake of

> There is no mistaking the meaning of the metaphor here as the elements of war are piled up on top of one another.

faith, is challenging. How do we handle this language, after the many wars fought in the name of the Lord or in the midst of wars being waged today? Another challenge lies in the perceived antithetical juxtaposition of this image of soldiers for God for the sake of being able to "proclaim the gospel of peace" (6:15). This seemingly paradoxical claim points to our own battles, supposedly for peace. Whether it be skirmishes, clashes, and hostilities in the "households" of our lives, or national and international combat, to what extent is the battle cry, "Onward, Christian soldiers!" used in the very same call for peace and reconciliation?

THE GOSPEL
JOHN 6:56-69 (RCL)
JOHN 6:60-69 (BCP, LFM)

This week after Pentecost brings us to the end of the Bread of Life Discourse. Once again, the verses in the RCL selection show the difficulty with splitting up the discourse into four separate Sundays, as verses 56-58 were included in last week's reading. While the lectionary sets the end of the reading at verse 69, there is good reason to extend the boundaries through the end of the chapter, that is, through verse 71. Verses 70-71 are difficult to hear, for "the one that would betray him" (6:64) is revealed as Judas and he is now no longer "the one who would betray him" but "a devil," which is probably the reason for leaving these verses off. Yet the fact that it is one of the members of Jesus' innermost circle who would betray him is critical to understanding how Judas is portrayed in the Fourth Gospel. The focus on just the disciples at the end of this discourse (6:60) and the introduction of Judas with the disciples here foreshadows the contrast between Judas and Mary at the anointing of Jesus (12:1-8) and the depth of Judas's betrayal

180

THE SEASON
AFTER PENTECOST
─────────
KAROLINE M.
LEWIS

as he departs from the last meal with Jesus ("And it was night," 13:30). Jesus has provided a meal for five thousand people at which even the disciples were guests and not the hosts. The anointing of Jesus and the foot washing by Jesus also take place around meals with Jesus.

Indeed, even the disciples have difficulty with Jesus' words, emphasized as the first verse of the BCP and LFM selected text. We are told that because of Jesus' challenging words, "many of his disciples turned back and no longer went about with him" (6:66). Then addressing just the Twelve, Jesus asks them if they, too, wish to go away. Peter's response is well known in liturgical denominations as the Gospel Acclamation prior to the reading of the Gospel: "Lord, to whom can we go? You have the words of eternal life." Peter's confession here recalls the similar incident in the Synoptic accounts at Caesarea Philippi, yet there it is Peter, not Judas, to whom Jesus says, "Get behind me, Satan."

> For John, there is no explanation for Judas except that he does not believe. He is a thief, one who tries to enter into the sheepfold by some other way.

This passage is the first mention of Judas in the Gospel and it is important to note that he is initially referred to as "the one who would betray him" (v. 64) and not by *name* (see also 6:71; 12:4; 13:2, 11, 21; 18:2, 5). Judas identified first by what he does and not by his name reveals several important issues about this character in John and related themes and it is worth considering the effect of introducing Judas in this way here, in this discourse, so early on in the narrative.

First, it foreshadows much about the portrait of Judas according to John, which on its own is worth investigating in comparison to Matthew's remorseful Judas, whose motive is explained by greed and whose rejection is muted by his suicide. For John, there is no explanation for Judas except that he does not believe. He is a thief (12:6), one who tries to enter into the sheepfold by some other way (10:1).[2] He will disappear into the night (13:30), into the realm of unbelief, and will not be heard from again, literally. When Judas returns to the narrative, he comes to the garden where Jesus had entered with his disciples, accompnied by a cohort of Roman soldiers (approximately six hundred men) bearing *lanterns* and *torches* and *weapons*, ironically to arrest one man, the light of the world. And as if to signify the depth of Judas's unbelief, Judas does not identify Jesus to the officers by saying "Rabbi" or kissing him. Instead, Jesus comes out of the garden—the good shepherd will not let the thief into the fold—and asks, "Whom are you looking for?" (18:4, 7). Indeed, this is the question throughout this Gospel, for Jesus' very first words to his disciples are virtually the same, "What are you looking for?" (1:38).

> That Judas is acknowledged first by what he does and not by his name immediately questions his discipleship, for followers of Jesus are called by name.

That Judas is acknowledged first by what he does and not by his name immediately questions his discipleship, for followers of Jesus are called by name (10:3). At the arrest, then, the fact that Judas is identified by name and as "the one who betrayed him" is a poignant reminder that he was a disciple but is now in the darkness. The arrest scene is the first time in the Gospel that he is called "Judas, the one who betrayed him," holding these in tension. In a sense, it is a new "name" and one that will be remembered. The last verse of chapter 6 echoes the beginning of this long discourse on Jesus as the bread of life. Verse 6:71 reads, "He was speaking of Judas son of Simon Iscariot, for he, though one of the twelve, was going to betray him." In the first section of the discourse, the disciples ask, "What must we do to work the works of God?" Jesus answers, "This is the work of God, that you believe him whom he has sent" (6:28-29). For Judas, this was the only work, and it was for the sake of "greater works than these" (14:12).

Notes

1. See E. Elizabeth Johnson, "Ephesians," in *The Women's Bible Commentary*, ed. Carol A. Newsom and Sharon H. Ringe (Louisville: Westminster John Knox, 1998), 430.

2. Note that the term *thief* only appears these two times in the Gospel.

THIRTEENTH SUNDAY AFTER PENTECOST

Revised Common (RCL)	Episcopal (BCP)	Roman Catholic (LFM)
Deut. 4:1-2, 6-9 or Song of Sol. 2:8-13	Deut. 4:1-9	Deut. 4:1-2, 6-8
Psalm 15 or 45:1-2, 6-9	Psalm 15	Ps. 15:2-3a, 3b-4a, 4b-5
James 1:17-27	Eph. 6:10-20	James 1:17-18, 21b-22, 27
Mark 7:1-8, 14-15, 21-23	Mark 7:1-8, 14-15, 21-23	Mark 7:1-8, 14-15, 21-23

FIRST READING

DEUTERONOMY 4:1-2, 6-9 (RCL)
DEUTERONOMY 4:1-9 (BCP)
DEUTERONOMY 4:1-2, 6-8 (LFM)

Deuteronomy 4:1-9 is a call to obedience of the entirety of the commandments of God, neither adding nor taking away any part (4:2). As Moses and the Israelites stand able to see Canaan, on the brink of a new chapter in their relationship with God, time almost stands still, as if signaling the import of this transition. They have come this far, from slavery under Pharaoh, to a harrowing escape from the Egyptians, to wanderings in the wilderness, but before their entry into the promised land Moses impresses upon the Israelites to remain obedient to God and God's ordinances.

This selection of text can be divided into two parts. 4:1-4 looks backward, to the role of the law in the life of the people up to this point. The law is a gift and connects the Israelites to their ancestors (v. 1). The law is also that which preserves them, keeps them safe, and secures the deliverance of the Lord (vv. 3-4). 4:5-9 looks forward to the function of the law in the new land. Observing the law will demonstrate the "wisdom and discernment" of the Israelites to the inhabitants of Canaan (v. 6). The occupants of the land need only hear the statutes to which God's people are called to follow and will know the Israelites as a "great nation" (v. 6), for following the commandments of the Lord sets the Israelites apart as a great nation (v. 8). Moreover, the ordinances of God communicate to the Israelites God's presence. "For what other great nation has a god so near to it as the

LORD our God is whenever we call to him?" (v. 7). The statutes of the Lord bear the very nearness of God, God's constancy, and God's means of relationship.

Those who live in the Twin Cities of Minneapolis and Saint Paul often say Minnesota has only two seasons: winter and road construction. At the writing of this commentary we are in the latter season, which makes travel of all kinds, especially by car, difficult. At one point during this season that seems as long and as painful as winter, a sign said, "Road construction on 35W South. Road closed. Use other routes." Use other routes? What other routes? What if you do not know any other routes? How are you supposed to get to where you planned to go? God's law is not just any other route. It maps out in great detail the route to the destination of the Israelites. But the main direction is to listen and obey, "Israel, give heed to the statutes and ordinances that I am teaching you to observe, so that you may live to enter and occupy the land that the LORD, the God of your ancestors, is giving you" (v. 1).

> God's law is not just any other route. It maps out in great detail the route to the destination of the Israelites.

SONG OF SOLOMON 2:8-13 (RCL ALT.)

The Song of Solomon (Song of Songs or Canticles) offers a provocative choice for preaching on a number of levels. Unlike any other book in either testament, this compilation of love poetry is as exigent as it is erotic. Numerous meanings and strategies for interpretation have been put forward to get at its genre, purpose, and message, without any one enjoying a consensus. In the end, the effect of the words and images creates the very feeling of that which they are describing—sensuous love between a man and a woman. This is a "no-holds-barred" passion, where the lovers are equal and express their desires openly and with great intensity.

The section of the book selected for this Sunday is from the point of view of the woman who describes a visit from her lover. He comes to her window and invites her to come away with him for some frolicking in the newness of springtime. The winter has past (2:11) and the earth is alive with new blooms, new songs, and new sensations of spring. If one chooses to preach on this text, the pericope should be extended through verse 17, where the comparison of the man to a gazelle or young stag returns to verse 8 and bookends the pericope.

Why preach on such a text? As one commentator notes, "A sensual sermon illustration is sure to make the person dozing in the third pew take notice of the remainder of the sermon."[1] Certainly, a sermon on sex would no doubt get the attention of one's parishioners. And perhaps, that effect alone is worthwhile. When do we talk about this particular gift from God, the romantic, sensual,

184

THE SEASON
AFTER PENTECOST
──────────
KAROLINE M.
LEWIS

passionate love, and the articulation of that love? How can lifting up the intense, intimate, expressive candor of these two lovers ask us to reflect on how we convey our own feelings in relationships?

Another reason to preach the Song of Songs is because of its function in the canon as a whole. "Without the Song of Songs, the prevailing stories in the Bible about women would be those where women are penalized and scandalized for their sexuality, confined to procreation without fulfilling sex, and forgotten because of their submission to repressive gender roles."[2] This is not to say that a sermon on the Song of Songs would be a sermon just for women or just about women. Rather, it is an opportunity to reflect on what it means to be the wholly human, incarnate, and carnal beings we were created to be. This is a contribution to our canon that "advocates balance in female and male relationships, urging mutuality not domination, interdependence not enmity, sexual fulfillment not mere procreation, uninhibited love not bigoted emotions."[3] It would be a sermon about God, who wants to rejoice with us in the love we have been given, as it is relished, enjoyed, and celebrated.

> A sermon on the Song of Songs is an opportunity to reflect on what it means to be the wholly human, incarnate, and carnal beings we were created to be.

RESPONSIVE READING
PSALM 15 (RCL, BCP)
PSALM 15:2-3A, 3B-4A, 4B-5 (LFM)

Psalm 15 reflects similar themes to those in the first reading from Deuteronomy. The ones who are able to enter into the sanctuary of God are those who follow the qualifications set out in this psalm. Psalm 15 is representative of an entrance liturgy and may have been used as worshipers came into the Temple in a call-and-response ritual. Recognizing its genre calls attention to how it might by preached. As J. Clinton McCann Jr. notes in his commentary on the Psalms, "What does God desire from the worshipper?"[4] Indeed, while we spend a good amount of energy in our worship planning around the desired effect of the worship experience, what is God's desire of us as we enter into worship?

PSALM 45:1-2, 6-9 (RCL ALT.)

The RCL alternative responsive reading pairs this unique psalm with the text from the Song of Solomon. Attributed as a royal psalm, its assumed function was in honor of or use in the wedding of a king. A number of study Bibles title this psalm "Ode for a Royal Wedding." It is unique in the psalter because it is not addressed to God, but to the bridegroom, the king, yet verses 10-16 are addressed to the queen and describe her new duties in the match-up. The superscription for the psalm names it a love song, which may also suggest its pairing with the Song of Songs reading. If this is indeed the intimated parallel, these two readings might be the basis for exploring biblical expressions of love, especially when, in most churches, the only time we hear about love is at a wedding, and through the lens of repeated "wedding" texts (such as 1 Corinthians 13, which, of course, has nothing to do with marriage). In the context of James and the reading from Mark, another possible connection is to consider how outward manifestations of professed beliefs correlate. Does our behavior match what we confess to believe, to hold as true, or our values?

SECOND READING

JAMES 1:17-27 (RCL)
JAMES 1:17-18, 21B-22, 27 (LFM)

As noted in the introduction above, this Sunday begins a set of readings through the letter of James. The most salient connection to the Gospel reading from Mark is the concept of virtue and even purity, yet for each author the emphasis is located in a different set of issues. For James, a virtuous life is grounded in the existence of faith. As doers of the word, faith is not faith unless it manifests itself in visible expression.

After an introduction that some commentators would take through verse 18, and not verse 16 as the lectionary selection suggests, the focus of the latter part of the chapter introduces the main theme of the letter through several different metaphors. Verse 18 locates works done through faith as participation in and fulfillment of God's plans as God's created beings. As "first fruits" of God's creatures, we are to set ourselves as examples of God's giving and God's righteousness (v. 20). The figure of the "implanted word" (v. 21) is intriguing. Assuming that the author equates the implanted word with the gospel, the image might suggest two things. First, the Greek term here for "implanted" (*emphytos*) is the only time the term is used in the New Testament. It has the sense of being implanted by nature or inborn. In other words, the word of the gospel is an innate, inborn reality. Second, given the reference to "first fruits" in 1:18, these first fruits are the "above ground" result of this implantation. Indeed, for James, works are almost an organic process or result. In his preface to his commentary on Romans, Luther writes, "Thus it is impossible to separate works from faith, quite as impossible as to separate heat and light from fire."[5]

> The tragedy is that one's very profession of faith, which seems convincingly genuine to the confessor and the hearer, is actually a sham, a fraud, that deceives oneself and God.

Perhaps the most commanding verses in this opening chapter of the letter are verses 22-24. These verses can function as a primary lens through which to read the whole of the letter, but also speak on numerous levels to our contemporary situations of professed faith that seem only demonstrable in insincere religiosity. As Luke Timothy Johnson notes, "For faith to be real, it must be translated into deeds. . . . Otherwise, one's faith is only self-deception."[6] This is, in fact, the tragedy. It is not only that any profession of faith which does not follow with works is empty. It is that one's very profession of faith, that seems convincingly genuine to the confessor and the hearer, is actually a sham, a fraud, that deceives oneself and God.

EPHESIANS 6:10-20 (BCP)

For commentary on this text, see the second reading for the Twelfth Sunday after Pentecost, above.

THE GOSPEL

MARK 7:1-8, 14-15, 21-23 (RCL, BCP, LFM)

After five Sundays with readings through the sixth chapter of the Gospel of John, we return to Mark where we find ourselves in the same narrative place as we were four weeks ago, after the feeding of the five thousand and the event of Jesus walking on the water. Critical to interpreting and preaching this pericope is to recognize the geographical location of this discussion with the Pharisees and the scribes. Jesus and his disciples are in Gennesaret, having landed on this northwestern side of the Sea of Galilee after Jesus walks on the water. In Gennesaret, they are still in the Galillean region, still in acceptable territory, so that the Pharisees and scribes are able to come to Jesus, *from* Jerusalem. While with Jesus, they notice that some of Jesus' disciples are not observing certain rituals having to do with purity and question Jesus about these breeches of conduct, tradition, and law.

> We would benefit from remembering the core element of this argument between Jesus and the Pharisees: that life before God, in God, and because of God lays claim on how we go about living.

While such matters seem uninteresting and even ridiculous to our modern ears, they were every bit vital and essential for Jews living in first-century Roman-occupied Palestine and for the Pharisees who were charged with carrying on the interpretation of the Torah. At stake for these keepers of the law was both the continuity of and commitment to God's commands, but also the holiness of all of life before God.[7] We would benefit from remembering the core element of this argument between Jesus and the Pharisees: that life before God, in God, and because of God lays claim on how we go about living. This system of holiness was critical for Israel, not only for the sake of obedience to God's commands but also because of the political reality of first-century Palestine. Ever since the Babylonian captivity, the Jewish people had faced the issue of maintaining identity in the face of encroaching political, social, cultural, and religious ideas from the Greco-Roman world. It is these purity laws and holiness codes that set them apart from their Gentile neighbors. And yet here is Jesus, who seems to defy purity law at every turn, who "makes an onslaught against these purity rules and regulations."[8] This will not be the first or the last time that we see Jesus in a situation where the boundaries of holiness are violated for the sake of the kingdom of God. We would do well to ask ourselves, To what extent do we engage in the same kind of "boundary crossing"? Or do we spend most of our time building them and then protecting them with all of our might? This story in Mark reminds us of a different calling.

Here we see what happens when people abrogate purity rules, cross boundaries, or redraw them. Whereas the authorities in Mark's story guarded boundaries, Jesus and his followers transgressed boundaries. Whereas the leaders saw boundaries as means of protection, the Jesus movement saw boundaries as oppressive and limiting. Whereas the leaders withdrew from uncleanness, the Jesus movement attacked or ignored uncleanness. Whereas Pharisees avoided contact with that which defiled, Jesus and his followers sought contact. The leaders had power by staying within the ordered boundaries. The Jesus movement, as depicted by Mark, treated boundaries as lines to cross, redraw, or eliminate.[9]

> The leaders had power by staying within the ordered boundaries. The Jesus movement, as depicted by Mark, treated boundaries as lines to cross, redraw, or eliminate.

We might also question to what extent Jesus' issue is not with the keeping of traditions, but to what extent they replace, excuse, or justify actions, judgments, or claims that might limit God's activity in the world. As Donald Juel notes, "Traditions themselves are not the problem; people cannot live without form and structures. Such traditions, however, cannot guarantee fidelity to God. They can become a refuge within which even the most devoted evade God's will."[10]

After further commentary for the Pharisees (7:9-13), the pericope picks up with Jesus' address to the crowds and not just the Pharisees (v. 14), and Jesus turns his attention specifically to the disciples (vv. 17-23). Jesus explains his point: it is not what comes into a person that defiles but what comes out. In sum, the issue "is a matter of the heart and not the digestive system."[11] A *Calvin and Hobbes* comic strip once had Calvin ask Hobbes, "Hobbes, do you think our morality is defined by our actions or what's in our hearts?" Hobbes replies, "I think our actions *show* what's in our hearts." The next frame finds Calvin with a blank stare in response to Hobbes's answer. In the final frame, Calvin yells out, "*I Resent That!*" Indeed, isn't that our response as well? How much easier it would be to allow said traditions to dictate our actions, or, as the story of the Syrophoenician woman will illustrate, how we allow them to determine God's actions, God's will—which is to extend beyond Gennesaret and go into the region of Tyre, to cross the boundaries and go into Gentile territory, and then, maybe, to come back to Gennesaret and tear down the borders themselves. To what extent do we resent Jesus, like the Pharisees, for the fact that he raises the stakes, makes us accountable, and causes us to take a good long look in the mirror (James 1:23)?

Notes

1. Renita Weems, "Song of Songs," in *The New Interpreter's Bible,* vol. 5 (Nashville: Abingdon, 1997), 381.

2. Renita Weems, "Song of Solomon," in *The Woman's Bible Commentary*, ed. Carol A. Newsom and Sharon H. Ringe (Louisville: Westminster John Knox, 1998), 168.

3. Ibid.

4. J. Clinton McCann Jr., "Psalms," in *The New Interpreter's Bible,* vol. 4 (Nashville: Abingdon, 1996), 734.

5. Martin Luther, "Preface to the Epistle of St. Paul to the Romans," in *Luther's Works* 35, ed. E. Theodore Bachmann (Philadelphia: Muhlenberg, 1960), 371.

6. Luke Timothy Johnson, "James," in *The New Interpreter's Bible*, vol. 12 (Nashville: Abingdon, 1998), 189.

7. Donald H. Juel, *Mark*, Augsburg Commentary on the New Testament (Minneapolis: Augsburg, 2000), 102.

8. David Rhoads, "Social Criticism: Crossing Boundaries," in *Mark and Method*, ed. Janice Capel Anderson and Stephen D. Moore (Minneapolis: Fortress Press, 1992), 149.

9. Ibid., 154.

10. Juel, *Mark*, 103.

11. Ibid., 106.

FOURTEENTH SUNDAY
AFTER PENTECOST

TWENTY-THIRD SUNDAY IN ORDINARY TIME /
PROPER 18
SEPTEMBER 6, 2009

Revised Common (RCL)	Episcopal (BCP)	Roman Catholic (LFM)
Isa. 35:4-7a or	Isa. 35:4-7a	Isa. 35:4-7a
Prov. 22:1-2, 8-9, 22-23		
Psalm 146 or 125	Psalm 146 or 146:4-9	Ps. 146:7, 8-9a, 9b-10
James 2:1-10 (11-13)	James 1:17-27	James 2:1-5
14-17		
Mark 7:24-37	Mark 7:31-37	Mark 7:31-37

FIRST READING
ISAIAH 35:4-7A (RCL, BCP, LFM)

The reason for the selection of this first reading from Isaiah is the clear link between 35:5, "and the ears of the deaf unstopped," and Jesus' healing of the deaf man in Mark 7:31-37. The snippet of text is certainly meant to have the resonance of the Gospel text behind it, before it, or within it, but it would be important to consider including the whole of the chapter as the designated reading. Set in the context of exilic Israel, the reading from Isaiah is an oracle of hope that imagines the homecoming to Zion, where Israel is rescued from her plight and will be able to go back to Judah. The glorious return comes to full expression in the last verse of the chapter, "And the ransomed of the LORD shall return, and come to Zion with singing; everlasting joy shall be upon their heads; they shall obtain joy and gladness, and sorrow and sighing shall flee away."

On its own, this first reading from the prophet Isaiah affords the preacher with several possibilities for sermon topics. Preaching on the prophets in general is most certainly a worthwhile effort, not only for their lack of attention in most pulpits, but also for the ways in which these figures mediated the word of the Lord in extraordinarily contextual situations. Expanding understanding of the prophets beyond predictors enables an insight into the promise of God's presence for God's people in the here and now and not just in the future. The prophetic literature gives voice to God's judgment but also God's salvation in the very depths of real despair and in the glory of witnessing God's promises being fulfilled.

Pairing this text with the Gospel reading from Mark gives a different perspective or profundity not only to the healing of the deaf man but also to the vision of healing and wholeness in the passage from Isaiah. Whereas one might view the healing envisioned in Isaiah on a more spiritual level and the healing in Mark as truly a physical miracle, reading these texts together suggests that such mutually exclusive categories do not exist with the in-breaking of the kingdom of God. Strictures placed on where, how, and when healing can lead to wholeness and what wholeness can mean are most certainly challenged, if not set aside, when God, and the presence of God in Jesus, is at work for the sake of restoration.

PROVERBS 22:1-2, 8-9, 22-23 (RCL ALT.)

The selected verses from this chapter in Proverbs focus on treatment of the poor and might be helpfully interpreted through a verse not included in the lectionary designation, verse 16: "Oppressing the poor in order to enrich oneself, and giving to the rich, will lead only to loss." Enriching oneself may be seen as the means by which one ensures a "good name" (v. 1), yet a good name is found in one's reaching out to the poor, remembering that they are no different than the rich in God's eyes (vv. 2, 23). Indeed, when one's reputation is made at the expense of others, especially the poor, calamity will follow (v. 8).

> When one's reputation is made at the expense of others, especially the poor, calamity will follow.

This Proverbs selection is clearly chosen with both the reading from James and the Gospel lesson in mind. Chapter 2 of James opens with the very same issue: favoritism for those like us and mistreatment of those different from us (2:1-4). In many respects, the reading from Proverbs can provide a helpful way to give even more particularity and specificity to the main point in the reading from James, that faith by itself, without works, is dead (2:17). Proverbs 22:22 is a sober indictment of Jesus' own response to the woman in the Gospel reading from Mark. To what extent do his words "crush the afflicted at the gate"?

RESPONSIVE READING

PSALM 146 (RCL)
PSALM 146:4-9 (BCP)
PSALM 146:7, 8-9A, 9B-10 (LFM)

Psalm 146 is classified as a song of praise and resonates with the other readings of the day—specifically in verse 7, that God is the one "who executes justice for the oppressed, who gives food to the hungry." It is tempting when interpreting or preaching on the psalms to use their individual classification as a means of summation or understanding of the psalm. Psalm 146 is a helpful corrective to generalization or reduction of the imaginative, figurative, and evocative language that arose from Israel's worship. In reading and interpreting this psalm, therefore, it is important to note for what the psalmist is particularly thankful in offering praise to God. Verse 3 provides additional reflection on the nature of riches and wealth addressed in the readings from Proverbs and James, that these are mortal, transient things, only temporary compared to the lasting reign of God and the permanence of faith (see James 1:9-11). Verses 8 and 9 give voice to the praise of God who is a God for the downtrodden in every possible way that such a state may occur. Psalm 146 is indeed a call to praise, but perhaps more important in our day and age, it is a "call to life."[1]

PSALM 125 (RCL ALT.)

A communal lament or prayer for help, Psalm 125 confirms trust in God in the face of surrounding enemies. A probable lectionary connection to the readings for the day is the reference to righteousness and wickedness in verse 3 and to good versus wicked in verse 5. There is a sense in this psalm of those outside forces ("scepter of wickedness") that might lead the righteous astray. In conversation with the other lections, the psalm asks the question, What are those influences that prevent us from doing good, from acting out our faith? And what is it that these influences or forces offer, do, or suggest that would take us down a different path? Faith calls for discernment and decision when it comes to working itself out in living lives of faith.

SECOND READING
JAMES 2:1-10 (11-13) 14-17 (RCL)
JAMES 2:1-5 (LFM)

Following the charge to be doers of the word and not just hearers (1:22), the author explicates this challenge with very concrete examples of what this looks like. Verse 2, "your assembly," sets up the situation in which James places his audience, and a situation that in fact could very well have taken place. In this gathering (*synagōgos*), if you profess to have faith, yet welcome the rich and discriminate against the poor—even making them subservient to you ("sit at my feet," v. 3)—you have usurped the very law of God, "you shall love your neighbor as yourself" (Lev. 19:18). The concern for the poor builds on 1:9-11, for in fact the rich will pass away, but the poor are always in need. These first verses of chapter 2 call attention to major issues that are not only illustrative of whether or not one's belief in Christ shapes behavior, but also name specific kinds of behavior that need to be called into question. Moreover, the issues named—favoritism (vv. 1, 9), placing people below you ("sit under my footstool," v. 3), and judging others (v. 4)—are not simply elemental to one's individual works of faith, but are detrimental to another. A critical point in these opening verses of chapter 2 is that the works of faith are not just about the individual but have an impact on the community.

> A critical point in these opening verses of James 2 is that the works of faith are not just about the individual but have an impact on the community.

The effect on the other that comes from one's works is emphasized further in verses 14-17. The author addresses the assembly as "brothers and sisters" and offers an illustration that uses one of the members: "If a brother or sister is naked. . . ." The interjection of these intimate terms intensifies the argument and what is at stake. Now, the person to whom you are to show mercy is not someone from the outside (vv. 1-5) but is someone from the inside. Indeed, this is also a word of judgment for us (v. 13). To what extent do we find it easier to help those we can keep at a distance, whom we can send on their way again, whom we do not have to see again? In what sense do our acts of charity become acts of partiality themselves, only seeking to help a select few and not others? This portion of the letter of James summons us to mercy that brings our faith to completion, to fulfillment, to perfection, (v. 22).

JAMES 1:17-27 (BCP)

For commentary on this text, see the second reading for the Thirteenth Sunday after Pentecost, above.

THE GOSPEL
MARK 7:24-37 (RCL)
MARK 7:31-37 (BCP, LFM)

The selected Gospel readings for this Sunday present two very different challenges depending on the preacher's denominational commitments. The RCL reading includes two stories, the healing of the Syrophoenician woman's daughter and the healing of the deaf man in the region of the Decapolis. Both the BCP and LFM readings do not include the first healing, thereby eliminating a difficult text and the difficult interpretive role of holding these two stories together. If we are honest, the interaction between Jesus and the Gentile woman presents a portrait of Jesus that does not fit well with our versions of the Savior we have come to know and love. In fact, Jesus' response to the woman of Tyre might even border on a Jesus we do not particularly like. In thinking about these texts for preaching, we will examine each healing individually and then ask about their relationship to one another, as the RCL reading sets up.

Critical to interpreting and preaching this pericope is to hold Gennesaret (the location of the discussion between Jesus and the Pharisees in last Sunday's Gospel lesson) and Tyre together. In 6:53, Jesus and his disciples have landed at Gennesaret, after the event of Jesus walking on water and calming the winds. In Gennesaret, the Pharisees and scribes come to Jesus, *from* Jerusalem, and question Jesus about issues regarding purity. Jesus then calls the crowd (7:14) and essentially summarizes his point. From this conversation with the Jewish leaders on defilement, Jesus himself turns defilement or purity on its head by going into the Gentile territory of Tyre, a coastal city in Phoenicia and north of the Galilean region. There, he enters a house, not wanting anyone to know where he is.

The woman who comes to Jesus is first described as just that, a woman—which provides information about her class as a citizen—who has a possessed daughter, who had heard about Jesus. Then we learn just what kind of woman she is. She is a Gentile, emphasizing Jesus' location in Gentile territory. We also learn that she is Syrophoencian, which tells her specific nationality, but also gives further accent to her "outsider" status. As a result, Jesus is quite far from Galilee and even farther from Jerusalem, as if to illustrate that defilement and purity are not determined by mere physical, attributable, or demonstrative components, which was the argument of the Pharisees. Yet, ironically, they are. That is, that which determines purity or risks defilement is not about what one eats (v. 15) or from where or who one is (vv. 24, 26)—but at the same time, purity is ultimately assessed by that which one says and does (v. 15). Jesus' geographical location after his conversation with the Pharisees does not seem to be either meaningless or coincidental. Rather, situating Jesus deep in Gentile country, and then conversing with a Canaanite woman in that region, suggests that what should defile does not. Juxtaposing Tyre with Gennesaret calls into question traditional views of defilement and purity. Indeed, Jesus calls us to the same questioning. What are our operating assumptions of defilement or corruption? How do we determine and define what is pure and wholesome?

> Juxtaposing Tyre with Gennesaret calls into question traditional views of defilement and purity.

In preaching on this lectionary text from Mark, it is helpful to note the differences between this story in Mark and Matthew. Matthew inserts another parable from Jesus, about which Peter asks for an explanation. Then follows the parallel sections in both Gospels on what defiles (Matt. 15:16-20; Mark 7:17-23). In Matthew, the woman's request of Jesus is narrated, "Have mercy on me, Lord,

Son of David; my daughter is tormented by a demon" (Matt. 15:22). In Mark, her first words are her response to Jesus' comment. In Matthew, the disciples want her sent away (15:23) for, to all intents and purposes, she is in a constant state of defilement and impurity according to the standards set by her location and the official representatives from Jerusalem. Jesus responds to her, "I was sent only to the lost sheep of the house of Israel" (15:24), to which she says, "Lord, help me."

In Mark, the conversation is shortened. Jesus speaks first, a metaphorical comment that can only be interpreted as disdain for the woman. Instead of leaving in disgrace, her response is really the only one of its kind in Mark's Gospel.[2] Her "yes, but" challenges Jesus, and for Mark, it is not her faith that is acknowledged, but her "clever and daring retort."[3] Literally, Jesus says to her, "Because of this word, go" (not, "you *may* go" as the NRSV translates). She goes home and finds her daughter healed. Yet, even without Matthew's redaction, "Great is your faith!" (15:28), the woman's persistence of faith is typically recognized. For Mark, however, her persistence is of a different kind and maybe for a different reason. She persists in an encounter that makes her an object of defilement, yet she shows what is in her heart (7:19-21). Her words and her actions are the embodiment of what it looks like and sounds like when matters of the heart come to the surface.

In effect, it is the Syrophoenician woman who becomes the explanation of the parable for which the disciples ask. She is the model of what it looks like when what is in the heart and what comes out of the mouth correlate. But Jesus reveals that traditions and traditionalism are worthy of and demand questioning and rethinking, by entering into a land that represents impurity and by granting the woman's request. The woman's presence and persistence, therefore, are not only representative of that which comes from her heart but suggest her own questioning and rethinking of traditional boundaries, ideas, and rituals. We might even wonder if Jesus' response is not only to her challenge to him but also to her challenge of and willingness to call into question tradition as he has done. His location, actions, and words challenge the set traditions, limitations, and boundaries and reveal that discipleship will be about doing the same (7:2). The Gentile woman from Tyre, of Syrophoenician origin, is a model of discipleship in the end. Aware of her location and the limitations placed on her, she does not succumb to them but brings them into the light and calls them into question, saying "Sir, even the dogs under the table eat the children's crumbs." Jesus calls us to this kind of discipleship, a discipleship that pushes and exposes the boundaries of others and those we place on ourselves, a discipleship that is willing to go past these boundaries to journey into Tyre,

> In effect, it is the Syrophoenician woman who becomes the explanation of the parable for which the disciples ask.

because it is a discipleship that, in the end, will have to believe that God will break the most imposing and impossible boundary of all—death.

The healing narrated in 7:31-37 brings Jesus back to the eastern side of the Sea of Galilee, having gone through Sidon, a coastal city about twenty miles north of Tyre. In the region of the Decapolis, ten cities located on the southeast side of Galilee, Jesus is brought a deaf man who also has a speech impediment. The miracle itself is rather straightforward. Jesus heals the man by touching his ears and tongue and with the command, "Be opened." "And immediately his ears were opened, his tongue was released, and he spoke plainly" (7:35). While Jesus orders silence, as he has done before, the command is ignored and they "zealously" proclaim Jesus' actions. The term for "zealous" literally means going beyond the usual or expected number or size, also "extraordinary" or "remarkable." The response of the crowd matches the acts that Jesus' performs, which is indicated by the words in 7:37. Extraordinary acts call for extraordinary response. The word for "beyond measure" has the same root as "zealously." They were astounded beyond measure and proclaim beyond measure the works of Jesus.

Preaching on just this healing from Mark should be situated within the context of the incident in Tyre and the entirety of the issues in chapter 7. Jesus has come full circle, back to the region of Galilee, but in the middle of the journey, extraordinary things have happened. The response of the crowd in 7:37 in many respects is a response to yet another boundary that Jesus has crossed, for he can make even the deaf hear and the mute speak. Any boundary put in the way of Jesus will be crossed for the sake of God's mission in the world. As disciples of Jesus, we are called to the same boundary crossing and the same proclamation without measure.

> Any boundary put in the way of Jesus will be crossed for the sake of God's mission in the world.

Notes

1. J. Clinton McCann Jr., "Psalms," in *New Interpreter's Bible,* vol. 4 (Nashville: Abingdon, 1996), 1265.

2. Mary Ann Tolbert, "Mark," in *The Women's Bible Commentary*, ed. Carol A. Newsom and Sharon H. Ringe (Louisville: Westminster John Knox, 1998), 356.

3. Ibid. See also Hisako Kinukawa, "Mark," in *Global Bible Commentary*, ed. Daniel Patte (Nashville: Abingdon, 2004), 374.

FIFTEENTH SUNDAY AFTER PENTECOST

TWENTY-FOURTH SUNDAY IN ORDINARY TIME / PROPER 19
SEPTEMBER 13, 2009

Revised Common (RCL)	Episcopal (BCP)	Roman Catholic (LFM)
Isa. 50:4-9a or Prov. 1:20-33	Isa. 50:4-9	Isa. 50:4-9a
Ps. 116:1-9 or Psalm 19 or Wisd. of Sol. 7:26—8:1	Psalm 116 or 116:1-8	Ps. 116:1-2, 3-4, 5-6, 8-9
James 3:1-12	James 2:1-5, 8-10, 14-18	James 2:14-18
Mark 8:27-38	Mark 8:27-38 or 9:14-29	Mark 8:27-35

FIRST READING

ISAIAH 50:4-9 (BCP)
ISAIAH 50:4-9A (RCL, LFM)

Isaiah 50:4-9 is considered to be the third of the Servant Songs (42:1-4, 49:1-7, 52:13—53:12) with the fourth having been connected to Jesus early on in Christian interpretation of Isaiah. Isolating these sections of text from their literary context and the identity of the servant are both debated issues in scholarship. Nevertheless, the general themes and concerns that link these passages can be a helpful lens through which to read and interpret them. The choice of this text for this Sunday directly relates this Servant Song to the suffering of Jesus. The Gospel text narrates the first of the three Passion predictions in Mark (8:31, 9:31, 10:33-34). The dynamic that is present in both the Isaiah passages and the reading from Mark is God's vindication of the servant who experiences humiliation and persecution for the sake of being faithful to God.

It is important to note that the main issue of this passage from Isaiah is not complaint about the suffering, that the suffering will provide some justifiable benefit for the sufferer, or that the suffering is due to God's punishment. There is not even the description of suffering itself but the declaration of God's presence and help (50:7, 9) in the midst of the distress. Rather than "Song of the Suffering Servant" the passage might better be titled, "Individual Psalm of Confidence."[1]

PROVERBS 1:20-33 (RCL ALT.)

The RCL alternate reading for this week provides a unique opportunity to focus a sermon on a genre rarely read, heard, taught, or preached in most churches. Wisdom literature in the Bible (Proverbs, Job, Ecclesiastes) poses the risk of being misinterpreted through definitions, categories, and expectations of contemporary perspectives on wisdom. Whereas modern constructions of wisdom might reduce its benefits to knowledge alone, biblical wisdom is intimately connected with God. Wisdom is sought through instruction, education, and sage advice but it is grounded in the observable workings of God through creation and human life. It is worth a preacher's time to delve into the complexities and

> Wisdom is sought through instruction, education, and sage advice but it is grounded in the observable workings of God through creation and human life.

particularities of the wisdom tradition and how such reflection might shape ways of talking about and speaking to issues of morality, making right choices, and consequences of our actions.

One of the most compelling elements in the wisdom tradition is Woman Wisdom, found in the text selected for this Sunday. Here, wisdom is personified, meaning that a concept or an idea is represented not by abstractions or generalizations but is embodied as a person. In this sense, the concept or idea "comes to life." Proverbs 1:20-33 is the first of three extended speeches of Woman Wisdom in the book (see also 8:1-36, 9:1-6). She stands in the streets, at the busiest corner of the intersection, and calls out to all to listen to her voice.

It is significant that this image of wisdom appears at the beginning of the book. She is a public persona, calling in the midst of the busyness and bustling of daily life. Who will hear her voice? Who will suspend the task, goal, intention that necessitated a trip to the city to listen to what Wisdom has to say? The setting is significant in the interpretation of this passage. In the middle of our needs, in the hub and bustle of our ordinary, necessary, daily goings-on, Wisdom calls to us, yet we are unable to hear her counsel amidst the purposefulness and priorities of life. Notice me, pay attention to me, listen to me, Wisdom cries.

RESPONSIVE READING

PSALM 116 OR 116:1-8 (BCP)
PSALM 116:1-9 (RCL)
PSALM 116:1-2, 3-4, 5-6, 8-9 (LFM)

Psalm 116 is an individual song of thanksgiving. Its opening phrase, "I love the LORD," indicates from the very beginning the themes and mood of this praise to God and can be a lens through which to read the entire psalm. Considered one of the *Hallel* psalms (113–118), Psalm 116 is used during the Passover liturgy, in particular, following the Passover meal. The title for the psalm in some study Bibles is "Thanksgiving for Recovery from Illness," signaling a way to respond to the healing of the possessed child in Mark 9:14-29, and in fact, might also be heard as the imagined response of the silent crowd. The psalm gives voice and language to those in our midst who indeed feel death reaching out to grab them (v. 3).

PSALM 19 (RCL ALT.)

Preachers will recognize the last verse of this psalm as a well-used and well-loved opening prayer for sermons. In many respects, this last verse of the psalm holds the entire theological claim of the poem together. The opening verse of the psalm calls forth the image that the heavens themselves tell of the glory of God, so that the created extols the wonder of the Creator. Indeed, the last verse of the psalm is our same joy—telling the glory of God. For those preachers who use this sermon opening on a regular basis, it would be a worthwhile exercise to take the literary context of the words seriously, reflecting on the function of this verse as the end of the particular words of this psalm.

WISDOM OF SOLOMON 7:26—8:1 (RCL ALT.)

The RCL alternate responsive reading for this Sunday pairs with the alternate first reading from Proverbs on Woman Wisdom. The reading from the Wisdom of Solomon narrates similar characteristics for Wisdom, including her personification as woman and her role as a spokeswoman for God. The selected text for this Sunday is from the second of three parts into which the book is typically organized. This middle and central section (6:22—10:21) focuses on Wisdom as representative of the divine nature, intimately connected to God and endowed by God. Choosing to preach on this apocryphal book would elicit a number of fascinating and worthwhile directions for a sermon.

First, in conjunction with the reading from Proverbs, there is an opportunity to explore the concept of wisdom here over and quite against contemporary understandings of the meaning and function of wisdom as noted in the discussion above. Without necessarily delving into the complexities of wisdom in Jewish and Greco-Roman thought, wisdom as a central attribute of God might challenge domesticated understandings of wisdom and even those of God.

Second, the particularities of wisdom expressed in this passage would offer a number of ways to explore the concept of wisdom. In this respect, it would be important to include 7:22b-24 in the pericope. The opening adjectives describing the nature of Wisdom situate the grounds and rationale for why Wisdom can be portrayed as the image of God's goodness (7:26).

SECOND READING
JAMES 2:1-5, 8-10, 14-18 (BCP)
JAMES 2:14-18 (LFM)

For commentary on this text, see the second reading for the Fourteenth Sunday after Pentecost, above.

JAMES 3:1-12 (RCL)

The RCL second reading from James has some connection to the first reading and the RCL alternate responsive reading. Controlling one's speech was a common concern in wisdom literature. In keeping with the concern for faith that does not produce works, the author of James moves to the same kind of demonstrative element concerning the "works" of the tongue. Just as a person's faith should be visible in works, a person's true self can be heard and is manifested in words. It is helpful to situate the discussion in chapter 3 within the context of the unique term introduced at the beginning of the letter and used throughout, "double-minded" (1:8). One of the central themes of this letter is the correlation between that which is on the inside of a person and the observable display witnessed by the outside. This critical correspondence is called forth not only because of an expected kind of life before God but also for the sake of the other (2:8). When there is no verifiable evidence for the parallel between the "implanted word" (1:21) and actions, looking in a mirror will tell the truth of this duplicitous life (1:23).

> One of the central themes of this letter is the correlation between that which is on the inside of a person and the observable display witnessed by the outside.

This section of the letter focuses on speech as representative of the whole of the person by using the tongue as a spokesperson. The detail with which the author works out this evocative point not only illustrates the central meaning, but also exemplifies rhetorical skills for preaching. The tongue as a "small member" capable of having an enormous impact is worked out through the use of several images: the bit in a horse's mouth (v. 3); the rudder of a ship (v. 4); and the small flame that can set a forest on fire (v. 5). These are vivid, pithy examples, yet represent a depth of meaning that encourages engagement, exploration, and imagination if preaching on this passage.

The effects of uncontrolled speech have disastrous consequences again for the community of faith (vv. 9-10). We all know that the chant, "Sticks and stones may break my bones but names will never hurt me," while a good retort to the bully on the playground, is profoundly not true. Words do hurt, tremendously. We have certain words we do not let our children use and we remind them to come from a place of kindness. We can all recall a time when we were called a name, when something not true was said about us, when hopes and visions were dashed with just one word. *Just one word* is the point of this portion of the letter of James. The tongue can stain the whole body (v. 6), it has effects beyond that which was meant to be said. In a return to the theme of the letter in a quite figurative and imaginative way, 3:12 reminds us that just as our works are demonstrative of our faith, our words are equally so. In some respects, this can be a connection to the Gospel lesson from Mark. In what sense is prayer the utterance of faith, the speech of faith? To what extent is faith dead when prayer is absent?

THE GOSPEL

MARK 8:27-38 (RCL, BCP)
MARK 8:27-35 (LFM)

Caesarea Philippi is a defining moment for the Synoptic Gospels, although only Matthew and Mark name this specific location for Peter's confession, "You are the Messiah." Indeed, for the Gospel writers as post-Easter interpretations, reflections, and perspectives, who Jesus is constitutes the most important question for deliberation in those early communities who claimed belief in Jesus. It is important to note that in putting the question on the lips of Jesus, it becomes a question for all believers, and which all believers must answer for themselves. The text itself indicates this deliberate move, not only in content, but also in form. Jesus first asks the question from a third-person perspective, "Who do people say that I am?" But then the grammar shifts to the second person, "Who do you [second person plural] say that I am?" Jesus directs the question to all of the disciples together, but only Peter stands up to answer. Yet, the distinction between a general address and the individual response suggests that each believer must answer individually. It is not enough to say what other people think, to repeat what other people say, to accede to popular assent. It is necessary, in fact, to confess it on your own, for yourself, and out loud. Confession demands belief, but it also necessitates articulation—for the sake of one's own affirmations, but also for the sake of that which is confessed. Peter's answer is not only important for what it is, but for what it does.

> Confession demands belief, but it also necessitates articulation—for the sake of one's own affirmations, but also for the sake of that which is confessed.

In Matthew, Mark, and Luke, Peter's answer to Jesus' question, "But who do you say that I am?" is followed by the first of Jesus' predictions of his suffering and death, of different number in each account. Traditional commentary on this event in the Gospel narratives emphasizes Peter's misunderstanding or the clarification that Peter needs in order to understand what it means to confess Jesus as the Christ. It means, of course, Jesus' own suffering and death, for which Peter rebukes Jesus, but it also means that anyone who follows Jesus will also be required to take up their own cross (Matt. 16:24-26; Mark 8:34—9:1; Luke 9:23-27). It is interesting to note that Peter's rebuke is not in response to his own possible suffering, but to the suffering of Jesus. Does he again not understand what Jesus means, and in this case, is he not able to comprehend what Jesus intimates by taking up your cross? Or, in what sense is his own suffering more acceptable than that of his master? Is it that Peter's idea of the Messiah is being challenged, and the new portrayal is not one that he can accept? Or, is it the case that acceptance will secure his own fate? Indeed, this is a critical avenue of meaning for the Gospel writers and for the meaning of discipleship today. It is not enough to offer the confession, "You are the Christ." One also has to know what it means to claim it.

It is essential to note that Peter's confession, stated before the realities of what that confession will mean both about Jesus and about discipleship, signifies several important truths through which to view the life of faith. First, the confession itself must be confessed. It must be said out loud. It must be articulated, as noted above. When something is said out loud, that act of speech, of confession, of declaration calls that which is said into existence. This is not to say that Jesus as Christ is dependant on our confession, but it is to affirm that Jesus as Christ needs to be claimed, according to the Gospel writers. The authors of the four Gospels were not simply writing to affirm their own confession, but for the sake of the ongoing confession of generations of believers, for the sake of the proclamation of the good news, which by its very definition is meant to be spoken and heard and not kept silent. Second, being able to confess Jesus as Messiah is one thing, a critical thing, but having a sense of what that means is an ongoing process. The character of Peter becomes illustrative of this very point. It is not simply that Peter just doesn't get it—one wonders if he, or we, is ever meant to. How that confession of Jesus as Christ is lived out in the life of faith is an unfolding, a revealing, that is not meant to have its meaning self-contained in the confession alone. This is what Jesus means, in part, about taking up our cross, about losing our lives for the sake of finding them again.

Finally, confessing Jesus as Christ before acknowledging Jesus as crucified Messiah suggests that confession is indeed about proclamation of faith and not comprehension of faith. In the end, to answer for ourselves, "You are the Christ," is

> When something is said out loud, that act of speech, of confession, of declaration calls that which is said into existence.

to claim victory over death, the promise of the resurrection, and the reality of *new* and present life now. When confession just becomes knowledge, information, or proposition, it is then that the cross is just what it is, death on a tree, and nothing more. It is then that we may have to say to ourselves, "Get behind me, Satan."

MARK 9:14-29 (BCP)

The BCP alternate Gospel reading in Mark 9 has parallels in the Synoptic Gospels (Matt. 17:14-20; Luke 9:37-43). Immediately following the healing Jesus predicts his death a second time. There will be only one other healing before Jerusalem, the healing of the blind beggar Bartimaeus (10:46-52), and it is the last of four exorcisms in Mark's narrative (see 1:21-28, 5:1-20, 7:24-30). While the exorcism itself is worthy of note, other elements in the story indicate critical themes for this Gospel, especially two chapters shy of Jesus' entry into Jerusalem. The detail about the child's condition in this story is extraordinary and seems deliberately paced, as if to highlight the moving dialogue between the father of the child and Jesus (vv. 21-24) and between Jesus and the disciples (vv. 28-29).

Jesus' words in 9:19 seem more directed to the disciples than to the surrounding crowd. His cry, "How much longer?" (literally, *until when*), not once, but twice reveals Jesus' apparent exasperation, and also calls attention to the chronological reality that there is not much more time before Jerusalem. The prediction of his suffering and death in the verses directly after the healing highlights the fact that time is running out—for Jesus, for those with whom he comes in contact, for the disciples. His question to the father, "How long has your son been this way?" is acutely tender. Though not in the same Greek construction as Jesus' question to the "faithless generation," there is a contrast here, especially given the fact that the father *does* have faith. The question is not just about the boy; it is also for the father. "How long have you suffered, to see your son this way?[2]

> The question is not just about the boy, it is also for the father: "How long have you suffered, to see your son this way?"

When the father asks for Jesus' help, "*If* you are able," Jesus' response, "*If* I am able," is not derogatory—as if to say, "Are you kidding me? Do you know who I am? Do you know what I have already done?" Jesus' words reveal the heart of the matter, "All things can be done *for* the one who believes"—not *by* but *for*![3] This is not up to the father. He has done enough. This is up to God.

"I believe! Help my unbelief" is one of the most affecting verses in the entire biblical witness. As much as it is the father's cry, it is so much our own. The Greek construction is important here. In the first part of the phrase, "I believe," believing is a present indicative verb (*pisteuō*). When the father says, "my unbelief," the word is a noun, translated "unbelief" or "lack of faith." Just because the

203

FIFTEENTH
SUNDAY AFTER
PENTECOST
───────────
SEPTEMBER 13

father admits to a lack of faith in this moment does not negate the ongoing process of his belief.[4] We continue to believe even when we experience moments that bring unbelief into our lives.

The story ends with the disciples wondering why their attempt at healing the boy had failed. Jesus responds as if to say, "Yeah. This one was really hard. You needed prayer for this one."[5] Previously in Mark the disciples have not been around or are asleep when Jesus prays (1:35, 6:46, 14:37-40). So how are they supposed to know? They were not. Jesus will bring up the issue of prayer a few chapters later (11:24), but here, Jesus makes a connection for them that they were not able to make before. Jesus is not saying that the disciples were lacking faith or unbelieving, but rather that prayer will be needed for what lies ahead.

Notes

1. Christopher R. Seitz, "The Book of Isaiah 40–66" in *The New Interpreter's Bible*, vol. 6 (Nashville: Abingdon, 2001), 436.

2. Elizabeth Strothers Malbon. *Hearing Mark: A Listener's Guide* (Harrisburg: Trinity, 2002), 62.

3. Ibid.

4. Ibid., 63.

5. Ibid.

THE SEASON
AFTER PENTECOST /
OF ORDINARY TIME

PROPER 20 THROUGH PROPER 28
DAVID F. WATSON

The readings on which I comment here occur in the midst of "Ordinary Time." During this time of the year, "each Sunday stands on its own as the Lord's Day and should be considered in the light of the Scriptures to be read that day."[1] In other words, worship services are not shaped by an overarching seasonal theme that focuses on a particular mystery of Christ, as they are during Advent, Christmas, Lent, and Easter. Rather, the Scripture readings for each Sunday shape the emphases of the liturgical celebration. Ordinary Time is not "ordinary," in the sense of there being nothing special about it. The word *ordinary* is taken from the word *ordinal* because we designate these Sundays numerically. Those planning worship can enjoy a bit more creative freedom during this less-structured time. We have the opportunity to celebrate the fullness of Christ's saving work through our hymnody, prayers, sermons, eucharistic celebrations, and other aspects of the liturgy.

This season is also called "Kingdomtide" and leads up to the Sunday called "Christ the King." The Markan material of this final part of the season, drawn from chapters 9, 10, 12, and 13, presents God's kingdom to us in a variety of ways. Sometimes Jesus teaches directly about this, such as we see after James and John make their request to sit, one at his right hand and one at his left, in his glory (10:35-45). Sometimes Jesus points out people who are good or bad examples of the righteous life, such as we see in the juxtaposed stories of the scribes who seek honor (12:38-40) and the poor widow who gives her last two coins (12:41-

44). At other times we see people exhibit great trust in Jesus and receive blessings because of their faith. In Mark 13, Jesus issues a prophecy of events that are rejections of God's righteousness—war, persecution, and suffering—which persist until the vindication of God's holy ones. In preaching this material, we have the opportunity to invite parishioners to receive God's kingdom in faith and humility.

There is, likewise, abundant material in the other readings each week that teach us about lives of holiness. Stories from Numbers and Esther relate the burdens and responsibilities of righteous leadership. The readings from Ruth invite us to reconsider our assumptions about "insiders" and "outsiders" and to follow Ruth's example of covenant faithfulness. Those from Job afford rich material for meditation on suffering and human finitude. The psalmists cry out to God in distress, praise God for blessings, and pledge to God fidelity and righteousness. Readings from James treat our tendency to "double-mindedness," as well as the plight of the poor and the guilt of those who oppress them. Then there are the selections from Hebrews, which talk about Christ's atoning work as both priest and sacrifice, our justification before God, and the lives of faith and righteousness to which we are called. The theme of righteous living suffuses this material.

It is no wonder, then, that many preachers take the opportunity during this time to talk about the church's mission in the world. During Pentecost, God sent the Holy Spirit. Now we consider the work of the Spirit within and through the body of Christ. We are reminded during this time that our salvation is not simply about receiving our heavenly reward. Rather, to be saved is to be born anew. By the work of the Holy Spirit, our values change; our desires, priorities, and volitions are not what they once were. The people whom our world says do not matter—the weak, the least, the impoverished, the outcast—are now VIPs. Salvation means a reordering of our lives according to God's to-do list. Ordinary Time, then, is really a time of invitation and celebration, during which our sermons are occasions to lead our parishioners into a deeper understanding of what it means to be "kingdom people."

Note

1. Hoyt L. Hickman, et al., *The New Handbook of the Christian Year* (Nashville: Abingdon, 1992), 241.

SIXTEENTH SUNDAY AFTER PENTECOST

TWENTY-FIFTH SUNDAY IN ORDINARY TIME / PROPER 20

SEPTEMBER 20, 2009

Revised Common (RCL)	Episcopal (BCP)	Roman Catholic (LFM)
Wisd. of Sol. 1:16—2:1, 12-22 or Jer. 11:18-20 or Prov. 31:10-31	Wisd. of Sol. 1:16—2:1 (6-11) 12-22	Wisd. of Sol. 2:12, 17-20
Psalm 54 or Psalm 1	Psalm 54	Ps. 54:3-4, 5, 6-8
James 3:13—4:3, 7-8a	James 3:16—4:6	James 3:16—4:3
Mark 9:30-37	Mark 9:30-37	Mark 9:30-37

FIRST READING

WISDOM OF SOLOMON 1:16—2:1, 12-22 (RCL)
WISDOM OF SOLOMON 1:16—2:1, 6-11, 12-22 (BCP)
WISDOM OF SOLOMON 2:12, 17-20 (LFM)

The Wisdom of Solomon envisions a twofold reward for those who receive Wisdom and the righteousness she produces. First, a life rightly lived on this earth is a reward in itself. Second, the righteous will receive eternal life with God. By contrast, the ungodly who shun Wisdom condemn themselves to death. By "death," the author means both the corruption that characterizes the present existence of the ungodly and the physical death that marks the end of their existence.

The ungodly have invited death because they have "reasoned unsoundly" (2:1). In a kind of self-fulfilling prophecy, their characterization of life as "short and sorrowful" with "no remedy" when it comes to an end leads them on the path to just such a life (v. 1). If only they reasoned properly, they would see that righteousness is the key to fullness of life in the present and immortality in the future. They are, however, strangers to Wisdom, and their hopelessness leads them to a life of futile pleasure seeking (vv. 6-11).

The discussion of pleasure seeking probably relates directly to problems facing the original audience of this text. Many scholars believe that the Wisdom of Solomon was written in first-century Alexandria, Egypt, where the Jewish community, though quite large, was still a minority. Traffic with Gentiles was unavoidable, and relations between Jews and Gentiles could be tense and sometimes violent. One source of this tension was that the lifestyle of Gentiles differed markedly from that of Jews. Apart from the fact that the Gentiles did not share the Jewish respect for the Torah, there were philosophical groups that endorsed lifestyles inconsistent with Jewish sensibilities. For example, the Epicureans were concerned chiefly with the seeking of pleasure and their lifestyle could be characterized by the motto, "Live untroubled." Some Jews may also have abandoned their ancestral customs and become such pleasure seekers. If so, the Wisdom of Solomon warns these lapsed faithful that their pleasure seeking comes at a price. This text provides the preacher ample material to discuss both the hopelessness and obsession with pleasure so common in our own culture.

> This text provides the preacher ample material to discuss both the hopelessness and obsession with pleasure so common in our own culture.

In 2:6-9, the writer describes the revelry of the ungodly. Verses 10-11 describe the consequences of their self-indulgence: the oppression of the righteous poor, the refusal to spare the widow, and a lack of regard for the aged. A life focused on personal pleasure necessarily neglects the needs of others. As the ungodly consume greedily, less is available for the more vulnerable members of society. Just as is the case today, overconsumption by the powerful (v. 11) resulted in the deprivation of others.

The righteous man who opposes the ungodly endures persecution (2:12-20; see also Isa. 52:13—53:12). He is "inconvenient" to the wicked (v. 12), reproaching them for their moral failings. He professes special knowledge of and a special relationship to God (v. 13). He lives differently (v. 15) and looks down upon the ungodly (v. 16). Therefore the wicked plot against him (vv. 19-20). Again they reason wrongly, blind as they are to the insights of Wisdom. The writer perceives a vicious circle in the life of the ungodly: lack of wisdom leads to an evil life, which in turn creates an even greater lack of wisdom.

JEREMIAH 11:18-20 (RCL ALT.)

Prophetic witness can be a dangerous business. God has revealed to Jeremiah the plans of the prophet's enemies. Though the faithful prophet is like a tree that bears fruit, they wish to cut him off "from the land of the living" (v. 19). They wish, moreover, to erase the memory of his name (v. 19), an abhorrent prospect for ancient Israelites since they believed one lived on after death through the memory of one's name. Jeremiah's opponents may be optimistic prophets who are blind to God's judgment and claim that all will be well with Judah.[1] If this is their claim, they are quite wrong. Judgment is coming. Jeremiah thus asks God, who knows the heart and mind, to judge righteously: bring retribution down upon the heads of his persecutors. God assents to this request in verses 22-23.

PROVERBS 31:10-31 (RCL ALT.)

Within the ancient Israelite household men and women had specific roles. A woman who was both wife and mother not only cared for and taught children, but managed the household and was second only to the father in authority.[2] The poem of Proverbs 31:10-31 should be seen in light of the crucial role the wife and mother played in the well-being of all members of the household.

The virtues of the "capable wife," however, are not limited to her domestic duties. She is also characterized by righteousness and wisdom. She cares for the poor (v. 20), shows strength and dignity (v. 25), "opens her mouth with wisdom" (v. 26), teaches kindness (v. 26), and fears God (v. 30).

The ideal wife of this passage is modeled on the figure of Woman Wisdom, mentioned elsewhere in Proverbs (see, for example, 1:20-33, 3:13-18, 8:1-36). Both Wisdom and a capable wife must be "found" (see 8:17, 31:10). Both are more precious than jewels (see 3:15, 8:11, 31:10). Both will bring gain to a man (see 8:18, 21, 31:11). Just as Wisdom is a teacher, so is the capable wife (see 8:10, 33-34, 31:26). Both embody strength (see 8:14, 31:17, 25). Both deploy servants (see 9:3, 31:15). Some interpreters have suggested that the wife of this passage not only displays characteristics associated with Woman Wisdom, but is in fact her embodiment.[3]

The role of the woman in this passage, though exalted by the writer, will seem confining to many modern readers. There is a great historical distance between ourselves and the writer of this passage, and it may help us to view this passage as primarily descriptive, rather than prescriptive. In fact, this passage is not written as a list of instructions, but as a hymn of praise.[4] It describes what it looks like from an ancient Hebrew perspective when wisdom is manifested in the actions of a wife and mother. Rather than attempting to impose ancient household structures on modern congregants, the preacher may wish to urge both men and women in the congregation to seek the guidance of divine Wisdom in their familial relationships and their relationship with God.

There is a great historical distance between ourselves and the writer of this passage, and it may help us to view this passage as primarily descriptive, rather than prescriptive.

RESPONSIVE READING

PSALM 54 (RCL, BCP)
PSALM 54:3-4, 5, 6-8 (LFM)

Here we have one of the psalms of lament, the largest category of psalms. Like other laments it contains a petition (vv. 1-2), a description of trouble (v. 3), an expression of confidence in God's help (vv. 4-5), and a vow (vv. 6-7). This psalm is identified as a "Maskil," though the precise meaning of this term is unknown and may be as generic as "artistic composition."[5]

The psalmist takes up the theme of the persecuted righteous person. The superscription of the psalm sets it during David's persecution by Saul and betrayal by the Ziphites (see 1 Sam. 23:15-29), though this psalm is general enough to apply to a variety of situations. The central conviction of the psalm is found in verse 4: "But surely, God is my helper; the Lord is the upholder of my life."

PSALM 1 (RCL ALT.)

Along with Psalm 2, Psalm 1 serves as an introduction to the psalter. Its basic message is that the righteous will enjoy happiness while the wicked will perish. The references to "law" in verse 2 are ambiguous, since the Hebrew word *tôrāh* has a number of meanings. It can refer to the Pentateuch but more generally means "teaching" or "instruction." It is sometimes used of legal statutes. One suggestion is that here *tôrāh* refers to the psalms themselves, which bring wisdom and instruction to those who pray them.[6] Such a reading is fitting in light of this psalm's position at the outset of the book.

Ancient Hebrews were aware that the righteous sometimes suffered and the wicked sometimes prospered; witness the many psalms of lament. In this psalm as in many others, the reality of suffering is balanced by a confidence that the truly good life is one lived in proper relationship with God. The righteous delight in God's instruction, and a life rightly lived is its own reward. God's instruction is like a life-giving stream of water (v. 3) that allows one's life to bear fruit. To reject God and the righteous life is to walk away from these life-giving streams. It is to choose a life of futility.

JAMES 3:13—4:3, 7-8A (RCL)
JAMES 3:16—4:6 (BCP)
JAMES 3:16—4:3 (LFM)

Not every way of thinking that bears the name "wisdom" is the wisdom that comes from God. There is "earthly" wisdom that is self-serving and "false to the truth" (3:14). There are apparently some people in the community to which James is writing who claim to be wise but do not demonstrate godly wisdom by their actions. True wisdom, according to James, will result in righteous works and gentleness. A more extensive list of the fruits of God's wisdom appears in 3:17.

Those who have received God's wisdom should display a way of thinking and acting that is different than those who have not. Yet James is fully aware (as are most churchgoers) that people within the church do not always exhibit the fruits of God's wisdom. Behavior characterized by conflicts and disputes is in keeping with "earthly" wisdom, but not with God's. One must choose between these. As James puts it,

> Those who have received God's wisdom should display a way of thinking and acting that is different than those who have not.

"Friendship with the world is enmity with God" (4:4). The earthly values that lead people to seek status and high reputation are opposed to the humility that characterizes the Christian life. James urges these Christians, then, to submit to God, resist the devil, and draw near to God. In so doing, they will open themselves to the leadings and fruits of God's wisdom.

THE GOSPEL

MARK 9:30-37 (RCL, BCP, LFM)

The Messiah of Mark's Gospel is no "gentle Jesus, meek and mild." He can be welcoming and compassionate, but he can also be fiercely demanding, uncompromising, and sharply critical of those who oppose his mission and teaching. Though many people have sentimentalized Jesus' treatment of children, this passage in Mark is meant as a challenge, along the lines of Jesus' demand that his followers "deny themselves and take up their cross" (8:34).

Much of the material in the section from 8:22—10:52 was deeply counter-cultural, perhaps even shocking to its original audience. Ancient Mediterranean people (and especially males) were very concerned with reputation and status, concepts that came under the umbrella of honor. In the modern West we tend to think of honor in terms of ethical integrity. A person can do the honorable thing even if everyone else is against him or her. This was not the case in the ancient world. Honor was a *socially acknowledged* claim to worth.[7] Regardless of the ethical nature of one's actions, without acknowledgment by other people one did not have honor. There were numerous ways to increase one's honor, from displays of valor to oratorical brilliance. One could gain honor through the giving of gifts or by being a well-known and respected teacher. Conversely, one could lose honor by being insulted, associating with the wrong sorts of people, being physically beaten, and in many other ways. Crucifixion represented an extreme loss of honor. In fact, the complete disgrace of the victim was a major part of its intent.

Given these cultural expectations, Jesus makes some rather unreasonable demands of his followers in this section. In the verses leading up to this week's passage he orders them to tell no one that they follow the Messiah (8:30) and Son of God (9:9). He states that his followers must "take up their cross" (8:34), and that they must not be ashamed of him after his crucifixion (8:38). Here in 9:30-37, he continues to teach this countercultural ethos.

> Crucifixion represented an extreme loss of honor. In fact, the complete disgrace of the victim was a major part of its intent.

In 9:31 Jesus issues the second of three predictions of his passion, death, and resurrection (see also 8:31 and 10:33-34). His disciples, however, do not understand what he means (9:32). By this point in the narrative the reader is probably not surprised at their lack of understanding. Earlier in the Gospel Mark writes that Jesus must explain all of the parables in private to his disciples (4:34). He castigates them for having no faith (4:40), and in 6:52 they are said to have hardened hearts. In 7:18 Jesus again expresses frustration over the disciples' inability to understand his teachings. In 8:4 the disciples appear especially obtuse, asking Jesus how one can feed so many people with bread in the desert, even though he has previously performed an almost identical miracle (6:30-44). Jesus' frustration with the disciples turns to exasperation (8:17-21), and in 8:33 he has a heated conflict with Peter. The disciples' failure to understand (9:32) therefore continues a well-established pattern in the narrative.

In 9:35 Mark narrates that Jesus' followers have been arguing with one another over which one of them is the greatest. In keeping with ancient Mediterranean concerns with status and honor, they attempt to establish a hierarchy among themselves and jockey for position (see also 10:35-45). This is another demonstration of their lack of understanding. Jesus tells them that that whoever wishes to become "first" must be "last of all and servant of all" (9:35). In the world in which Mark's Gospel was written, having authority over others was greatly to be desired, especially for males. It was a way of demonstrating prowess and acquiring honor. Serving was considered appropriate for people of low stature. This is to some extent the case in our own culture, though it was more overt and pronounced in the ancient Mediterranean world. The general expectation was that if a person was serving in a menial capacity, that person had no other choice but to do so. Servants and slaves did tasks that the more privileged members of society considered undesirable. Jesus, however, reverses these expectations. He teaches that, among his group of followers, to become highly honored one must humble oneself, taking on the conventionally menial role of the servant. Perhaps this is why Jesus attempts to pass unnoticed through Galilee (9:30). Crowds often flock to Jesus because of his teaching and healing (see, for example, 1:45, 2:2, 3:7-10, 5:21, 24, 6:31, 53-56, 8:1, 10:46, 11:8-10). This would undoubtedly enhance his reputation, but to receive freely such acclaim would be inconsistent with the ethos that he teaches and models elsewhere in this section of the Gospel.

The Greek word translated "servant" in the NRSV (9:35) is *diakonos*, the word from which we derive the English word *deacon*. Sometimes the verbal form of this word is translated "to minister." In Mark's Gospel, *diakonos* or its verbal form is used only of angels (1:13), Peter's mother-in-law (1:31), Jesus himself (10:45), and the women at the tomb (15:41). Though the Twelve are instructed to take on the role of a *diakonos* here in 9:35 and in 10:43, this word is never directly used of them. It seems that they never take to heart Jesus' teachings about service and humility.

> Jesus teaches that, among his group of followers, to become highly honored one must humble oneself, taking on the conventionally menial role of the servant.

Jesus continues in the same vein by comparing himself, and by extension God, to a child (vv. 36-37; see also 10:13-16). Modern interpreters sometimes understand Jesus' reference to the child in terms of childlike innocence. If we think of innocence as the absence of sin, however, this probably is not what is at stake in this passage. Rather, children were not the proper recipients of honor. They did not do the kinds of things that adults (and especially men) did to acquire honor. They did not seek to enhance their reputations by demonstrating prowess and beneficence. They did not exercise authority over others. In the honor-shame value system, they were nonentities. Now Jesus says that by welcoming one such insignificant person, you welcome him, and when you welcome him, you welcome God.

Jesus' demand that his followers become humble servants was difficult for the disciples, just as it is difficult for Christians today. We are taught by our culture that success means gaining for ourselves. It is no easy thing to make real sacrifices for others, to give of ourselves, to put aside our own interests and give up what our culture tells us is most important. Yet Jesus is clear that in God's kingdom, that is what is required.

Notes

1. See William L. Holladay, *Jeremiah 1: A Commentary on the Book of the Prophet Jeremiah, Chapters 1–25,* Hermeneia (Philadelphia: Fortress Press, 1986), 370.

2. See Leo G. Perdue, "The Israelite and Early Jewish Family: Summary and Conclusions," in Leo G. Perdue, et al., *Families in Ancient Israel* (Louisville: Westminster John Knox, 1997), 182.

3. See R. N. Whybray, *Proverbs* (Grand Rapids: Eerdmans, 1994), 425.

4. Ibid., 425–26.

5. Robert G. Bratcher and William D. Reyburn, *A Translator's Handbook on the Book of Psalms* (New York: United Bible Societies, 1991), 10.

6. See Richard J. Clifford, *Psalms 1–72* (Nashville: Abingdon, 2002), 40.

7. See Bruce J. Malina, *The New Testament World: Insights from Cultural Anthropology,* 3rd ed. (Louisville: Westminster John Knox, 2001), 29.

SEVENTEENTH SUNDAY AFTER PENTECOST

TWENTY-SIXTH SUNDAY IN ORDINARY TIME /
PROPER 21
SEPTEMBER 27, 2009

Revised Common (RCL)	Episcopal (BCP)	Roman Catholic (LFM)
Num. 11:4-6, 10-16, 24-29 or Esth. 7:1-6, 9-10; 9:20-22	Num. 11:4-6, 10-16, 24-29	Num. 11:25-29
Ps. 19:7-14 or Psalm 124	Psalm 19 or 19:7-14	Ps. 19:8, 10, 12-13, 14
James 5:13-20	James 4:7-12 (13—5:6)	James 5:1-6
Mark 9:38-50	Mark 9:38-43, 45, 47-48	Mark 9:38-43, 45, 47-48

FIRST READING

NUMBERS 11:4-6, 10-16, 24-29 (RCL, BCP)
NUMBERS 11:25-29 (LFM)

Chapters 11–25 of Numbers relate Israel's rebellion against God. Numbers portrays the old exodus generation as unfaithful, untrusting, and grumbling. The "rabble" mentioned in 11:4 are probably non-Israelites.[1] The Israelites follow their lead, however, in a fit of desire for fine dining. Apparently, the manna that God provides for the people is very tasty, like "cakes baked with oil" (11:8). Yet the people take for granted God's providential care, longing for the cuisine of their days in Egypt, and forgetting the hardship from which God has freed them.

Neither Moses nor God is pleased with this state of affairs. Moses has only recently interceded on behalf of the people, saving them from a fiery death (see vv. 1-3). Now they are grumbling again, God is angry, and Moses has grown frustrated with the burden of leadership. In verses 11-15 he issues to God a striking set of complaints. It is as if Moses says to God, "*You* should be fixing these problems. These are *your* people!" Moses compares God to Israel's mother and himself to Israel's wet-nurse. God has conceived and given birth to Israel, but instructed Moses, "Carry them in your bosom, as a nurse carries a sucking child" (v. 12). Moses claims that this burden is too great.

God concedes and offers Moses help. The spirit of God that the seventy elders receive in 11:25 brings with it a one-time gift of prophecy. Elsewhere in the Old and New Testaments we see God's spirit associated with prophetic action (for example, 1 Sam. 10:6, 19:20-24; Isa. 42:1, 61:1; Luke 4:18-19). Perhaps the point of this singular gift of prophecy in Numbers is to show through manifold voices, rather than only through Moses' voice, God's will for Israel. Moses still wishes to tender his resignation, but God's call to leadership is not something that one simply wishes away.

ESTHER 7:1-6, 9-10; 9:20-22 (RCL ALT.)

Though the Hebrew book of Esther never mentions God directly, Jews and Christians through the centuries have seen God's hand at work in the narrative. The deuterocanonical Greek Additions to Esther references God directly several times.

Esther is a story of courage and deliverance. In many biblical stories, the hero or heroine is an unlikely one, and Esther is no exception. It is normally men in the Bible who perform heroic deeds, but here it is a young woman. She is also an orphan, still living in the house of her cousin Mordecai. Yet she, like Moses, must deal with the burden of leadership, and as with Moses' intercessions before an angry God, Esther's actions have the potential to save Israel from destruction.

> Esther is a story of courage and deliverance. It is normally men in the Bible who perform heroic deeds, but here it is a young woman.

In chapter 5 she gambles with her life, entering the king's inner court uninvited, an offense punishable by death unless the king grants clemency. Now in chapter 7 the plan that began with her audience before the king comes to fruition. The king grants her a request, and she asks that her people be spared the slaughter that Haman has planned for them. Esther then indicts Haman before the king, and in a twist of dramatic irony, the wicked Haman is hung on the very gallows that he has ordered built for the righteous Mordecai.

The height of these gallows is ridiculous—fifty cubits, or about seventy-five feet. The term *gallows* may be something of a misnomer in Esther, as this may refer not to a device for execution by hanging, but to a large stake used for impaling. Regardless of the exact nature of the structure, the point of its great height is to make a public spectacle of Mordecai's death and thus increase the disgrace of Mordecai and his family. Now it is Haman who dies in disgrace.

The Jewish festival of Purim commemorates the story recounted in the book of Esther. During Purim the story of Esther is read aloud at a synagogue service. As we read in 9:24, the name of the festival comes from the Akkadian word *Pur*, which means "lot" (see also 3:7). Thus, the very name of the festival is ironic: the lot cast to determine the day on which the Jews would be killed has given its name to a festival celebrating their deliverance.

Responsive Reading

217

SEVENTEENTH
SUNDAY AFTER
PENTECOST

SEPTEMBER 27

PSALM 19:7-14 (RCL, BCP alt.)
PSALM 19 (BCP)
PSALM 19:8, 10, 12-13, 14 (LFM)

Psalm 19 is probably composed of two originally separate psalms, the first comprising verses 1-6, and the second verses 7-14.[2] Verses 1-4 express in beautiful poetic images that creation can teach us about God. Knowledge of God comes forth in a mysterious way, in a speech without words and an unheard voice. As John Calvin read this passage, "David shows how it is that the heavens proclaim to us the glory of God, namely, by openly bearing testimony that they have not been put together by chance, but were wonderfully created by the supreme Architect."[3]

As the psalm progresses, it moves topically from a discussion of the knowledge of God proclaimed through creation to a discussion of the law, beginning in verse 7. Perhaps the two psalms were combined because together they express that one can gain knowledge of righteousness through the creation (compare to Wisd. 13:1-9; Rom. 1:1-23).

In verses 7-10 the psalmist meditates on the perfection of the law and the benefits that it brings to God's people: it is life giving and brings wisdom, righteousness, enlightenment, purity, and truth. It is a joy, therefore, to keep the law of the Lord. One should desire to abide by God's ordinances even more than one would desire gold or honey. Christians, and especially Protestants, often have a negative view of "law," and we sometimes contrast it to grace. For ancient Jews, however, law and grace were of a piece. The law was not a burden, but a gift. It was considered an expression of Israel's covenant relationship with God and a way to live in harmony with the righteous world that God created.

> One should desire to abide by God's ordinances even more than one would desire gold or honey.

The final section of the psalm, verses 11-14, is a prayer for righteousness. The psalmist is "warned" by the law, but he realizes that he may inadvertently sin. He prays, then, that God will guide his thoughts, actions, and words in such a way that he will be acceptable to God.

PSALM 124 (RCL alt.)

The psalmist uses a variety of metaphors to describe the assaults of Israel's enemies. For example, they are likened to a beast with the capacity to swallow its victims alive. The psalmist also employs the metaphor of floodwater for Israel's enemies. In Genesis 7 floodwaters annihilate most of humankind, but the psalmist here celebrates Israel's deliverance. In verse 6, the psalmist returns to the metaphor of a predatory beast. Again quickly changing metaphors, he compares Israel to a bird that has escaped the fowler's snare. God is "blessed" for delivering Israel. The Hebrew *brk* expresses not just thanks, but solidarity.[4] The blessing reaffirms Israel's covenantal relationship with God.

Implicit in this thanksgiving is an element of warning: it is not just any god, but Yahweh (rendered LORD in most English translations), who has delivered Israel. Had it been some other god, Israel surely would have been devoured by the wicked (vv. 2-3). The worship of other gods will only bring destruction.

SECOND READING
JAMES 5:13-20 (RCL)
JAMES 4:7-12 (13—5:6) (BCP)
JAMES 5:1-6 (LFM)

As we read in James 4:7-10, righteous actions result from righteous inner states. Hence, James warns against being "double-minded," a term that describes the struggle between competing desires. One desires to do good on the one hand and evil on the other. As we read in 1:14-15, "one is tempted by one's own desire, being lured and enticed by it; then, when that desire has conceived, it gives birth to sin, and that sin, when it is fully grown, gives birth to death." Rather than allowing sinful impulses to grow into sin, the faithful should draw near to God, assuming an attitude of submission, repentance, and humility.

> Rather than allowing sinful impulses to grow into sin, the faithful should draw near to God, assuming an attitude of submission, repentance, and humility.

In verses 11-12, James warns against slander and judgment within the community of faith. He holds that slandering and judging others is the same as slandering and judging the law. The reference to the law here probably points to Leviticus 19:18: "You shall love your neighbor as yourself." James terms this the "royal law" (2:8; see also Matt. 22:39; Mark 12:31; Luke 10:27). To slander or judge others is to do the same to the "royal law" that prohibits such actions.

James then turns his attention to boasting. Those who boast focus on their own merit and strength, rather than God's providential care. James instructs believers not to boast of their own prowess, but rather to admit that the future is in God's hands.

The rich are the next on James's chopping block. They are accused of depriving laborers of just wages and committing fraud. Their wealth comes at the expense of others. Yet God hears the cries of the oppressed (see, for example, Deut. 24:17-22; Ps. 82:3-4; Isa. 5:7; Amos 2:6-7; Wisd. 2:12-20). Like those who boast, the rich rely on their own resources rather than on God's providential care.

Though our world is very different than the world in which the letter of James was written, the problems James discusses remain relevant. Slander, judgment, and self-aggrandizement still find their way inside the walls of the church, and the improper use of money is epidemic in many North American congregations.

In 5:13-20, James exhorts followers of Jesus to express both joy and suffering within the community of faith. He also holds that the Christian community is the only proper context for rites and prayers of healing. Ancient people did not have effective medical procedures, and the sick might turn to wandering magicians or pagan rites for healing. The writer appears to see a causal link between sin and sickness, which we find in other places in the Bible (for example, Lev. 26:16; Deut. 28:21-22, 27-28, 35; John 9:2). The pastor should exercise caution when dealing with such passages, since we know, as did many ancients, that the righteous are sometimes afflicted, and the wicked sometimes prosper.

THE GOSPEL
MARK 9:38-50 (RCL)
MARK 9:38-43, 45, 47-48 (BCP, LFM)

Jesus has just taught the disciples that their ways of understanding honor, reputation, and precedence are wrongheaded. To be great within Jesus' community of followers is to become like a servant and a child, people low on the hierarchy of status relations. Chapters 8, 9, and 10 are shot through with this countercultural understanding of values, though throughout these chapters the disciples are unable to understand Jesus' teachings. As is often the case with modern Christians, the disciples are so entrenched in their common cultural conventions that

> The disciples are so entrenched in their common cultural conventions that they cannot see the ways in which Jesus' message challenges their deep-seated assumptions.

they cannot see the ways in which Jesus' message challenges their deep-seated assumptions. Men, they believe, are supposed to seek precedence over one another. They are supposed to gain honor by one-upping other people. They are supposed to master others, rather than serve others. The episode of 9:38-41 shows again that they misunderstand Jesus' calling.

Jesus' disciple John calls to his attention that there is an exorcist casting out demons in Jesus' name, and that the disciples tried to stop this exorcist because he was not following "us." The disciples seem to have a distorted understanding of their own position. It is true that Jesus has given them special authority and responsibility. In 3:14-15 Jesus commissioned them to "proclaim the message, and to have authority to cast out demons." Likewise in chapter 6 he gave the Twelve authority over unclean spirits (6:7) and sent them out on a mission of proclamation (6:7, 11-12). He apparently also granted them the power to cure illness (6:13). Jesus has not, however, given them precedence within the group in such a way that other exorcists, or others who have faith in Jesus, have to "follow" the disciples. In other words, he never delineates a power structure within the group, except for the fact that he is the leader. Even as the leader, moreover, Jesus sets an example of service and humility. His followers should thus abide by his teachings and example, seeking to become servants rather than lording over other people. By seeking precedence themselves, in effect they deny Jesus' leadership.

The disciples also wish to delineate Jesus' group more exclusively than he does, but he corrects their error. Jesus holds that people can do deeds of power in his name even if they are not part of the group traveling with him through Galilee and without recognizing the disciples as leaders. These people who do deeds of power in Jesus' name will not be able to speak evil of him. The concept of "name" was very important in the ancient Mediterranean world. To act in the name of another person was to signal publicly an affiliation with that person. Sometimes names could be used simply as "magic words" in incantations, though this usage still signaled an affiliation with the person whose name was used. Jesus understands the use of his name in deeds of power as a contrast to those who are ashamed of him and of his words (see 8:38). Public acknowledgment of Jesus is important.

> The concept of "name" was very important in the ancient Mediterranean world. To act in the name of another person was to signal publicly an affiliation with that person.

Those who do not oppose Jesus and his followers, and specifically those who offer them hospitality, will receive their "reward." Jesus is more specific about this reward in 10:30, in which he describes entry into his community of followers in terms of receiving "houses, brothers and sisters, mothers and children, and fields, with persecutions." In other words, though there will be a cost to following Jesus (persecution), his followers will receive a new family of faith. They will also receive eternal life in the age to come (10:30).

There is no consensus as to the meaning of "little ones" in 9:42. Since much of the preceding discussion refers to status reversal, however, this phrase may refer to people of low status.[5] In other places, Mark refers to people of high station as *megistanes* (6:21, NRSV: "courtiers") and *megaloi* (10:42, NRSV: "great ones"), words that stand in contrast to the *mikroi* ("little ones") mentioned in verse 42. Along the same lines, "little ones" may refer to people who have adopted the humility and servanthood that Jesus exemplifies and teaches. Rather than despising low station and service, such people have deliberately humbled themselves and given up pretensions to greatness, precedence, and grand reputation. We may thus see Jesus' words in 9:42-48 as warnings against self-aggrandizing behavior and seeking conventional markers of high status and honor. One must not tempt others to glorify themselves (v. 42) and to live in accord with common social conventions.

The Greek word that the NRSV translates "cause to stumble" is *skandalizō*, which implies social offense and scandal. There was social pressure on early Christians to abandon the faith and return to conventional ways of living, thinking, and being religious. Those who would exert such pressure—whether outsiders to Jesus' group or unfaithful followers of Jesus—commit a grave offense. Aspects of one's life that keep one from following Jesus' example and teachings must be discarded, regardless of how painful it may be (vv. 43-48).

Jesus is quite serious about the consequences of sin. The images that he uses in verses 42-47 are indeed harsh: drowning under the weight of a millstone, the severing of limbs, and the gouging out of an eye. Yet such pain is not as bad as forfeiting one's eternal relationship with God. Again, Jesus uses strong images: the unquenchable fire of Gehenna, the worm that never dies. "Gehenna," or the valley of Hinnom, lay outside of Jerusalem. It was not far from the city and would have been a well-known image among those who had been to Jerusalem. It was a place where child sacrifice and idolatry had taken place (see 2 Kgs. 23:10; Jer. 32:35) and was used as a garbage dump where trash was burned. This unclean place associated with evil was a powerful metaphor for divine punishment.

> Aspects of one's life that keep one from following Jesus' example and teachings must be discarded, regardless of how painful it may be.

In 9:49-50 Jesus offers three sayings using the metaphor of salt. The first refers to being "salted with fire." Salt and fire have in common that they have the capacity to purify or destroy. Salt is also a preservative.[6] The connection with the preceding sayings (vv. 42ff.), other than the reference to fire (see 9:43, 48), seems to be that the harsh measures that Jesus mandates as preferable to eternal punishment are destructive, yet have the purifying effect of purging one of sin, and thus lead to eternal reward rather than condemnation.

The second saying, "Salt is good; but if salt has lost its saltiness, how can you season it?" is a way of describing the lives of righteousness that Jesus' followers are required to live. They should live differently than other people. They should exemplify humility, serve others, receive the outcast, and be willing to claim a crucified Lord. Just as salt that has lost its saltiness is missing that essential characteristic that makes it distinct, a follower of Jesus who will not become a humble servant is missing the essential characteristics that set Jesus' followers apart.

The third saying is related to the second. Those followers of Jesus who live as he requires, who have "salt" among themselves, will be at peace with one another. Conversely, those followers of Jesus who revert back to conventional ways of thinking and acting will not find peace (see 9:33-34, 10:41).

Notes

1. See Baruch A. Levine, *Numbers 1–20: A New Translation with Introduction and Commentary* (New York: Doubleday, 1993), 320–21.

2. See Hans Joachim Kraus, *Psalms 1–59: A Commentary*, trans. Hilton C. Oswald (Minneapolis: Augsburg, 1988), 268–69.

3. John Calvin, *Commentary on the Book of Psalms*, trans. James Anderson (Grand Rapids: Eerdmans, 1949), 307.

4. See Josef Scharbert, *brk*, in *Theological Dictionary of the Old Testament,* vol. 2, ed. G. Johannes Botterweck and Helmer Ringgren (Grand Rapids: Eerdmans, 1977), 279–308.

5. See Bruce J. Malina and Richard L. Rohrbaugh, *Social-Science Commentary on the Synoptic Gospels*, 2d ed. (Minneapolis: Fortress Press, 2003), 186.

6. On this saying, see Morna D. Hooker, *The Gospel According to Saint Mark* (Peabody, Mass.: Hendrickson, 1991), 233.

EIGHTEENTH SUNDAY AFTER PENTECOST

TWENTY-SEVENTH SUNDAY IN ORDINARY TIME / PROPER 22

OCTOBER 4, 2009

Revised Common (RCL)	Episcopal (BCP)	Roman Catholic (LFM)
Gen. 2:18-24 or	Gen. 2:18-24	Gen. 2:18-24
Job 1:1, 2:1-10		
Psalm 8 or 26	Psalm 8 or 128	Ps. 128:1-2, 3, 4-5, 6
Heb. 1:1-4; 2:5-12	Heb. 2:(1-8) 9-18	Heb. 2:9-11
Mark 10:2-16	Mark 10:2-9	Mark 10:2-16 or 10:2-12

FIRST READING

GENESIS 2:18-24 (RCL, BCP, LFM)

Genesis 2:4-25 relates a second account of creation, often attributed to the "Yahwist" (or "J") source. This is an etiological narrative, one that explains how things came to be the way they are. In this passage, there is not only an account of the origin of woman, but of marriage and sexuality.

The word for "woman," *ishshah* (v. 23), designates her as one who comes from man, *ish*. She is created, the text says, as a "helper and partner." Historically, this has been one of the "proof texts" used to subordinate women. Yet, as Christina De Groot comments, "Although the woman is derived from the man, it is not correct to assume that the woman created to be a helper is created to be man's subordinate. The Hebrew word *ezer*, in Genesis 2:20 is also used to describe God as our Helper or Deliverer (see Gen 49:25)."[1] She points out that the context of the word *ezer* determines its use. "In the context of Genesis 2, the man needs help to alleviate his aloneness. . . . In this context, being a helper does not mean being man's subordinate but rather means being his partner and companion."[2] In fact, Genesis tells us that the husband's rule over his wife comes not from this original order of things, but as a result of the first sin (3:16). Restoration of the original order of creation, then, would mean a return to mutuality, rather than subordination.

"Then the man said, 'This at last is bone of my bones and flesh of my flesh; this one shall be called Woman, for out of Man this one was taken.'" For this reason, the text says, a man leaves his father and mother and cleaves to his wife, and the two become one flesh. Sexuality, then, is not an aberration, but a return to the perfection of God's original creation. Later in the story, however, sexuality is somehow corrupted by a particular understanding of it, an understanding that was meant for God, but not for humans (3:1-24). As this story tells it, the relationship between man and woman was once perfect, but through disobedience the first man and the first woman corrupted it.

JOB 1:1, 2:1-10 (RCL ALT.)

In the worldview of the book of Job, heavenly beings are behind the fortunes and misfortunes that affect human life. In this case, it is Satan who afflicts Job, though only with God's permission. Satan, whose name means "accuser" or "adversary," is a member of the heavenly court. Unlike later texts in which he is God's archenemy, here Satan seems to have a particular function—to bring to God's attention the disloyalty of human beings (see also Zech. 3:1-5). He holds that Job's righteousness is the result of self-interest, and that if Job were afflicted he would curse God. The Almighty disagrees, and a sort of experiment ensues: How true is Job's devotion to God?

The book of Job challenges the idea found in many Old Testament writings that suffering is the result of sin and good fortune the result of righteousness. Here is Job, blameless and righteous, who suffers mightily. He refuses to curse God, but still he suffers even more. We can see from works such as Job and Ecclesiastes that the problem of human suffering is an ancient and perplexing issue. In the end, the book of Job does not solve this problem, but rather asserts that God's ways are beyond human understanding.

> The book of Job challenges the idea found in many Old Testament writings that suffering is the result of sin and good fortune the result of righteousness.

RESPONSIVE READING
PSALM 8 (RCL, BCP)

The psalmist celebrates the exaltation of humankind as a manifestation of God's grace and goodness. The meaning of verse 2 is unclear, though it may underscore the sovereignty of God who is able to silence enemies with even the babbling of infants. Human beings seem small and insignificant in comparison to the God who established the moon and stars (vv. 3-4), but, says the psalmist, "You have made them a little lower than God" (v. 5). The word *elohim*, translated "God" in the NRSV, can actually be translated in a number of ways, such as "angels," "the gods," "heavenly beings," "a god," or "divine."[3] The Septuagint (followed by Hebrews) renders this word in Greek as *angeloi*, which we normally translate as "angels."

Richard J. Clifford comments on an aspect of this passage that distinguishes ancient Hebrew thought from that of other Near Eastern peoples: "Ancient cosmogonies without exception told how human beings were created as slaves of the gods; their job was to maintain the universe for their divine masters and see to their food, clothing, and honor. Biblical cosmogonies differ. Human beings are not mere slaves because the biblical God is not needy in the same sense as the gods of the extrabiblical consmogonies."[4] The exaltation of humans, then, is the gracious gift of the sovereign God.

PSALM 26 (RCL ALT.)
PSALM 128 (BCP ALT.)
PSALM 128:1-2, 3, 4-5, 6 (LFM)

Psalm 26 is a response to an accusation of unrighteousness. Ancient Mediterranean people were much more group oriented than modern Westerners. The people with whom one affiliated and one's public activity were considered accurate indicators of character. One who consorted with sinners was seen as a sinner. The psalmist thus protests that he does not consort with the unrighteous (vv. 4-5). Those who question the psalmist's righteousness should observe his singing thanksgiving and praise at the altar of the Lord (vv. 6-7).

A cause-and-effect theology seems to lie behind verse 9. The sinful and bloodthirsty person will be swept away; this is probably a reference to death resulting from sin. The psalmist prays that God will not count him among the unrighteous (vv. 9-10) and asks that God "redeem" him (v. 11). In other words, he asks for vindication in an act of judgment upon his accusers.

Psalm 128 also expresses a cause-and-effect theology. The psalm is directed to a man who labors in the field and has a wife who has borne children. In the agricultural society of ancient Israel, fields that yielded bountiful harvests and a faithful wife who bore children were considered rich blessings indeed. There are, however, voices in the Bible that question the common understanding that the righteous prosper and the wicked suffer. As noted above, the book of Job addresses the issue of righteous suffering. Qoheleth ponders the issue, noting that "there are righteous people who perish in their righteousness, and there are wicked people who prolong their life in their evildoing" (Eccles. 7:15). The theological problem of human suffering was as acute in the ancient world as it is today.

> There are voices in the Bible that question the common understanding that the righteous prosper and the wicked suffer.

HEBREWS 1:1-4; 2:5-12 (RCL)
HEBREWS 2:(1-8) 9-18 (BCP)
HEBREWS 2:9-11 (LFM)

Hebrews leads with its Christology. There was a time, long ago, when God spoke through prophets, but a greater messenger has come along—not a prophet, but a Son. Verses 2-4 convey a variety of christological themes that are important for the larger argument of Hebrews. Jesus shares in the divine nature. He is the agent through whom creation came into being. Yet he allowed himself to be abased when he made purification for sins, and therefore God has exalted him far above even the angels. The reader should understand the inestimable value of what God has communicated and accomplished through this Son.

It is crucial to the larger argument of Hebrews to show that the message about Jesus, which originated with Jesus himself (2:3), supersedes the "message declared through angels," or the Torah. (Extrabiblical Jewish tradition held that the Torah was given to Moses by angels.) What is at stake in this admonition is the very salvation of the audience. At the core of the message of Hebrews is the claim that Christ, who is both high priest and sacrifice, has accomplished once and for all through his death the act of atonement necessary for human beings to achieve righteousness before God. No further sacrifices are necessary (see 10:12-14). If these Christians—probably Jewish Christians—attempt to achieve righteousness according to the stipulations of the Torah, they will neglect the salvation available to them through Christ. To continue in the old sacrificial system is to deny the efficacy of Christ's atoning death.

> To continue in the old sacrificial system is to deny the efficacy of Christ's atoning death.

Hebrews 2:6-8 contains a citation of Psalm 8:4-6, though the NRSV translation obscures the significance of the cited passage. The NRSV uses the plural noun "human beings" in this passage, but in Greek the subject, "the human being," is in the singular, and the pronouns referring back to him are singular and masculine. Thus, the citation begins, "What is a human being, that you are mindful of him / or a son of humanity [or "son of man"] that you care for him?" (2:6). Making these nouns and pronouns plural obscures the fact that this section of Psalm 8 functions here as a prophecy about Jesus. In other words, this passage from Psalms is not about humankind, but about a particular human being, Jesus.

More specifically, Hebrews interprets this passage as a reference to Christ's condescension to humankind, as we read of in 2:17. Being made "lower than the angels" (v. 7) means becoming human. Because of his condescension and abasement, Christ has been "crowned" with "glory and honor" and "all things" have been made subject to him (see also 1:3). The Son, who is the "exact imprint of God's very being," has shared the flesh and blood of humankind (2:14) and endured suffering and death (2:10, 14) so that "he might destroy the one who has the power of death, that is, the devil, and free those who all their lives were held in slavery by the fear of death" (2:14-15).

The Gospel

MARK 10:2-16 (RCL)
MARK 10:2-9 (BCP)
MARK 10:2-16 or 10:2-12 (LFM)

The Pharisees' question to Jesus in verse 2 is puzzling, since we know of no general prohibition of divorce among Jews in Jesus' day (but see the special cases in Deut. 22:19, 29). The assumptions behind their question are unclear. It does seem clear, though, that their request is not an innocent attempt to elicit Jesus' opinion on a matter of law. When the Pharisees attempt to "test" (*peirazein*) Jesus, their intention is to embarrass him in public debate (see also 8:11, 12:13-15). Perhaps the idea is that they know that Jesus' position on divorce is very unusual and appears inconsistent with the regulations of Deuteronomy 24:1-4, which allow divorce at the discretion of the husband. Divorce seems to have been quite common in Jesus' day.[5] By his prohibition of divorce, Jesus puts himself at odds with popular sentiment and practice.

The Pharisees ask only if it is lawful for a man to divorce his wife, and not whether a wife can divorce her husband. Roman law and custom allowed wives to divorce their husbands, but whether or not wives could initiate divorce in ancient Israel is unclear. Deuteronomy 24:1-4 does not allow a wife to divorce her husband, but later traditions may have. We do know of instances in which Jewish wives initiated divorce, though this evidence comes from Elephantine, Egypt, rather than from Israel, and it is much earlier than Mark's Gospel. We do not know, moreover, whether this practice was confined to Elephantine or whether it took place more widely.[6] In the absence of evidence to the contrary, it is probably safest to assume that in Israel divorce was primarily or exclusively the prerogative of the husband. The wording of the Pharisees' question seems to support this view.

In response to the Pharisees' question, Jesus elicits a Scripture reference from them. Deuteronomy 24:1-4 mentions a certificate of divorce. The main purpose of such a certificate was probably the protection of the divorced wife. Without such a certificate she could lose money that was owed to her in the divorce. There could also be uncertainty regarding her eligibility for remarriage.

Jesus concedes, then, that it is lawful for a man to divorce his wife. Even though divorce is lawful, however, it is not the ideal. The option to issue a certificate of divorce is a concession made because of human hardness of heart. Since men will put their wives out of their households, the certificate of divorce is necessary. To make his point, Jesus engages in a practice common in rabbinic debate: he cites Scripture against Scripture. Yes, the Pharisees have on their side Deuteronomy 24:1-4, but Jesus counters with two references to passages in Genesis. The first, which appears in Mark 10:6, is from Genesis 1:27: "God made them male and female." The second, which appears in Mark 10:7-8, is from Genesis 2:24: "For this reason a man shall leave his father and mother and be joined to his wife, and the two shall become one flesh." While his opponents may appeal to what is allowed by the Law of Moses, Jesus appeals to the original order of creation. His argument is that, because God has created human beings male and female, a man leaves his father and mother and is joined to his wife. In the joining together of these two, they become one flesh. Therefore, husbands who put their wives out of their households are separating what God has joined together in the order of creation.

> The option to issue a certificate of divorce is a concession made because of human hardness of heart.

This manner of biblical interpretation will strike some modern readers as strange. Jesus quotes from passages contained within two different creation stories. In the first, found in Genesis 1:1—2:4a, man and woman are created together. In the second, found in Genesis 2:4b-25, the first woman is created from the rib of the first man. In this second creation story, the fact that woman is created from man provides the rationale for the man's leaving his father and mother and being joined to his wife. Jesus has provided a different rationale, however, one drawn from the first creation story: the very fact that God created humankind male and female. By the standards of modern biblical interpretation, one might say that Jesus has taken these passages out of context. Neither Jesus nor the author of Mark, however, was a modern biblical interpreter. To ask either to interpret Scripture by the standards of the Western intellectual tradition is unreasonable.

Once in the house, the disciples ask Jesus privately about this teaching (see also 4:10, 7:17, 9:28, 13:3). They are probably perplexed given the unconventional nature of his teaching. Jesus' response to them, however, actually treats a different topic. In his debate with the Pharisees, Jesus discussed whether or not divorce was in keeping with God's will for humankind. In verses 11-12, however, Jesus discusses the issue of remarriage after divorce. He describes adultery here in an unusual way. Adultery occurred when a married woman had sex with a man who was not her husband. Jesus, however, expands the definition of adultery: just as a wife can commit adultery against her husband, a husband can commit adultery against his wife.

In the next passage (10:13-16), Jesus maintains his unconventional posture. Ancient Mediterranean men did not have much interaction with little children. (The Greek word for child used here, *paidion*, is diminutive in form—hence the description of these children as "little.") According to Aristotle, men regarded children and animals with contempt.[7] Ancient Mediterranean men were deeply concerned with public honor, status, and reputation. Children—and especially those of other people—could offer no help in this regard. One did not rise in status or enhance one's reputation by associating with children. The disciples' reaction is therefore understandable. Yet Jesus has already taught the disciples once about children: "Then he took a little child and put it among them; and taking it is his arms he said to them, 'Whoever welcomes one such child in my name welcomes me, and whoever welcomes me welcomes not me but the one who sent me'" (9:36-37).

Jesus' teaching is thus deeply countercultural. He welcomes these people who, by conventional standards, do not matter very much. Not only does the kingdom of God belong to these children, but "whoever does not receive the kingdom of God as a little child will never enter it" (10:15). Therefore, those who wish to follow Jesus must give up their conventional pretensions to greatness. It is not the people who have grand reputations, high status, and honor who find favor in God's sight. God does not judge people according to common human values. The people who "don't matter" may come to Jesus, and they should be able to come to his followers, as well.

> Jesus expands the definition of adultery: just as a wife can commit adultery against her husband, a husband can commit adultery against his wife.

Notes

1. Christina De Groot, "Genesis," in *The IVP Women's Bible Commentary*, ed. Catherine Clark Kroeger and Mary J. Evans (Downers Grove, Ill.: IVP, 2002), 6.

2. Ibid.

3. Robert G. Bratcher and William D. Reyburn, *A Translator's Handbook on the Book of Psalms* (New York: United Bible Societies, 1991), 82.

4. Richard. J. Clifford, *Psalms 1–72* (Nashville: Abingdon, 2002), 70.

5. See John J. Collins, "Marriage, Divorce, and Family in Second Temple Judaism," chap. 3 in Leo G. Perdue, et al., *Families in Ancient Israel* (Louisville: Westminster John Knox, 1997), 115.

6. See Adela Yarbro Collins, *Mark: A Commentary,* Hermeneia (Minneapolis: Fortress Press, 2007), 459–64.

7. See Aristotle, *Rhetoric* 1.11.16, trans. John Henry Freese, Loeb Classical Library (Cambridge: Harvard University Press, 1959).

NINETEENTH SUNDAY AFTER PENTECOST

TWENTY-EIGHTH SUNDAY IN ORDINARY TIME / PROPER 23
OCTOBER 11, 2009

Revised Common (RCL)	Episcopal (BCP)	Roman Catholic (LFM)
Amos 5:6-7, 10-15 or Job 23:1-9, 16-17	Amos 5:6-7, 10-15	Wisd. of Sol. 7:7-11
Ps. 90:12-17 or 22:1-15	Psalm 90 or 90:1-8, 12	Ps. 90:12-13, 14-15, 16-17
Heb. 4:12-16	Heb. 3:1-6	Heb. 4:12-13
Mark 10:17-31	Mark 10:17-27 (28-31)	Mark 10:17-30 or 10:17-27

FIRST READING

AMOS 5:6-7, 10-15 (RCL, BCP)

These passages from Amos occur within the context of a funeral song. The song is for "maiden Israel," and it is a prophecy of what will occur if she continues to turn away from God. The very life of Israel is contingent upon her seeking God's will (v. 6), which in these passages has to do with the treatment of the poor. In the mid-eighth century B.C.E., prior to the Assyrian exile, a wealthy elite in Israel and Judah acquired land and property that was formerly distributed among families and passed on through inheritance. Some people became much wealthier while others lost their land. The loss of family land was quite serious in this agrarian economy and was regulated in the Torah (see Leviticus 25). The situation Amos describes is one in which the prosperity of the few comes at the expense of the many. The wealthy have the resources to "trample on the poor" and they do so. God, however, will not abide this state of affairs.

Amos's prophecy is perhaps even more relevant today than in the time in which it was first uttered. As the number of people who worship the God of Israel has increased, so has our responsibility to care for those who lack vital resources to maintain a reasonable standard of living. The Western church is in a position to make a tremendous difference in the lives of the poor, both at home and abroad. Amos's prophecy is a reminder that complacency in the face of need is a grave sin.

The philosophy that "people get what they deserve" has been around for a long time. Job's "friend" Eliphaz has just accused him of considerable wrongdoing, mainly in the form of oppression of the poor. Eliphaz is stuck in a kind of thinking that the book of Job rejects, one that holds that suffering is necessarily the result of sin. Job, however, knows that Eliphaz is wrong. "I have kept his way and have not turned aside," he says. "I have not departed from the commandment of his lips" (23:11-12; see also 1:1, 8).

Job wishes to make his case before God, confident that God will acquit him of any wrongdoing. He even makes the audacious claim that he would come to God's own dwelling if he could, laying his case before God. Yet he does not know how to gain an audience. "If I go forward, he is not there; or backward, I cannot perceive him; on the left he hides, and I cannot behold him; I turn to the right, but I cannot see him" (vv. 8-9).

Job mournfully expresses what so many people feel in times of distress: a deep feeling of God's absence.

> Job makes the audacious claim that he would come to God's own dwelling if he could, laying his case before God. Yet he does not know how to gain an audience.

He wishes only to plead his innocence, to prove that he has done no wrong. He is met, however, with silence, and his desire to make his case before God collapses into despair. "If only I could vanish in darkness, and thick darkness would cover my face!" (v. 17). Many people in church each week have similar questions: Where is God? Why aren't my prayers answered? What have I done wrong? The time to help people deal with suffering is not only after tragedy has struck, but in the process of Christian formation that takes place each week through preaching, teaching, and liturgy.

WISDOM OF SOLOMON 7:7-11 (LFM)

This passage gives a first-person voice to the story of Solomon's prayer for wisdom and God's response (1 Kgs. 3:6-15). Solomon says that he preferred wisdom to all kinds of material blessings (Wisd. 7:8-10; see 1 Kgs. 3:11). Even though Solomon did not ask for these material blessings, however, he received "all good things," including "uncounted wealth" (Wisd. 7:11; see 1 Kgs. 3:13). Wisdom is more precious than other blessings for which people pray, but she can lead to many other blessings. For the preacher, this text affords the opportunity to talk about the good life that comes from prayerfully receiving God's wisdom, even if Christians think of the good life in terms other than material wealth.

RESPONSIVE READING

PSALM 90:12-17 (RCL)
PSALM 90 OR 90:1-8, 12 (BCP)
PSALM 90:12-13, 14-15, 16-17 (LFM)

Psalm 90 begins and ends by acknowledging God as a refuge in times of distress (vv. 1, 13-17). The verses between this beginning and end contrast God's greatness, eternity, and power with the frailty and ephemeral nature of human beings. Time is of no concern for God. Human beings, on the other hand, live lives of toil that in the large scope of time last for the blink of an eye. They are powerless before God's wrath and learn wisdom by becoming aware of their frailty and mortality.

Verses 13-17 express utter dependence upon God. Humans may be weak and mortal, but God's favor can bring blessing. The context is some type of distress: "Make us glad as many days as you have afflicted us, and as many years as we have seen evil" (v. 15). The psalmist does not entrust the future of Israel to human ingenuity, but to God's favor. In our culture of independence and rugged individualism, the psalm provides a reminder of our dependence upon God's good gifts.

PSALM 22:1-15 (RCL ALT.)

The first fifteen verses of this psalm of David alternate between complaint and statements of trust. In verses 1-2, the psalmist laments God's apparent absence with words that will be familiar to most congregants because of Jesus' cry from the cross (see Matt. 27:46, Mark 15:34). In verses 3-4, God's covenant relationship with Israel shows God's faithfulness. Verses 6-8 further develop the psalmist's complaint—he is an object of scorn, mocked by others who sarcastically refer to him as the one in whom the Lord delights. The psalmist then returns in verses 9-11 to statements of faith, now coupled with the petition, "Do not be far from me." Since God was with him at the moment of his birth, he asks that God will likewise be with him in this moment of need. With verses 12-15, the psalmist continues his list of grievances. He likens his enemies to strong bulls of Bashan (known for its hearty livestock) and lions. In verses 14-15, he seems to collapse into despair.

> The structure of the psalm takes the reader from one emotion to the next in a pattern that bespeaks total reliance on God in the midst of severe hardship.

This psalm brings together a variety of emotions: shame, sadness, loneliness, awe, hope, and faith. The structure of the psalm takes the reader from one emotion to the next in a pattern that bespeaks total reliance on God in the midst of severe hardship. Though the lectionary reading ends on a note of despair, the psalm taken as a whole ends with joy and hope. This ending makes quite a difference for the psalm's overall message.

SECOND READING
HEBREWS 4:12-16 (RCL)
HEBREWS 4:12-13 (LFM)

In 2:3 Hebrews asks, "How can we escape if we neglect so great a salvation?" Here is the same sentiment expressed in different terms. The word of God is "able to judge the thoughts and intentions of the heart" (4:12). Nothing can be hidden from God's judging word, which, like a sharp, two-edged sword, penetrates the deepest recesses of our very being.[1] God knows not only our actions, but our thoughts and intentions. Human beings have the opportunity to enter the "rest" that God has promised, but only if God, who sees all and knows all, judges them favorably (4:1).

Even though no one can escape God's judgment, believers have a great high priest, Jesus, who has made atonement on their behalf (vv. 14-16). By holding fast to their confession of faith, believers avail themselves of the salvation that is made available to them by the sacrifice of their high priest. Jesus the high priest is merciful; though he did not sin, he can sympathize with human weakness because he himself has been tested just as every human is. His throne is one of grace—of gifts freely bestowed to those who will accept them.

> Jesus the high priest is merciful; though he did not sin, he can sympathize with human weakness because he himself has been tested just as every human is.

Christians have wrestled with the issue of atonement since the earliest days of the faith. Many Christians today find atonement doctrines confusing. Yet, to paraphrase C. S. Lewis, we can understand what Christ has done without understanding exactly how he has done it.[2] God has poured out self-giving love through Christ and offers us eternal salvation through the events of the incarnation, crucifixion, and resurrection. Many people today carry guilt and fear, or feel that their lives really do not matter. The Christian narrative of salvation, however, tells them that they do.

HEBREWS 3:1-6 (BCP)

This passage from Hebrews reiterates a theme to which much of the first two chapters are dedicated: the message of the gospel supersedes the message of the Torah. Hebrews traces the message of the gospel back to the proclamation of Jesus (1:1-2, 2:3), who in this passage is called both "apostle" and "high priest." Nowhere else in the New Testament is Jesus called an "apostle," a term that probably refers to his role as the one who first proclaimed the Christian gospel. Jesus' role as "high priest of our confession" is crucial for the larger argument of Hebrews. The Jesus of Hebrews is both priest and sacrifice, but he is not like the mortal priests of Israel, nor is he like the sacrifices that they offer again and again. He is a priest who offers himself as a sacrifice in a once-and-for-all atoning act, never to be repeated. Jewish followers of Jesus who continue to practice rituals associated with sacrifice in the Jerusalem Temple are denying the efficacy of Christ's atoning work, and therefore rejecting what Christ has done. Those who truly believe the community's confession of faith in Christ, which surely included something about his atoning work, will be saved because they have faith. The old way is the way of Moses, a servant. The new way is the way of Jesus, a son.

Though there is rich theological material in Hebrews, it is a work that must be handled with care. Theologies according to which Christianity has utterly superseded Judaism have had devastating consequences. The pastor who preaches from Hebrews should keep in mind that it expresses one of many views in the New Testament toward God's covenant relationship with Israel.

THE GOSPEL
MARK 10:17–31 (RCL)
MARK 10:17–27 (BCP)
MARK 10:17–30 OR 10:17–27 (LFM)

In the ancient Mediterranean world, a public compliment or some other sort of praise increased the reputation, and therefore the honor, of the recipient. The cultural expectation was that an honorable person would offer some favor in return for this increase in reputation. In other words, to receive public praise was to become obligated to the person who offered the praise. An accolade is thus a kind of challenge to the recipient: return the favor, or show yourself to be dishonorable.

> Jesus' role in this passage is to hold this man accountable for his actions, rather than to exchange slaps on the back with him.

There was, however, one other course that an individual could take: to reject the accolade, thereby rejecting the obligation that came with it. This is the option that Jesus chooses. He rebuffs the compliment, and therefore the obligation. For Jesus to become obligated to this man could compromise his ability to call him to true righteousness. Jesus' role in this passage is to hold this man accountable for his actions, rather than to exchange slaps on the back with him.

This passage is working with two concepts related to wealth. The first can be described in terms of "limited good."[3] Ancient Mediterranean people believed that, with any given commodity, there was only so much to go around. If one person had more, other people had less. To a significant extent, this perception was probably accurate. In this preindustrial economy, the production of goods was slower and more labor intensive. One did not simply run out to the supermarket to pick up milk, bottled water, and fresh produce. Most goods—including food, potable water, farmable land, and textiles—were in limited supply. Those who enjoyed an abundance of such resources did so at the expense of other people.

In light of this "limited good" approach to resources, Jesus' treatment of the rich man becomes clearer. The commandments that Jesus mentions all have to do with the treatment of one's neighbor: "You shall not murder; You shall not commit adultery; You shall not steal; You shall not bear false witness; You shall not defraud; Honor your father and mother" (Mark 10:19; the commandment not to defraud is not one of the Ten Commandments, but is perhaps a reference to passages in the Torah such as Deut. 24:14-15). Commendably, the man has kept the commandments since his youth. Yet Jesus holds him to an even higher standard: the rich man must make amends for the ways in which he has contributed to the deprivation of others. He must sell his possessions and give the proceeds to the poor. The rich man reacts to Jesus' teaching with shock and grief.

> Jesus holds the rich man to an even higher standard: he must make amends for the ways in which he has contributed to the deprivation of others.

Jesus then uses the occasion as a "teachable moment." He says to his disciples that it is easier for a camel to go through the eye of a needle than for a rich man to enter the kingdom of heaven. Interpreters of this passage have attempted various exegetical gymnastics to keep it from saying what it clearly says. One common explanation is that "the needle" was a gate in Jerusalem, through which camels had to bend down to enter the city. On this reading, for a rich man to enter the kingdom of heaven is somewhat inconvenient. Clearly this is not what Jesus means. Rather, he means that the rich cannot enter the kingdom of heaven because their lifestyle involves the exploitation and deprivation of the poor. In the kingdom of God, the least and the last are exalted, not deprived.

Though we live in a different economy and culture than the first followers of Jesus, it is still the case that overconsumption by some contributes to the deprivation of others. In preaching from this text, the pastor may take the opportunity to speak to issues of consumerism, the care of the poor, and responsible living. Though some congregants may bristle at sermons that touch on their finances, the proper use of money is a common topic in the New Testament and a key component of faithful discipleship.

Unlike Jesus, who calls attention to the exploitative aspects of wealth, the disciples seem to think that material blessings are the fruits of righteousness. According to this perspective, both the rich and the poor deserve their respective lots. When the disciples ask, "Then who can be saved?" (v. 26), they are basically asking, "Who will God save, if not these people whose righteousness is so evident by God's material blessing of them?" Jesus responds that it is impossible for mortals to achieve their own salvation. He has just taught in 10:15 that the kingdom is something that one receives, not something that one creates by one's own actions. One must receive the kingdom, moreover, as a child—as one without status, power, and honor.

To enter into God's kingdom may mean the loss of everything that Jesus' followers thought important before. As Peter says, the disciples have left everything to follow Jesus (v. 28). Presumably this includes family, property, and possessions. Though it would be painful for many modern Westerners to break ties with family, we today are much more individualistic than ancient Mediterranean people were. Ancient people were highly group oriented, and the group that mattered most was one's family. The breaking of family ties would have been exceedingly difficult.

Jesus, however, offers a new kind of family, the family of faith (see also 3:31-34). Put in more technical terms, Jesus establishes what is sometimes called a "fictive kin-group."[4] Basically, this is a group that takes over the functions of the family. This is where one finds loyalty, trust, honor, protection, shared goods, and other characteristics of relationships between blood relatives. Jesus acknowledges that his followers may have to leave "house or brothers or sisters or mother or father or children or fields" for his sake and for the sake of the good news (v. 29).

> In the here and now, followers of Jesus will receive a fictive family many times larger than the natural families that they have left behind.

Yet they will receive in return "a hundredfold now in this age—houses, brothers and sisters, mothers and children, and fields with persecutions—and in the age to come eternal life" (v. 30). In the here and now, followers of Jesus will receive a fictive family many times larger than the natural families that they have left behind. Note the absence of the mention of fathers in verse 30. In this new family there is one true Father, God. Moreover, followers of Jesus will receive fields and houses that are shared among the family of faith, and in the age to come they will receive eternal life.

"Many who are first will be last," Jesus says, "and the last will be first" (v. 31). To be a Christian was to join a group of people who were held in low regard. In the abundance-sharing of Jesus' new family, there will nonetheless be persecutions (v. 30). Yet those who have lost everything for Christ, who have given up the common ambitions for reputation, widespread honor, and possessions, will receive a hundredfold what they have lost. Those who are "last" by the standards of outsiders will be "first" in God's kingdom.

Notes

1. See Harold W. Attridge, *Hebrews,* Hermeneia (Philadelphia: Fortress Press, 1989), 133–34.

2. See C. S. Lewis, *Mere Christianity* (New York: MacMillan, 1952), 58.

3. For a fuller explanation, see Jerome H. Neyrey, "Limited Good," in *Handbook of Biblical Social Values*, ed. John J. Pilch and Bruce J. Malina (Peabody, Mass.: Hendrickson, 1998).

4. See Bruce J. Malina, *The New Testament World: Insights from Cultural Anthropology*, 3rd ed. (Lousiville: Westminster John Knox, 2001), 214–17.

TWENTIETH SUNDAY AFTER PENTECOST

Twenty-Ninth Sunday in Ordinary Time / Proper 24
October 18, 2009

Revised Common (RCL)	Episcopal (BCP)	Roman Catholic (LFM)
Isa. 53:4-12 or Job 38:1-7 (34-41)	Isa. 53:4-12	Isa. 53:10-11
Ps. 91:9-16 or 104:1-9, 24, 35c	Psalm 91 or 91:9-16	Ps. 33:4-5, 18-19, 20-22
Heb. 5:1-10	Heb. 4:12-16	Heb. 4:14-16
Mark 10:35-45	Mark 10:35-45	Mark 10:35-45 or 10:42-45

FIRST READING

ISAIAH 53:4-12 (RCL, BCP)
ISAIAH 53:10-11 (LFM)

In this fourth and final "Servant Song" (52:13—53:12), Isaiah describes a servant who suffers vicariously on behalf of others. One often finds in the Old Testament the idea that sinners bring upon themselves their own suffering, yet in this passage the servant suffers because of the sins of other people. In fact, his life is made "an offering for sin," a strange concept since the Torah prescribes the sacrifices of animals as sin offerings (see Leviticus 4–5, 16). The text affirms repeatedly in 53:10-12 that the servant's suffering and death will remove the guilt of sins that others have committed. Yet, somehow, even though "he was cut off from the land of the living, stricken for the transgression of my people" (53:8), the servant will prosper because of his sacrifice. He will "see his offspring" and "prolong his days" (53:10). It is not just the servant who will prosper, moreover, but the will of God. This concept of exaltation because of willing suffering for others has probably influenced New Testament texts such as Philippians 3:5-11 and Hebrews 1:3-4, 2:9.

If the language in this oracle seems vague, it is because this is poetic language and its purpose is not to offer a coherent proposal on vicarious suffering. The more specific we try to get in articulating the theological concepts embedded in this passage, the more the text resists our efforts. There is much that is uncertain about this oracle. As one scholar has commented, the prophet "speaks in riddles and mysteries."[1]

Among these mysteries is the identity of the servant. This has long been a topic of debate. Some scholars have suggested that the servant is Israel, suffering in exile. Another option is that the servant is the prophet whom we today call Deutero-Isaiah.[2] Christian interpreters have long seen prophecies of Christ in this passage. In fact, it is quite possible that Jesus understood himself in the terms described in this Servant Song. Jesus may have seen himself as Israel's representative, a kind of embodiment of the people. Something like this may also be at work in Jesus' use of the

term "Son of Man," a self-referential term for Jesus in the Gospels, but a term for God's holy people in Daniel 7. Regardless of whether we think that this passage from Isaiah is a prophecy about Christ or we see Christ as embodying the description of the servant in the prophecy, we are confronted with the centrality to our faith of service, even to the point of suffering, on behalf of others.

JOB 38:1-7 (34-41) (RCL alt.)

In chapters 29–31, Job makes his final defense. It is as if he says, "I don't deserve this! God has dealt unfairly with me!" Job has been righteous. He has followed God's commands, and yet he is stricken. He loses his property, his children, and his health. His reputation as an honorable and righteous man has been destroyed, and now he is the object of mockery (see 29:1—30:15). In 30:24-26 he cries, "Surely one does not turn against the needy, when in disaster they cry for help. Did I not weep for those whose day was hard? Was not my soul grieved for the poor? But when I looked for good, evil came; and when I waited for light, darkness came." In other words, Job has cared for those in need, but God has not.

Beginning with 38:1, Job finally gets what he has wished for: an audience before God. Yet Job never makes his case because God shows him the weakness of human power and the limitations of human understanding. God is the creator of all things, the source of all life. The wisdom and knowledge and power of God are utterly beyond human understanding. Job, God says, speaks "words without knowledge" (38:2). The point of the speech is summed up in 40:2: "Shall a faultfinder contend with the Almighty?" Though the book of Job rejects some explanations of suffering—for instance, that suffering is necessarily tied to unrighteousness—it never provides a rationale for suffering that would justify God's actions. In fact, it says, God's ways are inscrutable. They are simply beyond our comprehension.

Many modern readers will struggle with the book of Job. People will inevitably ask questions about suffering and God's will, if not out loud, then silently. Job reminds us that, in asking questions about the mind of God, we must recognize that the human intellect is finite. Our vision is limited. That can be a difficult pill to swallow. Yet cognizance of our finitude is a component of understanding the divine-human relationship. Job reminds us in no uncertain terms that we are not God. We do not have to be satisfied with the limitations of our reasoning, but they are there nonetheless.

RESPONSIVE READING
PSALM 91:9-16 (RCL, BCP ALT.)
PSALM 91 (BCP)

The psalmist describes God as a refuge for those who live in covenant relationship with God. Most of this psalm is a statement of faith, meant to exhort others to faithfulness as well. In verses 14-16, however, God responds in an oracle of covenant faithfulness. To those who have faith, God will give deliverance, honor, long life, and salvation. In the ancient world of the psalmist, there were many gods, but for Israel there is only one, named by the psalmist in verse 2: Yahweh (NRSV: LORD). Those who know God's name will receive divine protection. God will answer them when they call.

> Job reminds us that, in asking questions about the mind of God, we must recognize that the human intellect is finite.

PSALM 33:4-5, 18-19, 20-22 (LFM)

"The whole earth," says the psalmist, "is full of the steadfast love of the LORD" (v. 5). The word translated "steadfast love" is *ḥesed*. This word is difficult to render in English, though we might also translate it as "covenant faithfulness." Two qualities of *ḥesed* are righteousness and justice (v. 5), which are simply basic elements of creation.[3] God's faithfulness, love, righteousness, and justice are woven within the very fabric of the universe. God watches those who place their hope in God's *ḥesed* and delivers them from death (vv. 18-19). The faithful wait in trust and call upon God to be with them in the steadfast love, faithfulness, righteousness, and justice that are the basis of their hope.

HEBREWS 5:1-10 (RCL)

Melchizedek only shows up twice in the entire Old Testament. His first appearance is in Genesis 14:18-20. In this passage, he blesses Abram and is described as a priest of El Elyon (NRSV: "God Most High"), a Canaanite deity. His second appearance is in Psalm 110:4: "The LORD has sworn and will not change his mind, 'You are a priest forever according to the order of Melchizedek.'" These two passages are crucial for the argument of the letter to the Hebrews. The author attempts to show that Jesus has made a sacrifice of himself that will atone for sin forever and needs never to be repeated. Yet in making this claim the author has to get past a few theological hurdles. To begin with, the Jewish priests, who offered sacrifice, were required to be from the tribe of Levi, and early Christian tradition held that Jesus was of the tribe of Judah, descended from David. How then, can Jesus offer sacrifice, since he is not a levitical priest? Further, Hebrews wishes to show that the "old covenant," expressed in the statues of the Torah, is "obsolete," "growing old," and "soon to disappear" (8:13). If Jesus offers sacrifices of atonement in the matter mandated in the Torah, then he is maintaining the old covenant, not superseding it.

Psalm 110:4, reinforced by the episode recounted in Genesis 14:18-20, provides the solution to these problems. Jesus is a different kind of priest, one authorized by God, but not a levitical priest. Rather, he is a priest according to the order of Melchizedek. Since the Old Testament is silent on the duties and roles of a priest according to the order of Melchizedek, Hebrews fills out the picture of such a priest with a particular version of early Christian atonement theology.

Understanding the role of the priestly order of Melchizedek in Hebrews is crucial for understanding the message of this work, but it might not make for the most inspiring sermon material. Fortunately, there is other material in here that relates much more directly to the person sitting in the pew. This passage is about Jesus' sufferings, his prayers and supplications to God, and his submission to God's will. Jesus suffered, just as we suffer. Jesus was called by God to do things that he did not want to do, just as we often are. Moreover, Jesus became "perfect" by his submission and obedience to God. "Perfect" here has the sense of "complete": Jesus became what God called him to be, fulfilling the task God called him to fulfill. In the same way, Christians can become the people God has called us to be by submission and obedience to God's will. That may not always be easy, but it is the path to perfection.

> This passage is about Jesus' sufferings, his prayers and supplications to God, and his submission to God's will.

HEBREWS 4:12-16 (BCP)
HEBREWS 4:14-16 (LFM)

Human weakness, humility, and suffering for the sake of others are major themes in the lectionary readings for this week. These themes are important for the Christology of Hebrews. In 2:9, Hebrews tells us that Christ "for a little while was made lower than the angels," meaning that he became human. Because of this, he was tested (or tempted), and though he did not sin, he knows what it is like to feel the allure of sin. Christ knows us. He knows what it is like to be one of us, and has made sacrifice on our behalf so that, despite the fact that we have sinned, we can experience salvation. The incarnation and Christ's self-sacrifice are testimonies of God's redeeming love and desire for us to come into proper relationship with God. (See also commentary on Proper 23, Nineteenth Sunday after Pentecost, second reading [RCL, LFM], below.)

THE GOSPEL
MARK 10:35-45 (RCL, BCP, LFM)
MARK 10:42-45 (LFM ALT.)

A good preacher knows that repetition drives a point home. Mark knew this as well. This is a story that, like a sermon, was meant to be heard, rather than read, and important points had to be repeated or were likely to be missed. The blindness of the disciples to Jesus' teaching is clearly an important point for the evangelist. In chapters 8–10, the failures of the disciples, though at times apparent earlier in the narrative (for example, 4:40, 6:52), become more common and therefore more pronounced. After the first two passion predictions (8:31, 9:30-31), the disciples fail to respond appropriately. Following the first, Peter "rebukes" Jesus (8:32). After the second, the disciples squabble over which of them is the greatest (9:34). Now, after the third and final passion prediction of 10:33-34, the disciples show once again that they do not understand Jesus' teaching. Jesus has taught that his followers must take up the cross (8:34). If any are ashamed of this crucified Jesus, he will be ashamed of them (8:38).

> The way to be with Jesus in glory is the way of the cross. Exaltation in the new age is left to the plans of God.

They must give up their worldly ambitions for status, honor, and privilege (for example, 9:35). He has told them that they must receive the kingdom as children if they wish to enter it at all (10:15). And yet here are the sons of Zebedee, asking Jesus to grant that they may sit one at his right hand, one at his left, in his glory. They still fail to grasp that the essence of discipleship is not personal glorification, but servanthood.

243

TWENTIETH
SUNDAY AFTER
PENTECOST
────────────
OCTOBER 18

Instead of simply denying their request or scolding them, however, Jesus turns the discussion toward the true cost of being his follower. He asks if they are prepared to drink the cup from which he drinks, or to be baptized with his baptism. They say that they are, but, as Jesus tells them, they do not know what they are asking. The "cup" and "baptism" to which Jesus refers are ways of talking about his passion and death. Jesus has already told his followers that they must take up the cross (8:34). He makes the point again here. The way to be with Jesus in glory is the way of the cross. In fact, Mark makes a point of saying that two bandits were crucified with Jesus, "one on his right and one on his left" (15:27). Exaltation in the new age is left to the plans of God.

Though James and John lead the way, the other disciples soon follow suit. They are angry because James and John have tried to exalt themselves above the other ten. Once again, Jesus attempts to correct their misunderstanding. He uses the example of those whom the Gentiles recognize as their rulers. These rulers "lord it over" their followers, and their "great ones" are "tyrants" over them. Among Jesus' followers, however, this is not to be, for "whoever wishes to become great among you must be your servant, and whoever wishes to be first among you must be slave of all" (vv. 43-44). This passage echoes the teaching of 9:35: "Whoever wants to be first must be last of all and servant of all." Terms like "great" (*megas*) and "first" (*prōtos*) were used by the ancients to describe people widely considered important in their society, such as royalty, leading citizens, heroes, and priests. On the other hand, words like "servant" (*diakonos*), "slave" (*doulos*), and "last" (*eschatos*) were used for the people who performed menial tasks, were under the authority of others, and were low in status. Jesus is asking his followers to turn their common cultural assumptions regarding greatness and prestige upside down. In God's kingdom, the people who serve, put others first, and demonstrate the kind of self-denying love that Christ showed are the truly great ones.

> In God's kingdom, the people who serve, put others first, and demonstrate the kind of self-denying love that Christ showed are the truly great ones.

What makes this hard is that the world will not recognize such people as great. There is a vast difference between life as a follower of Jesus and life apart from Jesus.

Jesus calls his followers to a difficult task. Yet he himself is the true exemplar of the ethos that he teaches. The NRSV omits a small but important word from its translation of verse 45: *kai*, which here is best translated as "even." If this word is included, the text reads, "For *even* the Son of Man came not to be served but to serve, and to give his life a ransom for many." Even one so great as Jesus, who could rightly claim all glory and honor, has come to serve others—at the expense of his own life no less. Jesus' use of the term "Son of Man" in this passage is an allusion to Daniel 7:13-14, where the Son of Man is given "dominion and glory and kingship," but must suffer before his exaltation. The reference to Jesus' life as a "ransom for many" may be an allusion to the servant of Isaiah 52:13—53:12, whose life is described as "an offering for sin" (Isa. 53:10). Mark uses these scriptural allusions to underscore Jesus' role as one who could claim all the markers of privilege for which humans strive, but instead chooses to take on the role of a servant, subjecting himself even to the degradation of the cross.

It is a difficult but important part of preaching to help parishioners to question their long-held assumptions about what is important, what they should strive for and value. The kind of self-giving service exemplified in Jesus' ministry simply does not come naturally to most of us. Whether in the ancient world or the modern one, people commonly have an interest in serving themselves first. The way of Christian discipleship calls for a new set of values, one contrary to the philosophy of "looking out for number one." After all, even the Son of Man came not to be served, but to serve.

Notes

1. See Joseph Blenkinsopp, *Isaiah 40–55: A New Translation with Introduction and Commentary* (New York: Doubleday, 2002), 355.

2. Ibid., 356.

3. See Konrad Schaefer, *Psalms* (Collegeville, Minn.: Liturgical, 2001), 82.

TWENTY-FIRST SUNDAY AFTER PENTECOST

THIRTIETH SUNDAY IN ORDINARY TIME / PROPER 25

OCTOBER 25, 2009

Revised Common (RCL)	Episcopal (BCP)	Roman Catholic (LFM)
Jer. 31:7-9 or Job 42:1-6, 10-17	Isa. 59:(1-4) 9-19	Jer. 31:7-9
Psalm 126 or 34:1-8 (19-22)	Psalm 13	Ps. 126:1-2a, 2b-3, 4-5, 6
Heb. 7:23-28	Heb. 5:12—6:1, 9-12	Heb. 5:1-6
Mark 10:46-52	Mark 10:46-52	Mark 10:46-52

FIRST READING

JEREMIAH 31:7-9 (RCL, LFM)

The Babylonian exile lasted for fifty years and had a lasting impact upon Israelite life, including religion. The people of Israel saw their homeland as a gift from God that demonstrated God's covenant loyalty to them. The loss of that land and the destruction of the Temple in Jerusalem in 587 B.C.E. were devastating. The prospect of returning to Israel, though it turned out to be a long and difficult process, was cause for rejoicing, not least because it reaffirmed God's covenant faithfulness.

Jeremiah 31:7-9 relates a prophecy of the return of a remnant to Israel. This return will be God's doing: "See, I am going to bring them back from the north . . . . With weeping they shall come, and with consolations I will lead them back" (31:8a, 9a). Hence, even people for whom this arduous journey would be most difficult—the blind, the lame, pregnant women, and women in labor—will return. It is noteworthy that there is no mention here of rulers. In earlier prophecies in Jeremiah, God calls to account the house of David (21:11-14) and the sons of Josiah (22:11-30). Israel's kings are called "shepherds who destroy and scatter the sheep of my pasture" (23:1). It is not through the might of kings, but through the hand of God, that Israel will be saved.

God, the oracle says, has become a father to Israel. Though the language of God as Father is common in the Christian tradition, it is rather uncommon in the Old Testament. By saying, "I have become a father to Israel, and Ephraim is

245

my firstborn" (v. 9), the prophecy depicts God as one who is to be honored and obeyed by Israel, and Israel (Ephraim) as the special recipient of God's favor. God will not abide unrighteousness and neglect of the covenant, but human wickedness cannot nullify God's covenantal love and faithfulness.

JOB 42:1-6, 10-17 (RCL ALT.)

Job has just gotten a good dressing-down. God has contrasted the power, wisdom, and knowledge of the Almighty with the frailty and limitations of human understanding. Job recognizes that he cannot respond to God, and so he recants. He admits that he spoke of things that he did not understand (42:3). The NRSV translates the beginning of verse 6 as "therefore I despise myself," but Job is not talking here about self-loathing. The verb translated as "despise" literally means "melt away" or "sink down."[1] The New Jerusalem Bible provides a better translation: "I retract what I have said."

In 42:1-6, Job responds to God with humility and submission. Yet it is hard to find any note of satisfaction in his response. Interestingly, in 2 Esdras, a later Jewish work that was edited and supplemented by Christians, Ezra complains to God about Israel's suffering, and he receives an answer similar to the one Job receives. Yet unlike Job, who is humbled by God's words, Ezra falls on his face and responds, "It would have been better for us not to be here than to come here and live in ungodliness, and to suffer and not understand why" (2 Esd. 4:12). The book of Job teaches us about the limits of our understanding, but cognizance of our intellectual limitations does not often cause our pain to go away.

> The book of Job teaches us about the limits of our understanding, but cognizance of our intellectual limitations does not often cause our pain to go away.

In the end, God provides Job with twice his original fortune. His family returns to him, though one wonders where they were when he was in need. Regardless, Job forgives their abandonment of him and provides a feast for them in his own home. Job receives twice the livestock that he owned before, and he has seven sons and three daughters, the same number that he had before tragedy befell him. The story concludes with an ending that might well read, "And they all lived happily ever after." Yet the darkness that Job experienced remains in the background. Job is compensated for his losses, but is it the case that "all's well that ends well"? The God of Job is mysterious, utterly beyond our comprehension, and may bring good or ill on humankind—even upon the very righteous—for reasons that we do not understand. God is all-powerful, and we humans are frail, and both blessing and tragedy are parts of life.

Sin creates a gulf between God and humankind. This, says Isaiah, is what has happened to Israel. Yes, God's hand can save them, and God can hear them. God is not the problem. Rather, "your iniquities have been barriers between you and God" (v. 2). Israel wishes to experience God's salvation, to know God's justice, but, as the prophet says, "Justice is turned back, and righteousness stands at a distance" (v. 14). The unrighteous have lost their spiritual sight (v. 10). They grope and stumble, unable to perceive the path that will lead to the fullness of God's salvation. Even those who attempt to turn from evil cannot do so because of the pervasive wickedness around them (v. 15).

The second half of verse 15 begins a new oracle with a difference topic—God's vindication of Israel. There was no human savior to intervene on Israel's behalf, "so his own arm brought him victory" (v. 16). Here God is a warrior who rushes forth against Israel's enemies like a pent-up stream that has been undammed. Those who oppress Israel are God's enemies, and with fury and vengeance God will repay their deeds in kind.

> Whether Israel or Israel's oppressors are the culprit, God calls to account those who have no concern for righteousness.

Many Christians, especially in mainline Protestant circles, do not like to speak of God as seeking retribution or vengeance, or acting in fury. Yet these oracles show that unrighteousness—here described as human violence (vv. 3, 13), unjust use of the law courts (v. 4), lying (vv. 4, 13), and oppression (v. 13)—is an affront to God. This is not an "anything goes" God who has no concern that people act justly. Whether Israel or Israel's oppressors are the culprit, God calls to account those who have no concern for righteousness.

RESPONSIVE READING

PSALM 126 (RCL)
PSALM 126:1-2A, 2B-3, 4-5, 6 (LFM)

Each psalm from 120 to 134 is labeled a "Song of Ascents." Exactly what this term means is unclear, but most scholars understand it to refer to the ascent up to Mount Zion. If this is the meaning of the term, these songs were sung by pilgrims on their way to Jerusalem.[2]

The psalmist looks to a time when God restored Israel after tragedy. Not only within Israel, but among the other nations as well, it was said that Israel's God had done great things for her. Israel is honored among the nations because of God's providential care. God's blessings were like a dream, seemingly too good to be true, but true nonetheless.

Verses 4-6 form a petition for God to restore Israel once again. The circumstances of the current crisis are not clear. What is clear, however, is that God's care for Israel in the past offers hope that God will care for this people in the present crisis. Like the wadis of the Negeb Desert, which are dry most of the year but become fertile and green with flash floods, so God's providential care can turn Israel's suffering into cause for rejoicing.[3] The God who restored Israel and made her honored among the nations can turn tears into shouts of joy.

PSALM 34:1-8 (19-22) (RCL ALT.)

Though there is a particular historical circumstance attached to this psalm (see 1 Sam. 21:10-15, although the king is Achish, rather than Abimelech), the superscription that specifies the historical circumstance was probably a later attachment. The psalm is general enough to apply to a variety of situations.

The first ten verses praise God for deliverance in a time of need. With verse 11, the psalm moves from praise to exhortation. The fear of Yahweh is the key to a full life. Those who live righteously will enjoy God's blessing of protection. The rest of the psalm, beginning with verse 15, is a meditation on righteousness and wickedness. The righteous may be afflicted, but God will rescue them. The God of Israel is a redeeming God who will not forsake those who keep the covenant. In contrast to the righteous, however, the wicked will suffer death and condemnation. As we read verse 16, God will "cut off the remembrance of them from the earth." This was indeed a terrible fate from the Israelite perspective, since it was through one's remembrance and descendants that one lived on after death. The only life that can truly be called good, and the only life in which one can experience God's salvation, is the one that is lived in service to God.

> The God who restored Israel and made her honored among the nations can turn tears into shouts of joy.

PSALM 13 (BCP)

The question, "How long, O LORD?" is common in psalms of lament. To the psalmist, it seems that God is absent, a frightening prospect to anyone who trusts in God's providential care. The psalmist suffers unrelenting pain and sorrow while his enemies are exalted. In verse 3, however, the lament gives way to petition (vv. 3-4), and the petition blossoms into a declaration of trust in God (vv. 5-6). The psalmist has called upon a God in whom he has faith, a God who can be trusted. God will bring salvation to and deal bountifully with the one who trusts in God's steadfast love. Like many psalms of lament, then, this psalm takes the reader through a range of emotions: sorrow, desperate supplication, and trust.

HEBREWS 7:23-28 (RCL)

Hebrews repeatedly asserts Jesus' superiority as a high priest over leviti-cal priests who made sacrifice in the Jerusalem Temple. The levitical high priests are mortal, are many in number, and must make sacrifices repeatedly, including sacrifices for their own sin. Jesus, however, is not a levitical high priest, but a high priest according to the order of Melchizedek, appointed not through the law but through God's oath (see Heb. 7:28; Ps. 110:4). He is immortal and utterly unique. His sacrifice need never be repeated, and he has no need to offer sacrifice for his own sin, since he is sinless. (See also comments on the second reading under Proper 26, Twenty-Second Sunday after Pentecost, below.)

HEBREWS 5:12—6:1, 9-12 (BCP)

Among the community for which Hebrews was written, some people have forgotten or rejected some of the basic aspects of the faith. The writer lists these basics in 6:1-2: "repentance from dead works and faith toward God, instruction about baptisms, laying on of hands, resurrection of the dead, and eternal judgment." The writer chastises these Christians: though they "ought to be teachers" by this time (5:12), they themselves need to be taught once again, having become "dull in understanding" (5:11). They need milk, as for an infant, not solid food, which is for the mature.

Having warned readers about the great danger of falling away from the faith, the writer expresses confidence that these Christians will receive salvation. God will remember their good works and love within the community of faith. God's salvation, promised in Scripture, is theirs for the taking if they will become imitators of the saints who have gone before them.

It is easy to forget sometimes why our formation in the faith, including learning basic Christian belief, actually matters. In fact, in some Christian circles, "doctrine" has become a term with negative connotations. Indeed, doctrine can be abused, especially when it is not coupled with works of justice and mercy. Yet Hebrews reminds us that we learn the truths of the faith because they are soteriologically valuable. They lead us into the life of God. Learning about God helps us to know God, who is the author of our salvation.

> Learning about God helps us to know God, who is the author of our salvation.

HEBREWS 5:1-6 (LFM)

For commentary on this text, see the second reading (RCL) for Proper 24, Twentieth Sunday after Pentecost, below.

The Gospel

MARK 10:46-52 (RCL, BCP, LFM)

For several reasons, the episode of the healing of Bartimaeus occupies a position of strategic importance in Mark's narrative. First, this is the final healing story in Mark's Gospel and the final story before Jesus enters Jerusalem. Though Jesus has spent much of the narrative so far performing healings and exorcisms, once he enters Jerusalem the plot turns to the events leading up to his passion, death, and resurrection. Second, the healing of Bartimaeus completes a major section of the Gospel that contains a significant amount of teaching by Jesus about the life to which he calls his followers (8:22—10:52). This is a life of humility in serving others. It is characterized by a willingness to endure the shame of outsiders in order to be honored by God and Jesus' followers. Third, it is no accident that the Bartimaeus episode is juxtaposed with the story of the request of James and John (10:35-45); the two stories are meant to contrast with one another. Fourth, the story of the healing of Bartimaeus also forms the latter part of a narrative "bookend," the first part of which is the story of the healing of the blind man at Bethsaida (8:22-26).

Sight as a metaphor for understanding is a key concept in this episode, especially in light of its larger narrative context. Mark explicitly links sight and understanding in Jesus' criticism of the disciples in 8:17-18, and the section that follows, bookended by these two stories of blind men, highlights the disciples' increasing blindness. They cannot seem to grasp what Jesus teaches them, especially when it has to do with rethinking their own honor and status. Early in this section of the narrative, Jesus tells Peter, who is the representative of the other disciples, that Peter has his mind set on human things, rather than divine things (8:33). By the time we come to the story of Bartimaeus, this has not changed.

> The disciples cannot seem to grasp what Jesus teaches them, especially when it has to do with rethinking their own honor and status.

Bartimaeus calls to Jesus using the royal messianic title "Son of David." The title "Son of David" carried messianic significance for early Christians and called to mind the figure of Solomon, shown in the Old Testament to be a generous benefactor and known in Jewish tradition to have healing powers.[4] Bartimaeus believes that Jesus can heal him and persists in petitioning Jesus even when people in the crowd attempt to silence him. His persistence is meant as a contrast to the disciples, who have been with Jesus all along, and yet fail to exhibit faith (4:40), fail to recognize Jesus in a moment of need (6:47-52), and fail to recognize Jesus' ability to provide for those who need his help (8:4).

Bartimaeus shows faith by his persistence, and it is his faith, Jesus says, that makes him well (Greek: "saved" him). Faith is an interesting concept in Mark. Jesus chastises the disciples for lacking faith (4:40), and the people of Jesus' hometown who know him cause him to be amazed by their lack of faith (6:6). It is normally minor characters in this Gospel who show tenacious faith in Jesus. The hemorrhaging woman who pushes her way through the crowd just to touch Jesus' clothes shows faith that he can heal her (5:25-34). Jairus persists in his belief that Jesus can heal his daughter even when he is told that she is already dead (5:21-24, 35-43). Those who lower a paralytic to Jesus through the roof of a house show faith (2:1-12), as does the Syrophoenician woman of 7:24-30. The father of a demon-possessed boy struggles with faith, crying out, "I believe; help my unbelief!" (9:24), which is enough to warrant the exorcism of the demon from his son. In Mark, faith is not simply belief, in the sense of intellectual assent. It is trust in Jesus' willingness and ability to care for those who need his help.

> In Mark, faith is not simply belief, in the sense of intellectual assent. It is trust in Jesus' willingness and ability to care for those who need his help.

The Bartimaeus episode, then, reinforces what has become a theme in Mark: faith shows up among people in need—the desperate, the outcast, and the unclean. Perhaps this is because for such people the "cares of the world" (4:19) have lost their meaning. To a woman who has been hemorrhaging for twelve years and has spent all of her money, to a father who is in danger of losing his daughter, or another father whose son is possessed by a demon, wealth, prestige, and reputation no longer hold sway. Serious crises tend to put our values in perspective.

Values, in fact, are at the heart of discipleship in Mark. The question that Jesus asks Bartimaeus in 10:51, "What do you want me to do for you?" is more significant than it might at first appear. In the preceding episode (10:35-45), Jesus asks James and John the same question, using wording that is almost identical in Greek. How one answers this question is crucial because it reveals what one truly values. James and John asked to be seated, one at Jesus' right and one at his left, in his glory. Despite Jesus' teaching, they seek their own exaltation.

> To follow Jesus is to stop setting our mind on human things, and turn our thoughts and hearts to the things of God.

Bartimaeus, by contrast, asks only to regain his sight. He does not ask for riches or status. He does not seek his own honor as the disciples do. In fact, though Jesus releases him from obligation by telling him to go away, he follows Jesus "on the way" (v. 52). The "way," of course, is the way into Jerusalem, where Jesus will be arrested, beaten, humiliated, and crucified. One is reminded of Jesus' words in 8:34: "If any want to become my followers, let them deny themselves and take up their cross and follow me." By following Jesus "on the way" into Jerusalem, Bartimaeus embodies the way of the cross about which Jesus spoke in 8:34ff.

The question that Jesus asks James, John, and Bartimaeus is deeply relevant for Christians today. What do we wish for Jesus to do for us? Why is Jesus important to us? What do we value? James and John wanted Jesus to make them great by the standards of the world in which they lived, but Bartimaeus wanted only his sight, and when he received his sight, he followed Jesus on the way. Bartimaeus allowed himself to be transformed, and this is a key element of discipleship in Mark's Gospel. To follow Jesus is to stop setting our mind on human things, and turn our thoughts and hearts to the things of God.

Notes

1. See William D. Reyburn, *A Handbook on the Book of Job* (New York: United Bible Societies, 1992), 772.

2. Robert G. Bratcher and William D. Reyburn, *A Translator's Handbook on the Book of Psalms* (New York: United Bible Societies, 1991), 1047.

3. See Konrad Schaefer, *Psalms* (Collegeville, Minn.: Liturgical, 2001), 306.

4. See Dennis Duling, "Solomon, Exorcism, and the Son of David," *Harvard Theological Review* 68 (1975): 235–52; idem, "The Therapeutic Son of David," *New Testament Studies* 24 (1978): 392–410; idem, "Matthew's Plurisignificant 'Son of David' in Social-Science Perspective: Kinship, Kingship, Magic and Miracle," *Biblical Theology Bulletin* 22 (1992): 99–116.

ALL SAINTS' DAY / SUNDAY

November 1, 2009
Henry G. Brinton

Revised Common (RCL)	Episcopal (BCP)	Roman Catholic (LFM)
Isa. 25:6-9 or	Sir. 44:1-10, 13-14 or	Rev. 7:2-4, 9-14
Wisd. of Sol. 3:1-9	2:(1-6) 7-11	
Psalm 24	Psalm 149	Ps. 24:1-2, 3-4, 5-6
Rev. 21:1-6a	Rev. 7:2-4, 9-17 or	1 John 3:1-3
	Eph. 1:(11-14) 15-23	
John 11:32-44	Matt. 5:1-12 or	Matt. 5:1-12a
	Luke 6:20-26 (27-36)	

FIRST READING

ISAIAH 25:6-9 OR WISDOM OF SOLOMON 3:1-9 (RCL)
SIRACH 44:1-10, 13-14 OR 2:(1-6) 7-11 (BCP)
REVELATION 7:2-4, 9-14 (LFM)

One Degree of Separation

Many of us have heard the term "six degrees of separation." That's the theory that we are all connected to one another by no more than six stages of relationship. But how about "Six Degrees of Kevin Bacon"? This is a game devised by a trio of Pennsylvania college boys—young men with *far* too much time on their hands. The goal of the game is to connect the actor Kevin Bacon to any other performer in the entertainment industry, linking them together in six degrees or less.[1] We get a kick out this game because we've all had small-world experiences, discovering that we are linked to complete strangers by surprisingly small networks of relationships. Small-world experiences give us a sense of security, and they satisfy our desire for connection, so that we won't feel lost in this complex, confusing, and often cruel world. But there's one area of life in which we don't want six degrees of separation, and that's our spiritual life. In terms of our relationship with God, we want the size of our separation to be as small as possible—one degree of separation.

In this search for a shorter link to the Lord, the saints of God can show us the way. In Revelation (LFM), John has a vision of heaven, and in it he sees a great multitude from every nation standing before the throne and before the Lamb of God, robed in white, with palm branches in their hands. They cry out in a loud voice, saying, "Salvation belongs to our God who is seated on the throne, and to the Lamb!" (7:9-10). These saints are standing in the presence of God, proclaiming that salvation belongs only to God and to the Lamb of God, Jesus Christ. There is an ancient Latin phrase for their particular position, *coram Deo*, which means "before the face of God," or "in the presence of God." Standing *coram Deo* is described by Isaiah when he says "the LORD God will wipe away the tears from all faces" (25:8, RCL); by the promise of the Wisdom of Solomon that "the souls of the righteous are in the hand of God" (3:1, RCL); and by Sirach when he advises, "My child, when you come to serve the Lord, prepare yourself for testing. . . . Cling to him and do not depart, so that your last days may be prosperous" (2:1, 3, BCP). To live *coram Deo* is to realize that God is working to forgive, heal, strengthen and save us—sometimes through trial and testing. *Coram Deo* is, quite simply, one degree of separation from the source of salvation.

> To live *coram Deo* is to realize that God is working to forgive, heal, strengthen and save us-sometimes through trial and testing.

Our challenge is to follow the saints in behavior that shows the world that we are living *coram Deo*. Presbyterian theologian Shirley Guthrie believes that we can do this by the way we drive our cars on expressways, and by the way we treat checkout clerks, garbage collectors, and food service workers. We can do this by the way we keep hoping and working for change in people and in institutions, when others say that nothing can be done. We can do this by the way we remain calm when others panic, and show deep dissatisfaction when others are complacent. We can do this by being glad when the cause of justice, freedom, and peace is advanced—by our own efforts, or by the efforts of others.[2] All of these actions and attitudes show that we believe that God is alive and well in our complex, confusing, and often cruel world, and that we are living in the presence of God, with no more than one degree of separation.

PSALM 24 (RCL) OR 24:1-2, 3-4, 5-6 (LFM)
PSALM 149 (BCP)

God's Faithful Ones

"Who shall ascend the hill of the LORD?" asks Psalm 24 (RCL, LFM). "And who shall stand in his holy place?" (v. 3). The answer is, "Those who have clean hands and pure hearts, who do not lift up their souls to what is false, and do not swear deceitfully" (v. 4). These are the saints who will receive blessing from the Lord, like the "faithful ones" of Psalm 149 (vv. 1, 5, 9, BCP). Old Testament scholar Walter Brueggemann notes that Psalm 24 regards Torah obedience as a qualification for access to God in the sanctuary—a standard that many would find overly legalistic today, in a world of nuance and ambiguity. But since life in these psalms is theologically secure and comprehended in coherent categories, it is appropriate "that access to God be measured in terms of conformity to what is known, trusted, and found reliable."[3] Even today, in congregations made up of people with unclean hands and impure hearts, faithfulness can be defined by reliance on a God who is known and reliable. We are God's faithful ones not because of our moral purity, but because of our trust in a completely faithful Lord.

SECOND READING

REVELATION 21:1-6A (RCL)
REVELATION 7:2-4, 9-17 (BCP)
EPHESIANS 1:(11-14) 15-23 (BCP ALT.)
1 JOHN 3:1-3 (LFM)

Santo Subito

When Pope John Paul II died in 2005, over a million people filed past his plain cedar coffin to pay their respects. About four million flooded into Rome to attend his funeral or watch the service on giant video screens placed across the city. Around the world, hundreds of millions of people watched the funeral on television. In Rome, a cry began to spread through the crowd, "*Santo subito* . . . *santo subito.*" Translation: "Sainthood immediately." The fans of John Paul II want the Vatican to cut through its normal red tape and pronounce the pope a saint right away. He's clearly a saint, they say—so let's make it official.[4]

All Saints' Day is the day each year we give thanks for the saints of the church, those great role models for faithful discipleship who now enjoy everlasting life with God. But why is it that people tend to focus on saints in heaven? Take a look at the Bible, and you see that the emphasis is on the saints that are living right here on earth. In his letter to the Ephesians (BCP), Paul writes, "I have heard of your faith in the Lord Jesus and your love toward all the saints" (1:15). Whenever Paul speaks of saints (*hagios*, "holy ones"), he is talking about members of the church—people who have been chosen by God and set apart to do God's work in the world. Saints are holy people, but their holiness does not come from achieving moral perfection. Instead, they have a holiness that comes from being marked as God's people. God "chose us in Christ before the foundation of the world," insists Paul, "to be holy and blameless before him in love" (v. 4).

> Whenever Paul speaks of saints, he is talking about members of the church—people who have been chosen by God and set apart to do God's work in the world.

God chose us and set us apart—this is such an important insight into saintliness. We know that the Lord God is holy because God is set apart from the world, and different from everything that God has created. Follow that logic, and you discover that we Christians are holy because God has set us apart from the world and given us a mission that is different from other earthly assignments. To be holy is not necessarily to be better than other people. Just different. Saints are people who long for "a new heaven and a new earth" (Rev. 21:1, RCL) . . . who look for the Lamb of God to be their shepherd (Rev. 7:17, BCP) . . . who "see what love the Father has given us, that we should be called children of God; and that is what we are" (1 John 3:1, LFM). *Santo subito* . . . sainthood immediately. The challenge for us is to live a *santo subito* life, among saints who are at work in the church and the world.

THE GOSPEL
JOHN 11:32-44 (RCL)
MATTHEW 5:1-12 (BCP) OR 5:1-12A (LFM)
LUKE 6:20-26 (27-36) (BCP ALT.)

The Sainthood Diet

Life is often brutal and short in the Third World. But the people of Micronesia, in the western Pacific Ocean, are now dropping dead in their fifties—and not for reasons commonly associated with the developing world. There is no famine here and little evidence of the diseases that cut life short in places such as Africa. The big killer, according to *The Atlantic Monthly*, is what some epidemiologists are calling "New World Syndrome"—a group of maladies brought on not by viruses or microbes or parasites, but by the assault of rapid Westernization on traditional cultures. Micronesians are just now beginning to face the diseases that knock us off here in the United States: diabetes, heart disease, and high blood pressure. They are facing these problems because they have been introduced to our fatty, sweet, and salty foods: Spam and corned beef and Vienna sausages, cake and muffin mixes, soda and beer and candy bars and potato chips. Go into a Micronesian grocery store, and you can find plenty of unhealthy imported food, but you can't buy fresh bananas, papayas, breadfruit, coconut, or mangoes.[5]

Welcome to the promised land of diabetes, heart disease, and high blood pressure. Of course, our New World problems are not purely physical—our spiritual diet is bad for us as well, and it is hurting us at younger ages all the time. We're victims of our own brand of New World Syndrome, getting sick from all the junk that we ingest in our rapid-fire, multitasking, individualistic, consumer-oriented culture. Evidence: church membership is declining, and a shrinking number of people are being nourished by the fruits of traditional religious culture.

> We're victims of our own brand of New World Syndrome, getting sick from all the junk that we ingest in our rapid-fire, multitasking, individualistic, consumer-oriented culture.

At the same time, a hunger for personal spirituality—cut off from religious institutions—has been soaring. Americans are feeling spiritually dead, like Lazarus in the tomb, and they are searching for life in online chat rooms, in exotic religions, and in the self-help sections of shopping mall bookstores.

What's missing is a spiritual lifestyle that will create a church of saints—people who are healthy and holy servants of Jesus Christ. In Matthew 5 (LFM, BCP) and Luke 6 (BCP), Jesus offers a "Sainthood Diet" that is not too salty, sweet, or fatty, but provides us with the spiritual nourishment we need for abundant life, now and forever. "Blessed are those who hunger and thirst for righteousness," says Jesus, and happy are those who are merciful, pure in heart, and working for peace (Matt. 5:6-9)—these are the elements of a spiritual diet that will lead to a life of health and wholeness as children of God. If you are feeling sick from your own strain of New World Syndrome, follow the Sainthood Diet's instructions to "Love your enemies, do good to those who hate you, bless those who curse you, pray for those who abuse you" (Luke 6:27-28). This spiritual approach is as countercultural as a meal plan that substitutes carrot sticks for potato chips, and it has equally healthy results.

To grasp the full significance of this Sainthood Diet, take a careful look at the story of the raising of Lazarus in John 11:32-44 (RCL), and gain a deeper understanding of how Jesus confronts—and then conquers—the powers of sickness and death. For starters, it is clear that Jesus is not untouched or unmoved by physical and spiritual destruction. He takes fatal illness seriously, and personally. Going to the tomb of his dead friend Lazarus, Jesus encounters the sisters Martha and Mary, and when Jesus sees Mary weeping, he is greatly disturbed in spirit and is deeply moved. He begins to weep himself, prompting some onlookers to say, "See how he loved him!" (v. 36). What a powerful image this is: God's own Son, the King of Kings and Lord of Lords, so overcome by grief over the loss of his friend and by anger over the destructive power of death, that he breaks down in tears.

Illness and death are not minor annoyances for Jesus. They affect him so profoundly that he is overwhelmed by emotion and cries. And just as he weeps over Lazarus, he weeps over physical deaths in Micronesia and spiritual deaths in our country. But then, suddenly, another group of onlookers in the story speaks up and makes a less sympathetic observation: "Could not he who opened the eyes of the blind man have kept this man [Lazarus] from dying?" (v. 37). It's a question that a great many people ask every day, in a variety of forms. Why doesn't the universe-creating God create miraculous cures for little children with cancer? Why doesn't the death-conquering Christ beat the heart disease of our elderly church members? Why doesn't the infinitely powerful Spirit of God eliminate the pain of the suffering poor? Just why do innocent people suffer? Why do bad things happen to good people? Why doesn't God protect us from violence and illness and death?

> What a powerful image: God's own Son, so overcome by grief over the loss of his friend, and by anger over the destructive power of death, that he breaks down in tears.

Within the church, we know that answers come only when we seek nourishment from God's Word together. In John 11, Jesus puts one key ingredient—belief—at the heart of the Sainthood Diet when he says to Martha, "I am the resurrection and the life. Those who believe in me, even though they die, will live, and everyone who lives and believes in me will never die. Do you believe this?" (v. 25). This is not a guarantee of a straightforward physical healing, but instead it is a promise of new life based on belief. Rather than promising Martha a miracle, he invites her to trust him to work for new life. There's a big difference between these two. Instead of saying, "I'm going to step in and make everything okay," Jesus says, "Those who believe in me, even though they die, will live." He promises that the dead will rise, but he doesn't predict exactly how. So what does Martha do in response to this invitation? She says yes. She believes. She proclaims, "Yes, Lord, I believe that you are the Messiah, the Son of God, the one coming into the world" (v. 27).

The very same invitation is extended to us today. Jesus says to us, in the midst of our physical and spiritual illnesses: "I am the resurrection and the life. . . . Do you believe this?" (vv. 25-26). Do you believe that I am working for radical new life? Do you believe that I am the Resurrection, the One who conquers death? Do you believe that I am leading you, right now, in so many unexpected ways, from dying to rising? "Did I not tell you that if you believed, you would see the glory of God?" (v. 40). It's impossible to predict what form this new life will take. But we can believe it will come.

When Sarah Hinlicky was studying for her Master of Divinity degree at Princeton Theological Seminary, she spent time visiting with her dying grandfather, a time of sadness and grief that was complicated by the fact that her grandfather was a pastor who really didn't approve of women in the ministry. On her last visit, she offered to pray with him, and then began to cry. "He opened his arms," she reports, and "I threw myself down on his chest . . . and he wrapped those dying arms around me. I gripped them. There was something miraculous about them. They were so unlovable, objectively speaking, so ugly and powerless. They looked like death. They pointed to death. They even called out for death. But to me, they were the embodiment of love, love right in the middle of death. . . . His yellow hands stroked my hair, and I started to pray, not very well, not very eloquently, not very coherently. He prayed too, calmly, quietly, humorously even. . . . But then, a confession

> Rather than promising Martha a miracle, Jesus invites her to trust him to work for new life.

and an admission. He prayed, 'Lord, I didn't know what to think of this business of letting women be ordained pastors. But I see that you have called my grand-daughter into it, so I think it must be a good thing after all.' And there it was, at the very end: the man who had baptized me was now blessing me to carry on his work in the world."[6]

When we face physical or spiritual death, there is only one approach that can improve our health: the Sainthood Diet. It comes from following the teachings of Jesus, from "Blessed are the poor in spirit, for theirs is the kingdom of God" (Matt. 5:3) to "Be merciful, just as your Father is merciful" (Luke 6:36). Most of all, it involves believing in Jesus, and trusting him to be at work for unexpected new life in every time, place, and situation. That's a lifestyle choice that will create a church of saints, a body made up of healthy and holy servants of Jesus Christ.

Notes

1. http://en.wikipedia.org/wiki/Six_Degrees_of_Kevin_Bacon, accessed July 29, 2008.

2. Shirley C. Guthrie Jr., *Diversity in Faith, Unity in Christ* (Philadelphia: Westminster, 1986), 88.

3. Walter Brueggemann, *The Message of the Psalms: A Theological Commentary* (Minneapolis: Augsburg, 1984), 42.

4. Jeff Israely, "John Paul II: How fast to sainthood?" *Time* magazine (April 3, 2007), http://www.time.com/time/world/article/0,8599,1606225,00.html, accessed July 17, 2008.

5. Ellen Ruppel Shell, "New World Syndrome," *The Atlantic Monthly* (June 2001), 50, http://www.theatlantic.com/doc/200106/shell, accessed July 17, 2008.

6. Sarah E. Hinlicky, "The Great Reunion Beyond," *Christianity Today* (February 3, 2001), 53, http://www.christianitytoday.com/ct/2001/february5/8.50.html, accessed July 17, 2008.

TWENTY-SECOND SUNDAY AFTER PENTECOST

THIRTY-FIRST SUNDAY IN ORDINARY TIME / PROPER 26
NOVEMBER 1, 2009

Revised Common (RCL)	Episcopal (BCP)	Roman Catholic (LFM)
Deut. 6:1-9 or	Deut. 6:1-9	Deut. 6:2-6
Ruth 1:1-18		
Ps. 119:1-8 or Psalm 146	Ps. 119:1-16 or 119:1-8	Ps. 18:2-3a, 3b-4, 47 + 51
Heb. 9:11-14	Heb. 7:23-28	Heb. 7:23-28
Mark 12:28-34	Mark 12:28-34	Mark 12:28b-34

FIRST READING

DEUTERONOMY 6:1-9 (RCL, BCP)
DEUTERONOMY 6:2-6 (LFM)

The foundational statement of Jewish faith occurs in Deuteronomy 6:4: "Hear O Israel: Yahweh is our God; Yahweh is one." This is called the *Shema*, which in Hebrew is the first word of the command, "Hear." As indicated in the NRSV footnote, there are various ways of translating this sentence. Translations are themselves interpretations, and each bears its own nuances of meaning. Yet, however we translate this sentence, its central message is that only Yahweh is the God of Israel. The following sentence, "You shall love the LORD your God with all your heart, and with all your soul, and with all your might," is a command to covenant devotion. Yahweh is to receive Israel's total allegiance. There is no room for worship of other gods or failure to abide by God's commandments.

"These words," the Ten Commandments, must be central to the corporate life of Israel. They are to be recited to children, passed down from generation to generation. They are to be recited whether one is at home or away, in the morning and in the evening. The command, "Bind them as a sign on your hand, fix them as an emblem on your forehead, and write them on the doorposts of your house and on your gates," led to the Jewish practice of wearing small boxes, called phylacteries, on the hand and forehead, and attaching boxes called mezuzahs to doorposts. Both phylacteries and mezuzahs contained passages of Scripture, among them these commands from Deuteronomy 6:4-5.

Israel is about to cross into the promised land. The gift of this land is a part of the covenantal relationship with God. It is crucial, then, that the people obey the statutes and ordinances that they have received from God through Moses. Both the land and the commandments are signs of the covenant, which is not simply for the generation that is with Moses, but for its descendants. The people of Israel must teach these laws to their children and to their children's children so that the covenant may be maintained in perpetuity. The promises that God made to their ancestors are being fulfilled, but the people of Israel must do their part to maintain the covenant.

As Christians, we believe that God's covenant love for Israel was made available to the Gentiles as well. The notion that Gentiles might come to know the living God is not just a Christian concept, but has precedent in pre-Christian Jewish tradition, such as we see in Isaiah 56:6-7. Covenant with God does not simply mean that God has forgiven our sins and receives us into the kingdom in exchange for our confession of faith. These are aspects of the covenant, but as we read here in Deuteronomy, our relationship with God should suffuse our lives. Whether at home or away, waking or sleeping, we are God's. The words of our mouths, the thoughts of our hearts, and the teaching of our children must be rooted in this covenant faithfulness.

> The promises that God made to their ancestors are being fulfilled, but the people of Israel must do their part to maintain the covenant.

RUTH 1:1-18 (RCL ALT.)

The book of Ruth tells a remarkable story and challenges readers to rethink their assumptions about insiders and outsiders. Ruth is not an Israelite, but a Moabite. Her mother-in-law, Naomi, is an Israelite, and the two of them, together with Orpah, experience great tragedy in the death of their husbands. When Naomi sends Orpah and Ruth back to the houses of their mothers in the hopes that they would find new husbands, she is acting in keeping with accepted convention. By returning to her family, Orpah simply does what was expected.

Ruth, on the other hand, does something quite unexpected, leaving her own people and her own gods to join Naomi's people and worship their God. In fact, she takes an oath to this effect. By saying, "May the LORD do thus and so to me, and more as well" (v. 17), she invokes God's curse if she ever leaves Naomi. Ruth's words in verses 16-17 are a touching statement of *ḥesed*, covenant faithfulness, which is a major theme in this story. In the ancient world it was no small thing to move to another culture. Barriers of language, custom, kinship, and religion, along with the difficulty and dangers of travel, tended to keep people within the cultures of their upbringing. Yet Ruth leaves behind her people, culture, and gods out of her love for and faithfulness to her mother-in-law.

In Ezra 9–10, foreign women and their children are expelled from life among the Israelites. They are rejected as unclean, and their presence is thought to bring sin upon the remnant returned from exile. This expulsion is not seen as cruel, but as the requirement of a God who demands purity among the covenant people. The book of Ruth, however, takes a different, more welcoming view of non-Israelites. Here the primary virtue is not purity, but faithfulness. Though Moabites were not held in high regard by the Israelites (see Num. 21:29; Deut. 23:3), Ruth is a model of covenant faithfulness. Her virtue is found not only in her love for and loyalty to Naomi, but in her willingness to adopt Israel's people and God as her own. She is even an ancestor of King David. Perhaps this story was meant as an explicit rejection of the attitudes present in the book of Ezra. Regardless, the story that Ruth tells teaches us that God's love and righteousness is not confined to one specific group of people. We must be open and willing to receive people into the family of faith from the most unexpected places.

> Ruth's virtue is found not only in her love for and loyalty to Naomi, but in her willingness to adopt Israel's people and God as her own.

RESPONSIVE READING

PSALM 119:1-8 (RCL, BCP ALT.)
PSALM 119:1-16 (BCP)

Psalm 119, the longest in the psalter, is an extended contemplation and celebration of the Torah. Each of the twenty-two stanzas of the psalm consists of eight lines. The first stanza (vv. 1-8) speaks of the happiness (or, perhaps more accurately, blessedness) of those who walk in God's ways. The good life is one lived in keeping with the ordinances of God's law, and such a life is the one for which the psalmist hopes. The Torah is not just a set of rules and regulations. It is a gift, a guide to a privileged way of living. Life that is ordered according to the statutes of the Torah is not encumbered by ignorance of God's will, but in every respect is in harmony with God's purposes.

The following stanza (vv. 9-16) expresses the same basic set of ideas. God's law is precious and the key to a good life. The psalmist prays that God will be his teacher. Deuteronomy 6:1-9 seems to lie in the background of this stanza. The reference to young people in the psalm may allude to the instruction in Deuteronomy 6:7 to recite the commandments to children. In Deuteronomy 6:6-9, the people of Israel are instructed to keep God's commandments in their heart, recite them aloud, and to bind them on their hands, on their foreheads, and on their doorposts. In similar fashion, the psalmist says that the law is to be sought with the whole heart, treasured, declared aloud, kept before one's eyes, and meditated upon.

There is real wisdom in this psalm. Today there are many voices telling us how to live the good life, but as Christians we believe that the good life is one lived in step with God's will. Like the psalmist, we are to seek God's will, meditate upon God's word, and seek the instruction of our divine Teacher.

PSALM 146 (RCL ALT.)

For commentary on this text, see the responsive reading for Proper 27, Twenty-Third Sunday after Pentecost, below.

PSALM 18:2-3A, 3B-4, 47 + 51 (LFM)

This psalm depicts God as a warrior (vv. 7-15) who comes to the aid of the faithful (vv. 20-24). In the opening verses the psalmist uses a variety of metaphors for the God who has saved him from the hand of his enemies: God is rock, fortress, deliverer, shield, horn of salvation, and stronghold. This is one of the "royal psalms," which concludes by praising and blessing God for the triumphs of King David over his enemies and God's ongoing love for the Davidic line.

SECOND READING
HEBREWS 9:11-14 (RCL)
HEBREWS 7:23-28 (BCP, LFM)

The writer of Hebrews has developed an argument so complex, so rooted in knowledge of the Old Testament, and so deeply indebted to his philosophical education that it is opaque to many modern readers (and one wonders about the ancient ones). To grasp the argument, one has to understand the contrast that the writer sets up between the levitical priesthood and Jesus' priesthood. The levitical priests offered sacrifice in the "tent" (9:11), by which the author means the Temple of Jerusalem, the predecessor of which was the "tent of meeting" mentioned in Leviticus 16:16-17. Before offering a goat for the sins of the people, the high priest had to sacrifice a bull as a sin offering for himself (see Lev. 16:6-14). The priest also had to purify the sanctuary and the altar with blood because of the sins of the priesthood and the people (Lev. 16:14-19). Then the sins of the people were laid upon a live goat, which was sent out into the wilderness (Lev. 16:20-22). This ritual was repeated each year on the Day of Atonement.

> It is not simply that we are guiltless before God. Rather, Christ's death also has the power to lead us into holier lives.

Jesus, by contrast, is not a levitical high priest (like the "former" priests mentioned in 7:23), but a high priest according to the order of Melchizedek (see 7:15-17; Psalm 110). Further, Jesus is not only a high priest; he is also the sacrifice. If the blood of bulls and goats offered by sinful priests can atone for sin, the argument goes, how much more can the blood of the sinless Christ? When Jesus, "who through the eternal Spirit offered himself without blemish to God" (9:14) made atonement for human sin, he did so through a sacrifice that never needs to be repeated (7:27). As both priest and offering, he is perfect. Moreover, Christ's sacrifice does not simply remove the guilt of sin, but purifies one's conscience "from dead works to worship the living God" (9:14). In theological terms, we might say that the change effected by Christ's sacrifice is not simply justification, but sanctification. It is not simply that we are guiltless before God. Rather, Christ's death also has the power to lead us into holier lives.

THE GOSPEL
MARK 12:28-34 (RCL, BCP)
MARK 12:28b-34 (LFM)

Christians sometimes seem to think that Jesus was hostile to his own tradition. We sometimes see Judaism, and especially Pharisaic Judaism, as a "religion of law," and Christianity, beginning with Jesus, as a "religion of grace." Yet these are misconceptions. Jesus did not reject his own tradition. It does not appear that he thought Judaism to be too legalistic, nor is it evident that he intended to found a new religion that replaced law with grace. Jesus seems to have had a deep respect for the Torah, and careful readers of the Old Testament will see that it is shot through with God's grace. Jesus did, however, often interpret the Torah differently than many other Jewish people of his day, and his interpretation generated controversy.

> Jesus often interpreted the Torah differently than many other Jewish people of his day, and his interpretation generated controversy.

In this episode, a scribe comes to Jesus because he has heard Jesus debating the issue of resurrection with the Sadducees. The scribe is a legal expert and, having heard Jesus' answer, he has a question of his own. He wishes to know which commandment Jesus thinks is the "first," or most important. The purpose of the scribe's question in this passage is not to learn about the Torah. In the Gospels, when the people who are typically Jesus' opponents ask him questions, their point is normally to best him in public debate. Such "challenge-riposte" interactions are contests in which honor and reputation are won and lost.[1] Here the scribe wishes to elicit from Jesus a public statement of his views on the Torah. In truth, the question would not be an especially difficult one for any Jewish teacher. It is a "softball" with an expected conventional answer. People are watching, and if Jesus does not answer well, he loses both honor and credibility to his questioner. More specifically, if Jesus does not provide the expected answer, it shows him to be out of touch with some of the most fundamental tenets of the Jewish faith.

In fact, Jesus does provide the answer that most Jewish people of his day would expect him to give. Broadly speaking, the Ten Commandments are divided into two "tablets," or "tables."[2] The first tablet governs relationships between human beings and God. Hence, the people of Israel were forbidden to have other gods before Yahweh, to make idols, and to make wrongful use of God's name. They were also to order their lives according to God's calendar by resting on the seventh day, the Sabbath. The second tablet governs the interactions that human beings have with one another. The people of Israel must honor their parents. They must refrain from murder, adultery, theft, false testimony against their neighbors, and covetous intentions. There were many other laws as well, but they were thought to be derived from the Ten Commandments.

It was commonly the case that when Jews wanted to summarize the two tablets, they quoted two particular commands from the Torah. The first, which summarized the first tablet, was found in Deuteronomy 6:4-5, also called the *Shema*, "Hear [*Shema*], O Israel: The LORD is our God, the LORD alone. You shall love the LORD your God with all your heart, and with all your soul, and with all your might." The second passage, which summarized the second tablet, was from Leviticus 19:18b: "You shall love your neighbor as yourself." In fact, either of these passages by itself could be taken as a summary of the entire law. As E. P. Sanders states, "Jews who used one saying as a summary of the whole law were not excluding other parts of the law; they regarded all the commandments as being implied by one of the great commandments."[3] Hence, Paul says that "the whole law is summed up in a single commandment, 'You shall love your neighbor as yourself'" (Gal. 5:14; see also Rom. 13:8).

When the scribe asks Jesus, "Which commandment is the first of all?" Jesus answers with the two passages that summarize the Torah (see also Luke 10:25-28). With this answer, Jesus does not depart from common Jewish tradition or amend it in some way. Rather, his response situates him firmly within this tradition. He asserts, "There is no other commandment greater than these," because these commandments summarize the basis for the wider collection of Jewish laws. While Jesus' teaching is often unconventional, here his answer is quite commonplace. He affirms the bedrock claims of Israelite faith.

While the scribe has come to Jesus in order to test him publicly on his commitment to the basic teachings of their tradition, he ends up honoring Jesus by commending his answer.

While the scribe has come to Jesus in order to test him publicly on his commitment to the basic teachings of their tradition, he ends up honoring Jesus by commending his answer. Jesus, in turn, ends up pronouncing a favorable judgment on the scribe, saying to him, "You are not far from the kingdom of God." This may sound like Jesus means that the scribe is still outside the kingdom, but Jesus' statement is a figure of speech, a form of understatement called a *litotes*.[4] It is like a person responding to a compliment by saying, "You're not too bad yourself." Jesus means to indicate the scribe's positive relationship to the kingdom of God.

Christians today do not generally regard the statutes of the Torah as necessary components of righteousness. Righteousness in the Christian tradition comes first and foremost from Christ's atoning work on the cross. Justification is God's gift, and our salvation comes from our accepting this gift. Yet we also believe in the importance of righteous living. Christ died for our sins, and yet this does not mean that our actions are of no consequence. Indeed, we are to seek God's help in living the kinds of lives to which we are called. God provides this help not only through the work of the Holy Spirit and the community of faith, but also through the guidance of Scripture. Here, in the words of Jesus, we find basic but invaluable guidance: we are to worship only one God, love God with our whole hearts, and love our neighbor as ourselves.

Notes

1. For an account of challenge-riposte interactions, see Bruce J. Malina and Jerome H. Neyrey, "Honor and Shame in Luke-Acts: Pivotal Values of the Mediterranean World," in *The Social World of Luke-Acts*, ed. Jerome H. Neyrey (Peabody, Mass.: Hendrickson, 1999), 29–32.

2. On the summarizing of the two tablets, see E. P. Sanders, "Jesus and the First Table of the Jewish Law," in *The Historical Jesus in Recent Research*, ed. James D. G. Dunn and Scot McKnight (Winona Lake, Ind.: Eisenbrauns, 2005), 225–37.

3. Ibid., 227.

4. See Adela Yarbro Collins, *Mark: A Commentary,* Hermeneia (Minneapolis: Fortress Press, 2007), 577.

TWENTY-THIRD SUNDAY AFTER PENTECOST

THIRTY-SECOND SUNDAY IN ORDINARY TIME / PROPER 27
NOVEMBER 8, 2009

Revised Common (RCL)	Episcopal (BCP)	Roman Catholic (LFM)
1 Kgs. 17:8-16 or Ruth 3:1-5; 4:13-17	1 Kgs. 17:8-16	1 Kgs. 17:10-16
Psalm 146 or Psalm 127	Psalm 146 or 146:4-9	Ps. 146:7, 8-9a, 9b-10
Heb. 9:24-28	Heb. 9:24-28	Heb. 9:24-28
Mark 12:38-44	Mark 12:38-44	Mark 12:38-44 or 12:41-44

FIRST READING
1 KINGS 17:8-16 (RCL, BCP)
1 KINGS 17:10-16 (LFM)

Elijah is a powerful man of God. His name in fact means, "My God is Yahweh." In this passage he goes to the home of a widow in Zarephath whom God has appointed to feed him. Zarephath is far to the north of the Sea of Galilee, on the coast of the Mediterranean Sea. It is in Sidonian territory, where Baal is the principal deity. Baal was a Canaanite storm and fertility god, thought to control the seasonal cycles that affected the harvest. From this perspective, Baal had power over life and death. If he brought rain at the appropriate times of year, there would be a harvest and people would eat. If he did not bring rain, people would starve and die.

The widow in Zarephath has given up. God has caused a drought, and there is no food to be had. Now this widow is down to her last few crumbs, and she is ready to make a paltry meal, after which, she believes, she and her son will starve. Elijah, however, tells her not to be afraid. Yahweh, the God of Israel, will provide for them by filling the jar of meal and the jug of oil until this same God brings the drought to an end. This story of God's provision of food, along with the previous story in which Elijah calls a drought upon the land (17:1-7) and the following story in which he brings the widow's son back from the dead, show that the rain, the seasons, the harvest, and life and death are not in the hands of Baal, but Yahweh. Even in this area where Baal is so widely worshiped and people do not worship the God of Israel, God can and does provide.

RUTH 3:1-5; 4:13-17 (RCL ALT.)

Ruth has been gleaning in the field of her kinsman by marriage, Boaz. Deuteronomy 24:19 mandates that during the harvest sheaves that are forgotten in the field should be left for the alien, the orphan, and the widow (see also Exod. 23:11; Lev. 19:9-10). This was a way of caring for people like Ruth and Naomi who were left without other means of providing for themselves. Boaz is a righteous man, and exceeds the requirements of the law in his treatment of Ruth (see 2:8-16). Out of his regard for her faithfulness to Naomi, he encourages Ruth to glean only in his fields and to stay near the young women of his household for protection. He provides her with food and water and lets her glean among the standing sheaves, rather than simply to gather those that have been missed in the harvest. He even has his workers hold back some of the harvest for her.

Yet even though Boaz shows special kindness to Ruth, gleaning the fields was a tenuous sort of existence, a way of living hand to mouth without security for the future. Therefore, Naomi and Ruth form a plan to bring Boaz and Ruth together in marriage. Exactly what takes place on the threshing floor between Ruth and Boaz is unclear and has been the source of much speculation and debate. There are sexual overtones in this story, and some interpreters have suggested that the word translated "feet" in this passage is a euphemism for genitals. Such a meaning is possible, but it is not clearly the case, and the author seems to convey the sexual overtones of the story more subtly than this.[1] The word here translated "feet" (vv. 4, 7) can also mean "legs," and, as Frederic Bush notes, "Naomi most probably means that Ruth should uncover the lower half of Boaz's body and lie down there close beside him," as a husband and wife would lie together.[2] The NRSV translates Ruth's response to Boaz in verse 9 as "I am Ruth, your servant; spread your cloak over your servant, for you are next-of-kin." Yet the word *gō'ēl*, here translated "next of kin," really means "redeemer." In essence, Ruth asks Boaz for marriage, but the grounds on which she asks are unclear. Is she asking based on the rules of levirate marriage, or on some other grounds related to the care of family members in need? This is another topic of considerable debate.[3] The main issue, however, is that she is seeking security in the household of Boaz.

> This story shows how God's people can be blessed by one who was not born within the house of Israel. God can work through the most unusual people in unexpected ways.

To make a long (and unusual) story short, the plan works. Ruth and Boaz are married, and together they conceive a son, Obed. Ruth's *hesed*—covenant faithfulness—to Naomi brings them to a place of security and blessing. Israel is also blessed by Ruth, for Obed is the grandfather of David, Israel's greatest king. This is a story that celebrates covenant faithfulness and righteousness. Yet it also shows how God's people can be blessed by one who was not born within the house of Israel. God can work through the most unusual people in unexpected ways.

RESPONSIVE READING

PSALM 146 (RCL, BCP)
PSALM 146:4-9 (BCP ALT.)
PSALM 146:7, 8-9A, 9B-10 (LFM)

The God of Israel is a God of righteousness, and for this righteousness the psalmist sings praises. The psalm begins and ends with the word *hallelujah!* While the princes of this earth may seem powerful, they are mortals. They will die and their plans will accompany them to the grave. Only God's faithfulness is eternal, and God is our only true and lasting hope.

Righteousness is carried out in works of justice and mercy. The psalmist writes of God's justice for the oppressed, provision for the hungry, and release of prisoners. God gives sight to the blind, lifts up the downtrodden, watches over strangers, and cares for the widow and the orphan. God upholds and blesses these vulnerable ones as well as those who emulate God's acts of righteous toward them. The way of the wicked, however, leads only to ruin.

PSALM 127 (RCL ALT.)

Whatever one does, says the psalmist, one must do with God's help and blessing. Life apart from God is futile. The building of a house, the guarding of a city, and the day-to-day work that people do are all dependent upon God's providential care. Many modern readers would do well to heed the psalmist's counsel that anxious toil and overworking oneself are fruitless, for God is our true provider. Children are also God's gift. Here sons are highlighted because of their role in protecting family honor in legal disputes at the city gate.⁴ In all things, happiness and fulfillment come from God, rather than through our own efforts.

SECOND READING

HEBREWS 9:24-28 (RCL, BCP, LFM)

The writer of Hebrews emphasizes again and again that Christ's atoning sacrifice for sin is the ultimate sacrifice, and the sacrifices of levitical priests are no longer necessary. Christ is the perfect priest, as opposed to the human levitical priests. Christ made sacrifice in a heavenly sanctuary, while the levitical priests make sacrifice in a temple "made by human hands" (9:24). Christ's sacrifice was himself, whereas the levitical priests sacrifice bulls and goats. The point of this extended argument is to reinforce belief in the efficacy of Christ's atonement and discourage participation in traditional Jewish rites associated with sacrifice in the Jerusalem Temple. The writer believes that to continue to participate in these rites is to deny Christ's atoning work, which is effectively to deny one's own salvation.

Hebrews has just ended a discussion of the earthly and heavenly sanctuaries. Here the writer may be indebted to Platonic thought, in which the material things of this earth are only copies of the archetypes that exist in heaven. The sanctuary in the earthly temple, the writer holds, is simply a "sketch" and a "copy" of one that exists in heaven. The levitical high priests enter into the earthly sanctuary in the earthly temple and make imperfect sacrifices year after year. Christ, by contrast, who is a high priest according to the order of Melchizedek, entered into the true and heavenly sanctuary and offered himself in a sacrifice that needs never to be repeated. What has occurred in heaven is perfect, whereas what occurs on the earth is necessarily imperfect. Christ will return, the writer holds, not to make atonement again, but to judge.

As we think about the "supersessionist" theology of Hebrews, we need to remember that this work, probably written within forty years after the death of Jesus, reflects a time when the Christian faith was just emerging. In some places, the split between church and synagogue was still occurring, and this was a painful process. There were not many Christians in the world, and the churches held no political power at all. The writer of Hebrews could not have foreseen the terrible events that would come to pass in the relationship between Christians and Jews. He had no way of knowing of the considerable political power that Christian leaders would someday have at their disposal. Today, however, we have the benefit of hindsight, and our cognizance of negative attitudes and actions toward Jews through the centuries should lead us to consider carefully our treatment of texts such as Hebrews.

> The writer of Hebrews could not have foreseen the terrible events that would come to pass in the relationship between Christians and Jews.

The Gospel

MARK 12:38-44 (RCL, BCP, LFM)
MARK 12:41-44 (LFM ALT.)

At the heart of Mark's Gospel is conflict. Jesus is engaged in conflict from the first chapter of the Gospel until his death on the cross. He comes to defeat evil, which is often manifested in the demonic. Yet evil also inheres in common-place human values. Just as Jesus casts out demons from the possessed, he comes to purge human beings of sinful attitudes and practices. Here, as the Passion narrative approaches, Jesus once again enters into conflict, not just with the scribes whom he criticizes, but also with values, assumptions, and ways of living that devalue the vulnerable members of society.

The two episodes in Mark 12:38-44 are closely related thematically. In fact, it might be best to read them as one story, a kind of "compare and contrast." On several occasions in the narrative, especially in chapters 8, 9, and 10, Jesus has taught his followers to give up their aspirations for high honor, grand reputation, prestige, and pride of place. These are the kinds of markers by which ancient Mediterranean people commonly measured self-worth. Yet Jesus turns these values on their head, teaching his followers to become servants, to become like children, to put others first. Now, as he teaches in the Temple, he turns his attention toward scribes who exemplify all of the characteristics that he criticizes.

> Jesus enters into conflict, not just with the scribes whom he criticizes, but also with values, assumptions, and ways of living that devalue the vulnerable members of society.

The scribes were professional and respected interpreters of the law. They served an important function in the culture. Righteousness is at the very heart of the covenant between God and Israel, and skilled interpreters help to maintain the covenant. On several occasions in the narrative, they come to challenge Jesus (see, for example, 3:22, 7:5, 11:27-28, 12:28). This is not surprising, since as legal experts they are likely to enter into legal disputes. Now it is Jesus who challenges them (though not for the first time; see 12:1-12). He does so not because of their interpretation of Scripture, but because of their hypocrisy. A similar critique is at the heart of Matthew 23: the scribes and Pharisees "do not practice what they teach" (Matt. 23:3).

The scribes apparently like to "walk around in long robes, and to be greeted with respect in the marketplaces, and to have the best seats in the synagogues and places of honor at banquets." By walking around in long robes, the scribes show themselves to be of importance and high status. A long robe was an expensive garment and wearing it showed that one was a person of means.[5] The point of being greeted with respect in the marketplace is that the market was an arena of male public interaction. Other people can see these respectful greetings, and the reputation of the scribe as a person worthy of respect increases. Having the best seats in the synagogue and places of honor at banquets shows that these are people of considerable status.

The accusation that the scribes "devour widows' houses" is rather unclear. The scribes are educated people of high standing. As a result, they had the opportunity to take advantage of more vulnerable members of society, such as widows.

It could be that they were given responsibility for the care of a widow's estate, but exploited their position of responsibility for their own financial gain. Though they say long prayers, this is only "for the sake of appearance" (v. 40). Their piety is a façade. One must "beware" of them (12:38), because while they seem righteous, their actions are wicked. They wish to receive honor, but they have truly done nothing to deserve it.

In contrast to the scribes is a poor widow, the kind of person mentioned as a victim of the scribes' exploitation in verse 40. Into the treasury of the Temple she puts two copper coins called "lepta." The lepton was the smallest coin in circulation. If these two coins were the sum total of her wealth, she was very poor indeed, and her poverty would stand in contrast not only to the rich who contributed large sums, but to the grandiosity of the Temple itself. The Temple was a massive structure requiring vast resources for its upkeep and day-to-day activities, and its treasury held very large sums of money and goods. Jesus, however, does not measure her contribution according to its monetary value. In fact, he praises her above all those who have put in large sums of money.

It is just like Jesus to do such a thing. He touches a leper (1:41), calls a tax collector to be his follower (2:14), and shares table with tax collectors and sinners (2:15). On his way to help the daughter of a synagogue leader, he stops to bless a sick woman who has spent all of her money (5:30-34). He embraces children, who have nothing to offer him (10:13-16), and he calls the rich to account (10:17-27). Jesus takes time for beggars, the blind, and the otherwise disabled. Now he exalts a poor widow, who can contribute to the Temple almost nothing financially, over those who contribute large sums of money. He is always attending to the "wrong" people, those who can offer him none of the social currency so prized in his day. He refuses to recognize the cultural standards by which people were assigned importance. He has a deeply countercultural lens through which he views people.

Jesus is always attending to the "wrong" people, those who can offer him none of the social currency so prized in his day.

This woman, says Jesus, "out of her poverty has put in everything she had, all she had to live on" (12:44). The words translated "all she had to live on" can also be translated, "her whole life." She has held back nothing in her devotion to God. In the explanation of the Parable of the Sower (4:14-20), Jesus talks about impediments to the word's bearing fruit. Among these are "the cares of the world, and the lure of wealth, and the desire for other things" that "come in and choke the word, and it yields nothing" (4:19). Yet here is a woman who has almost nothing, and gives her last two coins to the Temple. Many people would think her foolish, but in Jesus' view the foolish people are those who are prevented by the "cares of the world" from entering into God's kingdom. The poor woman represents the "good soil" in which the word can bear fruit, "thirty and sixty and a hundredfold."

The contrast between the scribes whom Jesus castigates and the woman whom he praises is glaring. The scribes seek their own good. Their piety is affected and false. They take advantage of the poor to line their own pockets. The poor widow gives of herself in service to God. She makes no display of her gift. Indeed, from the common cultural perspective, there is no display to be made. What she has done amounts to virtually nothing, unless one views things from Jesus' perspective, in which case her gift is a contribution of great significance. One more time, Jesus tries to teach his followers to turn their values upside down.

In many ways we are different than the people who lived around the time of Jesus, but, both then and now, people act in their own interest at the expense of others. Jesus teaches us to question our assumptions about what is important, what we value, and how we should live. Our culture offers us certain markers of success, most of which involve the abundance of material possessions. Yet success from Jesus' perspective is not about gaining for ourselves, but about serving others, especially the least and the last.

> Jesus teaches us to question our assumptions about what is important, what we value, and how we should live.

Notes

1. See Frederic Bush, *Ruth, Esther* (Dallas: Word, 1996), 153.

2. Ibid., 152.

3. For a discussion of this issue and the debate around it, see ibid., 166–69.

4. See Konrad Schaefer, *Psalms* (Collegeville, Minn.: Liturgical, 2001), 307.

5. See Adela Yarbro Collins, *Mark: A Commentary,* Hermeneia (Minneapolis: Fortress Press, 2007), 583.

TWENTY-FOURTH SUNDAY AFTER PENTECOST

THIRTY-THIRD SUNDAY IN ORDINARY TIME / PROPER 28
NOVEMBER 15, 2009

Revised Common (RCL)	Episcopal (BCP)	Roman Catholic (LFM)
Dan. 12:1-3 or 1 Sam. 1:4-20	Dan. 12:1-4a (5-13)	Dan. 12:1-3
Psalm 16 or 1 Sam. 2:1-10	Psalm 16 or 16:5-11	Ps. 16:5 + 8, 9-10, 11
Heb. 10:11-14 (15-18) 19-25	Heb. 10:31-39	Heb. 10:11-14, 18
Mark 13:1-8	Mark 13:14-23	Mark 13:24-32

FIRST READING

DANIEL 12:1-3 (RCL, LFM)
DANIEL 12:1-4A (5-13) (BCP)

In this passage, Daniel provides an early Jewish articulation of the resurrection of the dead. Michael, Israel's angelic guardian (see also 10:13), will arise, and God's holy people, "everyone who is found written in the book," will be delivered. The book referenced here is the "book of life," mentioned several times in the Old Testament (for example, Exod. 32:32; Ps. 69:28; Isa. 4:3; Mal. 3:16). After the resurrection there will be a final judgment, and though they have suffered during their lives, the "wise" and "those who lead many to righteousness" will enjoy a reward of everlasting glory. The wicked, by contrast, will endure eternal shame and contempt. As is the commonly the case in apocalyptic literature, these revelations are to be hidden away until the proper time.

Verses 5-13 include later additions to the book, specifying the time "until the end of these wonders" (v. 6). An angel swears that it will be "a time, two times, and half a time" (v. 7), which means three-and-a-half years, a longer span of time than the 1,150 days predicted in 8:14. In verses 11 and 12, even longer lengths of time are offered. It seems that longer calculations were made when earlier ones proved incorrect.

Here in Daniel are some of the roots of the Christian belief in the resurrection of the dead. Daniel believes in a God who is just, and who abides eternally with the righteous. God has power over life and death, and death will not have the final word.

1 SAMUEL 1:4-20 (RCL ALT.)

The initial story of 1 Samuel tells of God's providential care for Hannah, who gave birth to Samuel. Samuel would grow up to be a prophet and judge, and he would anoint both Saul and David. Samuel is given over to God even before his birth when his mother takes a nazirite vow on his behalf (v. 11). A nazirite vow marked a special time of consecration (see Num. 6:1-21). One who had taken such a vow did not drink wine or cut his or her hair. This person would also make a special effort to avoid contact with a corpse. Samuel, like Samson (see Judg. 13:2-7), is an unusual case in that he does not take the vow himself. Further, while most nazirite vows were temporary, in the cases of Samuel and Samson there appears to be no limit on the time of consecration.

This is a story about God's care for the downtrodden. Hannah takes this unusual vow of consecration because she so desperately wishes to bear a son. Her husband, Elkanah, asks her, "Am I not more to you than ten sons?" The implicit answer is, "No, Elkanah, you are not." Hannah describes her anguished prayers as "pouring out my soul before the LORD," and "speaking out of my great anxiety and vexation" (vv. 15-16). In the worldview of this story, much of a woman's worth and honor was tied to her ability to give birth to children, and especially male children. To many modern readers, this will seem a very unhealthy perspective, but cognizant of the worldview assumed by the text is essential for understanding the depth of Hannah's sorrow and desperation. Yet God has not abandoned her. God answers the prayer of this despondent woman, and through her blesses Israel with Samuel's prophecy and leadership.

> God answers the prayer of this despondent woman, and through her blesses Israel with Samuel's prophecy and leadership.

RESPONSIVE READING

PSALM 16 (RCL, BCP)
PSALM 16:5-11 (BCP ALT.)
PSALM 16:5 + 8, 9-10, 11 (LFM)

This petition for protection is also a statement of devotion to the God of Israel. One finds security in the one true God, whereas those who go after other gods only add to their own sorrows. The psalmist affirms that he has not prayed to other gods or made offerings to them, but has been entirely loyal to Yahweh (v. 4).

God is the psalmist's counselor (v. 7), and the psalmist is always in God's presence (v. 8). In Sheol, where the dead abide, no one praises God (see Ps. 6:5), but the psalmist is not like those who have died. He praises God and enjoys the "fullness of joy" that one experiences in God's presence.

1 SAMUEL 2:1-10 (RCL ALT.)

"Hannah's Song" is a beautiful prayer of praise and thanksgiving. It is probable that this song was at one time independent of the story of Samuel's birth, but in the narrative context of 1 Samuel it contributes poetic expression to a theme already present in the story: God lifts up the lowly. The poem advises the reader, "Talk no more so very proudly, let not arrogance come from your mouth" (2:3). It is the humble, rather than the proud, whom God will bless. This poem encourages the reader to trust in God, rather than in one's own strength. Verses 4-7 develop this theme with a series of contrasts: the "bows of the mighty" contrast with the "feeble" (v. 4); the "full" contrast with the "hungry" (v. 5); the woman who has many children contrasts with the "barren" (v. 5); the rich contrast with the poor (v. 7). In each case, the less fortunate or weaker party prevails. It is God who "brings low" and "exalts." Human beings may think that they are powerful and secure, but true power belongs to God, and true security rests only with God.

> Human beings may think that they are powerful and secure, but true power belongs to God, and true security rests only with God.

SECOND READING

HEBREWS 10:11-14 (15-18) 19-25 (RCL)
HEBREWS 10:31-39 (BCP)
HEBREWS 10:11-14, 18 (LFM)

In the first century, becoming a Christian could involve considerable personal sacrifice. It sometimes meant the severing of family ties, the loss of job opportunities and income, and even arrest, torture, and execution. The Christians to whom Hebrews was written apparently endured "hard struggle with sufferings, sometimes being publicly exposed to abuse and persecution, and sometimes being partners with those so treated" (10:32-33). It seems that some of the Christians were imprisoned and others were robbed of their possessions. There were many reasons not to become a Christian, and if one did become a Christian, there were many reasons to recant. Hebrews therefore encourages perseverance. Do not, the author says, forfeit the salvation that is available in Christ. Those who "shrink back" will be lost (v. 38).

In verses 11-14, Hebrews describes the remarkable sacrifice of Christ in the heavenly sanctuary. This sacrifice is the perfect act of atonement and initiates a new covenant between God and humankind (v. 15). Hebrews draws upon the story of Moses' ratification of the covenant with blood (Exod. 24:3-8, though elements of some other stories are conflated with this one) as a precedent for God's forming a new covenant through Christ's blood. Because of this new covenant, believers may have full assurance that God will judge them favorably. The writer exhorts them, however, "Let us hold fast to the confession of our hope without wavering" (v. 23). In other words, they must maintain their belief in the effectiveness of Christ's atoning work on the cross, and their actions

> Hebrews draws upon the story of Moses' ratification of the covenant with blood as a precedent for God's forming a new covenant through Christ's blood.

must demonstrate this belief. If they go back to their old ways, if they do not demonstrate faith in Christ, then they will lose their salvation.

THE GOSPEL
MARK 13:1-8 (RCL)
MARK 13:14-23 (BCP)
MARK 13:24-32 (LFM)

As Jesus and his disciples are coming out of the Temple, one of them comments on the size of the stones and the buildings. This comment is quite understandable. The Temple was built up to tremendous proportions under Herod the Great. It must have been a magnificent structure, and its walls were built of massive stone blocks. Seeing even the ruins of the Temple today, one wonders how such a structure could have been destroyed without the use of modern machinery. Yet this is exactly what Jesus prophesies will happen. Not one stone will be left upon another, he says. In fact, this is what happened in 70 C.E., when the Romans, who had besieged Jerusalem in an effort to put down a revolt, made their way into the city, slaughtered the population, and destroyed the Temple. The destruction of the Temple must have taken quite some time, but the Romans were masters of intimidation and they quelled revolts without mercy.

The thirteenth chapter of Mark is sometimes called the "Markan Apocalypse," and it has often been taken to be about the end of the world. Yet the text itself tells us its topic: the events surrounding the destruction of the Temple. In verse 3, Jesus and his disciples have made their way to the Mount of Olives, from which the Temple would have been easily visible to the west. Jesus has just prophesied that the Temple will be destroyed. His disciples then ask the natural question, "Tell us, when will this be, and what will be the sign that all these things are about to be accomplished?" The discourse that follows is in answer to their question. In other words, the disciples ask how they will know when the Temple is to be destroyed, and Jesus tells them. He tells them, however, using the language of Old Testament prophecy, language that his followers might have understood and Mark's audience might have understood, but later readers from other cultures generally misunderstand.

"Beware," says Jesus, "that no one leads you astray" (v. 5). Many will come in the name of the Messiah saying, "I am he!" (v. 6). Jesus himself will make the same claim, but not until he is on trial before the council (14:62). His claim to be "the Messiah, the Son of the Blessed One" (14:61) is a confession that will lead to his death. To be the true Messiah, for Mark, means suffering. The Messiah is not one who claims power and conquers amid escalating violent conflict, but who, despite his great power, has come to serve others and to give his life as a ransom for many (10:45). Jesus' prophecy, then, relates to the false messiahs who would claim authority in the years leading up to and during the First Jewish Revolt (beginning in 66 C.E.). The language of nation rising up against nation, and kingdom against kingdom (v. 8), is relatively straightforward: there will be war between nations. Old Testament prophets used language of catastrophes in the natural world to talk about political events of great magnitude in the life of Israel. The mention of earthquakes (v. 8) is a way of talking about the coming disasters of war, just as in Isaiah 13:13. Famine is a consequence of war, for crops were burned, and farming and commerce were disrupted.

The "desolating sacrilege" set up in the Temple will be the sign that it is time to flee. In the background of this passage lie references to an "abomination that desolates" in Daniel 9:27, 11:31, and 12:11. Likewise, 1 Maccabees 1:54 refers to a "desolating sacrilege on the altar of burnt offering." Each of these references relates to the same event: the setting up of an altar of Zeus in the Jerusalem Temple at the command of the Seleucid emperor Antiochus IV. Mark has drawn on the language of these earlier writers, but exactly what he means by "desolating sacrilege" is unclear. There are, however, several theories as to what the "desolating sacrilege" might be. One relates to Caligula's order in 40 C.E. that his statue be placed in every temple in the empire. This would undoubtedly have been a "desolating sacrilege," and the Jews refused to obey this command. There surely would have been severe violence over this issue had Caligula not suddenly died. Yet this event occurred over two decades prior to the revolt, so its association with the events that foretell the coming destruction of the revolt is tenuous. Another theory is that the "desolating sacrilege" refers to the Roman troops, or

> The Messiah is not one who claims power and conquers amid escalating violent conflict, but who, despite his great power, has come to serve others and to give his life as a ransom for many.

perhaps the emperor Titus, standing in the Temple and setting up standards there after the Roman victory in 70 C.E.[1] This proposal is quite reasonable, but modern readers will have to be content with a degree of uncertainty as to the referent of the "desolating sacrilege" in Mark.

Despite the uncertainty of modern readers regarding this reference, it seems that Mark expected the original audience of this text to understand its meaning ("let the reader understand," 13:14). If this is true, then the "desolating sacrilege set up where it ought not to be" is a temporal marker: when this event takes place, it is time to flee. This flight, moreover, must be immediate. There will be no time to go back for possessions. Pregnant women and those with nursing infants will be especially at risk, since quick and unencumbered flight will be difficult or impossible for them (see Hos. 13:16). If it is winter, the journey will be even more difficult. The suffering will be great indeed, and everyone would die if God did nor shorten those days so that the elect could be saved (see Isa. 65:8).

As Jesus said in 13:6, false messiahs will arise. Here in verse 22 he also mentions false prophets. In such desperate times, people will be vulnerable to the deception of false leaders who claim to be sent by God. These false messiahs and prophets will produce signs and omens and might even lead the elect astray. Jesus' followers, however, have been forewarned (see Jer. 6:13-15; Deut. 13:1-3). They are to watch for these signs and recognize what is taking place.

Verses 24-26 draw heavily upon the language of Old Testament prophecy. Many interpreters have seen in this passage a prophecy of the end of the world. Given the way in which this kind of language is used in the Old Testament, however, Mark's Jesus is probably not speaking about the end of the world, but of political and national upheaval followed by redemption of the elect. Isaiah 13:10, for example, reads, "For the stars of the heavens and their constellations will not give their light; the sun will be dark at its rising, and the moon will not shed its light." In this passage, Isaiah is not talking about the end of the world, but

> Mark's Jesus is probably not speaking about the end of the world, but of political and national upheaval followed by redemption of the elect.

about the cataclysmic events of a war between Babylon and Assyria. A similar oracle occurs in Ezekiel 32:7-8: "When I blot you out, I will cover the heavens, and make their stars dark; I will cover the sun with a cloud, and the moon shall not give its light. All the shining lights of the heavens I will darken above you, and put darkness on your land, says the Lord God." This oracle relates to the defeat of Egypt by Babylon, but not to God's destruction of creation. In Joel 2:10 we read, "The earth quakes before them, the heavens tremble. The sun and the moon are darkened, and the stars withdraw their shining." A similar passage occurs in Joel 2:31: "The sun shall be turned to darkness, and the moon to blood, before the great and terrible day of the Lord comes." Neither of these passages, however, is about the end of the world, but each is about political turmoil, the threat of destruction, and God's redemption. When we read in Mark, "the sun will be darkened, and the moon will not give its light, and the stars will be falling from heaven, and the powers in the heavens will be shaken" (13:24-25), we are reading a prophecy about the events related to the First Jewish Revolt and the destruction of the Temple. Jesus here stands in the tradition of Israel's prophets, using poetic, metaphorical language to talk about national calamity.[2]

In the same way, verses 26-27 involve appropriations of Old Testament themes and language to speak about particular historical events. In Daniel 7, the Son of Man is a representation of God's holy ones, Israel. After a period of suffering (7:25), the holy ones are vindicated by God through God's giving them kingship and dominion (7:14, 27). In Mark, this prophecy is understood in terms of the vindication of the holy ones who follow Jesus. Jesus' followers are instructed not to follow false messiahs and prophets. They are not to fight, but to flee when the war comes. They will endure rejection and persecution because they follow Jesus (13:9-13), but God's protection will be around them. The ingathering of God's people (Mark 13:27) also has precedent in the Old Testament. For example, Isaiah 11:11 states, "On that day the Lord will extend his hand yet a second time to recover the remnant that is left of his people, from Assyria, from Egypt, from Pathros, from Ethiopia, from Elam, from Shinar, from Hamath, and from the coastlands of the sea" (see also Ezek. 39:28; Zech. 10:9-10). Those who take up the sword against Rome will suffer a great defeat, culminating in the destruction of the Temple. Those who follow Christ's teachings, however, will be vindicated, though they will have endured persecution and suffering for Christ. While their faith is not centered on the Temple, neither have they participated in the events leading to its destruction.

> Followers of Jesus are to trust in God's providential care even if the world around them seems to be falling apart before their eyes.

These are complex texts, deeply rooted in Old Testament language, history, and theology. Yet, despite the difficulties that they present, they are also powerful texts that teach us not to follow false messiahs and prophets. The dangers of over-zealous nationalism and reactionary violence are clear in this passage. Violence begets violence. Followers of Jesus are to trust in God's providential care even if the world around them seems to be falling apart before their eyes.

Notes

1. Both theories are briefly discussed in Morna D. Hooker, *The Gospel According to St. Mark* (Peabody, Mass.: Hendrickson, 1991), 314.

2. For a discussion of such figurative language, see G. B. Caird, "The Language of Eschatology," chap. 14 in *The Language and Imagery of the Bible* (Philadelphia: Westminster, 1980).

CHRIST THE KING / REIGN OF CHRIST

LAST SUNDAY IN ORDINARY TIME / PROPER 29
NOVEMBER 22, 2009
KAROLINE M. LEWIS

Revised Common (RCL)	Episcopal (BCP)	Roman Catholic (LFM)
Dan. 7:9-10, 13-14 or 2 Sam. 23:1-7	Dan. 7:9-14	Dan. 7:13-14
Psalm 93 or 132:1-12 (13-18)	Psalm 93	Ps. 93:1a, 1b-2, 5
Rev. 1:4b-8	Rev. 1:1-8	Rev. 1:5-8
John 18:33-37	John 18:33-37 or Mark 11:1-11	John 18:33b-37

FIRST READING

DANIEL 7:9-14 (BCP)
DANIEL 7:9-10, 13-14 (RCL)
DANIEL 7:13-14 (LFM)

For this last Sunday after Pentecost that celebrates the reign of Christ, or Christ the King, the first and second lessons are appropriately both representative of apocalyptic literature. This is not the case for Years A or C. Situating these texts within this literary genre lends a particularity of meaning and theological impact for this Sunday in the liturgical year. Contemporary readers find apocalyptic texts strange and unfamiliar, yet this would not have been the case for the audiences to which these texts were addressed. Coming to light in the intertestamental period, 200 B.C.E.–100 C.E., and arising from Judaic prophecy, this stylized medium offered comfort and encouragement in the face of ongoing battles for rule of Palestine. With the spread of Hellenism under Alexander the Great came the political reality of vying for control of Palestine, first under the Ptolemaic Empire, then under Antiochus Epiphanus and the Seleucids. While the Maccabbean Revolt temporarily put Palestine under the jurisdiction of the Hasmoneans, in 63 B.C.E. it was annexed by the Roman Empire. Only a little more than a hundred years into Roman rule, the Romans destroyed the Temple in response to increased Jewish resistance, which included the first Jewish Revolt (66–70 C.E.), and any further attempts at revolt would be unsuccessful (132–135 C.E.).

Apocalyptic literature met a particular need in the lives of God's people and might best be described as crisis literature. For the oppressed and persecuted, it provided an interpretation of the unfolding events that upheld the control of God over against and in the midst of the perceived control of other forces. The symbolism, visions, and images provided a view of the present situation whereby the dominion of God was affirmed even though every indication would suggest otherwise. The reign of God is in the midst of the crisis and beyond.

The appointed text from the book of Daniel for this Sunday is an example of response to the political situation narrated in the early part of the brief history outlined above. Daniel's vision secures the promise of God's reign in the midst of foreign control, in particular under the Seleucids and Antiochus IV. The first section of the pericope in part speaks to this very issue as judgment comes to the oppressive forces in the form of "the Ancient One." In verses 13-14 another figure joins the Ancient One, "one like a human being," or literally, "one like a son of man." From the perspective of faith in and witness to Jesus, verses 13-14 testify to this figure as Jesus. The Gospels designate Jesus as the Son of Man who descends from the heavens (see Mark 13:26, 14:62; John 1:51). On Christ the King Sunday, the dominion, glory, and kingship granted to Jesus can be located in the very real need to claim Jesus' reign, God's reign, when it appears that other forces are in control. This becomes a powerful declaration about Christ as king that positions this claim not as an over-and-against, hierarchical, hegemonic. Statement but as a testimony to the power and presence of God in spite of our despair and in the midst of our distress.

> On Christ the King Sunday, the dominion, glory, and kingship granted to Jesus can be located in the very real need to claim Jesus' reign when it appears that other forces are in control.

2 SAMUEL 23:1-7 (RCL ALT.)

The RCL alternate first reading comes from the second to last chapter of 2 Samuel, and while the text states, "these are the last words of David," the date cannot be determined, and literarily, this is not the case because David will speak again in the last chapter and again in 1 Kings until his death is narrated in 1 Kings 2:10. Since a good portion of the RCL alternative readings for Pentecost have been from the David story, recalling the kingship of David on this last Sunday of the season provides a sense of closure but also continuity as we look toward the birth of Jesus and the claims about his ancestry, kingship, and legacy.

This brief poem follows immediately after David's great song of thanksgiving (22:1-51) in which he exclaims the mighty acts of the Lord throughout his life and reign. While 23:1-7 may pale in comparison to the longer and weightier previous psalm, these words of David redirect his reflections from what the Lord has done *for* David to what the Lord has done *through* David.

PSALM 93 (RCL, BCP)
PSALM 93:1A, 1B-2, 5 (LFM)

This hymn of praise, or enthronement psalm (see also Psalms 29, 47, and 95), is a fitting responsive reading for Christ the King Sunday. The psalm celebrates the image of the Lord as king and provides specificity to the meaning and importance of this image for God in the worship life of Israel. In this psalm, the Lord as king is not simply the one who reigns over the nations, but the one who reigns over even the chaos of the world. The threefold repetition of "floods" in addition to waters, waves, and sea heighten the potency of the powers that the Lord has subdued in demonstration of sovereignty and rule.

PSALM 132:1-12 (13-18) (RCL ALT.)

This royal psalm is dedicated to the remembrance and importance of the rule of David, both in relation to God's promises and to obedience to God's covenant. The psalm celebrates David's bringing the ark to Mount Zion and the great blessings that God has bestowed for the future of Zion. While verses 13-18 are optional verses for the day, there is merit in including them in the responsive reading. Here God states directly the decision to make Zion the place where God dwells, and in verse 17 we read of God's intent to continue the reign of David forever. The reign of God, the kingship of God, inhabits a place, works through God's chosen ones, and will redefine what reign, kingship, and glory mean in God's Son.

SECOND LESSON

REVELATION 1:1-8 (BCP)
REVELATION 1:4B-8 (RCL)
REVELATION 1:5-8 (LFM)

For the few times the book of Revelation comes up in the lectionary, serious consideration should be given to preaching these opening verses of the letter. As discussed above in the commentary on the first reading, understanding the nature and function of apocalyptic literature is critical for the interpretation of these less-than-familiar texts. While Revelation is the only complete apocalypse in the New Testament, there are other portions of writings that are considered apocalyptic in nature (for example, Mark 13 and 1 Thess. 4:13-17).

Because of our lack of exposure to this genre and because few sermons are devoted to Revelation, it is frequently the most misunderstood and misinterpreted book in the Bible. Rather than understanding it as a specific letter to an alienated, exiled, or persecuted community of faith in the late first century, many people think of it as a divinely certified blueprint for the future. It is ironic that a letter so deeply embedded in the situational and occasional circumstances of these seven churches in Asia Minor is most often relegated to prophecy at its narrowest sense of prediction. A letter meant to bring comfort, hope, and a call for endurance (2:7, 11, 17, 26; 3:5, 12, 21) ends up being a vehicle of fear, judgment, and signs of the end of the world.

On a trip to the North Georgia mountains from our home in Atlanta, my husband and I passed on the winding road a small church with a prominent billboard that said on that particular day, "Do you know where you are going?" We soon realized that the question had nothing to do with our current trip when five miles up the road we passed another small church with another strategically placed sign that said, "Are you sure you want to go there?" This has been the kind of theology for which Revelation has been used—and abused. Yet, its use in the church testifies to its true purpose. In the *Lutheran Book of Worship*, for example, seventy-eight hymn texts are attributed to Revelation.

> A letter meant to bring comfort, hope, and a call for endurance ends up being a vehicle of fear, judgment, and signs of the end of the world.

One of the reasons to preach on this particular text from the book of Revelation is that a sermon could address a number of these issues. The name for the book arises from the very first word, *apokalypsis*, which means "revelation" in the singular—not "revelations," as the book is frequently called, thus leading to the assumption that it is a series of visions about the future. This revelation comes from Jesus and was made known to John. What follows is described as John's witness or testimony to the word of God, which is then communicated to the seven churches. Verse 4 reveals the other center of this book, that it really is a letter to seven specific churches. Like the letters of Paul, this is addressed to a specific audience in response to a specific situation and begins with the typical greeting for a letter. And, like Paul's letters, clues to the general thrust of the letter are present in the greeting. The expanse of the reign and rule of Christ spans the past, present, and future, "from him who is and who was and who is to come." This sweeping claim is also that of the Lord God: "'I am the Alpha and the Omega,' says the Lord God, who is and who was and who is to come, the Almighty" (1:8).

In addition, the main claim of the letter is also stated in these opening verses. Jesus Christ is the ruler of the kings of the earth (v. 5), and glory and dominion are his forever (v. 6). While it may seem that other entities (such as, the Greco-Roman Empire) rule the world, the battle for power has already been won: "Now have come the salvation and the power and the kingdom of our God and the authority of his Messiah" (12:10). The Lord is indeed the Almighty God.

One fruitful means of interpreting this text for preaching is to explore the tension between the genre of apocalyptic and the genre of a letter. For the claim of this unique writing in the canon is that God's revelation to God's people is inextricably tied to the everydayness of the needs of God's people. God's answer to the plight and peril of each of these churches is a word on target but is also a word that transports them and unites them to a common vision of God's purpose. It is important to remember that this letter is addressed to seven churches so that each congregation knew of the matters that existed in the others. Why is this the case? What is the function of such an address? What might result from hearing the issues in other churches? God's response to all is this shared revelation and so makes these churches God's kingdom on earth (1:6).

> God's answer to the plight and peril of each of these churches is a word on target but is also a word that transports them and unites them to a common vision of God's purpose.

In the liturgical context of Christ the King Sunday or the Reign of Christ, we can look to this introduction to Revelation for ways to unpack what kingship can signify. General propositions that claim Christ as king are not helpful for our congregations. What difference does such a claim make? So what? Why should that matter? How this text articulates the meaning, purpose, and possibilities for understanding this title for Jesus can lead to thinking, imagination, and dialogue around power, politics, and faith.

The Gospel

JOHN 18:33-37 (RCL, BCP)
JOHN 18:33b-37 (LFM)

This section of text from the Fourth Gospel comes early on in the trial narrative of John's Passion story. John 18:28—19:16a is devoted to Jesus' trial before Pilate, after already having been interrogated by Annas (18:13-27). At the same time that Jesus stands before Annas, Peter denies Jesus. The narrative moves back and forth between Jesus' interrogation and Peter's interrogation, creating the effect of simultaneous "trials" for Jesus and Peter. It is Peter's "final verdict" that immediately precedes the beginning of Jesus' interrogation by Pilate. "One of the slaves of the high priest, a relative of the man whose ear Peter had cut off, asked, 'Did I not see you in the garden with him?' Again Peter denied it, and at that moment the cock crowed" (18:26-27). While Peter's denial alone is critical to this last scene before Jesus is taken to Pilate, the reference to the garden is also important for the drama that is to follow. Two references to Jesus' arrest are mentioned—(1) Peter cutting off the ear of Malchus, the slave of the high priest, and (2) "in the garden." These two details of the arrest of Jesus are unique to John.

286

THE SEASON
AFTER PENTECOST
─────────
KAROLINE M.
LEWIS

Only John provides the name of the slave and only John locates Jesus' arrest in a garden. The garden becomes the kind of enclosed space that will be worked out in the narrative that follows. In the arrest scene (18:1-13a), Jesus and his disciples enter *into* the garden. When Judas arrives with the representatives of the Jewish authorities and the cohort of Roman soldiers (a cohort is over six hundred men), Jesus comes *out* of the garden (the NRSV translates the Greek verb "come forward") to meet the mob and their weapons, leaving his disciples inside the garden, safely in the fold (10:3).

After Peter's third denial of Jesus, the narrative returns to Jesus where he is brought to Pilate's headquarters (in Greek, "*into* the praetorium"). "They," which later we discover represents the Jewish leaders (18:31), do not enter the praetorium because of ritual defilement, especially on the Day of Preparation for the Passover. These two locations, inside Pilate's headquarters and outside the praetorium, become the two stages on which the unfolding drama in seven scenes (18:29-32, 18:33-38a, 18:38b-40, 19:1-3, 19:4-7, 19:8-12, 19:13-16a) will take place.

> These two locations, inside Pilate's headquarters and outside the praetorium, become the two stages on which the unfolding drama in seven scenes will take place.

The selected text for Christ the King Sunday is scene two in the drama, although most scholars extend this scene through verse 38, and the setting is inside the praetorium. The first scene (18:29-32) is *outside* the headquarters. Pilate is forced to come out to meet the Jewish leaders since they would not come in because of concerns for ritual purity. He first questions the authorities about the charge they are filing against Jesus. The authorities defer to Pilate—essentially saying, "Why would we bring him to you if there was not a capital offense?"—because in the next verses we discover that indeed, they abrogate the death penalty, in part for the sake of their own political standing with Rome.[1] Pilate then goes back into his headquarters to question Jesus about the offense (18:33), thus bringing us into scene two and the reading for Christ the King, Year B.

For each of the canonical Gospels, Jesus as king is an important element of the Passion narrative, but for the Fourth Evangelist more so than the Synoptic accounts. In each Gospel, Jesus' first encounter with Pilate has the procurator asking Jesus the same question, "Are you the King of the Jews?" (Matt. 27:11; Mark 15:2; Luke 23:2-3; John 18:33). Whereas the Synoptic accounts then place this title for Jesus in the context of his crucifixion, as the charge engraved on the plaque above his head and on the lips of those who mock Jesus while he is on the cross, John clusters them in the trial scene with Pilate no less than nine times. The only time the term *king* is used during the crucifixion itself in John is at the debate over the signage above Jesus' head (19:19, 21) and never in a mocking way by passersby.

John 18:33, therefore, is the first such use, paralleling the other Gospel narratives. While in Matthew, Mark, and Luke Jesus responds, "You say so" (Matt. 27:11; Mark 15:2; Luke 23:3), in John, Jesus answers with a question, "Do you ask this on your own, or did others tell you about me?" essentially putting Pilate on the defensive. Now who's on trial? Pilate's answer in the NRSV translation ineffectively captures the negative answer that the Greek construction expects, since Pilate's question is rather the emphatic and contemptuous statement, "Certainly, I am not a Jew!" In Jesus' response to Pilate, it is important to understand the meaning of "kingdom" in the context of the larger themes of the Fourth Gospel. The term for "kingdom" can also be translated "kingship" and this better captures Jesus' sense here. For the Gospel of John, there is no "the kingdom of heaven is like" because Jesus himself brings the very revelation of God, from God, to the world in the incarnation. As a result, at stake for Pilate is whether or not he will recognize that Jesus' reign has nothing to do with kingdoms but, rather, with origins.[2] Where Jesus comes from is the truth (18:38) and not his identity as king. Yet, the latter is exactly what Pilate sees: "So you are a king?"

> For the Gospel of John, there is no "the kingdom of heaven is like" because Jesus himself brings the very revelation of God, from God, to the world in the incarnation.

Jesus' answer, "You say that I am a king," is similar to the Synoptic accounts, yet with one noticeable difference. While in Matthew, Mark, and Luke, Jesus responds, "You say so," in John he says, "You say that I am a king." With the added clause, "that I am a king," the "I am" statements in the Gospel, both predicate and absolute, stand behind "I am a king." Moreover, Jesus extends his answer, that he is witness to the truth and that anyone who belongs to the truth listens to his voice. Standing behind this claim are chapters 9 and 10, where first the blind man hears Jesus' voice and is then healed and recognizes Jesus as Lord (9:38), followed by Jesus' discourse on the healing, which takes up the issue of hearing through the figures of the shepherd and the sheep. The sheep, who are in the fold, hear the voice of the shepherd. In chapter 11, Lazarus heard the voice of Jesus as his name was called, and came out of the grave. And back in the garden after Jesus' crucifixion, Mary will hear Jesus' voice when he calls her name, and she will announce to the disciples, "I have seen the Lord." Those who belong to the truth are the ones who recognize God in Jesus, who has come to make God known (1:18), who can confess with Thomas, "My Lord *and* my God" (20:28). When Pilate questions Jesus, "What is truth?" he asks the very question of this Gospel and exposes the final verdict of his own trial—guilty. The lectionary reading most certainly should be extended through 18:38 for this reason alone.

On its own, this second scene in Jesus' trial before Pilate is an extraordinary text quite apart from its liturgical setting for the day. It is important that the

288

THE SEASON
AFTER PENTECOST
────────────
KAROLINE M.
LEWIS

uniqueness of this text not be overshadowed by its lectionary locale. On this Christ the King Sunday, however, this text provides an abundance of possibility for exploring the church's claim for this last Sunday of the ecclesiastical year. As noted in the commentary on the Markan passage below, Jesus as king is situated in the context of the Passion narrative. This literary and narrative placement suggests that understandings of Jesus as king that do not take this into account risk seeing Jesus' kingship as "of this world" and not "not of this world."

MARK 11:1-11 (BCP ALT.)

The BCP alternate Gospel text is Mark's account of Jesus' entry into Jerusalem. Either the reading from John or the reading from Mark creates a moving contrast between the celebratory claim of Christ as king by situating his reign in the context of the reality of Jesus' death. Calendrically and liturgically, as the last Sunday of the church year, we are reminded that the birth of the king will also come with his death. In this sense, the church holds the incarnation and the crucifixion together at once. We are met again with the certainty that what becomes flesh must die, even the begotten God. We move into Advent with the awareness that part of preparing for Jesus' birth is also preparing for his death.

It is in the midst of this reality that we are called to remember that declaring Christ as king requires subtle and solid exegesis and expression. Christ's reign is not of this world. This is not the kind of kingship that we have ever known or experienced. For the first audiences of the Gospel narratives, however, kingship was known and experienced, yet with the particular and powerful meaning of history, tradition, and covenant. For Mark's Gospel, therefore, Christ the King is not at first "Jesus is king," but "Jesus, Son of David" (10:47-48). It is only after this messianic claim, after connecting Jesus to the kingship of David, that the Gospel portrays him as king.

As a result, Jesus' "triumphal" entry into Jerusalem is so designated because of the royal description of the procession. The "colt" alludes to Zechariah 9:9, where the coming king arrives riding a donkey, the common animal of transportation for royal figures. The fact that the colt has never been ridden indicates the cultic purity of the animal (see 1 Sam. 6:7). Cloaks and branches are spread onto the road, which recalls processions of royal figures and during festivals (2 Kgs. 9:13; 1 Macc. 13:51; 2 Macc. 10:7). The shout of "Hosanna" praises God and is a call to God for deliverance, because it literally means "save now." The words that follow come from Psalm 118:25-26, which had a critical role in Jewish religious life, both for pilgrims going to Jerusalem and for use during the Feast of Tabernacles and Passover.[3]

The attention to the details of the entry stand out in striking contrast to the pace of the story up to this point. Mark moves at a breathtaking rate, as Jesus "immediately" does most everything. Yet, of the forty-two times the term is used in the Gospel, only six are found after Jesus enters Jerusalem, and the last occurrence is in 15:1, when Jesus is brought before Pilate. After this encounter, "immediately" is never used in the Gospel again. Once the chain of events leading to Jesus' crucifixion is set in motion, the narrative comes to a striking halt, almost outside of time and space. Indeed, it is no wonder that Mark's Gospel has been called a "Passion narrative" with an extended introduction.

In Mark, the only time that Jesus is given the title "King of the Jews" is during his trial and crucifixion. The first occurrence is in 15:2 (see also 15:9, 12, 18, 26), where Jesus stands before Pilate, who asks him, "Are you the King of the Jews?" The last time Jesus is called "King" is when he is on the cross, being mocked by the passersby, the chief priests, and the scribes, who said "He saved others; he cannot save himself. Let the Messiah, the King of Israel, come down from the cross now, so that we may see and believe" (15:31-32). It is just after this that Jesus dies (15:33-37). With this final pairing of the term *king* with "Israel," the full impact of who Jesus was is realized. The abundance of God's covenant, God's promises, and God's love for God's people, through history, through relationships, through revelation is found not in a crown, but a cross, not in a temple, but a tomb, and not in earthly sovereignty, but resurrection glory. This is what it means to confess that Jesus Christ is our king.

> Once the chain of events leading to Jesus' crucifixion is set in motion, the narrative comes to a striking halt, almost outside of time and space.

Notes

1. Gail R. O'Day, "John," in *The New Interpreter's Bible,* vol. 9 (Nashville: Abingdon, 1995), 816.

2. Ibid., 817.

3. Donald H. Juel, *Mark,* Augsburg Commentary on the New Testament (Minneapolis: Augsburg, 2000), 154.

THANKSGIVING DAY

NOVEMBER 26, 2009 (USA) /
OCTOBER 12, 2009 (CANADA)
HENRY G. BRINTON

Revised Common (RCL)	Episcopal (BCP)	Roman Catholic (LFM)
Joel 2:21-27	Deut. 8:1-3, 6-10 (17-20)	Deut. 8:7-18 or 1 Kgs. 8:55-61
Psalm 126	Psalm 65 or 65:9-14	Ps. 113:1-2, 3-4, 5-6, 7-8 or Ps. 138:1-2, 2-3, 4-5
1 Tim. 2:1-7	James 1:17-18, 21-27	Col. 3:12-17 or 1 Tim. 6:6-11, 17-19
Matt. 6:25-33	Matt. 6:25-33	Mark 5:18-20 or Luke 12:15-21 or Luke 17:11-19

Quiet Cathedrals: A Thanksgiving Travelogue

What the world needs now are pilgrims. Not Mayflower pilgrims—they're history. What we really need today are people on a pilgrimage, people on a spiritual journey, people who have a passion to come into God's presence with thanksgiving. People who want to make a joyful noise with songs of praise!

For more than nine centuries, pilgrims traveled in multitudes to the majestic Canterbury Cathedral in England, trekking from all over Europe. It came to be known as the mother church of the global Anglican faith. But in the twenty-first century, the faith that drove these pilgrims is seriously diminished. Journalist T. R. Reid reports that at Morning Prayer on a typical Sunday, the vaulted ceiling of Canterbury Cathedral looks down on a grand total of thirteen worshipers. A midday communion service does better, with about three hundred people on hand, counting a cluster of tourists with video cameras. But that still leaves most of the seats unused. Western Europe is just full of quiet cathedrals.

The reasons for this drop-off are not entirely clear. Some feel that Holy Scripture has been replaced by blue-ribbon committees. Some blame quantum physics, modern genetics, and other scientific advances. Others sense that modern life in Western Europe has become so easy and comfortable that people can avoid facing the big issues of life and death. Says Michael Chandler, a priest at Canterbury,

"You can get to age 50 or higher without ever facing the death of somebody close to you."[1]

There simply aren't many Europeans these days responding to the words of the prophet Joel in the RCL first reading, "You shall eat in plenty and be satisfied, and praise the name of the LORD your God" (2:26). A slim minority is remembering the obligation in the BCP's Psalm 65, "Praise is due to you, O God, in Zion; and to you shall vows be performed, O you who answer prayer!" (v. 1). Europeans are doing even worse than the ten lepers who were healed by Jesus in the LFM's Gospel reading from Luke—at least one of the ten returned to Jesus to give thanks and praise God with a loud voice (Luke 17:11-19)!

But are we Americans doing much better? Many of us are not. This creative approach to a Thanksgiving sermon, "Quiet Cathedrals," offers a travelogue through the various texts appointed for this great American holiday. Preachers of various traditions should be able to glean a wealth of insights to help them answer the question of why our churches have become so quiet on Thanksgiving, instead of being places full of vigorous praise and heartfelt worship.

FIRST READING
JOEL 2:21-27 (RCL)
DEUTERONOMY 8:1-3, 6-10
(17-20) (BCP) OR 8:7-18 (LFM)
1 KINGS 8:55-61 (LFM ALT.)

Travelogue Stop One: Our Spiritual History

As we gather for worship on Thanksgiving, I have to wonder how it is that the early colonists' top religious history has evolved for so many people into a celebration of feasting and football. Through most of our history, Thanksgiving has been our one truly American sacred holiday, a day of worship that crosses denominational boundaries. But today, apart from a quick prayer before the turkey is carved, it seems fewer and fewer people are interested in spending any part of the day in expressions of gratitude for the blessings of life.

> We have lost touch with our spiritual history, in which God's judgment is followed by divine mercy, and our response is always to give thanks for God's abundant blessings.

Across the country, a diminishing number of religious pilgrims are making the trek to church to give thanks to the Lord. The call of Joel to national repentance is falling on deaf ears, as is his invitation to the children of Zion to "be glad and rejoice in the LORD your God; for he has given the early rain for your vindication . . . . The threshing floors shall be full of grain, the vats shall overflow with wine and oil" (Joel 2:23-24, RCL). We have lost touch with our spiritual history, in which God's judgment is followed by divine mercy, and our response is always to give thanks for God's abundant blessings. More and more, it seems that a sense of gratitude is fading from both our church and our culture, even though we live in a time in which our threshing floors are full of grain and our vats are overflowing with wine and oil.

Back in Puritan New England, Thanksgiving was the number-one holiday of the year, a day of churchgoing and prayer in a religious culture that considered Christmas and Easter to be inferior holidays—celebrations polluted with pagan customs. As recently as thirty years ago, interdenominational Thanksgiving services still drew good crowds, and there was the sense that people of many backgrounds could be united by the wish to come together and express thanks to a God we all shared. Sure, there are still community Thanksgiving gatherings going on across the country, and some are quite popular, but such services seem to be the exception rather than the rule. On Thanksgiving Day in America, we're now seeing too many of Europe's empty pews.

This is distressing, since the history of the Hebrews teaches us not to forget God in a land of prosperity. Looking ahead to the promised land, Moses tells the people that "the LORD your God is bringing you into a good land . . . a land where you may eat bread without scarcity, where you will lack nothing" (Deut. 8:7-9, BCP, LFM). This is a land of flowing streams, wheat, barley, fig trees, olive trees, honey, iron, and copper—a place of abundant natural resources. Moses says that God offers all this goodness to the people, and asks only that they remember the source of their blessings and give thanks: "Do not say to yourself, 'My power and the might of my own hand have gotten me this wealth.' But remember the LORD your God, for it is he who gives you power to get wealth, so that he may confirm his covenant that he swore to your ancestors, as he is doing today" (Deut. 8:17-18, LFM).

Like the ancient Hebrews, our responsibility is to remember the covenant, eat our fill, and bless the Lord our God for the good land that God has given us (v. 10). Our spiritual history demands that our churches not be quiet, but instead loud with the sounds of praise. "Blessed be the LORD," said King Solomon, in a powerful voice to all the assembly of Israel, "who has given rest to his people Israel according to all that he promised; not one word has failed of all his good promise, which he spoke through this servant Moses" (1 Kgs. 8:56, LFM).

> Our spiritual history demands that our churches not be quiet, but instead loud with the sounds of praise.

PSALM 126 (RCL)
PSALM 65 OR 65:9-14 (BCP)
PSALM 113:1-2, 3-4, 5-6, 7-8 (LFM)
PSALM 138:1-2, 2-3, 4-5 (LFM ALT.)

Travelogue Stop Two: Our Sense of Entitlement

Giving thanks and praise has always been one of the pillars of a worship service, an action that is seen repeatedly in the book of Psalms. "Praise the Lord!" says Psalm 113 (LFM). "Praise, O servants of the Lord; praise the name of the Lord" (v. 1). God is to be praised for God's sovereign power, "high above all nations" (v. 4), but also because of the care God shows to the downtrodden: "He raises the poor from the dust, and lifts the needy from the ash heap" (v. 7). Praise and thanksgiving is to be offered by people at every level of society, even the kings of the earth (Ps. 138:4, LFM), because God's words are powerful and the Lord's glory is great. "I give you thanks, O Lord, with my whole heart," says the writer of Psalm 138; "before the gods I sing your praise; I bow down before your holy temple and give thanks to your name for your steadfast love and your faithfulness" (vv. 1-2). In the face of such power, care, glory, love, and faithfulness, is there any better response than praise and thanks?

Yet it seems that people come to church today with a different set of expectations. Instead of seeking out opportunities to express gratitude, many Christians are looking for comfort, inspiration, stimulation, and community. Now these aren't bad things, but they line up more with self-improvement than with thanksgiving, and the end result is that we develop a blindness to our blessings. We come to see the good things of life as an entitlement, rather than a gift, and we lose the sense of wonder and surprise that gives birth to true thankfulness. "I think when we recognize that we are being given a gift, we feel joy," observes my friend John Sandel, a pastoral psychotherapist in Milford, Connecticut. "And gratitude is the experience that flows from this joy."

> People come to church today with a different set of expectations. Instead of seeking out opportunities to express gratitude, many Christians are looking for comfort, inspiration, stimulation, and community.

When we receive a gift, we feel joy—and gratitude is the experience that flows from this joy. Unfortunately, like so many who have come to expect a life of ease and comfort, we've lost the sense that each day on this earth is a wonderful gift. We now feel entitled to have a comfortable home, a dependable car, a decent salary, a full refrigerator, a complete wardrobe, and the latest home entertainment center. We have begun to see our well-being as a right, rather than as a gift—and this is a dangerous trend. It steers us away from the truth of Psalm 65 (BCP), which understands God to be the source of every good thing and offers thanksgiving for the earth's riches: "You crown the year with your bounty. . . . The pastures of the wilderness overflow, the hills gird themselves with joy, the meadows clothe themselves with flocks, the valleys deck themselves with grain, they shout and sing together for joy" (vv. 11-13). In this celebration of God's abundance, even the pastures, hills, meadows, and valleys join together in praise.

If we can rediscover that all of our blessings are a gift from God, we will experience the harvest of joy described by Psalm 126 (RCL), a raucous celebration of laughter and rejoicing based on the realization that "the LORD has done great things for us" (v. 3). There can be no quiet cathedrals when the people of God "come home with shouts of joy, carrying their sheaves" (v. 6).

SECOND READING
1 TIMOTHY 2:1-7 (RCL)
JAMES 1:17-18, 21-27 (BCP)
COLOSSIANS 3:12-17 (LFM)
1 TIMOTHY 6:6-11, 17-19 (LFM ALT.)

Travelogue Stop Three: Our Christian Theology

"The year that is drawing towards its close, has been filled with the blessings of fruitful fields and healthful skies," wrote Abraham Lincoln in his Thanksgiving Proclamation of 1863, in the middle of the Civil War.[2] "To these bounties, which are so constantly enjoyed that we are prone to forget the source from which they come, others have been added, which are of so extraordinary a nature, that they cannot fail to penetrate and soften even the heart which is habitually insensible to the ever watchful providence of Almighty God." Little did Lincoln know how "habitually insensible" we would become to the providence of God, and how blind we would be to the source of life's bounties.

Today, young children are showered with so many toys that holiday presents are not recognized as gifts, but are seen as things that they deserve. Working teenagers and young adults increasingly use their earnings to load up on the latest TVs, computers, clothing, and cars—they race toward a level of prosperity that previous generations took years and years to achieve. Living at home for longer periods, often free of any responsibility for room and board, they end up with an illusory sense of material well-being, a phenomenon social scientists call "premature affluence." Then, once they are out in the world on their own, they feel disappointment—not gratitude—as they adjust to a lower standard of living.

We've come a long way—and not in a good direction—since the Mayflower Pilgrims felt a deep sense of gratitude for simple survival. It is hard to imagine a politician today, in the middle of a wrenching civil war, pausing to give thanks for "the blessings of fruitful fields and healthful skies."

So, what can we do to regain a proper perspective and refill the pews of our quiet churches? A critical step is to reconnect with our Christian theology, which never fails to point us toward the source of every good and perfect gift. "As for those who in the present age are rich," writes Paul in his First Letter to Timothy, "command them not to be haughty, or to set their hopes on the uncertainty of riches, but rather on God who richly provides us with everything for our enjoyment" (6:17, LFM). As Christians, we are to live a new life in Christ, one defined by compassion, kindness, humility, meekness, patience, forgiveness, and love, according to Paul in his letter to the Colossians (3:12-17, LFM)—"And whatever you do," he recommends, "in word or deed, do everything in the name of the Lord Jesus, giving thanks to God the Father through him" (v. 17). Thanks to God is to be the foundation of everything we do as brothers and sisters in Christ.

> As Christians, we are to live a new life in Christ, one defined by compassion, kindness, humility, meekness, patience, forgiveness, and love.

James encourages us to "be doers of the word, and not merely hearers who deceive themselves" (1:22, BCP), while Paul urges that "supplications, prayers, intercessions, and thanksgivings be made for everyone, for kings and all who are in high positions" (1 Tim. 2:1-2, RCL). This is because God "desires everyone to be saved and to come to the knowledge of the truth" (v. 3), with a focus on what God has done for us in Jesus, "who gave himself a ransom for all" (v. 6). This offering of Jesus Christ, more valuable than "fruitful fields and healthful skies," is at the heart of our Christian faith, and is the gift that should inspire our deepest gratitude.

THE GOSPEL
MATTHEW 6:25-33 (RCL, BCP)
MARK 5:18-20 OR LUKE 12:15-21 OR LUKE 17:11-19 (LFM)

Travelogue Stop Four: The Goodness of God

One challenge for us today is to help people turn their attention away from the pursuit of "stuff" and see the nonmaterial gifts of God. When Susan Andrews was pastor of Bradley Hills Presbyterian Church in Bethesda, Maryland, she and a group of lay leaders held small weekday services that focused on reflection and thanksgiving. Worshipers gave thanks not only for moments of success or joy, but also for the blessings that can be found in the midst of events that might be stressful or painful—such as the mother of a troubled teenager finding patience, or a retiree surviving cancer against all odds. Susan saw a real hunger in these busy professional lives, a hunger to experience the presence of God in the ordinary moments and events of life. Together, they avoided the mistake of the rich fool in Luke 12:15-21 (LFM), who stored up material goods for himself but was "not rich toward God" (v. 21).

On Thanksgiving, it is important to give thanks for the presence of God in everyday life, in the moments that we discover unexpected healing and wholeness. We should not be like the nine lepers in Luke 17:11-19 (LFM) who are healed by Jesus but then wander off without a word. Instead, we should be like the tenth, the one who returns to Jesus, thanks him, and praises God with a loud voice. Jesus makes it clear that this thankful leper is the one with true faith, for he sends him away with the words, "Get up and go on your way; your faith has made you well" (v. 19). Are we among the nine, who take their health for granted? Or are we like the tenth, who makes a pilgrimage simply to give thanks?

> On Thanksgiving, it is important to give thanks for the presence of God in everyday life, in the moments that we discover unexpected healing and wholeness.

In the Sermon on the Mount, Jesus tells us not to worry about food, drink, or clothing, because our good God knows that we need all these things. "But strive first for the kingdom of God and his righteousness," says Jesus, "and all these things will be given to you as well" (Matt. 6:33, RCL, BCP). We are encouraged to turn away from anxiety about material things, and to turn in faith toward the nonmaterial gifts of our good and gracious God. Like the Gerasene demoniac in Mark 5 (LFM), we can hear Jesus saying to us, "Go home to your friends, and tell them how much the Lord has done for you, and what mercy he has shown you" (v. 19). Instead of sitting in quiet cathedrals, our challenge is to go into the world as pilgrims on a journey of thanksgiving, full of appreciation for what the Lord has done for us. God's goodness is a gift, and if we receive that gift with wonder and joy, then our natural response will be overflowing gratitude—gratitude that will be felt both inside and outside the church.

Notes

1. T. R. Reid, "Europe's Faithful Few," *The Washington Post National Weekly Edition,* May 14–20, 2001.

2. Abraham Lincoln, "Thanksgiving Proclamation (1863)," found in the second volume of Lincoln's collected papers in the Library of America series (*Abraham Lincoln: Speeches and Writings, 1859–1865* [New York: Library of America, 1989]), 520–21, http://members.aol.com/calebj/proclamation.html, accessed July 10, 2008.

APRIL 2009

Sunday	Monday	Tuesday	Wednesday	Thursday	Friday	Saturday
			1	2	3	4
5	6	7	8	9	10	11
12 Easter Sunday	13	14	15	16	17	18
19 Second Sunday of Easter	20	21	22	23	24	25
26 Third Sunday of Easter	27	28	29	30	31	

MAY 2009

Sunday	Monday	Tuesday	Wednesday	Thursday	Friday	Saturday
					1	2
3 Fourth Sunday of Easter	4	5	6	7	8	9
10 Fifth Sunday of Easter	11	12	13	14	15	16
17 Sixth Sunday of Easter	18	19	20	21 Ascension of the Lord	22	23
24 Seventh Sunday of Easter	25	26	27	28	29	30
31 Day of Pentecost						

JUNE 2009

Sunday	Monday	Tuesday	Wednesday	Thursday	Friday	Saturday
	1	2	3	4	5	6
7 First Sunday after Pentecost	8	9	10	11	12	13
14 Second Sunday after Pentecost Body and Blood of Christ (LFM)	15	16	17	18	19	20
21 Third Sunday after Pentecost	22	23	24	25	26	27
28 Fourth Sunday after Pentecost	29	30				

JULY 2009

Sunday	Monday	Tuesday	Wednesday	Thursday	Friday	Saturday
			1	2	3	4
5	6	7	8	9	10	11
12 Fifth Sunday after Pentecost	13	14	15	16	17	18
19 Sixth Sunday after Pentecost	20	21	22	23	24	25
26 Seventh Sunday after Pentecost	27	28	29	30	31	
Eighth Sunday after Pentecost						

AUGUST 2009

Sunday	Monday	Tuesday	Wednesday	Thursday	Friday	Saturday
						1
2 Ninth Sunday after Pentecost	3	4	5	6	7	8
9 Tenth Sunday after Pentecost Transfiguration (BCP/LFM)	10	11	12	13	14	15
16 Eleventh Sunday after Pentecost	17	18	19	20	21	22
23 Twelfth Sunday after Pentecost	24	25	26	27	28	29
30 Thirteenth Sunday after Pentecost	31					

SEPTEMBER 2009

Sunday	Monday	Tuesday	Wednesday	Thursday	Friday	Saturday
		1	2	3	4	5
6 Fourteenth Sunday after Pentecost	7	8	9	10	11	12
13 Fifteenth Sunday after Pentecost	14	15	16	17	18	19
20 Sixteenth Sunday after Pentecost	21	22	23	24	25	26
27 Seventeenth Sunday after Pentecost	28	29	30	31		

OCTOBER 2009

303

Sunday	Monday	Tuesday	Wednesday	Thursday	Friday	Saturday
				1	2	3
4 Eighteenth Sunday after Pentecost	5	6	7	8	9	10
11 Nineteenth Sunday after Pentecost	12 Thanksgiving Day (Canada)	13	14	15	16	17
18 Twentieth Sunday after Pentecost	19	20	21	22	23	24
25 Twenty-First Sunday after Pentecost	26	27	28	29	30	31

NOVEMBER 2009

Sunday	Monday	Tuesday	Wednesday	Thursday	Friday	Saturday
1 All Saints Day Twenty–Second Sunday after Pentecost	2	3	4	5	6	7
8 Twenty–Third Sunday after Pentecost	9	10	11	12	13	14
15 Twenty–Fourth Sunday after Pentecost	16	17	18	19	20	21
22 Christ the King	23	24	25	26 Thanksgiving Day (USA)	27	28
29	30					